JUSTICE REQUIRED

JUSTICE REQUIRED

POLICE SHOOTINGS AS
LEGALIZED VIOLENCE

———

ROBERT J. DURÁN AND ORALIA LOZA

Columbia University Press
New York

Columbia University Press
Publishers Since 1893
New York   Chichester, West Sussex

Library of Congress Cataloging-in-Publication Data
Names: Durán, Robert J. author | Loza, Oralia author
Title: Justice required : police shootings as legalized violence /
Robert J. Durán and Oralia Loza.
Description: New York : Columbia University Press, [2025] |
Includes bibliographical references and index.
Identifiers: LCCN 2025009798 (print) | LCCN 2025009799 (ebook) |
ISBN 9780231202107 hardback | ISBN 9780231202114 trade paperback |
ISBN 9780231554398 ebook
Subjects: LCSH: Police shootings—United States | Police brutality—United States |
Discrimination in criminal justice administration—United States |
Racial profiling in law enforcement—United States
Classification: LCC HV8141 .D87 2025 (print) | LCC HV8141 (ebook) |
DDC 363.20973—dc23/eng/20250728

Cover design: Noah Arlow
Cover image: Lewis Tse/Shutterstock

GPSR Authorized Representative: Easy Access System Europe, Mustamäe tee 50,
10621 Tallinn, Estonia, gpsr.requests@easproject.com

THIS BOOK IS DEDICATED TO THE LIVES STOLEN
BY STATE VIOLENCE
AND TO GREATER HUMANITY, DIGNITY, AND JUSTICE

CONTENTS

PREFACE

The collaboration between Dr. Robert Durán and Dr. Oralia Loza began from a federally funded research training program that worked to build interdisciplinary networks to conduct and apply for grants, particularly those of the National Institutes of Health (NIH). The program was the Interdisciplinary Research Institute Training (IRTI) (NIH-NIDA R25 DA026401), based at the University of Southern California, School of Social Work. After we completed our training, we joined the National Hispanic Science Network (NHSN) to study drug abuse among Latina/o/x populations. Durán participated in the 2011 cohort, and Loza, in the 2007 and 2013 cohorts.

Every other year, the institute hosted a conference that brought fellows from different cohorts together to meet, learn about one another's research skills and expertise, and network. In 2011, Durán was one of the only sociologists who attended. Most of his work focused on studying Latina/o/x communities on the topic of gangs, violence, policing, drug markets, and community resistance. Policing was a topic that he had regularly studied, but as he moved toward publishing, the data he had collected on officer-involved shootings became more challenging to analyze qualitatively. He met a level of peer-review resistance that he previously had not experienced because reviewers and editors demanded a quantitative analysis of the data and indicated in their reviews that they did not believe the qualitative themes outlined.

When Durán shared this with Loza at the 2014 IRTI follow-up meeting in Miami, Florida, she offered to collaborate and lead the database management to prepare the data for quantitative analysis. Loza had training in applied statistics and experience in statistical consulting before starting doctoral work in public health epidemiology. She was not new to stepping into existing projects and conducting secondary data analysis. Loza had recently presented findings from a collaborative project and shared her role in getting the work out at conference presentations and via publications; Durán could see how this collaboration could work. More important, she thought the work was meaningful and wanted to be involved. Although she did not have an academic background on the topic, it was not new to her or the community she grew up in, Decoto, in Union City, California.

During our time as collaborators, we continued to find a lack of support from journal editors, and in the end, Durán genuinely believes the reasons are because the findings and the analysis provided are shocking to traditional viewpoints about policing and American democracy. To date, this dataset is one of the most extensive analyses on officer-involved shootings in one city and county and also in other locations in the South and Southwest. The killing of George Floyd brought wider attention to the relentless work of the Black Lives Matter movement to eradicate racism in policing and US society. Academia is also a location of tremendous underrepresentation of faculty of color and the domination of many research areas by white academics who determine which research is acceptable and unacceptable. For example, only 2 percent of full professors in the United States were Hispanic in 2020. On many points, white elitism is wrong, and we are tremendously thankful to Columbia University Press for being a venue for us to share these data and insights. There is no reason why the study of police violence should remain silenced because there is an overrepresentation of Black and Brown victims. The data presented in this book include every police shooting in Denver, Colorado, between 1983 and 2020. A total of 298 cases are included. It also includes insights gleaned from counties in the regions of the Rocky Mountains (Utah), Borderlands (New Mexico and Texas), and the South (Tennessee).

The quantitative and qualitative data presented in this book include characteristics of the person shot, the police officers who did the shooting, and the scene. These data were collected from various sources, including archival government documents, ethnographic interviews and observations, and news and internet sources. Using these data, we report the patterns of the shootings by race/ethnicity, gender, age, foreign-born status, and time. The methodology of these efforts is described in detail in appendix 1. These analyses can serve as a blueprint for providing an evidence-based approach to collecting data and assessing such patterns in other cities and counties. The policies and some of the laws over these thirty-eight years have altered in terms of how police shootings are documented, and the process by which one can gain access to the data changed over the course of the data-collection process. Nevertheless, the importance of transparency regarding the number of lives taken by the state remains important if the United States continues to claim to be a democratic nation.

Depending on our background and privilege, when we think of gun violence, we may not think it includes people in law enforcement. However, gun violence includes gun violence by police. Gun violence by police *is* a public health problem, specifically for Latina/o/x, Black, and Indigenous people and people of color. The approaches used in analyzing these data include those used in studies assessing racial and ethnic health disparities. The case studies presented include a range of shootings. With some of the shootings, it was difficult to see an alternative response, but for the majority, the violent response was questionable. Moreover, a small but sizable number of shootings were problematic, and it is with reference to the questionable and problematic shootings that we think this book is of greatest importance. As long as there is official inaction and a lack of transparency, the authors remain concerned about the future detriment to marginalized communities and individuals across the country: no justice.

INTRODUCTION

s a graduate student attending a local university, all of my time (Durán) was devoted to researching gangs. I never saw myself becoming interested in officer-involved shootings. Such a lack of critical awareness did not last long. April 25, 2003, was a clear and sunny day.[1] While cleaning my apartment bedroom in a suburb a block north of Denver, I began to hear several popping noises that, at first, made me think of fireworks. I became aware that these were gunshots at the same time I realized my two children were playing outside. My wife followed me as we rushed outside to see what was happening. We noticed several police vehicles positioned near a minivan with its windows shot out. Police and ambulance sirens erupted in the background as emergency personnel began to crowd the scene. We made our children come inside the apartment; then, I grabbed my video camera and went back outside. Over the previous two years, I had been observing the police with a local community advocacy group. I realized that recording this police encounter and talking with witnesses would be one of the most important moments in my life. My interest in documenting this event was complicated by my reluctance to capture a homicide victim on my video camera.

As I continued recording, an emergency response team took the young man away on an ambulance stretcher. He was alive but hurt, covered in blood and in obvious pain. A chopper appeared, hovering in the sky, and I recognized it as the local media. A white male police officer began taping off the crime scene and asked whether anyone had seen anything. Many of my neighbors were outside, but no one stepped forward. It was clear that the police lacked rapport within the community. Many of us perceived the police as untrustworthy and dangerous. No one wanted to get involved. The working-class residents were primarily Latino/a, white, Asian, and Black.[2] When I watched the news that evening, I learned the man's name was Michael Grimaldo; he was listed as being alive.[3] The police maintained a crime scene around Michael's van as investigators sifted through the evidence. I felt a sense of relief the man hadn't died, especially because my neighbors claimed the shooting was unjustified.

The next morning, I picked up the newspaper and learned the man had died from his gunshot wounds shortly after arriving at the hospital. The "Special District Attorney Decision Letter" stated that Michael had been shot three times while fleeing from the police.[4] The DA suspected Michael was preparing to use drugs when he was startled by two police officers while parked in an abandoned bowling alley a block south of my apartment. Christopher Mace, an officer with seven years of experience, believed his life was in danger when Michael attempted to get away in his vehicle and made threatening arm motions.[5] Officer Mace fired several shots, but Michael continued driving away. The two officers lost Michael when they notified dispatch that shots had been fired and that the suspect was perceived to have been hit. Officer Karl Scherck, a twenty-year veteran, heard the call and drove to the vicinity.[6] An update was given that the suspect was parked in my apartment complex. When Officer Scherck came to a screeching halt in his patrol car, he hopped out of the vehicle and ordered the bloodied Michael to put his hands in the air. According to Officer Scherck, Michael did not respond and reached toward the center of his vehicle; at that point, Scherck fired two shots. Michael, after being shot a total of four times, continued to remain unresponsive to commands. Officer Scherck fired a third shot, the fifth bullet to hit Michael, who fell to the ground with his arms underneath him. Afterward, Officer Scherck reported thinking that Michael was reaching for a gun. No such weapon existed. The autopsy reported the twenty-three-year-old Michael died of multiple gunshot wounds, and thus the death was declared a homicide.[7] The DA noted that toxicology results were positive for cocaine and cannabinoids in Michael's system but that he was not under the influence of alcohol or drugs at the time of the shooting.

In reaching a legal decision, the special prosecutor did not want to participate in "Monday-morning quarterbacking," and thus, based on the totality of the facts, there was no reason to conclude a "reasonable likelihood of proving beyond a reasonable doubt that Officer Scherck committed a criminal act."[8] The outcome was primarily placed on Michael because he had "repeatedly refused" to comply with reasonable and lawful commands from a police officer.

Michael was the same age as my younger brother, making me feel connected to the events. A few days later, several individuals came to the scene of the shooting, and I walked over to see what they were doing. I learned they were Michael's family members, including his pregnant wife and his in-laws, trying to understand what had happened. I told them what I had observed and recorded at the time of Michael's shooting. They thanked me for my help and invited me to attend Michael's funeral viewing. As I sat near the back, I watched family members mourn as they approached the casket. I saw the effect of losing a family member to legitimized police violence. I wondered how the police could enter my neighborhood, shoot an unarmed Latino, and face no legal consequences.[9] Several additional shootings of Blacks and Latinos over the summer of 2003 made me want to learn more about who gets shot by the police and why. What determines whether a shooting is considered legally justifiable? Had there been questionable shootings in Denver similar to Michael's that had also been lawfully considered justified, and if so, why?

LEGALIZING DEADLY FORCE

The official decision making regarding who deserves the punishment of death has a long history of controversy in the United States. In the early 1900s, Ida B. Wells and W. E. B. Du Bois protested against the acts of lynching in the South, where Blacks were overrepresented as victims of these brutal attacks.[10] In the twenty-first century, we have learned how Latinas/os were also targeted, particularly in the Southwest, in addition to immigrants of Chinese and Italian descent.[11] In this form of punishment, community members, often with the help of or led by law enforcement officers, enacted their form of extrajudicial violence for individuals accused of criminal wrongdoing. After the increased production of fire-arms, a new form of death at the hands of law enforcement began to emerge: officer-involved shootings.[12] The production of firearms has increased since the nineteenth century, allowing this deadly tool to be used for self-defense, discretionary enforcement of laws, suicide, and other acts of violence.[13] The Small Arms Survey described armed violence as an epidemic that continues to affect communities around the globe.[14] In 2024, the US surgeon general declared firearm violence to be a public health cri-sis.[15] Most firearm research has focused on civilian interpersonal vio-lence, even though agents of the state have also employed this object, resulting in a higher number of deaths.[16]

Law enforcement officers hold the only position within the criminal justice system where the state allows employees to use deadly force on the public. An officer's discretion over whether to shoot a suspect with a fire-arm occurs before any court proceeding, without a legal framework for determining guilt or innocence, and lacking an adversarial system.

Several legal and research articles explain how law enforcement's jus-tification to use deadly force when apprehending a suspect is based on a common-law ruling existing as far back as England in the 1200s.[17] Dur-ing these times, breaking the law resulted in forfeiture of life. Accurate data on how often these crimes and deadly apprehensions occurred may not have been assessed or documented. In the United States, most felo-nies and homicides do not result in the death penalty.[18]

For centuries, each state had its own legal precedents and policies regarding the use of deadly force. The 1985 Supreme Court case of *Ten-nessee v. Garner* formally established federal ground rules for law enforce-ment officers. In this case, a Memphis, Tennessee, police officer shot and killed an unarmed fifteen-year-old Black youth named Edward Garner, who was fleeing from a nighttime burglary.[19] The eighth grader attempted to jump a six-foot fence; the officer reported thinking the suspect would get away, and he shot Edward in the back of the head. A Tennessee stat-ute and police department policy allowed the officer to use deadly force in a burglary despite Edward only stealing ten dollars and a purse. Edward's father challenged this practice, but the lower courts agreed with the police department and state in finding no criminal wrongdoing in the officer's decision to shoot. However, the US Supreme Court argued that the Fourth Amendment's reasonableness requirement did not include a seizure of this type. The outdated common-law practice of allowing the use of deadly force for any felony was no longer realistic. The court ruled that police officers cannot shoot a nondangerous fleeing suspect unless probable cause exists that the suspect poses a significant threat of death or serious injury to the officer or other individuals. Three years later, the Supreme Court decision in *Graham v. Connor* (1988) ruled that under the Fourth Amendment, law enforcement officers possess an "objective reasonableness" standard that must be judged by a reasonable officer on the scene, thus protecting the discretionary use of force when deemed necessary. Hence, we see many legal justifications for officer-involved shootings today.

THE STUDY OF OFFICER-INVOLVED SHOOTINGS

Despite causing outrage, particularly in racial- and ethnic-minority communities, there has been very little research devoted to officer-involved shootings until after the shooting death of Michael Brown in 2014. This does not mean, however, that there had been no previous attempts to change this lack of attention. As early as 1974, the sociologist Paul Takagi critiqued the lack of research on police killings of citizens. He outlined patterns of racism, showing how the police killed Black men at a rate of nine to ten times higher than white men, which effectively was the continuation of an institutionalized practice of genocide on Black citizens. James Fyfe, a former police officer who later became a researcher and joined Takagi's investigations, critiqued the absence of research on police use of deadly force during his earlier career. The country does not accurately report how often its own agents kill or injure its citizens, which Fyfe described as a failure of democracy.[20] In 1988, Fyfe reported that only a few individuals were studying police use of deadly force, which was "dwarfed by the volume of studies on most other (and less critical) decision points in the criminal justice process."[21] Fourteen years later, in 2002, Fyfe outlined how the existing scholarship lacked systematic data and noted that the *Washington Post* had done the best job accumulating information for several cities.[22] To address this data gap, Fyfe believed the requirement of a federal mandate similar to the Uniform Crime Reports would be necessary to get law enforcement agencies nationwide to begin providing information.

In 2008, two additional criminologists, Michael White and David Klinger, concurred with these previous research studies, stating that police shooting research was virtually nonexistent until the 1970s.[23] Empirical data sources to understand law enforcement shootings were less accessible than other secondary datasets. Researchers primarily relied upon data sources that included (1) FBI supplementary homicide reports, (2) National Center for Health Statistics, and (3) police-generated data. Other researchers sought out additional sources of data such as death certificates, police internal affairs records, and newspaper stories, all containing different types of flaws for an accurate understanding of police shootings.[24] Because of the limitations in the consistency and availability of data, researchers cautioned against comparing cities by using Uniform Crime Reports and other vital statistics. They encouraged the National Center for Health to improve its data collection systems. Nevertheless, without better alternatives to hand, researchers used the data available to study national patterns.[25] Other researchers focused on the cities where they could gain access to police department records, including cities such as Chicago, Los Angeles, Memphis, New York City, and Philadelphia.[26]

Feeling frustration regarding police violence and the lack of justice, a collaboration formed between the October 22 Coalition to Stop Police Brutality, the National Lawyers Guild, and the Anthony Baez Foundation, resulting in the book *Stolen Lives: Killed and Brutalized by Police* in 1997.[27] The book was unique because it emphasized that "there is an epidemic of police brutality in the United States," and rather than allow the violence to be hidden, the authors listed the name, age, nationality, date killed, and location of murders by police from 1990 to 1997, for several US states.[28] They highlighted that the victims were primarily Black, Latino, and other people of color, and they issued a call for people to share these stories in an effort to expose and stop the brutalization. The ninety-nine-page book ends with several photographs of those killed by police, starting with the fifteen-year-old Angel Castro, a Puerto Rican youth, shot in the back of the head by Chicago police officers. The autopsy photos and report drive home the devastating reality of police violence.[29] The second edition, *Stolen Lives: Killed by Law Enforcement*, came out soon after, featuring over two thousand cases.[30] The editor of the introduction, Karen Saari, reported that authorities were not gathering or reporting this information. Thus, it became "up to us," the people, to gather and report it. The second edition included additional cases and a section at the beginning titled "The Faces of Stolen Lives," which provided photos of the person killed along with their name, location, and date of death.

Public interest increased after the killing of eighteen-year-old Michael Brown in Ferguson, Missouri, by Darren Wilson in August 2014. Michael, who was Black, unarmed, and walking down a street, was confronted by the twenty-eight-year-old police officer when an argument ensued. The officer shot Michael six times.[31] Black Lives Matter, which began one year earlier, after the killing of Trayvon Martin, continued to shed light on how Blacks were unjustly being murdered and how state and federal officials refused to collect data on killings by law enforcement. A UK-based news outlet, the *Guardian*, began sharing data on the number of killings by law enforcement in 2015. Contrary to what federal officials had been estimating, the number of killings by law enforcement was nearly three times higher: 1,146 deaths in 2015.[32] Several additional organizations joined the data collection effort to document the number of killings by law enforcement; these included the *Washington Post* (on their website *Fatal Force*) and other crowdsourced internet websites such as *Fatal Encounters* and *Mapping Police Violence*. The Centers for Disease Control and Prevention also began documenting homicides by police.[33]

TRADITIONAL EXPLANATIONS FOR POLICE SHOOTINGS

Before this more recent increase in the amount of data available to analyze, most of the researchers in disciplines such as criminology, criminal justice, and sociology primarily attributed the reasons why police shootings occurred to one of four factors: (1) the community, (2) the suspect, (3) the organization (i.e., the law enforcement agency), or (4) systemic racism.[34]

Blaming the community revolved around describing the "dangerous settings" where officers were forced to work.[35] The support of the argument for increased danger included arrest rates and homicide rates. In such a context, it was argued that police use of deadly force could protect all groups from violence and that law-abiding citizens benefit from this form of public safety.[36] The police must control a violent population and react to urban conditions, making the enforcement of laws more difficult. Researchers were finding that as the frequency of dangerous criminal incidents increased, so did police killings of civilians.[37]

The second explanation offered for why police shootings occur was based on the disproportionate involvement in violence, particularly for minority groups, which yields a higher number of use-of-force encounters with law enforcement.[38] Based upon a framework used for understanding homicide victimization called victim precipitation, researchers argued that "criminals" who were killed by law enforcement caused their deaths because they resisted arrest, did not follow legal directives, or reached for a weapon.[39] It was for these reasons that the overrepresentation of Blacks could range anywhere between six to twenty-nine times higher than officer-involved shootings of whites. The summation of this argument could be officers encountering "dangerous criminals." Officers were viewed as moral and professional employees who held no ill will toward residents and, therefore, felt "forced" to use their weapons to deescalate situations. From this perspective, the officers became "victims" of having to endure the trauma of killing or injuring another human being.

The third explanation was to blame the organization, which attributes the responsibility of police shootings mainly to the hands of administrators who control policies, training, and guidelines for officers. The criminologist James Fyfe argued that elective shootings (e.g., instances where officers have a choice) were more influenced by policy, whereas nonelective shootings (e.g., no options available) were attributable to the social environment.[40] Based on this research, the internal working environment played a critical role in influencing discretion in elective encounters but had less of an effect in nonelective encounters, where situational and environmental influences were more important. In addition, the organizational culture could influence officers to develop justifications regarding when to shoot based on the circumstances, characteristics of the victim, or a higher purpose.[41] The racial and ethnic composition of the police force was recognized as being important. Still, there were indications that minority officers may have been overrepresented in police shootings because of assignment, residence, and socialization.[42]

The fourth explanation, systemic racism, was emphasized the most by the criminologist Paul Takagi and several of his colleagues.[43] He stated that it was the perception of the Black community that officers were engaging in the genocide of Black people.[44] Takagi stated, "Coercive force has been invoked in the very communities where people have experienced super-exploitation and the long-term effects of racism and has created a dialectic through which people have acquired character in their struggles with the antagonists."[45] Mainstream solutions, in his view, only served to maintain the view of holding individuals accountable and expanding administrative duties in response to "bad apples" rather than addressing the political-economic and institutional racism aspects of police-caused homicides. Criminologists mystified and concealed racial and class oppression in the name of free scientific inquiry. Several other researchers agreed, and they criticized the traditional explanations given for why police shootings occur.[46] These authors argued, "The aggressive patrol practices of the police, concentrated in working-class neighborhoods, implemented in racist ways, rely in substantial part on the popular fear of police violence."[47] Such actions were but a piece of the total level of state brutality directed at residents.

James Fyfe reported, "Only the ingenuous and the naïve can conclude from these figures that racism is not involved in police use of deadly force."[48] But rather than being a societal anomaly, he argued that racial disparities exist in a wide range of social phenomena, including life expectancy, incarceration rates, etc. He found Blacks were more likely to be shot in elective encounters (e.g., instances where officers have a choice) than whites but that policies and training could change this. Less optimistic about police reform, the historian and scholar Robin Kelley described how the police have often acted as an occupying army in Black and Latino communities.[49] From slave patrols, black codes, lynchings, and race riots to police homicides, brutality, COINTELPRO (counterintelligence programs), and urban uprisings, law enforcement officers have been central participants in differential treatment. Until the implementation of systematic change, Kelley recommended dismantling police departments and the criminal justice system; this was a precursor to the movement to abolish the police that developed after the killing of George Floyd.

A MINORITY PERSPECTIVE ROOTED
IN SOCIAL JUSTICE

The foundation for the information presented in *Justice Required* is based on a minority perspective rooted in social justice. It seeks to build on the call for a "minority perspective" expressed by Paul Takagi in 1981.[50] At the time, Takagi was a criminology professor at the University of California, Berkeley, and he argued that there was a crisis in academia because much of the research was contributing to racially discriminatory criminal justice policies rather than acknowledging that such policies were acts against humanity. He himself had lived such abuse according to policy and procedure when he lived in a Japanese internment camp during World War II. Takagi stated that Alvin Gouldner's "sociology of the underdog" was a helpful starting point because it represented a commitment to sympathy and compassion for racial minorities.[51] Takagi critiqued the methods used to reach conclusions regarding minority communities and questioned how many studies were obtained without the inclusion of the thoughts and experiences of people of color living in these communities.

The sociologist Alvin Gouldner's article "The Sociologist as Partisan" expressed a perception that most academics were on the side of the "overdog," as their lives were more similar to officials enacting policies beneficial to their own interests.[52] In contrast, a minority perspective offered insights from those who were oppressed and offered solutions that often ran counter to ones suggested by those in power. Such a critical stance was rare because the tenure-track positions and research funding often depended on maintaining the status quo. In Gouldner's view, objectivity in the social sciences should be more focused on what contribution it made in fostering human unity. Moreover, social science should not ignore human suffering or make peace with any form of human unity that accommodates itself complacently to or imposes suffering.

The points that Gouldner and Takagi were making in the 1960s and 1980s were issues that had been encountered since the start of the twentieth century. At that time, many social science disciplines, in an attempt to demonstrate objectivity, distanced themselves from offering policy suggestions or guidance. In the discipline of sociology, this laissez-faire style of personal detachment is evident in the foundation of the Chicago School, especially in its contrast to the social justice–oriented Atlanta School of the early 1900s.[53] Unlike most white academics, Black scholars did not have the luxury of sitting idly by when fellow Black residents were being lynched in the United States. When Ida B. Wells expressed much effort to "self-help" and create a "remedy" to stop the barbarism of lynching, she did not accept that it was okay to ignore these horrors.[54] She even emphasized how Black families should keep a firearm over their mantel for self-protection because the law or law enforcement could not be relied upon. The sociologist Aldon Morris's research on W. E. B. Du Bois quoted one of Du Bois's writings: "Speaking of a horrific lynching, after which he saw the victim's knuckles on display in the window of a local grocer, Du Bois wrote: 'One could not be calm, cool, and detached scientist while Negroes were lynched, murdered and starved.'"[55]

To develop a social science that would be an advocate for the underdog, much had to be done. Several researchers have outlined how criminology and criminal justice programs that specialize in the study of crime and institutions designed to respond to illegal behavior have primarily lacked a critical orientation.[56] Takagi, along with several of his colleagues at UC Berkeley, focused on developing radical or critical criminology; their efforts were shut down by 1976. The faculty members involved were relocated to other departments or left the university, but research critical of the system continued. Around the same time as UC Berkeley's criminology program was being closed, the development of critical race theory (CRT) began as lawyers, activists, and legal scholars began critiquing law and racism in US society.[57] CRT holds that racism is foundational in the history and common everyday practices of the United States. Interested individuals joined together to hold their first workshop in the summer of 1989 in Madison, Wisconsin; this has since grown to become a movement of activists and scholars engaging in the study and transformation of race, racism, and power. One of CRT's four central tenets has also emphasized the importance of a voice-of-color thesis that acknowledges differential histories and experiences with oppression that whites may not know.

In London, the criminologists Coretta Phillips and Benjamin Bowling were in agreement that a racial- and ethnic-minority perspective was needed. They were working to build on Katheryn Russell's development of "black criminology" and feminist perspectives.[58] They reported how the term "minority" allowed for the inclusion of other marginal and excluded statuses, such as sexual and gender minorities, including lesbian, gay, bisexual, and transgender (LGBT) populations and even white academics. Phillips and Bowling also stressed that it was important that British criminology be able to reflect on whether it was institutionally racist and evaluate practices at all levels to ensure that prejudice and discrimination were not dominating the empirical and theoretical approaches of the discipline. Such evaluations and assessments were needed in departments, on editorial boards, in policy groups and task forces, and when awarding grants.

RACIALIZED SOCIAL CONTROL

To merge a minority perspective rooted in social justice with traditional social theory begins by filling a scholarly gap in order to develop the concept of racialized social control. An early founder of sociology, Emile Durkheim, explained how social positions and social relationships in society were ordered based upon a structure that humans cannot necessarily observe with the human eye but rather is visible in the patterns that produce and reproduce behavior. Durkheim outlined three forms of "deviation," that is, when society's integration and regulation were not functioning properly: He termed them the "altruistic," "anomic," and "egoistic." In Durkheim's analysis, these three types were the most common, but there was a fourth form of deviation, which he described in a footnote as "fatalistic." Durkheim defined fatalism as "persons with futures pitilessly blocked and passions violently choked by oppressive discipline."[59] He believed rules could also be "the cause of evil."[60] This concept was considered the opposite of "anomie," or normlessness, a concept that has been frequently used in criminology. For the timeframe in which Durkheim lived (1858–1917), as a white cisgender male growing up and residing in France, he may have been blind to the role of imperialism in creating a "fatalistic" society. Frantz Fanon (1925–1961), born in the Caribbean, in the French colony of Martinique, described the violence and psychological harm that resulted from colonization. He joined with others in efforts to decolonize various nations across the globe, which is reflected in the scholarship of postcolonialism.[61] The sociologist Julian Go has emphasized how these forms of analysis were reflective of different perspectives shaped by their social location within a hierarchy: the standpoint of power (i.e., social science), on one hand, and the standpoint of marginality, on the other.

In his dissertation and first book, Durán used Durkheim's framework to develop a racial oppression model titled "fatalistic social control," wherein three components ensured that marginalized groups had their futures pitilessly blocked and their passions violently choked by oppressive discipline.[62] Durán theorized that control required (1) hierarchies of power that differentiate people as dominant and those socially constructed as less equal and less deserving, (2) segregated geographic environments that heighten privilege and disadvantage, and (3) laws and policies that ensure that resistance to inequality results in increased control. Thus, developing Durkheim's concept of fatalism with the inclusion of postcolonial scholarship allows for the opportunity to provide new forms of analysis. The merging of the notions of "fatalistic" with "racialized" primarily identifies the groups who have been targeted, the most marginalized in US society, as falling into a racial caste system: This is, in brief, racialized social control. The political scientist Sandra Bass corroborated these themes when she outlined how "racial social control" has developed into a new Jim Crow involving a war on drugs and quality-of-life policing that continues to disproportionately affect Blacks.[63] The law professor Michelle Alexander's award-winning book *The New Jim Crow* built upon Bass's scholarship by emphasizing how the racial caste system locks people of color into second-class citizenship.[64]

In an effort to contribute to postcolonial theory, two other caveats will be included in this book: (1) an analysis of social dominance theory (SDT) and (2) the emphasis on public health. First, SDT argues that all human societies are structured in systems of group-based hierarchies. The small number of dominant groups influences the ideologies of what is socially valued, primarily through three stratification systems including (1) age, (2) gender, and (3) "arbitrary sets," which include caste, clan, ethnicity, race, religion, or other socially relevant group distinctions. These theorists argue that law enforcement is a hierarchy-enhancing occupation, with employees with primarily antiegalitarian beliefs seeking to uphold (and receive privileges for upholding) dominant group interests.[65] The second caveat is our desire not just to theorize a solution but to support interdisciplinary efforts to address violence. Currently, the field of public health appears to be the most suited for such a task. According to the

American Public Health Association, "public health promotes and protects the health of all people and their communities" and seeks to improve "our quality of life, helps children thrive, reduces human suffering and saves money."[66]

FIREARM VIOLENCE: SOCIAL DEATH AND STATES OF DENIAL

Although we are interested in stopping other practices of law enforcement misbehavior, such as assault, criminal activity, and harassment, along with other forms of violence and harm, we believe the most time-sensitive issue should be the use of firearms. David Hemenway, a professor of health policy, has described gun violence as a modern-day public health epidemic that requires the use of science.[67] Hemenway reported that improving the safety of motor vehicles and the roads they are driven on is the best example of progress. In the past, more emphasis was placed on the driver, not the vehicle. However, after many tragic accidents, it was discovered that vehicles could be modified with technical improvements to make them safer. Based on data on suicides and homicides, it is clear that gun violence is a public health problem that may, in part, require similar technical solutions.

Studies on settler colonialism have emphasized how the use of violence has been crucial in obtaining power.[68] The sociologist C. Wright Mills once wrote, "All politics is a struggle for power; the ultimate kind of power is violence."[69] Indigenous populations and racialized others become targeted for extermination, incapacitation, or removal, but accomplishing that task always requires overcoming various legal and ideological hurdles. US society has been built on violence. In its pursuit of democracy, becoming more inclusive will require addressing blind spots in how violence has been used by the state. Officer-involved shootings are a blind spot where violence has been and continues to be used, and it primarily targets those who have been marginalized. The ethnic studies scholar Lisa Cacho describes the vast scholarship regarding individuals and groups denied personhood and who have been deprived of rights, criminalized, and left in a perpetual "inalienability problem," in which all power and decision making continue to be in the hands of the dominant group.[70]

Such a standpoint has pushed us to analyze how such a stance aligns with states of denial and emphasizes the importance of recommending and creating better ways to address social problems with social science.[71]

THIS STUDY

This mixed-method study incorporates data qualitatively collected and coded. The compiled data sources were then analyzed using not only that methodology but also quantitative analyses. Most researchers have used national data sets that have not provided the opportunity to examine qualitative or quantitative differences based on actual case studies. Denver, Colorado, served as the foundation for this study; it then branched out to other locations. A more detailed overview of the methods and data can be found in the appendix. The initial purpose of the study was to describe the officer shootings that occurred in the city and county of Denver, Colorado, between January 1, 1983, and December 31, 2020. The goal was to develop greater research clarity in regard to the patterns and trends involved in officer-involved shootings in an attempt to explore three themes (suspect characteristics, officer characteristics, and contextual factors) that highlight differences in officer-involved shootings involving whites, Blacks, and Latinos and discuss the possible reasons for these violent encounters.

Shootings were analyzed in terms of frames or stages based on previous research that examined the situation that led to law enforcement being alerted, the interaction between the suspect and the officer, the decision for the officer to use deadly force, and the outcome.[72] The researchers gathered the data by compiling district attorney summaries, police shooting files, video interviews of officers and witnesses, and newspaper articles. The authors thoroughly reviewed each shooting incident first to provide a narrative outlining racial and ethnic patterns and second by coding the data to conduct bivariate analyses to compare how these patterns merge with other individuals of similar racial and ethnic backgrounds. Denver provides a unique setting to study these patterns because it has a proportionate Black population similar to the national average and twice the size of a Latino population. Although whites are the numerical and political majority, the city has a racial and ethnic history of protest for improving rights for minority groups.[73] As of 2022, the city and county of Denver had a population of 713,252 residents.[74] It is located in the Rocky Mountain region of the United States and is considered the nineteenth-most-populated city in the country. According to census data, Denver continues to be racially, ethnically, and economically segregated.[75]

The model adopted in Denver was then brought to other counties where Durán was living, working, and studying various social issues. Thus, the analysis also includes insights from another Rocky Mountain area, Weber County, Utah; the Borderlands of Doña Ana County, New Mexico; and El Paso County, Texas, along with a county from the South: Knox County, Tennessee. These four different counties were included to highlight how officer-involved shootings affect communities across the nation. The selection of these counties was not based on the desire to generalize but rather to explore the extent of this social issue in communities beyond Denver. Police violence is broad, and to analyze the extent of the problem will require more data gathering and analysis. We encourage and seek to participate in these efforts.

ORGANIZATION OF THE BOOK

Each chapter in *Justice Required* begins with a story, drawing from critical race theory's emphasis on the importance of storytelling. Chapter 1 outlines the historical context for the use of state violence in Colorado and how it later led to the condoning of police shootings in Denver despite public protests and civil lawsuits. Denver city and county leaders had institutionalized a process for which "the law" could protect their interests along with providing legal protection for those who carried out these actions. As the geographic site for the most comprehensive data collected of the five sites studied, it was important in this book to outline the history of policing, racial and ethnic inequality, and racialized violence.

Chapter 2 provides an analysis of the descriptive patterns obtained regarding officer-involved shootings in Denver, Colorado, from 1983 to 2020. A special focus is devoted to analyzing bivariate characteristics of age, sex, and foreign birth. These characteristics highlight the importance of intersectionality when studying and understanding officer-involved shootings.

In chapter 3, we provide an analysis of racial and ethnic differences regarding who is shot by law enforcement officers. We focus on differences between Blacks, Latinos, and whites in the city and county of Denver. Building on Paul Takagi's concept of "two trigger fingers," we examine whether officers perceive the actions of certain individuals as more dangerous based on visible cues of racialized social status.

In chapter 4, we provide an overview of the range of shootings, using the categories of "problematic," "questionable," and "less controversial." We primarily focus on the issues surrounding the legal decision making involved when district attorneys do not file criminal charges against officers in controversial officer-involved shootings. Community members desired justice and accountability, whereas public officials primarily managed to shift the focus toward notions of legality and policy shrouded in the terminology of justification that centers blame on the person shot. Victimization literature often describes this as "blaming the victim," but for officer-involved shootings, most individuals who are shot and wounded or killed are deemed unworthy of "victim" status. In a strange twist of decision making, officers become described as the "victims" in their having had to use deadly force.

Chapter 5 explores the patterns involving which officers in Denver, Colorado, have shot someone, whether on duty or off duty. Most officers were employed by the Denver Police Department (DPD), but many other federal, state, and local agencies have also been involved in their own incidents. The chapter includes a special focus on fourteen DPD officers who had participated in three or more shooting incidents from 1983 to 2020. Some of these shootings span an entire career, whereas one officer was involved in three shooting incidents in one year alone. This chapter will highlight that despite similarities between law enforcement organizations and street gangs in terms of bonding and behavioral attitudes, the institution of a law enforcement agency ensures that this organization has a level of power, influence, and lack of accountability that is not available to marginalized social organizing.

Chapter 6 extends the research focus of officer-involved shootings from Denver, Colorado, to counties in Utah, New Mexico, Texas, and Tennessee. The chapter begins with the shooting incident in Uvalde, Texas, where nineteen students and two teachers were fatally killed; it took law enforcement seventy-seven minutes to intervene. We highlight how most officer-involved shootings are very different from the "active shooter" scenario in Uvalde, and thus, conflating these two issues should be avoided. Examining each of the counties in this chapter highlights how each community has its own historical legacy of violence that deserves greater attention. Police violence extends beyond one county and is a nationwide problem.

Chapter 7 examines the importance of federal, state, and local officials to act in order to stop police violence. We recommend several studies on how the organization of law enforcement can be reformed but question what effects can realistically be obtained. Finally, we propose guidelines for studying officer-involved shootings under a social-ecological model influenced by epidemiological criminology.

We conclude with an analysis of racialized social control and discuss how officer-involved shootings highlight the racial state of expendability, which is more reflective of settler colonialism than it is of democracy. The ramifications of such a model of governance hold extremely adverse outcomes for members of racial and ethnic minority groups and individuals experiencing mental health crises or suffering from alcohol and or drug addictions.

1

THE CONTEXT OF POLICE SHOOTINGS AND PROTEST

Denver

I t is the summer of 2003, and I (Durán) am walking toward a planned candlelight vigil for the police shooting death of fifteen-year-old Paul Childs.[1] Six days earlier, during a temporary family crisis, Paul's sister called the police to report that her brother was following her mom around with a knife. Considered to be slightly mentally disabled, Paul was on several forms of medication. He regularly visited the hospital, and his family often called the police to help with his behavior. When the police arrived, they ordered everyone out of the home. After the family members were behind the officers, Paul came to the door holding a knife. He took one step forward and was shot four times by Denver Police Officer James Turney.[2] Paul died shortly after being rushed to the hospital. This was the second Black teen with disabilities that this officer had killed in the past year and a half. The Black community of Denver is frustrated and angry. I walk with other neighborhood residents down the street toward the park. Northeast Park Hill is one of the neighborhoods with the highest concentration of Black residents in the city. Everyone I see is Black.[3] As a light-skinned Chicano in my mid-twenties, I receive some glances as to who I may be. I am aware that I am not dark skinned or perceived as Black, but no one questions my presence. I'm not a cop, and I'm sorry to learn of this shooting. I march in solidarity for Black and Brown coalition building against police terror.

When I arrive at the park, I hear speeches amplified via bullhorn as several leaders in the community share commentary. The expressed sentiment of the crowd is that there is too much police violence. Some in the crowd suggest that maybe there needs to be some form of retaliation against cops who target the Black community with brutality and death. Allegedly, an anonymous flier has been circulated stating that people should start shooting police officers.[4] The outgoing mayor for the past twelve years, Wellington Webb, is present at the vigil.[5] As Denver's first Black mayor, he encourages residents to have faith in the legal system and asserts that the law will correct this wrong. The community seems skeptical, but Webb's political authority, his ongoing presence within the community, and his physical build as a six-foot-five Black man help calm down the crowd to focus on the tasks ahead. The day becomes dusk, candles are lit, and the mourning continues, but the protests are far from over.

Over the next six months, several more protests are held after it is learned that Officer Turney will not face any legal consequences from the district attorney's office for shooting Paul Childs or Gregory Smith, the other young man a year earlier. Bill Ritter, the DA, was under the opinion that he would be unable to convince a jury of twelve people to convict the officer.[6] As a result of this statement by the DA's office, several civil rights and faith-based organizations engage in civil disobedience in front of the police department building. Three individuals are arrested for trespassing.[7] The Childs family files a civil suit, and it is initially led by Johnnie Cochran, the nationwide famous attorney and member of the dream team who helped O. J. Simpson be found not guilty beyond a reasonable doubt. One of my friends from Denver Copwatch, Shareef Aleem, creates Operation Get Turney, a grassroots effort to push for accountability for the officer who killed Paul Childs. At the annual Martin Luther King "Marade" held in January, Mr. Aleem heckles the new mayor, John Hickenlooper, with a bullhorn for not doing enough.[8] He shouts, "Fire Killer Cops" and "Justice for Paul Childs."[9] On April 15, 2004, the Denver Police Department's manager of safety finds that Officer Turney violated several police department rules and regulations and suspends him for ten months.[10] This was later reaffirmed by the Denver Civil Service Commission in 2007 despite a couple of rulings that swung back and forth between that decision and a lighter punishment.[11] Before this reaffirmation, Paul Childs' family was awarded a $1,325,000 settlement in a civil suit: at the time, it was the second-largest settlement in Denver's history.[12]

During the fall of 2003 there are five more separate officer-involved shootings: The victims are Sergio Medrano, Teresa Perez, Brant Murphey, Luis Acuña, and Raymond Martinez. Based on the analysis used to review these shootings, several incidents appeared less controversial (Martinez, Murphey, and Perez), one shooting was ranked as questionable (Acuña), and one shooting was evaluated to be reflective of misconduct (Medrano).[13] The officer who shot Mr. Medrano, Karl Scherck, is the same officer who had shot Michael Grimaldo four months earlier. Both cases are examples of the officer thinking the suspect had a gun when no gun existed. The DA, Bill Ritter, stated in the decision letter: "To put this in context, in the ten years that I have been the Denver District Attorney, there have been 79 officer-involved shootings in Denver. Of those, there have been only three 'I thought he had a gun' cases. I am unaware of any Denver Police Officer in the last 30 years who has been involved in two 'I thought he had a gun' cases during his or her entire career."[14]

Despite this observation, DA Ritter does not file criminal charges. The families of Acuña and Medrano file civil lawsuits but are unsuccessful in court. Each shooting case became intertwined with a call for change in policing. The following summer, another polarizing incident occurs; this time it is the shooting death of sixty-three-year-old Frank Lobato. The officer assumed the man he saw was holding a gun, but it was later established that it may have been a Pepsi can.[15] More protests occur; this officer also does not face any legal consequences. Combined, police shootings reflect the ongoing nature of police violence, community frustration, a legal system that rarely pursues criminal charges, and law enforcement agencies that infrequently discipline officers. On the contrary, officers were more likely to be recognized with commendations praising their bravery.

Geographically, the city and county of Denver is a midsized community in the United States. It resides within the Rocky Mountain region of the nation, with mountains to the west and high plains to the east. Denver experiences the four weather seasons of fall, winter, spring, and summer. The county had a growing population, with 492,365 residents in 1980 within 111 square miles (near the data collection start date of 1983), rising to 715,522 residents within 155 square miles by 2020 (when data collection ends).[16] In 2022, Denver was considered the nineteenth-largest city in the United States based on total population.[17] According to the US Census, Denver was racially and ethnically diverse (55 percent white, 29 percent Hispanic, 10 percent Black, 4 percent Asian, and 2 percent Native American).[18] However, the neighborhoods where people live were considered segregated; Black people were more likely to live in Northeast Denver, Latinos in West and North Denver, and whites in South Denver.[19] Gentrification has been an ever-increasing issue since the 1960s; less affluent residents have been pushed out of certain neighborhoods and higher income white tenants have moved in.[20] One study of the nation's fifty largest cities found that Denver gentrified at the third fastest rate from 1990 to 2000 and seventh highest from 2000 to 2013.[21]

In response to various racial and ethnic challenges, people in Denver established several civil rights organizations. Some of the leading groups included the Crusade for Justice, Denver branches of the American Indian Movement (AIM), the Black Panther Party, and the National Association for the Advancement of Colored People (NAACP).[22] This chapter will use Denver as its primary site of data collection and explore how the police department, district attorney's office, and city and county have evolved along with a use-of-force policy allowing law enforcement officers the legal authority to use deadly force. Providing this contextual foundation will set the stage for chapter 6, where we will analyze other regions of the country.

EARLY HISTORY OF DENVER, RACE RELATIONS, AND THE DENVER POLICE DEPARTMENT

Denver was settled by white gold miners in 1858.[23] Two historians described Denver as "largely the preserve of white men"; Asians, Blacks, Mexicans, and Native Americans were not widely welcome.[24] As part of the Kansas Territory, it was integrated into the Missouri Compromise, which was designed to limit the number of slave states. Thus, Colorado was considered part of the Union. The southern half of Colorado was seized by the United States after the Mexican-American War. The negotiation for peace required the 1848 Treaty of Guadalupe Hidalgo, which resulted in Mexico ceding half of its territory to the United States.[25] Although many political governments had laid claim to the land (France, Mexico, Spain, Texas, and the United States), it was the various Native American tribes who had lived in the area for at least 13,000 years that considered this land home.[26] Mesa Verde, Colorado, is one of the oldest archeological sites in North America.[27] Early encounters with European and Spanish trappers and hunters were described as amicable, but as migrants continued to enter the area during the gold rush, the poaching of Native American lands escalated. White migrants' continual violations of legal treaties escalated, triggering increased conflict with Native Americans.[28]

The Sand Creek Massacre was the culmination of Colorado's federal desire to remove native people from the land. In 1864, the Arapahoe and Cheyenne tribes thought they were at peace, as they had surrendered and were considered prisoners by military officials.[29] They were even stationed near a federal fort and received food rations. Before the massacre, the governor of the territory of Colorado, John Evans, applied for and received permission to organize a militia to respond to the "Indian threat." Governor Evans selected John H. Chivington to lead the battalion. As Methodists, both men viewed Native Americans as "savage others" for which Anglo Americans had the "right of conquest" to "the promised land."[30] The historians Lyle Dorsett and Michael McCarthy reported the military attack on the Arapahoe and Cheyenne thus: "One hundred and five women and children, plus twenty-eight men (many of them aged) were shot, scalped, and mutilated on the orders of the fanatical colonel."[31] The historian Gary Roberts noted that the atrocities continued for two days:

> Scalping and more extensive mutilation of the dead continued. Soldiers cut off ears and fingers and the genitals of both men and women. One pregnant woman was slashed open and her unborn child cut from the womb. The body of White Antelope was extensively mutilated. He was scalped several times, his ears were taken, and his scrotum cut off to make a tobacco pouch. Men and women who feigned death or lay

wounded tried to defend themselves when the scalpers came, but they could not.[32]

Body parts were taken by the military battalion as trophies. By 1865, the Sioux, Cheyenne, and Arapahoe retaliated, only to receive a sustained military response.[33] Despite a federal investigation finding wrongdoing regarding the atrocities at Sand Creek, no criminal charges were filed, thus forever confirming that the early peoples of this region of the country had been marked by the government for genocidal removal.[34] Although Chivington's political career was ruined, he was never legally charged with a crime and continued to be celebrated in Colorado.[35] His new occupation was as an Arapahoe County undersheriff.

As the community of Denver began to grow, white male leaders took an interest in addressing drunken disorder, particularly in regard to migrants entering the town. At least one-third of the early businesses were saloons.[36] These establishments were considered multifunctional, providing various resources such as food, room and board, mail service, and entertainment. According to the historian Eugene F. Rider, the formation of the Denver Police Department was preceded by the creation of a city government in 1860 that coincided with the establishment of a law enforcement marshal. The marshal oversaw eight officers, who worked to reduce lawlessness. This law enforcement agency eventually evolved into the Denver Police Department.[37] The other law enforcement entity was the Arapahoe County Sheriff's Office, as Denver at the time was not its own county. This caused many jurisdictional disputes for the next half century. Several months later, a jail site was chosen to house individuals who had been arrested. During this era, frontier justice occasionally emboldened citizens to take the law into their own hands. In so doing, the police often stood aside when individuals arrested for sensational crimes were forcibly removed from the jail and lynched. There were also legalized public hangings before they were moved behind closed doors in penitentiaries.[38] An estimated three thousand people attended the vigilante hanging of L. H. Musgrove in 1868 and the legal public hanging of Theodore Myers in 1873.[39] The former district attorney Mitch Morrissey and his coauthor Norm Brisson reported in *Denver District Attorney's Office: A History of Crime in the Mile High City (1869–2021)* that several additional killings were driven by decisions made by "People's Courts" or "Vigilante Committees." These actions, according to Morrissey and Brisson, demonstrated the need for an organized government in the area, including a prosecutor's office.

According to Rider, the primary use of firearms by law enforcement officers was to shoot "unmuzzled canines."[40] Stray dogs had become a public nuisance and occasionally attacked people. The shooting of wandering dogs lasted until at least 1884, when public uproar finally resulted in the creation of a pound, where unleashed animals could be housed or euthanized outside of public view. Since the creation of the Denver Police Department, there had been difficulties with corruption and ongoing political influence.[41] The elected mayor appointed the police chief, who then influenced officer recruitment. In addition, city leaders and police officers encountered various levels of vice, primarily saloons that offered drinking, gambling, and prostitution. Such a market primarily catered to transitory single Anglo men brought to the city by the railroad in search of gold and work. Over time, the police department adopted uniforms that mirrored New York City's. Officers were provided billy clubs, but they had to purchase their own revolvers.

Despite working to build the railroad, the Chinese were not entirely welcome to live and work in the city. Chinese men had moved into a segregated neighborhood known as "Hop Alley."[42] The men mainly worked as laundrymen. The historian Thomas Noel wrote that although Blacks were seen as inferior, the Chinese were perceived as subhuman.[43] Such perceptions resulted in the anti-Chinese riot of October 31, 1880. After a personal dispute, many white residents attacked Chinese people and their businesses, resulting in the beating death of Look Young.[44] Law enforcement did little to intervene. Afterward, Noel described how Chinese bigotry continued with shootings and attacks by mobs. The persecution drove some residents to suicide. In 1882, Congress passed the Chinese Exclusion Act, curtailing Chinese immigration. The Chinese population continued to decline after these sustained exclusionary policies and white public opposition.

In 1880, with a city population of 35,629, Black citizens petitioned the city council for a Black officer to be put on the Denver police force. The man hired was Isaac Brown. Officer Brown held various jobs during his lifetime, including owning a saloon.[45] Despite this accomplishment for representation, the Black community's legal and social standing continued to remain precarious, as reflected in the legal hanging case of Andrew Green. Fifteen to twenty thousand men, women, and children in holiday attire attended his legal execution in 1886.[46] The author of *Going to Meet a Man*, William W. King, described how the twenty-five-year-old Green, a Black man, attempted to rob a streetcar driver, a white man, of his money box when Green's gun accidentally went off.[47] Although not the original suspect and offering a questionable confession, Green was found guilty in a two-day trial and executed two months after the incident. The "twitch up" hanging went horribly wrong; Green struggled to breathe for at least five minutes and was left dangling for twenty-two minutes to ensure he was dead. King described how various news agencies covered the reporting of the case differently, but ultimately, the brutal killing of Green was the last public hanging in the city, as it pursued a more progressive image similar to cities in the northeast and Europe. Members of the Black community also attended the execution and were there exposed to the fact that racist terror existed beyond the geographic region of the US South.

During that same year, according to Rider, a Denver police captain shot and killed a man who was holding a revolver at a pawn shop. The gun was not loaded.[48] The officer reluctantly resigned after extensive protest from the Irish community. Afterward, he moved to the state of Washington and was employed by a private detective agency. Several city initiatives in 1891 pushed for increased police department standards in physical fitness and mental health. For a short period of time, employment shifted toward performance rather than political influence, and there was increased oversight of on-duty officer behavior.[49] This, however, did not prevent controversial shootings. In 1894, a white Denver Police Officer shot and killed a Black Arapahoe County deputy sheriff and claimed self-defense.[50] The Denver officer's account of the incident didn't make sense: Smith was not only shot and killed but also beaten by several officers. The DA at the time pursued criminal charges, and the officer was found guilty of second-degree murder and given a ten-year sentence. The officer appealed his conviction, and the Colorado Supreme Court reversed the order. The DA's office never pursued a new trial. Afterward, the officer went to work with a fuel company to break up labor strikes.

A small handbook given to officers outlined when to use lethal force. The 1897 handbook stated:

Q.—Under what circumstances may a policeman use his pistol?

A.—He should never draw nor attempt to use his pistol except in extraordinary cases, such as the actual defense of his own life, when attacked with a deadly weapon, or in active pursuit of escaping criminals charged with great crimes, such as murder, burglary, arson, etc. Shooting at another is a crime except when proved to be done in self-defense.[51]

By 1899, the chief of police reported the need to properly train officers in how to use firearms. The chief believed such training could have been helpful in stopping an escaped fugitive.[52] In 1900, an off-duty officer named Charles S. Secrest was drinking at a saloon when he shot and killed a man during an argument.[53] The officer initially reported he was "trying out his new gun" before claiming self-defense. The DA did not file criminal charges. The same officer, once again off duty, shot and killed another man less than six years later while playing a dice game at another saloon. The DA filed charges, and the jury found the officer guilty of second-degree murder. He received a fourteen-to-twenty-year prison sentence but was paroled in 1913.[54]

Despite covering the time period of 1858 to 1905, Rider, writing in 1971, did not offer much commentary regarding the Denver Police Department's interactions with racial and ethnic minority groups other than this paragraph:

It is difficult to draw conclusions about Denver police treatment of minority groups, such as Negroes, Mexican-Americans, and the Chinese. Because race prejudice was pervasive then, not only in the city but throughout the nation, the press might well have overlooked incidents of police discrimination based on race. Nevertheless, it is apparent that some officers allowed their racial attitudes to influence them in the performance of their duties.[55]

In conclusion, Rider emphasized how various law enforcement agencies operated in Denver, not only Denver police officers. During the Civil War, a volunteer regiment enforced laws. Later, a merchant's police and private detective agencies ensured the protection of business establishments. In addition, extralegal groups such as vigilantes formed occasionally in response to perceived wrongdoing and encountered little to no legal consequences. Arapahoe County operated as the sheriff with arrest powers until 1902, when Denver became its own city and county. The Denver Sheriff's Office was created at the time, but only to provide security for the court and jail. At the opening of the twentieth century, the Denver Police Department had become the area's primary institutionalized law enforcement agency.[56]

In 1900, the Black population was nearly 2 percent of the city's population.[57] Many Blacks had moved to the Five Points neighborhood, the heart of the Black community, and worked hard to purchase their own homes; many whites in the area did not rent or sell to Blacks.[58] Although Denver was not located in the South, where Jim Crow laws prevailed, personal businesses and public institutions maintained de facto forms of segregation. Such forms of discrimination could be found in education, housing, policing, and public accommodations. Blacks were only allowed to sit in the balcony at movie theaters, were not permitted to rent public halls for social events, and had restricted times and days for visiting swimming pools, to name several examples. Denver's Blacks were also involved in various forms of civil rights organizing. In Lynda Dickson's dissertation, "The Early Club Movement Among Black Women in Denver: 1890–1925," she stated: "Denver's black community, like those in other urban areas, embraced the belief that in order to improve their condition, they must rely upon themselves."[59] The earliest organizations were churches, including the Zion Baptist Church and African Methodist Episcopal Church. Black women formed at least twenty-two clubs during this time, working to reflect the motto of "Lifting as We Climb" by supporting self-improvement, self-help, and racial unity. Men and women joined forces in 1914 to establish a Denver branch of the National Association for the Advancement of Colored People (NAACP). In 1925, this organization held its national convention in Denver.[60]

The historian Thomas Noel reported that one-fourth of Denver's population throughout the nineteenth century was foreign born.[61] Germans were the largest group of immigrants, then individuals from Ireland. German and Irish saloons helped immigrants from these two countries attain economic and political power. Although far fewer in number, Italians were not welcome in the city and worked some of the lowest-paying jobs as day laborers. They lived in shacks along the river. Italian immigrants were disliked by nativists because of their language, culture, and religion. One of the most brutal lynchings was of Dan Arata in 1893, reflecting the time's anti-Italian prejudice.[62] Arata, a manager/bartender, killed a sixty-two-year-old customer who was a Civil War veteran. A mob stormed the jail chanting "kill the Dago." They broke into the building and took Arata away to be hanged and shot. As the crowd grew, several participants who missed the original hanging wanted to repeat the murder. Arata was cut down and hanged again in a different location. The autopsy account stated the "hanging was done by parties unknown to the jury."[63] By 1900, nearly two-thirds of saloons were operated by immigrants, and thus, political and nativist fears were more than likely mobilized in attempts to restrict these businesses. Prostitution and gambling became illegal in 1912, and by 1916, four years before the national prohibition of alcohol, the city voted to outlaw the selling and distribution of liquor. This effectively led to the demise of saloons, initiated underground forms of police corruption, and paved the way for a new organization in the area based on hate and white Anglo patriotism.[64]

As the city of Denver continued to grow, the Ku Klux Klan (KKK) emerged onto the scene during the second wave of Klan organization occurring around the nation.[65] The state of Colorado housed the second-largest Ku Klux Klan membership, after the state of Indiana. According to the historian Phil Goodstein, the Denver chapter announced its presence in a local newspaper on June 17, 1921, as the "the very best citizens of Denver" devoted to improving the community.[66] They preached increased patriotism, religious influence, and uniting Protestant whites. They were against Blacks, Catholics, immigrants, and Jews. After several years, the Klan became a political powerhouse, reaching the height of its influence between 1924 and 1925.[67] They elected a Klan-supported mayor (Ben Stapleton), governor (Clarence Morley), and senator (Rice Means), along with many Denver police officers, including its chief of police (William Candlish), and various city council members, judges, teachers, and business leaders.[68] The fall of the organization began after several scandals involving its grand dragon, Dr. John Galen Locke, including tax evasion and the kidnapping of a fifteen-year-old high school student.[69] A Klansman judge, Henry Bray, dismissed the charges on a technicality, but Dr. Locke's reputation was tarnished.[70] The difficulties the KKK experienced in Denver and the state of Colorado reflected the nation-wide decline of the second wave of the organization's effort to seize and maintain power.[71]

By 1929, the Black population had increased slightly to 2.25 percent, and the Latino population began growing faster.[72] Employers actively recruited Mexican and Hispanic laborers from southern Colorado and northern New Mexico to work in the sugar beet fields.[73] In 1930, the Latino popu-lation increased to 2.4 percent of the city's 287,861 residents, an increase from 0.5 percent in 1920.[74] Similar to other racialized minority groups, Latinos were segregated into some of the poorest sections of the city. In a 1938 report, the Youth Survey Committee of the Adult Education Council of Denver found the geographic area along the Platte River had the highest rates of delinquency and unemployment. US Census data indicated that people of Mexican descent lived in this area, whereas the second-highest rates of delinquency and unemployment were in neighborhoods with a higher proportion of Black residents.[75] These living conditions and higher levels of interaction with law enforce-ment officers led to the increased targeting of Latino youth. In the early 1940s, when the city of Los Angeles, California, became involved in the Zoot Suit Riots, similar forms of harassment toward Latino/a youth were occurring in the city of Denver.[76] These were the years of a "war on gangs," and Latino/a youth were perceived as synonymous with gangs.[77] The Denver Police Department accelerated various community-sponsored initiatives to arrest and punish Latino youth for curfew vio-lations, loitering, and vagrancy. The police force only had one Latino and two Black officers; it was overwhelmingly composed of white offi-cers, who, at the time, were being criticized for police brutality and aggressive treatment of minority residents.[78] A 1947 study conducted by Mayor Newton's Interim Committee on Human Relations reported many instances of police brutality, which were described as a result of the lingering problems from the Klan days.[79]

Reflective of the times, a Denver police officer named Delmar Reed shot and killed a fifteen-year-old boy, who was Black, named Charles H. Wilson.[80] Charles had escaped his custody when Officer Reed said he fired his gun accidentally. The DA charged the officer with first-degree mur-der, but a jury acquitted him in 1951. In the late 1940s and mid-1950s, racial hierarchies became acknowledged within the city and county. Several city reports and newspaper articles described the dire conditions in which Blacks (2 percent of the population) and Latinos (10 percent of the population) were living.[81] The Denver Commission on Human Relations concluded, "Prejudice is an expensive luxury. The cost in dollars and cents is staggering. The cost in human misery is enormous."[82] The *Rocky Mountain News* published a seven-part series focusing on Denver's "Spanish-American Problem," which was recharacterized as "Spanish-Americans Move Onward" several years later, after receiving criticism about the earlier title.[83]

Despite a growing awareness of inequality, the Denver Police Department maintained a "get-tough" attitude. Denver had grown to 530,000 people, for which the police department had seven hundred police officers and 120 civilian employees. Comparable cities had a higher police-to-citizen ratio (Denver had 1.55 officers per thousand people, compared to other cities with two to three per thousand). The lack of manpower was the most significant critique made in a 1959 *Denver Post* article titled "How Good Is Denver's Police Force?" The writer, Lawrence Weiss, examined the department's low morale.[84] Weiss emphasized the good work officers were doing despite the challenges of a few bad apples. He was reluctant to believe most claims of police brutality, despite several officers being fired or resigning because of misbehavior, misuse of force, or instances of criminal involvement.[85] Weiss stated, "A good many people have a deep-seated hatred of policemen, and many citizens regularly blame the police instead of themselves when they get into trouble." Some people were simply "police-haters." Police officers desired greater public confidence, and the *Denver Post* writer encouraged the public to provide a vote of confidence for the department.[86] Nevertheless, the full extent of the number and severity of criminal charges against officers did not become public until the early 1960s.

LAW ENFORCEMENT ACTIVITIES OF THE 1960S AND 1970S

In the early 1960s, Denver gained a reputation as the "crooked-cop capital." Officers began to be charged with a very high number of burglaries.[87]

Over time, sixty-one individuals faced criminal charges, of whom fifty-four of the defendants were Denver police officers.[88] A former cop turned news writer, Mort Stern, described the process of an everyday police officer who obtains the job as an officer but becomes corrupted by those around him to illicitly earn additional money on the side.[89] A large part of the problem, according to Stern, was the ease of becoming a police officer in a labor market where not enough people were applying for this type of work. He advocated higher standards for becoming a police officer, better pay, and benefits. Other criticism was directed toward the police department's lack of supervision, which looked the other way when observing or receiving reports of officer wrongdoing.[90] It was estimated that almost 20 percent of the Denver Police Department had participated in the burglary ring.[91]

Criminal activity of police officers was not the only issue plaguing the city and county of Denver. Racial and ethnic relations that had historically been suppressed began to be publicly challenged more frequently by civil rights groups and the broader community. Denver was home to one of the four leading Chicano organizations in the nation, the Crusade for Justice, which originated to combat problems with the treatment of Chicana/o youth in schools and negative minority relationships with the police department.[92] In addition to the Crusade for Justice, splinter groups of the American Indian Movement (AIM) and Black Panther Party (BPP) were also formed in Denver to respond to issues with law enforcement. In studying the Denver Police Department, the political scientist David Bayley and his coauthor Harold Mendelsohn, a sociologist, reported in 1968, "The police seem to play a role in the life of minority people out of all proportion to the role they play in the lives of dominant majority."[93] Bayley and Mendelsohn conducted four public opinion surveys, including the general public, Blacks and Latinos, Denver police officers, and community leaders. Spanish-surnamed individuals were more critical than whites or Black people regarding policing in their neighborhoods. More than one-fourth of respondents of color reported that their police encounters were unfriendly or prejudiced, whereas only 4 percent of whites described similar feelings. The researchers found that despite higher levels of negative interactions and police brutality, minority group members were less likely to file complaints. Nearly half of the Spanish-surnamed individuals believed it would not do any good, whereas only 20 percent of whites thought their complaints would go unsupported.

Denver's Chicano historian Ernesto B. Vigil provided an overview of numerous instances of brutality, corruption, and cases of deadly force that distanced community members from the police and pushed community leaders to create civil rights organizations.[94] Vigil described the killing of nineteen-year-old Edward Larry Romero in 1962, who was shot in the back by an off-duty officer working at a bar.[95] Less than two years later, nineteen-year-old Alfred Salazar was killed after a police officer struck him on the head with a nightstick.[96] In 1967, additional controversial killings included Louis Piñedo, Eugene Cook, and Robert Gene Castro, resulting in protests and the eventual resignation of Police Chief Harold Dill.[97] At the time, issues of police violence were sparking nationwide protests and rioting.[98] The community in Denver advocated for a civilian review board, to no avail. According to George Kelly in the book *The Old Gray Mayors of Denver*, Mayor Thomas Currigan initiated two programs focused on the Denver Police Department, but these programs did not last long. First, Currigan created a Committee on City-Citizens Relationships that included minority representatives from the community instead of forming a citizen review board. Most of the community complaints received were directed at the police department, but the committee became bogged down with paperwork, and a lack of purpose resulted in its demise. The second program was based on the theory that the police department could improve community relationships. This resulted in a program named the Police Community Relations Bureau, established in 1965. According to Kelly, Denver Police Chief Harold Dill ensured the program's failure, as he did not support the captain in charge or offer resources for the program to move forward.

News reports from the 1960s reflect many challenges within the Denver Police Department. In 1965, the manager of safety announced the implementation of a new policy that required an officer to be suspended with pay after an officer-involved shooting to allow the officer to "collect himself."[99] The officer could return after the DA announced whether there would be any pending criminal charges. To protect themselves from civil suits, police officers were purchasing a particular type of insurance to reduce civil liability in cases of brutality or misconduct.[100] In addition, the police department was being encouraged to recruit and train minority officers.[101] The Denver Police Department had 826 officers, but only 3 percent were Black and 2 percent Latino in a city that was 14 percent Black and 20 percent Latino. Increasing the number of minority officers was a recommendation from the President's Commission on Law Enforcement in the Administration of Justice to reduce community tensions. However, the Denver Ministerial Alliance reported problems also existed because of a lack of minority officers in higher ranks in the department.[102] Most officers of color never rose above the rank of technician, whereas white officers were represented at all levels.

Vigil reported that killings by police continued into the 1970s with the shooting deaths of Luis Martinez in 1973, Arthur "Artie" Espinoza and James Hinojos in 1977, Felix Jaramillo in 1979, and sixteen-year-old Joey Rodriguez in 1979.[103] A grand jury indicted Officer David E. Neil for shooting Espinoza at the park, but he was acquitted.[104] The family later won a civil suit for an unknown amount. The DA held grand juries for the killing of Jaramillo and Rodriguez, both of which resulted in no charges. Such a climate led a Chicano writer for the *El Gallo* newspaper to sarcastically report, "Killing Mexicans has never been a crime [for the police]; [Mexicans] provide good target practice, and there are always plenty of them around."[105] In addition to Latinos, the killings of Carl Newland, who was Black, and Sidney Whitecrane, a Native American, highlighted the issue of police violence as a deep structural problem for the Denver Police Department.

In 1974, the Denver City Council considered establishing an "advisory panel" composed of four citizens and three police officers to review allegations against the police department.[106] The council was concerned that the Staff Inspection Bureau (SIB) had failed to investigate "citizen complaints fairly and thoroughly." Such a recommendation was opposed by the Denver Police Union and the Police Protective Association, and the police chief also reported that such a panel may raise legal concerns for non–law enforcement officers. Similar failed attempts at creating a civilian review board were described as occurring in 1964, 1968, 1971, and 1972. In 1976, the new mayor Bill McNichols used an executive order to establish the Citizens Police Advisory Review Committee in an effort to thwart a community initiative to establish a stronger civilian commission to be added to the ballot.[107] The citizens group Coalition Against Police Abuse did its best to advocate for the creation of a civilian commission with broader powers over the police department, including a say in who served in the role of police chief. Although they were unsuccessful, the five-member committee that was created by the mayor immediately began reviewing SIB reports; if found incomplete, they recommended further investigation. After eight months of reviewing files, the committee reported that certain policemen had reputations as "brutal" but that the department's response was primarily to discredit citizen complaints rather than investigate.[108] The committee sought to obtain personnel files from the police department in regard to several questionable cases, but the group's status continued to remain contested.[109] Of longer institutional longevity was Mayor McNichols and DA Dale Tooley's creation of the Citizens Appreciate Police (CAP) nonprofit organization, which recognizes Denver police officers who serve the public above and beyond the regular call of duty. As of 2020, the organization has recognized over four hundred officers with this award.[110]

CITY AND COUNTY LEADERSHIP AND EFFORTS TO REVIEW POLICE SHOOTINGS: 1983 TO 2020

The thirty-eight years of police shootings covered in this book include the time period between 1983 to 2020. During this timeframe, there were changes in leadership of the city and county, police department, and district attorney's office. These city officials were seen as more progressive and diverse compared to other midsize cities, but none of these leaders altered the law that justified enforcement force with a firearm, working instead primarily to ensure police-citizen encounters that were less publicly explosive. Law enforcement officers in Colorado were given legal authority to shoot someone in cases where the officer reasonably believed it was necessary (1) to defend himself or a third person or (2) effect the arrest or prevent the escape of an individual who has committed a felony or is fleeing with the use of a deadly weapon.[111]

From July 1983 to July 1991, Federico Peña served as the mayor of Denver. He was the first Latino mayor of this city. He was reelected for a second term but did not pursue a third term, as he became secretary of transportation under President Clinton. Norman S. Early was elected as the district attorney, the first African American to serve in this role. He was reelected three times and served until 1993. According to Morrissey and Brisson, Early wrote a letter in 1983 to the police chief urging him to overhaul police training; this was finally enacted in 2003, after the killing of Paul Childs. During this time, DA letters were made publicly available.[112] The chiefs of the Denver Police Department included Art Dill (1972 to 1983), Robert Shaughney (1983), Thomas E. Coogan (1983 to 1987), Rudy Phannenstiel (1987), and Aristedes "Ari" Zavaras (1987 to 1991). Art Dill was suspended and eventually resigned after an allegation of proceeds obtained from police department bingo games. Coogan resigned after a relationship with a policewoman under his command. They later married, and he became chief of police of the Littleton Police Department from 2007 to 2013. Ari Zavaras later became the safety manager and the director of the Colorado Department of Corrections.

From July 1991 to July 2003, Wellington Webb was the mayor of Denver. He was the first Black mayor of this city, and he served three terms. During this time, William "Bill" Ritter was elected district attorney, and he served in this role for three terms, from 1993 to 2005. He was later elected governor of Colorado and performed these duties from 2007 to 2011. The chiefs of the Denver Police Department included Robert Cantwell (1991), Jim Collier (1991 to 1992), David Michaud (1992 to 1998), Tom Sanchez (1998 to 2000), and Gerry Whitman (2000 to 2011). In June 1996, District Attorney Bill Ritter appointed an advisory team to review the policies and procedures of the Denver Police Department as to whether deadly physical force decisions should result in criminal charges.[113] A retired Colorado Supreme Court Justice, William H. Erickson, led the team of former law enforcement officers, elected officials, and community leaders. The decision for such a commission was pushed by the criticism the DA had received for not filing criminal charges on two off-duty officers involved in the Jeff Truax shooting. Truax was a young white man shot to death while attempting to flee a fight in his vehicle.[114] His passenger was also shot and wounded. The advisory team devoted a year to reviewing the procedures for shooting investigations and a total of eleven officer-involved shootings. In conclusion, the Erickson Commission "found no fundamental flaws in the procedures that are currently being followed."[115] However, they also compared police shootings in

Denver to twenty-five other similar-sized jurisdictions around the country and found that Denver's criminal law gave great latitude and freedom to law enforcement officers. Thus, greater change or progress was suggested to result in improved internal policies, procedures, and training.

From July 2003 to July 2011, John Hickenlooper was mayor of Denver. He was reelected but then resigned to become governor of Colorado. He served as governor until 2019 and then was elected to the US Senate in 2021. Mitchell R. Morrissey was the district attorney, and he was reelected three times (2005 to 2017). Despite the typical expectation that each mayor would select their own chief of police, Mayor Hickenlooper retained Gerry Whitman as the chief of the Denver Police Department. In response to criticism regarding the police shooting of Paul Childs in 2003, the incoming mayor, John Hickenlooper, initiated a thirty-eight-member task force composed of community activists, law enforcement officers, city government representatives, and other community members. The goal of the task force was to review policy strategies for reforming the Denver Police Department. The group met for a period of 104 days but struggled to agree on many recommendations.[116] In conjunction with the mayor and city council, the city and county of Denver established the Office of the Independent Monitor in 2004 to serve as a citizens' oversight of the Denver Police and Sheriff's Office.[117]

In 2008, the city and county contracted with the Police Assessment Resource Center (PARC) to review twenty-four officer-involved shootings from 1999 to 2003.[118] They concluded that Denver met and even exceeded national standards in many areas, "making the DPD one of a handful of American police departments becoming a national leader." Yet, most of this progress occurred after 2004.[119] PARC encouraged the Denver Police Department to hold officers accountable and learn from these incidents. They used the legal reasoning in *Graham v. Connor*, arguing the discretion of whether to use force "must be judged from the perspective of a reasonable officer on the scene, rather than with the 20/20 vision of hindsight."[120] The evaluators criticized the DPD for some of these cases, including contradictory crime scene investigations and lack of follow-up on some leads. They also encouraged better collection of physical evidence. Some investigative interviews were found to be rushed and often included improper leading questions.[121] Many of the interviews did not match the material evidence. The evaluators discouraged the granting of medals of honor or other awards for many of the law enforcement shootings because some of these incidents occurred as a result of tactical errors. Thus, rather than shooting the suspect, there should have been a demonstration of increased restraint by the officer. PARC discouraged officers from putting themselves in proximity to vehicles and endangering themselves.[122] Overall, this report replicated several assessments conducted over the past forty years that sought to determine whether officer decision making was objectively reasonable in light of the facts and circumstances. Legally, such decision making was relatively broad.

From July 2011 to July 2023, Michael Hancock was mayor. Mitchell Morrissey continued as DA until term limits prevented him from continuing beyond three terms. Beth McCann was then elected as DA (2017 to present). She was the first woman to serve as DA in Denver. A 2019 *American Bar Association Journal* featured her as one of the "Prosecutors Changing the Paradigm." The chief of police for the Denver Police Department was Robert White (2011 to 2018), followed by Paul Pazen (2018 to 2022), and then Ron Thomas (2022 to present). The mayor selected both police chiefs to improve relations between the police and the community.

⸺ ∞ ⸺

Each community in the United States has its own history, geography, and social climate, and these have shaped community relationships with institutions and city and county leaders. Law enforcement was but one institution existing in a social environment that was stratified and unequal. Rather than reducing inequality, law enforcement enhanced disparities, and that dominance was legally enforced. The historical context provided in this chapter highlights how the law has not uniformly protected everyone equally. Marginalized groups in Denver have received the brunt of differential treatment. Violence has been used to seize property and maintain racialized social control. Individuals acting on behalf of vigilante groups or working to enforce state terror could face legal oversight but were rarely found criminally liable or incarcerated. Instead, the murders were listed as a killing by "parties unknown." As society has evolved over the years, the use of public violence as a punishment has shifted behind closed doors, whereas law enforcement remains the only authority permitted to use deadly force on the general public in response to perceived life-threatening behaviors. The use of violence has remained a staple of US society in its ability to maintain power. In William King's book on the legal execution of Andrew Green in 1886, he questioned how the law could be used to allow violence toward specific groups and against others. What was the possibility of justice in a hierarchical society where justice was more of a process than an act?[123] The historian Stephen Leonard asked a similar question when attempting to understand the patterns of lynchings in the state of Colorado.[124] The defining characteristic in his analysis was the inability to hold the people actually participating in the lynching accountable.

2

DIVERGENT LIFE CHANCES FOR GETTIN' SHOT BY THE POLICE

You will very likely never be an eyewitness to an officer-involved shooting. Even the shooting that occurred outside my (Durán's) apartment complex, I was inside at the time and only after running outside after the shooting happened could I begin documenting the incident. Thus, the most significant portion of my data gathering on this topic has been the Denver district attorney's office (DA). For each shooting since at least 1983 the DA produces a decision letter if no criminal charges are filed, and they "invite" the public to view the investigative files if there are any questions or concerns. In the summer of 2022, I was attempting to gain access to the investigative files one last time to finalize the data collection analysis for this book. At that point, all the data had been collected and analyzed, but I didn't like the descriptive statistic stating that I had only reviewed 61.4 percent of the files at the DA's office. Since my weekly visits in 2007, 2008, and 2012, I had not been back. My effort to do so in 2022 was completely different. The listed person of contact by the new DA, Beth McCann as of 2017, was no longer in the office; I was told to contact the "communications director."

I imagined replicating my previous visits to the DA office; these had included the following process: I send an email using official letterhead requesting access, using my university and personal credentials ("PhD," "Professor"), and wait for a response. I have a phone conversation regarding the data I am seeking. I explain that I'm a sociologist who studies patterns and trends. We schedule a visit for me to physically view the files.

I dress in business casual clothes. I'm driven to the Wellington E. Webb Municipal Office Building in downtown Denver and get dropped off by my family. I walk in the door and pass through a metal detector. In a tray, I place metal objects, including my laptop. I take an elevator up to the DA's office, state my name and whom I am there to see at the glass window. I sit outside in the hallway and wait. The representative meets me at the door and walks me back to a cubicle near the DA's office, where I can begin reviewing the files. We engage in small talk, but once I am here, let the work begin! There are bankers boxes stacked in and around my work cubicle. Inside each box are several binders, one for each shooting. The newer cases have a DVD for which I can watch samples of interviews; the older cases occasionally contain a VHS tape. I compare the information with what I have in my Excel file and take a lot of notes. This is the routine for each day. I am told by the first assistant district attorney that only a small number of residents have entered this office to review files. It's clear why. This is not a library, and despite Denver's approach, which is not shared nationally, this is a contested space. The DA must decide whether "the totality of the facts" indicate there is "a reasonable likelihood that all of the elements of the crime charged can be proved beyond a reasonable doubt, to twelve jurors, at trial, after considering applicable defenses."[1]

In 2022, I am told the process is now different. The communications director tells me that "no one since 2018 has requested to review the investigative files" and that now the process must go as follows: (1) sign a confidentiality agreement, (2) review the material of interest, and (3) submit a records request, which required paying a fee. Denver, the city and county, which once had "prided" itself on having the most transparent officer-involved-shooting decision cases in the country, has changed into something much less so.[2] I must admit, decision letters are much better than news reports for data coding, but it is often the additional details not included in the DA's letter that are important for understanding the entirety of the case. Now, Denver is treating its officer-involved-shooting information with much more secrecy, and this prevents DA transparency and oversight.[3] Therefore, 61.4 percent of case files I reviewed can no longer be replicated; researchers no longer have access to even 1 percent of the case files.[4]

When I first began visiting the DA's office, the only common aspect of each shooting case (according to prosecutors) was that the officer felt his or her life in danger and had to make a split-second decision about which type of use of force to use in order to stop the threat. This book will complicate that claim. As I collected, coded, and analyzed each case, the number of cases in my files increased to the point that I needed the help of someone who analyzed statistics regularly and had much more knowledge of the process. Meet Dr. Oralia Loza.

Initially, when I (Loza) received this dataset, I approached it like any new dataset that I was not familiar with. The important but simple first step I took was to look at the data and become familiar with how the data is organized and labeled. It was initially sent to me in an Excel file. I next had to prepare it for import and use in a statistical software package. This involved ensuring all measures were numeric (e.g., coding yes/no responses to 1/0). For this dataset, each row represents an individual who was shot by police in Denver, Colorado, since 1983. For each individual (row), we had measures or variables (columns) describing the person shot, the officers who shot, the situation surrounding the shooting, how the case was handled by the police and DAs office, and the sources of data for each case. For the most part, I was not familiar with this type of data or information or how it is typically collected or organized by researchers who study police shootings. I learned how to prepare the dataset for analysis through conversations with Durán. I made suggestions, and he helped me understand what would be appropriate to do with the data. In some fields, the data is collected in a systematic way, using standardized questionnaires that are collected in the same way for every person in the study. This was not the case here.

Next, I ran descriptive statistics, which allows me to look at each variable, one at a time, and determine whether it is a categorical variable, with levels or options (e.g., sex is either male or female); a continuous variable, with units (e.g., age in years); or a count variable (e.g., number of times was a person shot). In some cases, the categorical variables had many options, and I made suggestions to Durán to reduce the number of levels by combining those that were similar. For example, if a variable had options that included spouse or partner in a gendered manner (e.g., wife/girlfriend vs. husband/boyfriend), I combined them (e.g., partner/spouse). This phase of the data utilization process is called database management. This is also the stage in which you address any inconsistencies in the data, particularly for related variables. For example, we have a variable for whether the case involved a lawsuit settlement (no, yes, attempted). For cases where there was a lawsuit settlement, we should have the lawsuit settlement amount. However, that information was missing in some cases. If a data point was missing, I labeled why it was missing—if we knew why. Data for a variable can be missing because of error (e.g., data should be in the dataset but is not), because it is not relevant in that particular case (e.g., if an officer was not shot, we do not record how many times they were shot), or because the information is restricted or not available for public or research use.

Once the data-cleaning process was completed, we moved on to the analysis stage. We wanted first to look at each individual variable and then look to see if the variables were associated with age group, sex, foreign-born status, and race/ethnicity of the person shot. For the analysis, we organized the measures in the following headers: Sociodemographic Characteristics of the Person Shot, Alcohol and Drug Use of the Person Shot, Shooting-Related Measures, Incident-Related Factors, Officers Who Shot, Sociodemographic Characteristics of the Officers Who Shot, Post-Shooting Outcomes, and Data Sources. After completing the analysis and reporting the results in a table format and as a text summary, I started reflecting on the implications of the results more deeply. This was in the back of my mind throughout this process, but it wasn't until it was time to write about the results and link them to not only what I know from the scientific literature on the topic but also what I know from the news and community did the results become meaningful. Because I primarily work with public health data (e.g., substance use, sexual risk behaviors for HIV, LGBTQ+ health, health disparities), I am always aware that the data I am working with represents people, human beings with certain characteristics that may be living with a disease, engaging in a behavior that has implications for their health, or exposed to a condition in their community or environment that affects their health. Data allows us to find patterns and potential points of intervention to prevent disease or negative health outcomes. More recently, however, the data I have been working with has implications for policy changes; without the policy changes, patterns will persist.

In most cases, the primary data source for the information presented in this chapter came from district attorney (DA) decision letters (93.3 percent). Additional sources included a review of the complete district attorney file (61.4 percent) at the DA's office; a review of DA videos (12.8 percent) that could include interviews with officers, witnesses, and crime scene footage; a copy of the autopsy (72.2 percent among those who died) provided by the Denver medical examiner for those who died from the gunshot or soon after from suicide; and news coverage (85.6 percent), primarily by local news agencies. The median number of newspaper articles for each shooting was three (1, 5).[5] In a separate analysis by time wave, there were significant differences for all the various data sources by time wave (p-value<0.001). These results are shown in table 2.1. The decision letter was available for most cases and for all time waves, except for a drop in 1991 to 2000 to 81.9 percent. As noted in the introductory paragraph, the review of DA files decreased from 96.9 percent (1983 to 1990) to 71.4 percent (2001 to 2012) and dropped to the review of only one case between 2011 and 2020. A review of video evidence held

TABLE 2.1. Bivariate Associations Between Data Sources and Time Wave for All Police Shooting Cases in Denver, Colorado, 1983–2020 (N=298)

Data sources	1983–1990		1991–2000		2001–2010		2011–2020		
	N	Frequency (%)	N	Frequency (%)	N	Frequency (%)	N	Frequency (%)	p-value
Decision letter	65	63 (96.9)	83	68 (81.9)	63	62 (98.4)	87	86 (98.9)	<0.001*
Review of DA file	65	63 (96.9)	83	74 (89.2)	63	45 (71.4)	87	1 (1.1)	<0.001*
Review of video	65	1 (1.5)	83	21 (25.3)	63	11 (17.5)	87	5 (5.7)	<0.001*
Copy of autopsy (among those who died)	28	2 (7.1)	34	33 (97.1)	38	27 (71.1)	50	47 (94.0)	<0.001*
News coverage	65	22 (33.8)	83	83 (100)	63	63 (100)	87	87 (100)	<0.001*

* Significant bivariate test results are noted. These were determined at alpha level 0.05 or p-value<0.05.
Note: A copy of the autopsy was requested for those who died as a result of the shooting or soon after by suicide (N=150).

at the DA's office was available for one case between 1983 and 1990 (1.5 percent), then increased to 25.3 percent between 1991 and 2000, and then
dropped to 5.7 percent between 2011 and 2020. Improved relations with
the Denver medical examiner's office resulted in an increase in autopsy
records. Only two cases (7.1 percent) were available from 1983 to 1990,
97.1 percent between 1991 to 2000, 71.1 percent between 2001 to 2010,
and then 94.0 percent between 2011 and 2020.[6] News coverage records
were available for 33.8 percent of the cases between 1983 and 1990 and
then 100 percent of the files after 1991.

POLICE SHOOTING RESULTS

The number and rate of police shootings per year (1983 to 2020) in Denver, Colorado, are displayed in figure 1.[7] The yearly number of incidents
was highest in 1983, at fourteen shootings. Given the city and county's population of 492,365, it also reflected the highest rate of shootings (2.84) per
100,000 residents. The lowest number of shootings per year was in 2005,
with a population of 600,158, making this one shooting the lowest rate at
0.17 per 100,000 residents. The only pattern observed from police shootings was a slight decline in law enforcement officers using force with a
firearm. The decade averages for the 1980s and 1990s were remarkably
similar (1.80 and 1.70), as were the averages for 2000 and 2010s (1.02 and
1.24). The average rate of shootings per 100,000 residents during this
thirty-eight-year time period was 1.41. Although there is currently no standardized definition or data source available at this time to compare
police shootings by city or county, there have been some developments in
state comparisons. Using data acquired by the *Washington Post* on fatal
police shooting encounters, the researchers Jon Shane, Brian Lawton, and
Zoe Swenson found that for the years 2015 to 2016, Colorado ranked ninth
highest in the country, with Denver one of the twenty riskiest cities for a
police shooting.[8] However, having data for only two calendar years makes
it difficult to compare across space and time.

Descriptive statistics, "statistical techniques for describing the patterns
found in a set of data," for all measures by age group are found in table
A2.1 in appendix 2.[9]

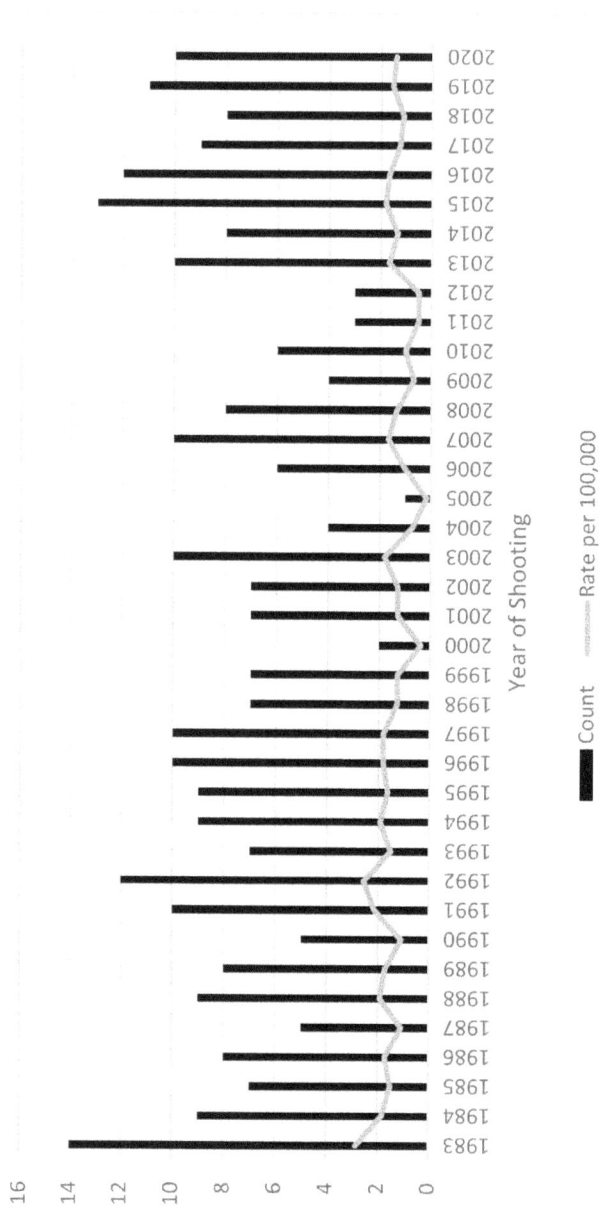

FIGURE 2.1. Count and rate per 100,000 for all cases of police shootings in Denver, Colorado, 1983–2020 (N=298).

A total of 298 officer-involved shootings occurred in Denver, Colorado, between 1983 and 2020. In Table A2.1, we provide descriptive statistics for all cases and measures. Given that most continuous variables were not normally distributed, we provide median and quartiles (Q1: 25th percentile, Q3: 75th percentile). After sorting the data from minimum to maximum value, quartiles break the data up into four equal parts, each holding 25 percent of the data. Between Q1 and Q3, we have the middle 50 percent of the data, or half of the cases. For categorical variables with levels or options (e.g., sex: male, female), we provide frequency and percent. Measures include sociodemographic characteristics and alcohol and drug use of the person shot and measures for the shooting, incident, officers involved, and postshooting outcomes.

SOCIODEMOGRAPHIC CHARACTERISTICS OF THE PERSON SHOT

Almost all the individuals shot by law enforcement were male (95.3 percent) and US-born (95.6 percent). The median age was 29 (22, 37) years old. In terms of race or ethnicity, 44.3 percent were Latino, 31.1 percent white, 21.6 percent Black, and 3.0 percent Asian/Native American/Multiracial or Nonwhite Other. Almost half of the cases were people who had a listed address in Denver (49.8 percent), a large portion lived somewhere in the state of Colorado (43.3 percent), a small proportion lived in the adjacent city of Aurora (3.2 percent), and the remainder had an address listed outside of Colorado (3.6 percent).[10] Comparatively, the individuals shot by the police contrast with city and county demographics for Denver. From 1980 to 2020, males averaged 49.7 percent of the population, and nearly nine-tenths were born in the United States (89.3 percent). Potential reasons why males and US-born residents were shot more frequently by law enforcement officers will be explored in the bivariate associations section of this chapter. Latinos and Blacks were both overrepresented in terms of the number of shooting victims within the city and county; whites were underrepresented.

Table 2.2 summarizes US Census data for 1980 to 2020 for Denver County, Colorado.[11] The table includes the total population and the percentage of the population that is Black, Latino, Non-Hispanic white, male,

TABLE 2.2. Population Size and Percent of Population for Denver County, Colorado, Between 1980 and 2020

Year	Population size	Black	Latino	White, non-Hispanic	Male	Foreign-born
1980	492,365	12.0%	18.7%*	66.7%	48.2%	6.2%
1990	467,610	12.9%	22.8%	61.6%	48.7%	7.4%
2000	554,636	12.0%	31.7%	52.6%	50.5%	17.4%
2010	600,158	11.7%	31.8%	52.5%	50.0%	N/A
2020	715,522	9.9%	29.0%	55.0%	50.4%	14.2%
Average	566,058	11.6%	27.3%	57.1%	49.7%	11.8%

* Persons of Spanish Origin for 1980
N/A: not available

and of foreign-born status. The population in Denver County has been consistently growing between 1980 and 2020. Since 1990, the percentage of Black citizens has been steadily decreasing, the percentage of the Latino population has fluctuated, and the percentage of male residents has been constant. The rate for those foreign born increased between 1980 and 2000 but then decreased in 2020; we note that data for 2010 was not available.

ALCOHOL AND DRUG USE OF THE PERSON SHOT

Alcohol and drug use measures include any alcohol or drug use as well as a measure for individual drugs, including alcohol, cocaine, heroin/opiate, marijuana/THC, and methamphetamine/amphetamine use. More than half of the persons shot had ingested alcohol and or drugs (55.3 percent) before encountering a law enforcement officer.[12] Toxicology tests were not collected or reported regarding whether law enforcement officers were under the influence of any substance.[13] Officers may work on and off duty in venues that sell alcohol, but policy regulations prohibit the use of this substance while working.[14] These data highlight how the interaction between police officers and residents often include someone under the influence of a substance that may alter behavior and perception. Based on toxicology examinations, over a third of cases included alcohol (35.8 percent). The National Institute on Alcohol Abuse and Alcoholism reported that excess alcohol use "interferes with the brain's communication pathways and can affect the way the brain looks and works. These disruptions can change mood and behavior and make it harder to think clearly and move with coordination."[15]

Thus, the perceptions of the individual shot may differ greatly from what an officer may be observing. For example, in one incident, a family was moving into an apartment complex when a man came over to talk. His breath smelled of alcohol; he was slurring his words and saying he was not a bad guy. He asked if he could give them a hug. As they were talking, a handgun fell to the ground, and the man walked off, holding his pants. The family became concerned the man might hurt himself, and they called the non-emergency line to the police department. When the police arrived to find a man matching the call description, they inquired whether he had a gun. The body-worn camera captured the audio and video of the police asking questions and the man inquiring what he did wrong. The officers stated the man did not comply with orders and reached for a gun, and thus, the three officers (Robert Krelle, Antony Gutierrez-McKain, and Dennis Liss) fired nine shots in response to the perceived threat. Identification of the individual took some time because his family lived out of state, and the man had never been previously arrested. Authorities discovered his name was Mac McPherson; his homicide by police occurred at the age of twenty-two. His blood alcohol level was 0.259, and he had THC in his system.[16] No obituary was found chronicling the loss to family and friends.

Although not analyzed for Denver, several scholarly studies have found that higher concentrations of alcohol outlets (e.g., liquor stores) yield higher rates of violent crime at the neighborhood level. For example, an ecological study based on census tract data from 2005 to 2012 determined there was a spatial correlation between alcohol outlets and violent crimes in Baltimore City: For every one-unit increase in the number of alcohol outlets, there was a 2.2 percent increase in the count of violent crimes.[17] Similar relationships were established in Washington, DC, between community-level alcohol outlet density and assaultive violence;[18] Austin and San Antonio, Texas, between alcohol outlet density and violent crime rates after controlling for neighborhood social structural characteristics and spatially autocorrelated error;[19] Atlanta, Georgia, between reduction in alcohol outlet density and reduction in exposure to violent crime;[20] and Baltimore, Maryland, between access to alcohol outlets and violent crime exposure.[21]

More than half of the persons shot had recorded use of alcohol or drug use (55.3 percent). The next most common drug used was marijuana/THC (18.2 percent), followed by methamphetamine/amphetamine (12.8 percent), cocaine (12.4 percent), and heroin/opiates (4.4 percent).[22] According to the National Institute on Drug Abuse (NIDA), in addition to activating brain cell receptors to produce a "high," THC alters senses and perceptions of time, causing changes in mood and impaired body movement, and has the potential to cause difficulty with thinking and problem solving, memory, hallucinations, delusions, and psychosis.[23] Methamphetamine and amphetamines are stimulants, like cocaine. NIDA indicates stimulants increase wakefulness, physical activity, breathing, blood pressure, and body temperature. In addition to a decreased appetite, all of these substances can produce a rapid and or irregular heartbeat. Stimulants increase the amount of the natural chemical dopamine in the brain, reinforcing drug-taking behavior and making the user desire to repeat the experience. Heroin, on the other hand, is an opiate. Prescription opioids and heroin produce euphoria or a rush and can lead to a fluctuation between consciousness and semiconsciousness. We note that there were instances when the person was under the influence of more than one drug at a time, known as polydrug use. Polydrug use also alters the effects of each individual drug on the brain and on behavior in ways that are not always predictable or safe.[24]

Among those shot by police officers, the rate of alcohol and drug use was higher for those killed compared to those wounded (see table 2.3). Specifically, the rates for all alcohol and drug use measures were statistically significantly higher (p-value<0.001) for those killed, except for heroin or opiate use (p-value=0.106), compared to those wounded. Although the rate of heroin or opiate use was higher for those killed compared to those wounded as a result of the shooting, the result was not statistically significant.

The use of psychoactive substances in the United States is extremely common.[25] Individuals are very likely to ingest some type of drug between birth and death. It is estimated that 85.6 percent of people over the age of

TABLE 2.3. Bivariate Associations Between the Rates of Alcohol and Drug Use for Those Wounded and Killed for All Police Shooting Cases in Denver, Colorado, 1983–2020 (N=275)

Alcohol and Drug Use of the Person Shot	Wounded		Killed		p-value
	N	Frequency (%)	N	Frequency (%)	
Any alcohol or drug	132	35 (26.5)	143	117 (81.8)	<0.001*
Alcohol	131	20 (15.3)	143	78 (54.5)	<0.001*
Cocaine	131	9 (6.9)	143	25 (17.5)	0.008*
Heroin/opiates	131	3 (2.3)	143	9 (6.3)	0.106
Marijuana/THC	131	5 (3.8)	143	45 (31.5)	<0.001*
Methamphetamine/ amphetamine	131	3 (2.3)	143	32 (22.4)	<0.001*

* Significant bivariate test results are noted. These were determined at alpha level 0.05 or p-value<0.05.

eighteen have drunk alcohol at least once during their lifetime, and 54.9 percent reported drinking in the past month.[26] In terms of illicit drug use, including marijuana, 21.4 percent of people over the age of twelve had used at least one substance in the past year.[27] Thus, a sizeable portion of the United States has consumed alcohol and/or drugs but was never shot by a law enforcement officer. However, as an interactive encounter, the unpredictability of drug-induced behavior may heighten the officers' discretion to react with greater force. Several studies have found that officers use a higher level of force on suspects displaying signs of alcohol or drug use.[28]

SHOOTING-RELATED MEASURES

Between 1983 and 2020, officer-involved shootings occurred each year in the city and county of Denver. The percentages of shootings that were analyzed for each time period were as follows: 21.8 percent between 1983 and 1990, 27.9 percent between 1991 and 2000, 21.1 percent between 2001 and 2010, and 29.2 percent between 2011 and 2020.[29] A trend test indicated these numbers were not statistically different. We found the length of time for analysis helpful for this study to recognize changes over time and for observing four decades of consistent trends.

After compiling the thirty-eight years of data, we found police shootings most frequently happened on a Saturday (18.8 percent) and at night between the hours of 11:00 PM to 5:59 AM (37.6 percent). Later in the evening and weekends are often celebratory times; the workday is over, and people have an opportunity to get together and socialize. Bars, clubs, and restaurants often have promotional events of live music or dancing or show sports games on televisions. These periods are often when alcohol consumption and drug use are at higher levels. Law enforcement officers may also be on more heightened alert and perceive a greater level of dangerousness, as it may be harder to visibly see and make sense of what is going on around them.[30]

In total, there were eleven incidents (3.7 percent) where a law enforcement officer shot two individuals in the same encounter. Sometimes, these individuals were fighting with each other or fighting together, but officers saw them both as a threat. There were also instances where additional persons were shot by the police beyond the intended target; in four cases (1.3 percent), one additional person was shot, and in one case (0.3 percent), three bystanders were shot. For example, two detectives were having lunch at a Vietnamese restaurant when a twenty-six-year-old man named Phuong Dang entered the kitchen with a shotgun through the back door in an attempt to rob the place and its patrons. In response to the threat, one of the detectives fired his gun at the same time as Phuong. The officers (Sgt. John Pinder and Detective Jesse Avendano) fired a total of twelve shots at Phuong, but in the encounter, three patrons were also hit. DA Mitch Morrissey emphasized that one of the individuals grazed by an officer's bullet thanked the two officers for saving their lives. This patron perceived that if it were not for the police, "everyone would have died."[31] Phuong is currently serving a prison sentence in a Colorado penitentiary and becomes eligible for parole in 2167.

The median number of minutes between when the police arrived and when the shooting occurred was five (Q1: 2, Q3: 13). As an outlier, there was one case where officers devoted 452 minutes (7.5 hours) to resolve the issue. Forty-two-year-old Kathleen Stege was one of fourteen females shot by the police in our dataset.[32] On Sunday, March 13, 1994, around 7:00 AM, a neighbor of Ms. Stege's in the Belcaro neighborhood (an almost all-white and low-poverty neighborhood) called the police and reported a loud noise and the sound of breaking glass.[33] An officer responded to the scene around 9:39 AM and made contact with the possible suspect, who reported she was on the phone long distance and couldn't talk to the officer. Although the officer reported that he found the response by Ms. Stege strange, he found a lack of evidence indicating criminal behavior and left the scene. Around 2:00 PM, the neighbor's daughter viewed a bullet hole in her mother's house and organized several additional neighbors to call to the police again. Two different police officers arrived and attempted to speak with Ms. Stege, but there was no response. The officers contacted a detective, who called Ms. Stege's home. Ms. Stege reported that she had shot at three hit men who were in her attic and that she would shoot anyone who attempted to come into her house. The police department called the Metro/SWAT unit, and a five-hour standoff ensued. Negotiators were unsuccessful at getting Ms. Stege to come outside, even after the deployment of five ferret rounds of CS gas. Officers contacted the hospital to learn more about Ms. Stege's mental condition. The hospital staff reported treatment for paranoia and delusional behavior and that she had been prescribed lithium and Mellaril (an antipsychotic).

Shortly after 9:00 PM, the Denver Police Department made the decision to initiate a surprise entrance of six officers into the home to arrest Ms. Stege. During the entrance of officers, the lead officer, Technician Ken Overman, a white male and twenty-two-year veteran, reported Ms. Stege entered the room and fired one round. He fired three shots in return. Medical emergency personnel took Ms. Stege to the hospital, where she died from multiple gunshot wounds. DA Bill Ritter described the entire incident as "unfortunate and ultimately tragic," but the officer's decision was necessary to protect those in the immediate vicinity of Ms. Stege from future harm. Based on the information in the file, the level of threat presented by Ms. Stege was completely hypothetical. However, the collective organizing of residents in a white neighborhood put law enforcement under pressure to act. The primary concerns were her possession of a firearm and unstable mental condition. Public officials praised the level of officer restraint and attempted to gain compliance by alternative methods; no public criticism was reported in the media or contained in the files held at the Denver DA's office.

Based on the individuals' perceived behavior, there was a community-initiated effort to flag down an officer or call 911 in over half of the cases (52.0 percent). The person who reached out the most frequently was a stranger observing the situation (36.9 percent), followed by a family member (16.1 percent) or a victim (16.1 percent). If the law enforcement officer wasn't directed to the encounter with a potential suspect, the most common reason for the officer to initiate contact was to execute an arrest warrant (29.3 percent). These could consist of attempting to serve the arrest warrant at the individual's residence or discovering an outstanding warrant during a traffic stop. The other two types of common situations in which an officer would initiate contact with a person of interest included gun incidents (19.2 percent, i.e., the officer hearing gunshots or observing a firearm) or observing a disturbance (17.5 percent).

Police shootings occurred primarily outdoors (76.8 percent) in public spaces (59.7 percent). Thus, a high number of shootings occurred in alleys, parking lots, sidewalks, streets, and toward individuals in vehicles. These are all places where bystanders, if present, could observe these encounters between officers and the suspect. Less frequent were shootings indoors (23.2 percent) and in personal living areas (40.3 percent) such as bedrooms, hallways, kitchens, living rooms, etc. These shooting incidents were more likely to be witnessed by or be in closer proximity to family, friends, or other household members. Indoor shooting locations also included banks and workplace settings.

Despite Denver's diversity, residents are segregated into different neighborhoods by class and race. Socioeconomic differences are reflected in which neighborhoods had a higher proportion of police shootings. Based upon census tract data from 1980 to 2020, neighborhoods were analyzed for whether the proportion of any racial or ethnic group exceeded 50 percent. We found nearly half of the shootings were occurring in census tracts that were white (49 percent) compared to Latino (40.5 percent) or Black (10.5 percent). As we presented county demographics earlier in the chapter, these data reflect that a lower proportion of white census tracts had a police shooting, Latino census tracts were overrepresented, and Black census tracts were similar to county population numbers. The proportion of poverty in the neighborhood where most of the shootings occurred was high poverty (49.5 percent), followed by medium poverty (29.0 percent).[34] A law enforcement shooting has occurred in sixty-seven of Denver's seventy-eight neighborhoods. The neighborhood with the highest number of shooting incidents (n=22) was Five Points, the oldest historically Black neighborhood in Denver, which increasingly became Latino and Black and has since been gentrified to become white. The second highest number of shooting incidents occurred in Westwood, a primarily Latino community.[35]

INCIDENT-RELATED FACTORS

Based on the infraction reported or observed, the authors calculated that the seriousness of these offenses was most frequently a felony (71.8 percent) and that the possible offense type was interpersonal violence (59.4 percent).[36] When individuals were shot, the suspects' behavior was described by officers as an active threat (59.4 percent), either from pointing or firing a gun or by using a vehicle as a weapon. In 30.5 percent of circumstances, law enforcement described the person as a perceived threat based on making threats, reaching for something, or holding a weapon. According to the Denver Police Department's Operations Manual Use of Force Policy:

> Officers may use lethal force only when all other means of apprehension are unreasonable given the totality of the circumstances and 1) The arrest is for a felony involving conduct including the use or threatened use of deadly physical force; 2) The suspect poses an immediate threat to the officer or another person; and 3) The force employed does not create a substantial risk of injury to other persons.[37]

In slightly less than 10 percent (9.7 percent) of cases, the person shot had fled from an officer, with the shooting then taking place in a different neighborhood from where the initial interaction took place. This low figure highlights how most individuals, even those making efforts to flee, were rarely able to remove themselves from the geographic context of where the encounter began. The outdoor presence of fences, sidewalks, streets, trees, vehicles, etc. functioned as objects that impeded movement, as did the tool of the officer's firearm, which quickly disabled the individual from continued travel.

When officers fired their weapons, individuals were shot in multiple body locations (44.1 percent). When officers fired one bullet, they hit the individual more frequently in the chest, shoulder, or pelvis (22.4 percent), followed by the head or neck (10.3 percent). Police were trained to shoot the center mass as the quickest way to stop the threat.[38] In one-quarter of the cases, another person was physically injured by the individual shot by law enforcement. These victims were most likely a stranger or a bystander (42.5 percent), followed by a police officer (21.9 percent) or partner/spouse (19.2 percent). These types of injuries ranged from physical assaults to less frequent incidents of homicide. In some incidents, the violence occurred before a law enforcement officer intervened, whereas other instances of aggression were based upon the individual's perception of what threat the officer might present to their activity.

The most common weapon possessed by the person shot was a gun (57.0 percent), followed by a knife (12.4 percent) or a vehicle (10.7 percent); 14.1 percent did not have a weapon. According to a Pew Research Center survey conducted in 2021, 30 percent of residents own a gun in the United States, and 40 percent live in a household where guns are present.[39] The most common firearms possessed by individuals shot by the police were various calibers of handguns, followed by rifles and shotguns. Sharp objects for the category of knives ranged from pocketknives and kitchen knives to swords. DA Norm Early emphasized to law enforcement officers that "if a knife wielding assailant closes to a distance closer than approximately twenty-one feet, shooting the assailant using a revolver may be insufficient to 'stop' an attacker from completing an attack, in that the attacker's forward momentum may not be stopped."[40] Vehicles ranged from sedans to sports utility vehicles and trucks. A Police Assessment Resource Center (PARC) report in 2008 described an increased risk of a higher number of shots fired at a person in a vehicle and the danger of the automobile's continuing to move forward by its own momentum. Both options increased the risk for innocent bystanders to become injured or killed. Thus, it was made a clear national standard for officers to move out of the way and refrain from engaging in shooting at a vehicle.[41] Although Denver officials developed policies to restrict shooting at tires or other sections of the vehicle other than the individual, the shooting of suspects in a vehicle continued to occur, but at a noticeably lower rate than in the 1980s and 1990s.

Other characteristics of the individual shot were not all gathered at the scene, known, or confirmed by police at the time of the shooting. Overall, 10 percent of the individuals shot by the police were described as having mental health issues, 14.5 percent reported suicidal ideation, 48.8 percent possessed a criminal record, 20.3 percent had previously been incarcerated in prison, and 9.4 percent had alleged gang involvement. These factors could potentially be important when preparing to arrive to the scene, initiate an arrest, or when responding to various crises. Particularly in the incident, these descriptions were important in justifying officer decision making.

POST-SHOOTING-RELATED MEASURES

In close to half of the cases (49.0 percent), the persons shot by law enforcement were killed; in 51 percent of cases, they were wounded. A prosecutor described how the DA office investigates shootings resulting in both death and injury because a significant factor for whether someone lives or dies was the medical response. The public health scholar David Hemenway agreed: "Most gun killings are indistinguishable from nonfatal gun shootings; it is just a question of whether a vital organ is hit, the caliber of the bullet, and how much time passes before medical treatment arrives."[42] Depending on the severity of injury, it was highly probable that the individuals who were shot by a law enforcement officer would suffer life-altering changes. A study of gunshot wound survivors found adverse physical and mental function outcomes years after being shot.[43] There were also studies highlighting the impact that various calibers of bullets have on the human body.[44]

A study by the criminologists Justin Nix and John Shjarback explored factors associated with victim mortality in four US states (California, Colorado, Florida, and Texas) for various time periods, with measures including mortality, race/ethnicity, gender, age, weapon, and access to trauma care.[45] They found that Colorado had the highest mortality rate, at 63 percent, compared to the other three states. Males were more likely to die from their wounds than females in California, Colorado, and Florida, but not in Texas. Individuals who were twenty-five years of age or younger were more likely to survive police shootings than older victims.

Unarmed victims were more likely to survive than those who were armed. Victims in Colorado, Florida, and Texas who were shot in a county with a level I or II trauma center were more likely to survive than those who were not. Various public health concerns of fatal police shootings were discussed, such as the cost (lost wages, medical bills, taxes, lawsuits), impact on communities both economically and psychologically, as well as nearby residents having a higher risk of high blood pressure and higher levels of depression or post-traumatic stress disorder.

After the shooting occurred, in just over a third of the cases (35.9 percent), there were reported disputes between law enforcement accounts of what transpired compared to witnesses or individuals wounded. Most of the coverage of these discrepancies was found when reviewing the entire case file, as much of this information was omitted or minimized in decision letters. Many of these disputes were not covered in the local news media. The most active local newspaper reporting disputes was *Westword*, whereas the *Denver Post* and *Rocky Mountain News* primarily concentrated on high-profile shooting cases. There was no statistical difference in the percentage of disputed cases by time wave (p-value=0.117). The percentage of disputed cases was lowest from 2011 to 2020 (27.6 percent), followed by 1983 to 1990 (32.3 percent), 1991 to 2000 (41.0 percent), and 2001 to 2010 (44.4 percent).[46]

If the individual survived, criminal charges for the incident that preceded the shooting were likely to follow. At least 33.1 percent of individuals who survived a shooting were found through a Colorado Department of Corrections inmate search.[47] After reviewing each case, it was estimated that 3.4 percent of the officer-involved-shooting cases had the potential to be pursued as a death penalty case but were not since the individual had been killed by the officer before a court hearing could be scheduled.[48] Not one of the individuals who survived a police shooting met the initiative or interest from prosecutors to pursue the death penalty. Thus, these shooting cases were not inherently considered the "worst of the worst." The state of Colorado abolished the death penalty in 2020. At that point in time, from 1983 to 2020, the state had executed one person, three men were on death row, and the punishment of death had been pursued in 130 cases.[49] Thus, death at the hands of the state primarily occurs at the discretion of law enforcement officers without the individual entering the adversarial court system to determine guilt or innocence.

Most of the officer-involved shooting cases were handled by District Attorney (DA) Norm Early (1983 to 1993), Bill Ritter (1993 to 2005), or Mitch Morrissey (2005 to 2017), which was reflective of the terms they were elected and reelected to. In terms of bringing a police shooting case before a grand jury to determine whether to file criminal charges, Norm Early and Bill Ritter each brought one case; Mitch Morrissey brought zero cases. Bill Ritter decided not to file criminal charges against Officer Ranjan Ford in the shooting death of Frank Lobato in 2004. Norm Early did pursue criminal charges against Officer Michael Blake for shooting and killing Steven Gant in 1992, but Blake was acquitted at trial. In total, it appears that two officers received criminal charges. A lot of information was gathered by the investigative agency in conjunction with the DA's office after the shooting to determine whether to file criminal charges against officers, but more effort was expended on what type of criminal charges to file against the suspect in the event the person survived the encounter. Together, factors such as alcohol and drug use, gang membership, mental illness, prior criminal record, or prison incarceration provided additional justification to confirm a police officer's claims of deadly risks presented by difficult individuals.

During the three-decade period, there were sixteen police chiefs (involving outside jurisdictions and the Denver Police Department) that had to await the legal outcome and examine whether any departmental policies had been violated in conjunction with the manager of safety's review. Although a clear disciplinary accounting was unavailable, news media accounts of these shootings report that nine officers were disciplined. These consequences included suspensions and termination for at least three law enforcement officers.[50] In addition, five mayors interacted with the public regarding these shooting incidents and provided official responses as toward different strategies to maintain control and oversight of the Denver Police Department.

Since there was only a small number of law enforcement officers who received criminal or disciplinary charges, many families attempted to pursue justice through civil lawsuits. When a civil lawsuit was achieved (9.9 percent), the median settlement amount was $332,500 (Q1: $70,000, Q3: $1,230,000) in US dollars. Thus, only one out of ten cases had a family member who could successfully make a claim in court that the law enforcement officers' behavior was inappropriate based on the circumstances. High-profile cases were often settled rather than bringing the case to trial and awaiting an unknown jury decision.

Adding an additional level of oversight, Durán coded each case based on reasons to support the decision making for the shooting or counter that assumption based upon the evidence presented from all available data sources. Durán found nearly half of the cases were questionable (48.3 percent) as to whether the officer needed to use deadly force, 20.8 percent were problematic, and 30.9 percent were less controversial based on the information presented.[51] Any additional information could alter the evaluation of each case; scores ranged anywhere from a negative 11 to a positive 7.[52] This evaluation contrasts with the criteria used by the DA's office of whether to pursue criminal charges (1.4 percent), the police department's use of discipline (3.0 percent), and the court documentation of successfully filed lawsuits (9.9 percent). This discrepancy is reflected in the lives of individuals shot, as they were more likely to be from marginalized backgrounds.

In the following sections, we present the bivariate analysis results for measures that statistically significantly differed by age group, sex, and foreign-born status. A bivariate relationship is defined as "a relationship between two variables."[53] Significant results were determined; the statistical tests used are outlined in the appendix.

BIVARIATE ASSOCIATIONS BY AGE GROUP

In the criminological literature, age has been found to correlate with criminal offending, and there are particular periods of life with a higher likelihood of contact with law enforcement officers. According to the "age fundamentals" described by the criminologist John Laub and sociologist Robert Sampson in their book *Shared Beginnings, Divergent Lives*, criminal offending begins in preadolescence, peaks during adolescence, and declines in young adulthood.[54] The earlier an individual becomes involved in criminal offending, the higher the risk of continued offending. Laub and Sampson followed the lives of five hundred males between the ages of ten to seventeen until the age of seventy. They found that even for active offenders criminal involvement declined with age and that individuals experiencing "turning points" such as marriage, employment, and military service led to greater desistance from crime than for those without such experiences.

Bivariate associations by age indicated many patterns of interest for a study into police shootings. Bivariate associations for all measures by age group are found in table A2.2 (see appendix 2). This summary refers to the measures in the study that differed across the age groups (<18, 18 to 27, 28 to 37, 38 to 47, 48+) of the person shot.[55] From the sociodemographic characteristics, the age of the person shot was associated with their race and ethnicity and their listed address. Among youth (age less than 18) and young adults (age 18 to 27) shot by police, the majority were either Black (39.1 percent and 30.7 percent, respectively) or Latino (39.1 percent and 46.5 percent, respectively), while older adults (age 38 to 47 and 48 years and older) were predominantly white (53.2 percent and 64.0 percent, respectively). These data highlight how age and race and ethnicity reflect a concerning trend where youth of color were more likely to be shot by a law enforcement officer, which could result in death or lifelong injuries. Such interactions could take a heavy toll on the individual shot and their families and friends. Across age groups, most persons shot were reportedly living in Denver (49.8 percent) or a residence in Colorado (besides Denver and Aurora); however, for older adults (age 48 years and older), the majority (83.3 percent) shot had an address listed in Denver. This may be in part attributable to people who are older having increased independence or established roots in the community. The proportion of any alcohol or drug use, alcohol, cocaine, and methamphetamine/amphetamine differed by age group. Rates were lowest for youth and highest for those aged 28 to 37, except for cocaine, which was highest for those aged 38 to 47.

From all the shooting-related measures, the time wave (ten-year intervals) when the shooting took place, contacting the police, and shooting details significantly differed by age group. Among youth shot by police, close to half (48 percent) were shot between 1991 and 2000. This time period coincides with Denver's "Summer of Violence," which increased the concern of city officials, the media, and the public over gangs and youth violence.[56] Initiatives were launched to create programs and provide greater punishment for offenders who broke the law. The proportion of cases in which there was a community-initiated engagement or someone calling 911 was lowest for youth (36.0 percent) and highest for adults 48 or older (80.0 percent). In those cases, a partner or spouse made the call for those aged 28 to 37, but it was most likely a stranger who called for those in the other age groups. Shootings took place primarily outside and in a public space at a higher rate for all age groups except for those ages 48 or older, who had higher rates of being shot indoors and in a living area.

From incident-related factors, there were significant age group differences in the location of the body where the person was shot and whether the person shot reported being suicidal, had a criminal record, or had been previously in prison. Among youth shot by police, the most common locations on the body were the arm and hand, followed by multiple locations on the body. For the other age groups, the most common locations on the body were the chest, shoulder, and pelvis, followed by multiple locations on the body. Rates for reported suicidality increased as the age group became older, from 4.2 percent to 32.0 percent. Those in age groups 28 to 37 and 38 to 47 had the highest rates of having a criminal record, at 57.1 percent and 55.6 percent, respectively, and having previously served time in prison, at 32.2 percent and 20.0 percent, respectively.

Based on postshooting outcomes, there were significant differences in outcome for the person shot, reported dispute between accounts, and district attorney by age group. The individuals shot by the police were more likely to die if they were aged 38 to 47 (61.7 percent) and 48 years and older (68 percent). This may reflect the decline in the body's ability to recover as people get older in age.[57] Reported disputes between accounts were most frequent for those under 18 years of age (60.0 percent) and least frequent for those aged 48 or older (24.0 percent), although not statistically significantly different. As the age group increases, so does the frequency of being deceased. According to the CDC's National Center for Health Statistics, the life expectancy at birth as of 2022 was 76.1 years.[58] Most of the individuals shot in Denver, whether killed or injured, have not lived to this age.

There were age group differences in how many police shooting incidents were reviewed by each district attorney. Bill Ritter reviewed almost half of the cases for youth (48.0 percent) and those aged 38 to 47 years old (46.8 percent). Norm Early handled close to a third of the cases for individuals between the ages of 18 to 27 (32.5 percent). For those 48 or older, most cases were handled by either Mitch Morrissey (36.0 percent) or Norm Early (40.0 percent). These numbers overlap with the time period for which David Michaud was chief of the Denver Police Department for the highest number of cases for those aged under 18 (44.0 percent) and 38 to 47 (24.3 percent), whereas Gerry Whitman was chief for those aged 18 to 27 (22.1 percent) and 28 to 37 (21.8 percent). News coverage and the number of news articles significantly differed by age group. Cases with a person 39 to 47 years of age had 97.9 percent news coverage; those who were 48 years of age and older had 68.0 percent coverage. The number of news articles was highest for youth (median=4); those 48 or older received the lowest coverage (median=2).

BIVARIATE ASSOCIATIONS BY SEX

Sex was a significant correlate with criminal offending and contact with law enforcement. Males are more likely to be involved in serious criminal offending and to be arrested compared to females.[59] However, an increasing number of studies have raised the awareness of the complexity of the gender category from simply being a binary difference.[60] A Pew Research Center survey found that 1.6 percent of US adults self-identified as transgender or nonbinary, whereas 5.1 percent of adults younger than the age of thirty did.[61] Sex assigned at birth is biologically defined; gender is socially constructed.[62] Therefore, the following summary refers only to the measures that differed by sex, meaning that the measures contrasted between the male and female persons shot. Gender was not collected in any of the data sources used to create the dataset for this analysis, and they were not gathered or included in datasets on police shootings, including *Fatal Encounters*, *The Counted*, *Fatal Force*, and *Mapping Police Violence*.[63] Without a measure for gender, we cannot systematically report it or identify whether the person shot was cisgender or transgender, the latter being the case with Jessie Hernandez, who was shot by two law enforcement officers in 2015.[64]

Bivariate associations for all measures by sex are found in table A2.3 (see appendix 2). There was evidence of sex differences in various police shooting outcomes, including mortality.[65] Based on shooting-related measures, there were significant sex differences in the number of additional people shot and the shooting incident's level of critique. In most cases among males who were shot, there were no additional people shot (99.3 percent). However, among females who were shot, one additional person was shot in over one-fifth of the cases (21.4 percent). A review of these case studies highlights how these shootings differ. For example, Teresa Perez, forty years of age, began firing a gun at her older male partner in front of the Denver Police Department's Gang Unit. When officers attempted to stop her, at least one of the bullets they fired hit Ms. Perez's boyfriend and grazed a fellow officer. Another case involved Anne Barnett, sixty years of age, who was pointing a gun at her adult son who was drunk and causing a disturbance. She was threatening her abusive son and demanding he leave the apartment. When two officers descended toward the second-floor balcony walkway, they noticed a gun, and the female officer shouted, "She's got a gun." Ms. Barnett turned toward the officers with the gun, and they began firing shots. One of the bullets ricocheted off a metal hand railing and hit the male officer in the forearm. Ms. Barnett was shot five times and died shortly after arriving at the hospital. DA Norman Early did not pursue any criminal charges against the officer but did express some regret for the case: "There are clearly no winners in tragic incidents like this, only victims. This is yet another tragedy associated with the massive presence of handguns in our community. Citizens must understand that they are in possession of a firearm, they may know that their intent is harmless, but those who encounter them may not."[66] The news coverage of the case documents a changing narrative that at first reported that Ms. Barnett had fired at officers. This claim was retracted after it was discovered it was the fellow officer's bullet ricocheting that caused injury to the male officer.[67] The son and the community were shocked that a sixty-year-old white woman in a comfortable middle-class area in southeast Denver could be shot by law enforcement.

From the postshooting outcomes, whether the person was currently in a Colorado prison between 2013–2022 or was now deceased differed by sex. Most of the males (74.5 percent) and females (80.0 percent) who were shot by a law enforcement officer were now deceased. Among the 202 men who survived, 21.4 percent were in a Colorado prison between 2013–2022; none of the ten women were incarcerated during that period.

In most cases, it was not clear that the officer's decision making entailed the same form of legitimacy for both males and females. The shooting incident level of critique was problematic and questionable for 19.4 percent and 48.9 percent of cases among males and 50.0 percent and 35.7 percent of cases among females, respectively. As females account for a smaller number of the overall shootings by law enforcement officers (n=14), these cases revealed more questions. For example, in 35.7 percent of the cases involving a female, the female who was shot was not the intended target and was unarmed. They were primarily in a vehicle with a male who was targeted or in the vicinity of a male perceived as a threat to law enforcement officers. When females were presenting a threat to another individual or to an officer, the weapons primarily involved a gun, followed by vehicles and, in one case, a knife.

Based upon these results, officers tend to perceive males as a greater threat to themselves and third parties. The exceptions, when they occur, include domestic disputes and efforts to remove themselves from encounters with male law enforcement officers. There was not one shooting where a female officer shot a female suspect.[68]

BIVARIATE ASSOCIATIONS
BY FOREIGN-BORN STATUS

Immigration status has been a politically contested topic since the creation of the United States. Native Americans have been the only indigenous people in the area for thousands of years; all other residents came from somewhere else, as reflected in the concept of settler colonialism. [69] The next longest-originated group of individuals are of Spanish and indigenous descent in the lands of the Americas that were once Spain and Mexico. It was only after the late 1800s that the United States began enacting comprehensive federal immigration law, and it was largely geared toward the regulation of migration of certain people.[70] In contemporary times, according to the US Census Bureau's American Community Survey estimates for 2021, slightly more than 45 million people were born outside of the United States, in a country of more than 334 million residents. The

Migration Policy Institute's analysis of the Census Bureau's data found that the state of Colorado's foreign-born population comprises 9.5 percent of its total population.[71] The place of birth was 49.6 percent Latin America, 25.0 percent Asia, 13.5 percent Europe, and 8.3 percent Africa. Forty-nine percent were naturalized citizens. The foreign-born populations speak a variety of languages beyond English, which can present communication challenges during interactions with the general public and in encounters with law enforcement. As police shootings revolve around perceptions, miscommunication, either nonverbal or verbal, has the potential to be an additional risk factor.[72]

Bivariate associations for all measures by foreign-born status are found in table A2.4 (see appendix 2). The following summary refers to only the measures that differed by foreign-born status, meaning that the measures differed between those born in the United States and those born outside the United States.[73] In terms of the sociodemographic characteristics of the person shot, there were significant differences in the race and ethnicity by the foreign-born status of the person shot. Among those who were shot and foreign born, the majority were Latino (92.3 percent), one was Black, and none were white or Nonwhite Other. Based on the alcohol and drug use of the person shot, there were significant differences in cocaine use by foreign-born status. Those who were foreign born (41.7 percent) had a higher rate of cocaine found in the body compared to those who were not (11.1 percent). A study by several researchers on individuals of Mexican origin found that "nativity, acculturation, and urban residence each contribute to increases in illicit drug use, with nativity having the strongest risk and protective effects."[74] These researchers were concerned about the erosive effects of socialization in the United States.

Based on shooting-related measures, significant differences were identified in the time wave when the incident occurred by foreign-born status. Those who were foreign-born had no reported shootings from 1983 to 1990. The time wave from 2001 to 2010 (61.5 percent) was when the frequency of law enforcement shootings of the foreign born was the highest; the year 2000 was when the proportion of this population was also at its greatest. In the state of Colorado, this was also featuring Tom Tancredo's anti-immigrant, particularly anti-Latino, politics as a member of the US House of Representatives from 1999 to 2009.[75] An officer working off duty was killed by an immigrant of Mexican descent in 2005, which only increased political anger. The nationwide right-wing backlash led to a push for legislation to turn undocumented residents into felons. In 2006, an estimated fifty thousand people marched on behalf of immigrant rights in Denver, along with millions in other cities across the nation.[76]

In the category of incident-related factors, when the person shot had a weapon, there was a significant difference in the type of weapon they had, based on postshooting discovery, by foreign-born status. A gun was the most common weapon to possess for those who were foreign born (53.8 percent), although this was slightly lower than for those who were born in the United States (57.2 percent). A significant difference in foreign-born status was found in the police district for the area of the census tract where the shooting occurred. Among those who were foreign born, more than half of all shootings occurred in southwest Denver (53.8 percent). Based on census tract data, a higher proportion of foreign-born residents lived in this section of the city.

In terms of postshooting outcomes, there were significant differences in reported disputes between accounts and whether there was a lawsuit settlement by foreign-born status. Those who were foreign born (92.3 percent) had higher rates of a reported dispute between accounts compared to those who were not foreign born (33.0 percent). A lawsuit settlement was achieved or attempted by 46.2 percent of the foreign born, compared to 10.3 percent for those who were not foreign born. Many of these cases involved discrepancies between what officers reported occurring compared to forensic evidence. These cases also reflected efforts to utilize foreign government consulates to ensure oversight.

A study by the criminologists Shytierra Gaston and Rashaan DeShay and the sociologist April Fernandes investigated the "macrolevel" contributors to police killings and how they relate to race, ethnicity, foreign birth, and sex.[77] The researchers used crowdsourced data from the *Mapping Police Violence* website, the FBI's uniform crime reports, and the US Census American Community Survey between 2013 and 2018. They found the foreign-born population percentage reduced the rate of police killing for white men by 12 percent but did not affect the rate for the other five racial and ethnic groups. An article by the sociologist Asha Layne examined the complex relationship between Black immigrants and the criminal justice system in the United States.[78] Layne describes how Black immigrants were often "Americanize[d]" in the mainstream media, whereas the experiences of Black immigrants were distinct. Several cases involving Black immigrants were primarily discussed as about the targeting of Blacks but not as about the experience of being a Black immigrant. Cases discussed included Alfred Olango, who was shot and killed near San Diego, California, in 2016, and Amadou Diallo, who was killed by police officers in New York City in 1999. Layne emphasizes the increasing population of Black immigrants and, thus, the importance of including citizenship status in future conversations regarding police violence against Black residents. Our data in Denver, Colorado, found Latino immigrants particularly affected by various forms of nativist decision making.

———— ∞∞∞ ————

With one or two people shot by the police per 100,000, several characteristics were disproportionately overrepresented. These patterns of overrepresentation were found for males, individuals from racial- and ethnic-minority groups, persons between the ages of eighteen to twenty-seven, US citizens, and neighborhoods with higher levels of poverty. Individuals who were under the influence of alcohol and drugs were more vulnerable, as were those outside at night between the hours of 11 PM and 6 AM and on Saturdays. Slightly more than half of these incidents were initiated with law enforcement by someone calling 911 or that person seeking out the attention of a police officer; the remaining portion of shootings were officer directed. These data highlight how a significant proportion of these incidents were activities that could potentially result in felony charges for the individual targeted by law enforcement based upon involvement in interpersonal violence. The presence of firearms heightened the threat level for law enforcement officers to respond by shooting the suspect. However, more than 95 percent of these cases were not severe enough for a DA to pursue the death penalty if such a punishment were available. Thus, it is important to understand that law enforcement shootings of residents cover a broad range of behaviors and types of interactions. Sometimes, the officer's decision to shoot ranged from questionable, inaccurate, or unintentional to incidents where law enforcement officers were responding to actual and imminent life-and-death encounters that were difficult to resolve without the use of a firearm.

Theoretically, these patterns reflect the concept of intersectionality: It is not one social status alone but rather the intertwining of multiple characteristics at the same time that leads law enforcement officers to perceive specific individuals as presenting a greater level of threat compared to others. The descriptive statistics and bivariate analysis provided in this chapter do not allow us to address intersectionality quantitatively because we were looking at only two variables at a time. However, in our mixed-method design we do want to introduce the concept of intersectionality, as developed by the critical race scholar Kimberle Crenshaw.[79] Crenshaw argued that instances of discrimination targeted against Black women were often unacknowledged in a court system focused on categories of race or sex because white women were used as the baseline comparison for sex. Crenshaw demonstrated how Black women experience discrimination in ways that were both different and similar to Black men and white women; thus, without an intersectional analysis, the problems of this complexity will go unaddressed. Patricia Hill Collins, a sociologist, has also worked toward examining these issues by utilizing the theory of intersectionality.[80] The critical theory we hope to employ in this book is one based on social action and social justice.

3

TWO TRIGGER FINGERS

An Examination of Racial and Ethnic Differences

I (Durán) grew up with a high number of negative interactions with police officers as a teenager.[1] When, as a young college student, I began working in law enforcement as a deputy juvenile probation officer, I never wanted to reach out to the police if there was an emergency. The court policy required calling the police department if any criminal incidents occurred during our observations. Since I occasionally worked with a white male or white female partner in an unmarked state car, I let my partner initiate and lead these interactions, but for the most part, I tried to resolve issues on my own. My experiences and perceptions were based on law enforcement's potential to cause more problems. Even working in law enforcement did not remove my suspicions about police officers. In one encounter at a statewide gang conference, it was presumed that I might be working undercover for a gang. My presence attending law-enforcement-only sessions prompted some questioning and requests to show my law enforcement badge. Even the badge did not prevent one of the gang officers from contacting my supervisor and inquiring about my status. My time working in juvenile probation and youth corrections was always presumed to be suspicious and somehow "criminal."[2] My goal was to change the system, but I realized over time that simply working in these institutions maintained a legitimacy that ensured a pattern of punishment for marginalized groups in society.[3]

When I began graduate school and started my doctoral training in how to study gangs, the policing of gangs remained one of my key areas of segregation, perceived social status, language, citizenship, age, sex, name, or perceived criminality, have a carryover influence on the use of discretion.

The early studies on police shootings from 1960 to 2013 found repeated instances of Black overrepresentation, compared to whites, as suspects shot by the police. The researchers were confused as to why these patterns were emerging from the data, given an absolute reluctance to suggest or comprehend how racism may be playing a role.[16] For example, the sociologist Gerald Robin examined police killings in Philadelphia from 1950 to 1960 along with data from nine other cities. He concluded that Blacks' contribution to the victim-offender relationship was six to twenty-nine times greater than the rate of whites. Thus, Robin concluded, "all these things make it clear that criminals killed by police officers generally are responsible for their own death."[17] Another sociologist, Marshall W. Meyer, didn't offer racially inflammatory comments and biased interpretations of the data in his study of police shootings in Los Angeles from 1974 to 1979. Instead, Meyer reported how measures for evaluating police shootings could lead to different interpretations as to why Blacks and Latinos were shot more frequently than whites. Another study by a team of researchers examined data on shooting incidents regarding an unnamed major metropolitan police department from 1970 to 1972.[18] They found that 64.4 percent of the shooting incidents involved Black suspects and 35.6 percent involved white suspects, despite the city being 25 percent Black and 75 percent white. However, since officers fired more shots at white suspects, the researchers believed that officers were not prejudiced against Blacks—in fact, possibly the contrary. Finally, a study by the researchers William Geller and Kevin Karales examined police shootings in Chicago from 1974 to 1978 and found that 70 percent of the individuals shot were Black in a city that was 33 percent Black. Twenty percent of the shooting suspects were white, despite the city being 60 percent white. Ten percent of the shooting suspects were Latino, in a city that was 7.5 percent Latino. After Geller and Karales considered various factors such as race of the officer and other reasonable comparison points (e.g., the officer's arrest rate, etc.), they concluded that a lack of data and the statistical analysis techniques they used did not find racism to be a motivating factor.

These four studies of police shootings highlight a pattern reflected in the early policing literature, in which white researchers obtained information from police departments while simultaneously living in a white habitus that was completely uncritical and unaware of how societal racism influenced their interpretation of the data. The sociologist Eduardo Bonilla-Silva describes the white habitus as "a racialized, uninterrupted socialization process that *conditions* and *creates* Whites' racial taste, perceptions, feelings, and emotions and their views on racial matters."[19] The social and spatial isolation of whites creates a sense of group belonging and produces negative views about Blacks and people of color. Therefore, these researchers referred to individuals shot by the police as civilians, criminals, and suspects but did not question law enforcement decision making. The explanation of these disparities often included blaming Blacks for disproportionate involvement in crime, particularly violent crime, and arguing that the communities in which Blacks live contain higher levels of illegal activities.[20] The law professor Katheryn Russell-Brown has commented on how US society has blamed Blacks for their own victimization or required them to establish themselves as good victims (i.e., employed, graduate, no criminal record, held in high esteem, and appearing as nonthreatening).[21] Such a standard continues to place a burden on victims and/or families to prove the worthiness of loved ones.[22]

At a time when unique access was being provided by several major metropolitan police departments to researchers to study police shootings, there were also attempts to understand the scale of police violence, referred to as "use of force," on a national level. The greatest challenge encountered in conducting national studies, as it was later reported, was the availability and completeness of data for analysis, which severely underrepresented the magnitude of the number of shootings. Nevertheless, the national studies focusing on race continued to find that Blacks were overrepresented as shooting suspects in comparison to whites, with the outcomes for other racial and ethnic groups unclear.[23] In an effort to provide greater clarity, one of the first "official" national reports on officer-involved shootings was disseminated by the US Bureau of Justice Statistics, utilizing FBI supplemental homicide reports (SHR).[24] The statisticians originally calculated that there were 373 individuals shot and killed by law enforcement per year, on average, between 1976 to 1998, and an average of 419 per year between 2003 and 2009. Most of the individuals killed were male, and Blacks were killed at higher rates than whites. In

1998, law enforcement officers shot Blacks at a rate four times greater than they shot whites. In 1978, the rate was eight times higher. In their report, the statisticians acknowledged the limitations of the data, but they did not seem to comprehend the scale of how many more police-shooting deaths were occurring each year. In addition, the statisticians who prepared the report used the language of law enforcement agencies, labeling the people shot by the police as "felons" and the killings by police as "justifiable homicides" despite no such adjudicatory decision having occurred. This highlights the problematic nature of the "official" study of police shootings and subsequent analysis.

After the police shooting death of Michael Brown in 2014, several news agencies and websites began to take a more critical examination of how often death occurs at the hands of law enforcement. Research studies have since benefited from these outlets to begin grasping the level of magnitude of overrepresentation by race and sex. In an effort to determine whether these shootings are equally distributed by race and ethnicity, a couple of different comparisons have been used: first, by county population; second, by county population and using the reference group of whites; and third, by a county population's contact with law enforcement as determined by arrest rates. The data analyzed has primarily consisted of those collected by the *Washington Post* on a database website named *Fatal Force*, the Centers for Disease Control (CDC), and the websites of *Fatal Encounters* and *Mapping Police Violence*.

According to the data provided by the *Washington Post's Fatal Force* database, an average of 1,043 individuals were shot and killed by the police per year between 2015 and 2024.[25] *Fatal Force* is a log of fatal shootings in the United States by police officers beginning in 2015 as a result of an investigation by the *Washington Post* that discovered that the FBI undercounts police shootings in the United States. The methodology used by this site consists of collecting data from various news accounts, social media accounts, and police reports. Reviewing these data for demographic characteristics, the individuals shot and killed by the police were primarily white (44.6 percent, yet 62.0 percent of the population per 2020 Census Bureau numbers), followed by Black (23.5 percent, yet 13.0 percent of the population) and then Latino (15.9 percent, yet 18.0 percent of the population). Other racial and ethnic groups were categorized as "other" and comprised 4 percent of all shooting deaths. One way to evaluate these results was to compare them to population percentages; doing so reveals lower numbers of police shootings for non-Hispanic whites, Blacks being overrepresented 1.8 times more than their population numbers would suggest, and Latinos with slightly lower numbers than their population would suggest. To determine fatal police shootings by race and ethnicity in rural and urban areas, the public policy professor David Hemenway and his colleagues utilized the *Fatal Force* database.[26] The study covered three years, from 2015 to 2017. These researchers found 2,945 fatal police shootings during this timeframe, and there was very little difference in the number of fatal police shooting rates between rural and urban areas. This was a surprising finding because it contrasted with the idea that violent crime, firearm violence, and homicides were more likely to be an urban problem. Hemenway and colleagues found that the rate at which Blacks were shot and killed was higher than for any other racial and ethnic group. They were most likely to be killed by police in an urban setting; fatal police shooting rates for whites and Latinos were higher in rural areas.

The epidemiologist Elle Lett and colleagues used *Fatal Force* data to examine the persistence of racial inequity in fatal US police shootings.[27] By assessing the primary outcomes of the death rate and years of life lost (YLL; the difference between life expectancy and age of death) per quarter per million (pqpm) from 2015 to 2020, these researchers found 4,740 police shootings. The majority shot were white (51.0 percent), followed by Black (26.7 percent) and Hispanic (18.8 percent). Compared to whites, the rate ratio (RR) for death was highest for Native Americans (RR: 3.06; 95 percent CI: 2.42, 3.86), Blacks (RR: 2.62; 95 percent CI: 2.41, 2.86), and Hispanics (RR: 1.29; 95 percent CI: 1.18, 1.42). The pattern rate ratio for years of life lost (YLL) was similar in order. Compared to whites, the rate ratio for YLL was highest for Native Americans (RR: 3.95; 95 percent CI: 3.11, 5.02), Blacks (RR: 3.29; 95 percent CI: 2.59, 4.17), and Hispanics (RR: 1.55; 95 percent CI: 1.22, 1.97). The rate ratio and years of life lost were lower for Asians, even when compared to whites. This outcome presented a challenge to the authors for using racism as an explanation because they were unclear on how Asians received a protective effect compared to other racial and ethnic groups. Overall, the authors considered police shootings a public health emergency.

The sociologists Frank Edwards, Hedwig Lee, and Michael Esposito have worked together to analyze the *Fatal Encounters* online database. *Fatal Encounters* is an online database created by the journalist/researcher Brian Burghart for the University of Southern California.[28] The website was started in 2014 to provide context to police shootings in the United States and identify "who is being killed by police." The database contains information on police-related shootings from January 1, 2000, to date. The data is collected primarily through paid researchers, public record requests, and a crowdsourcing effort of public records and various new sources, which are then verified by the researchers. In the first study by Edwards and colleagues that examined the *Fatal Encounters* data between 2012 and 2018, they found a total of 8,581 deaths attributed to police-civilian interactions, for which they focused on a total sample size of 6,295 cases where adult males were killed as a result of asphyxiation, beating, chemical agents, medical emergency, taser, or gunshot.[29] They found that Black men were killed at a rate of 2.1 per 100,000, Latinos at 1.0 per 100,000, and white men at 0.6 per 100,000. During this timeframe, police were responsible for 8 percent of all homicides of adult male victims in the United States. Edwards and colleagues reported how their analysis, accounting for geographic spaces, highlighted how racial inequalities on a structural level influenced the broader contextual environment in which policing occurs. Such a framework of understanding went beyond idiosyncratic circumstances and focusing upon individual choices that were often examined legally or described by the news media. In the second study by Edwards and colleagues, these same researchers focused on differences by gender, race, and age between 2013 and 2018.[30] They estimated that if the risk levels remained similar to the study period, the police would kill fifty-two of every 100,000 men and boys over a life course and about three of every 100,000 women and girls. Black men were 2.5 times more likely to be killed by the police than white men. Similar disparities existed between Black women and white women. Latinos and Latinas, along with Native American men and women, were also more likely to be killed than white men and women. Between the ages of twenty-five and twenty-nine, Black men were killed by police at a rate of between 2.8 and 4.1 per 100,000, whereas Latino men were killed at rates between 1.4 and 2.2 per 100,000. The authors concluded that inequalities exist in one's gender, race, and age and that such a pattern is a public health concern. Police violence was found to be a leading cause of death, especially for young men of color.

Another data source used to determine racial and ethnic disparities is the Centers for Disease Control and Prevention's National Violent Death Reporting System (NVDRS). Based on data from seventeen states in 2013, Blacks were found to be killed by law enforcement at a higher rate (0.6 per 100,000 population) compared to Latinos (0.3 per 100,000) and whites (0.1 per 100,000).[31] A separate study focusing on sixteen participating states from 2005 to 2012 found that Blacks, Latinos, and Native Americans experienced higher rates of law enforcement homicides than whites did.[32] Asians were the lowest among all racial and ethnic groups. One way to evaluate these results is to apply the model of a Relative Rate Index (RRI), which compares whether the rates match the comparison group, as used in studies on disproportionate minority contact, to assess racial and ethnic disparities in the juvenile justice system.[33] Therefore, analyses of the NVDRS data show that Black people were killed by law enforcement at a rate of 0.6 per 100,000 population, compared to Latinos at 0.3 per 100,000 and whites at 0.1 per 100,000. Using the rate for whites as the baseline for comparison, these results indicate a pattern in which Blacks were killed at a rate six times higher than whites and Latinos three times higher than whites. Hence, an analysis incorporating a comparison group heightens the level of racial and ethnic disparity. A third study by a public health researcher named James Buehler utilized data acquired from the Center for Disease Control and Prevention's Wide-Ranging Online Data for Epidemiologic Research (WONDER) system to estimate rates of racial and ethnic differences.[34] Buehler found 2,285 legal intervention deaths between 2010 and 2014. Ninety-six percent of those deaths involved a firearm being discharged by a law enforcement officer, and of those, 96 percent were male victims. Legal intervention death rates were highest among Blacks, followed by Hispanics, and the lowest rates were found for white individuals. Among males, Blacks were 2.8 times more likely to be killed compared to whites; similarly, Hispanics were 1.7 times more likely to die compared to whites. Among all age groups, Black males had the highest rates of legal intervention deaths.

The final data source examined more thoroughly by researchers to determine national patterns in police shootings that allows us to examine racial and ethnic disparities was *Mapping Police Violence*. This website documents police shootings and police killings regardless of whether a firearm was used.[35] The main concern for the creators of this database is that official reports and databases in the United States are underreported. The website contains data from 2013 until the present. In one study, several researchers explored the relationship between state-level racism and racial disparities between Blacks and whites in fatal police shootings.[36] They used fatal police shooting data from the *Mapping Police Violence* website for the time period between January 2013 and June 2017. They examined the level of racism in each state by examining five dimensions: residential segregation, gaps in incarceration rate, educational attainment, economic indicators, and employment status. Overall, these researchers found that in forty-nine states, Blacks were shot and killed by police at a rate 3.1 times higher than whites and that unarmed Blacks were shot at a rate 4.5 times higher than unarmed whites. They found racial residential segregation to be a statistically significant indicator in explaining Black and white racial disparities. These researchers hoped this article could aid in the theorizing of the relationship between structural racism and racial disparities in fatal police shootings. Finally, a study by the criminologists Shytierra Gaston and Rashaan DeShay and the sociologist April Fernandes using the *Mapping Police Violence* data between 2013 and 2018 gave greater attention to the role of gender and female victimization. They found that Black men had police killing rates three times higher than white men did and 2.2 times than those of Hispanic men. Black women were killed by police at a rate of 0.34 per 100,000, compared to 0.23 per 100,000 for white women and 0.18 per 100,000 for Hispanic women. Within each gender, Black men and Black women were at the highest risk of being killed by police, highlighting the importance of examining the racialized-gendered nature of police shootings.

Given these contemporary patterns and racial and ethnic disparities in police shootings, a number of arguments and statements have been made: (1) an acknowledgment that police shootings occur not only in urban areas but also in rural and suburban spaces, (2) the declaration of police shootings as a public health emergency, (3) the need to examine the broader contextual environment for racial and ethnic inequalities beyond individual choice and idiosyncratic circumstances, (4) the need for more comprehensive data collection efforts by local police stations and centralization of that data by the federal government, and (5) the analysis of the racialized-gendered nature of police shootings through multivariate adjusted analyses and studies that address or account for intersectionality in the factors that increase the risk of being a victim of a police shooting.

In recognition of these differential outcomes, we repeat here the sociologist Paul Takagi's blunt assessment, offered in 1974: "It is the actual experiences behind statistics like these that suggest that police have one trigger finger for whites and another for Blacks."[37] Takagi began his article by exploring how society's focus at the time was concerned with the killings of police officers but had neglected the killing of civilians by the police, considering them as isolated incidents. These resident encounters with police were described as "deadly force," thus legitimizing the decision making and neglecting the officer's role in violence. Takagi's argument regarding the two trigger fingers was reached after examining justifiable homicides from the CDC's Vital Statistics in the United States database and comparing these numbers to male civilians ten years and older. Takagi stated that the nation was moving more toward a "garrison state" that offered a false sense of comfort by upholding a belief that our society was still a democracy.

The sociologist Harold D. Lasswell coined the term "garrison state" as a developmental construct to describe a society in which the specialists of violence were the most powerful group in society.[38] It was a society that had cardinal virtues to obey, serve, and work. It was considered a dictatorial regime. At the time, Lasswell considered the United States as a "business state" but was concerned that China and Japan had moved more toward a garrison state.[39] The sociologist C. Wright Mills also examined various types of power elites in US society, describing that not one group holds all the power but outlining how various powerful interest groups collectively maintained power. One such group was the "warlords." Mills acknowledged that the United States was born in violence but that military leaders often used this background to obtain positions of power in other sectors of life, for example, economics or politics. Both Lasswell and Mills primarily considered the use of violence as an institutional tool of the military, but they did not examine how agents of the state working in law enforcement also used violence against its residents.

Such a description corresponds with the description of the militarization of the police offered by several researchers.[40]

RACIAL AND ETHNIC DIFFERENCES

In an effort to examine whether police officers had and have separate trigger fingers for whites, Blacks, and Latinos, the focus of this chapter will be on the bivariate associations by race and ethnicity. These findings will be complemented with case studies to provide context to the results, which were developed from analyzing each racial and ethnic group separately in comparison with census data.[41] As reported earlier, 44.3 percent of all shootings occurring in Denver from 1983 to 2020 involved Latinos, while the rest of the cases included 31.1 percent white, almost 22 percent Black, and 3 percent categorized as Nonwhite Other, which included Native American, multiracial, and Asian individuals. Although Latinos had the greatest percentage of shootings, police officers shot Black males at a rate 3.9 times more often than white males.[42] In Denver, Latino males were shot at a rate three times greater than white males.

BIVARIATE ASSOCIATIONS BY RACE
AND ETHNICITY

Bivariate associations for all measures by race and ethnicity are found in table A2.5 (see appendix 2). Only the measures that differ by race and ethnicity are presented. A full list of the measures under each section is presented in the Measures section of the Methods, which can be found in the appendix. During the coding of the 298 officer-involved shooting cases, the presentation of narratives from actual cases was developed to highlight statistically significant bivariate racial and ethnic differences that occurred, based on the intersection of suspect characteristics, officer characteristics, and contextual factors. The randomly selected ten narratives capture thematic differences such as running from officers, shootings in the back, the quickness with which officers shoot, and immediate-entry search warrants.

SOCIODEMOGRAPHIC CHARACTERISTICS OF THE PERSON SHOT

There were significant racial and ethnic differences across the age group of the person shot, the foreign-born status of the person shot, and where the person shot reportedly lived. Whites had the highest median age at the time of the shooting, 36 (26, 44), while Blacks had the lowest median age, at 22 (19, 30.5). This pattern of Blacks being shot at a younger age was consistent with a previous study described earlier in the chapter that emphasized a greater number of years of life lost from police violence.[43]

Among white adults, those aged 28 to 37 (27.2 percent) and 38 to 47 (27.2 percent) had the highest rates of being shot. Among Black (54.7 percent and 18.8 percent), Latino (40.5 percent and 36.6 percent), and Nonwhite Other (44.4 percent and 22.2 percent) individuals, most were shot as adults aged 18 to 27 and 28 to 37. Black youth (14.1 percent) were shot 3.3 times more often than white youth (4.3 percent). The foreign-born rate was the highest among Latino persons shot (9.2 percent) compared to the other groups (0 percent–1.6 percent). The distribution of the proportions of where people reportedly lived differed by race and ethnicity. Among white (45.6 percent), Black (44.3 percent), and Latino (54.2 percent) persons shot, most lived in Denver, but the rate was highest among those who were Nonwhite Other (87.5 percent).

There were no statistically significant differences in the percentage of cases that were disputed by race and ethnicity; however, those who were Nonwhite Other (55.6 percent) had the most disputes, followed by Black (39.1 percent), Latino (36.6 percent), and white (29.3 percent) persons shot. This was surprising because we had assumed, from general news coverage, that shootings primarily of Blacks would receive a higher number of disputes and news concerns. We found, however, that controversial law enforcement shootings were more equally distributed across racial and ethnic groups, indicating the difficulty for any shooting to undergo public scrutiny, even if it included someone of the white majority group. News coverage was consistent across each racial and ethnic group, ranging between 84.4 percent and 88.9 percent, with a median of three newspaper articles per shooting.

Sociodemographic factors intertwined with other features that often demonstrated a greater level of restraint, delay, and occasionally compassion shown for white suspects compared to Blacks and Latinos. Case files indicate encounters where law enforcement officers attempted a nondeadly outcome for white suspects. For example, on Friday, April 18, 1997, around 11:30 PM, a twenty-two-year-old white male named James Fleck shot and killed his nineteen-year-old common-law wife (Lana), who was pregnant.[44] Afterward, James drove his eight-month-old daughter to his grandfather's house in the Berkeley neighborhood (69 percent white and 28 percent Latino, with an 11 percent poverty rate), saying he wanted to die because he had shot and killed Lana.[45] Family members called the police when James left in his vehicle with two pistols. The four police officers were inside talking with the grandfather when they saw James exit his vehicle around 1:00 AM in front of the house. Officers repeated commands for James to drop his weapons. Instead of complying, James fired a shot into the air and then pointed the gun at himself and then at the officers. The officers retreated behind a car and shouted, "Put the weapons down," and "We can discuss this." James continued to approach officers and fired two additional shots into the air. James was shouting that he wanted to die. The four officers (Ed Frushour, Kenneth Manzanares, Phil Manzanares, and Robert Wilson), who were white and Latino, reported feeling that they no longer had an escape route and returned by firing seven shots. Three bullets hit James in the arm, chest, and head; he died from these wounds.

The DA, Bill Ritter, commended the officers for showing such great restraint. One witness stated that the officers must have shouted "Put down the weapon" more than twenty times times. The grandfather reported James was manic-depressive and suicide prone. One of James's guns had stovepiped, but the other gun was cocked and loaded. If police officers had arrested James, a prosecutor could have possibly pursued the death penalty. This case was unique because it was one of the rare cases (comprising only almost 3 percent of the total), where the suspect had been involved in a homicide before or during an encounter with officers. Reports of wanting to die at the hands of law enforcement, also known as suicide by cop, seemed common in the media but were found more frequently for whites (17.4 percent) and Latinos (16.7 percent), compared to Blacks (1.6 percent). There were five cases where the person shot had killed themselves before being shot by law enforcement or after coming into contact with law enforcement. Being unable to interview these individuals, it was difficult to discern whether they were suicidal, had escalated toward a more pessimistic outcome, or if there was some form of misconduct that covered up wrongdoing. For example, *Fatal Encounters* includes data regarding suicides that occurred after a police encounter.

Reviewing officer-involved shootings of Latinos and Blacks indicates that officers often acted more disrespectfully to the suspects before, during, or after the encounter occurred in comparison to whites. For example, on Saturday, January 23, 1988, twenty-three-year-old Antonio Castillo became involved in a dispute with a man on the bus in the Sun Valley neighborhood (65 percent Latino, 13 percent white, and 12 percent Black, with a poverty rate of 65 percent) and allegedly flashed a gun.[46] The man got off the bus a short distance away and noticed a police officer parked close by; he went over and told the officer what he had seen. The white male officer, Michael Calo, with three years of experience, observed the identified suspect. Antonio allegedly placed a small-caliber gun in his waistline. The officer began following in his patrol car and then exited with his gun drawn and shouted, "Police officer, stop!" Antonio continued walking with his girlfriend and then started running. The officer hopped back in his car and followed him; he then started chasing him on foot. The officer reported that as Antonio was running, he turned back toward the officer with the gun pointed. The officer responded by firing four shots. Most of the witnesses reported not seeing a gun, but DA Norm Early stated it was probably because it was a very small handgun and, given the angles, they did not observe the shooting. The gun was a .25 caliber Raven, and it did not have a bullet in the chamber. Several shootings of questionable conduct included a .25 firearm.[47] Antonio died at 4:35 PM from a single gunshot wound to his back left side two inches from the armpit. One of the witnesses reported it was "uncalled for" and claimed that after the shooting, the officer pulled the boy's head up by the hair and dropped his face back into the snow. DA Early stated that the witness accounts were not supported by the evidence. Mr. Early reported that the officer had a reasonable belief that the armed Antonio presented a danger to the officer's life.

ALCOHOL AND DRUG USE OF THE PERSON SHOT

Significant differences were identified in alcohol or drug use reported by race and ethnicity. Persons who were Nonwhite Other had the highest proportion of any alcohol or drug use (66.7 percent) as well as alcohol use alone (44.4 percent), whereas Blacks had the lowest rates (33.3 percent and 19.3 percent, respectively). In the United States, the criminal justice system has particularly targeted racial and ethnic minorities with punishment-focused consequences of arrest and incarceration driven by perceived differences in drug use.[48] One of the studies examining racial and ethnic differences in alcohol and drug use found that arrest rates for aggressive crimes were higher for Mexican Americans compared to Blacks or whites even though drug and alcohol use was observed for all ethnic groups.[49] They did report that the frequent use of alcohol increased the probability of arrest for an aggressive crime for males in general whereas drug use produced the opposite outcome. In this study, the researchers examined arrest rates and how they differed by race and ethnicity in the state of Texas by focusing on the cities of Dallas, Houston, and San Antonio. Rather than blaming "cultural difference," the authors emphasized the mixture of socioeconomic, environmental, and cultural factors that distinguish communities and the settings in which aggression may occur.

Scholars have often reported the importance of family in the Latino community as a primary site of resiliency against the experiences of colonization and migration.[50] However, maintaining a family under lower economic circumstances and affected by alcohol, drugs, jealousy, possessiveness, deportation, mass incarceration, or generations of exclusion was difficult to do well. For example, on Monday, April 30, 2000, Ralph Baca-Salcido, forty-four years of age, was involved in a domestic dispute in the Sloan's Lake neighborhood (51 percent white and 41 percent Latino, with an 18 percent poverty rate). Around 1:38 PM, Mr. Baca-Salcido's daughter called 911, stating her dad was yelling at her mother and swinging a knife at everyone. He left the scene, carrying a knife, before five officers arrived. His wife told the police that he is an excessive drinker and is abusive toward her and their five children. Earlier in the morning, Mr. Baca-Salcido had tried to choke her to death and threatened to kill her. Because of his behavior, she has been staying at a motel. The wife reported that her husband stated he could not live without her and was not going back to jail. He had previously served several years in prison for manslaughter.

Three officers were present in the front yard when Mr. Baca-Salcido pulled up in his vehicle at 1:47 PM. He exited with a beer bottle in his right hand and a large pipe and knife in his left hand. The officers drew their firearms as Mr. Baca-Salcido continued to advance. The officers yelled, "Drop the weapons!" Family members shouted, "He is drunk and won't do anything." The family pleads with their dad and the wife with her husband to drop the weapons, but he responds by saying he did not want to go back to jail. Two officers deploy mace. Family members stated he began swinging his arms wildly because he couldn't see, whereas officers reported the mace did not seem to have any effect. The two white male police officers (Hans Leven and Michael Mosco) fired five shots at 1:53 PM. Mr. Baca-Salcido fell face down, and officers held back family members as they called the ambulance. He later died from his injuries. His blood alcohol level was .240. The DA, Bill Ritter, stated in the decision letter, "It is tragic that Salcido chose to be violent with his wife and family. It was not the first time. They are the real victims in this case. You need to look no further than Ralph Salcido to lay one hundred percent of the blame for his own death."[51] This statement by Mr. Ritter was unsettling because while rightfully challenging the criminal behavior of Mr. Baca-Salcido, which may have led to a return conviction to prison, the district attorney, in essence, justified the punishment of death, a penalty that would not have been handed down in a court of law. This case also highlights the trauma that family members and children report when observing an officer-involved shooting resulting in death. Studies have noted symptoms of depression, grief, and PTSD resulting from having a loved one killed by violence.[52] The suddenness of the event makes it much more difficult to make sense of what transpired. The public scrutiny after the fact of the individual shot by law enforcement can also be traumatic. Moreover, officers rarely received criminal charges, making the search for accountability or simply closure unattainable.

SHOOTING-RELATED MEASURES

There were significant differences by race and ethnicity in two shooting-related measures, the time difference between the arrival of police and the shooting, as well as the proportion of race and ethnicity that was greater than 50 percent in the neighborhood where the shooting occurred. The time between the arrival of police and the shooting was lower for those who were Black at three (Q1: 2.0, Q3: 6.0) minutes compared to a median of five minutes for whites (5.0; Q1: 4.0, Q3:14.5), Nonwhite Other (5.0; Q1: 3.5, Q3: 23.8), and Latino (5.0; Q1: 2.0, Q3: 15.0) individuals. Whereas police officers often demonstrated restraint and negotiated with white suspects, law enforcement officers shot Black people more quickly. For example, on Saturday, November 27, 1999, nineteen-year-old Joseph Ashley went with his girlfriend to retrieve some money.[53] They drove to meet with two young men. The girlfriend got into their car; shortly after, Joseph hopped into the back seat, pointed a gun at the driver, and told him to drive. Joseph threatened to kill the two young men with a gun for disrespecting him earlier on the telephone. Joseph robbed both individuals of their material possessions. After driving around aimlessly for a period, Joseph released one of the occupants. This individual called the police around 6:35 PM. Police officers responded from two jurisdictions, given the origin of the call and later the location of the vehicle at a Burger King in the Lowry Field neighborhood (86 percent white, with 6 percent poverty), where Joseph's girlfriend had left her car. As officers approached the parking lot at 6:43 PM, they noticed Joseph driving the kidnapped suspect's vehicle. Officers blocked off the exits from the fast-food restaurant. Seeing he was going to be contained, Joseph rammed into a police car. The officer used his patrol car to push Joseph and the two occupants into a corner. Joseph's girlfriend encouraged him to give her the gun and surrender. As the police commanded "Put your hands up in the air" via loudspeaker, both the kidnap victim and girlfriend complied, and the gun fell to the floor. Police officers noticed Joseph was not complying. The kidnapping victim reported Joseph stating, "Fuck this! I'm going out like a soldier," as he stepped out of the vehicle and reached for the gun.

As Joseph started raising the gun, four white male officers (one Denver Police Department officer, Joseph Hamel, and three Aurora Police Department officers, Mark Jucha, Steve Oulliber, and Darin Parker) fired twenty-seven rounds, hitting Joseph ten times in the head, chest, groin, and forearm. The time was 6:46 PM, and officers reported only a four-to-five-second difference in time between when Joseph grabbed the gun and when officers fired shots. Joseph did not fire a bullet from his Tec-9 pistol, but the DA, Bill Ritter, commended officers for neutralizing this threat. Joseph's blood alcohol level was 0.155. This case highlights the difficulties of focusing primarily on officer-involved shooting data as it provided little information as to the reasoning behind Joseph's behavior and that of the officers in possibly creating an alternative outcome. It was, however, yet another example of the killing of Black males for which men and boys are disadvantaged because of their maleness.[54]

White male police officers' ability to establish rapport with white shooting victims contrasted with their continued confrontation with Black and Latino suspects. For example, forty-seven-year-old David Pratt, a white male, walks into a bank in the Baker neighborhood (54 percent Latino and 40 percent white, with a poverty rate of 31 percent) on Wednesday, October 28, 1992, around 9:40 AM and orders the teller to put the money in the bag.[55] Mr. Pratt wore a blue baseball hat and jacket and pointed a gun at the teller, who placed the money in the bag. The teller pushed the silent alarm as Mr. Pratt walked away. Another teller alerted a detective, who was working off duty, about the robbery and the suspect leaving out the bank doors. The detective, Michael Greer, a white male with seventeen years of experience, chased and yelled for Mr. Pratt to stop or he would shoot. Detective Greer saw Mr. Pratt reach for his gun, and he fired one shot, hitting Mr. Pratt in the left front leg. Mr. Pratt fell to the ground, and the officer placed him in handcuffs. While waiting for the ambulance, Detective Greer asked Mr. Pratt if he had any children, which he answered affirmatively. The detective stated it was a good day for both men: Their children still had fathers because neither man had been killed. The DA, Norman S. Early, stated:

The facts developed in this investigation show conclusively that Detective Greer acted swiftly, courageously and professionally to apprehend this armed bank robber. The threat presented by Pratt, armed with a loaded sawed-off 30-30 rifle, is obvious. . . . We commend Detective Greer, not only for his quick and decisive action in apprehending this clearly dangerous criminal, but also for the compassion he displayed after the threat was neutralized. These actions exemplify excellence in police work and a human decency that speaks for itself.[56]

Mr. Pratt was described by news reports as a self-styled mountain man who simply wanted to take out a "little loan" from the bank.[57] He had been living out of his truck, which was equipped with a camper that included a variety of living amenities. He robbed the bank because he'd run out of money, and despite not having a listed criminal record, police were looking into whether he had committed other unsolved robberies.

Immediate-entry search warrants resulting in officer-involved shootings were more common for Black and Latino suspects. The war on drugs has disproportionately targeted racial and ethnic minorities.[58] For example, on Wednesday, September 17, 1986, a judge issued an immediate-entry search warrant for a residence in the Curtis Park housing projects in the Five Points neighborhood (50 percent Latino, 24 percent white, 22 percent Black, with a poverty rate of 43 percent). A confidential informant reported the packaging and distribution of heroin occurring at the residence, along with the presence of guns. Police officers expected two Mexican nationals to be present during the raid, along with fifty-four-year-old Alfonso Mitchell, whom law enforcement officials described as having a history of concealing weapons. Thirteen officers from the Narcotics Bureau and Tactical Motorcycle Unit split into two teams. They enter the front and back doors of the residence around 3:35 PM. As officers enter the home, they yelled, "Police, freeze!" The police apprehend a Latino man from New Mexico, place him on a chair, and tell him to keep his hands in the air. A white male officer with eleven years of experience, Michael Thomson, sees an inner door partially open and possibly closed by a hook or chair. The officer kicks the door open and yells, "Police, don't move!" A Black male inside, Mr. Mitchell, moves his right hand, and the officer fires one shot to his upper right chest. Afterward, officers were unable to find a weapon, but the police suspected he was possibly attempting to stash a small bag of heroin. The DA, Norm Early, stated that it was reasonable for the police officer to believe Mr. Mitchell posed an immediate threat to his safety: "An officer has the right to act on appearances and does not have to wait for a citizen to injure or kill him before he acts to protect himself or a third party."[59] DA Early stated that Mr. Mitchell's movement caused the officer to shoot. The police found 27 grams of heroin and four thousand dollars in cash on the Latino male, in addition to a gun. Police officers were unable to find additional drugs or weapons in the residence, so it was unclear whether Mr. Mitchell really was attempting to hide some drugs or whether his perceived movement resulted in officers making an incorrect assumption.

Fights outside of bars or nightclubs were a more common feature for officer-involved shootings of Latinos and Blacks. For example, on Friday, March 7, 2003, twenty-four-year-old Luis Almeida Ponce was partying at the Tequila Le Club in the Regis neighborhood. Although the residential neighborhood was 74 percent white, the bar and nightclub located along the busy Federal Boulevard played primarily Spanish music. At 1:15 AM, an officer was filling out paperwork in a parking lot when a woman pulled up in her vehicle and stated that an individual was brandishing a firearm. The woman describes the suspect as a Hispanic male wearing blue jeans, a white shirt, and a white cowboy hat. Three officers in different patrol cars rush to the scene. Upon arriving, officers see two individuals struggling over an object in one of the individual's waistbands. The individuals break up as the officers shout, "Let me see your hands!" The officers report Luis reaching for his waistband and starting to raise an object. The three police officers (William Carr, Randy Murr, and Joseph Trujillo), who were white and Latino, fired twenty-seven shots, of which fourteen hit Luis, who fell to the ground. Several witnesses reported hearing police say "put the gun down" or "drop the weapon." One witness believed Luis was attempting to surrender by putting his hands in the air. The officers reported they feared the suspect was about to shoot them. During the autopsy, medical examiners found a 0.156 blood alcohol level for Luis. The DA, Bill Ritter, states:

> Almeida-Ponce is the only person who could know with certainty what his intentions were at the instant he pulled the weapon. The officers are not mind-readers. They must react to the quickly evolving circumstances which confront them. They do not have the luxury of pushing a pause button. . . . It is unfortunate that Almeida-Ponce chose to act as he did. His actions throughout this confrontation were non-compliant, aggressive and consistent with an intention to harm the officers. It is fortunate that no officer or citizen was injured in this life threatening confrontation.[60]

Public officials did not mention whether language or nationality differences might have influenced the shooting outcome or whether officers were too quick to shoot. Police officers shot at least thirteen immigrants, of whom 92 percent were reportedly from Mexico or other Latin American countries, during the thirty-eight years of this study. As the foreign-born population in Denver was at its highest in 2000, it put pressure on the police department to hire more bilingual Spanish-speaking officers and to provide increased incentives for developing language competency.[61]

INCIDENT-RELATED FACTORS

There were significant differences in incident-related factors by race and ethnicity that included a person injured in cases when someone else was injured, as well as the person shot listed as having a mental health issue, suicidality, a criminal record, or gang involvement. Counter to common assumptions regarding police shootings, only 24.8 percent of cases, or one-fourth of all shooting incidents, occurred after the individual shot had injured another individual. These differences were not statistically significant, but what was significant was the person whom the individual shot had injured. Whites were statistically more likely to injure a police officer (36.8 percent) or a partner/spouse (31.6 percent). This finding is important because although Blacks and Latinos were shot at a higher rate than whites, white males were a greater threat to law enforcement officers. Similar misplaced levels of a perceived threat compared to actual threats are pervasive in the criminal justice system. For example, lone wolf terrorists, school shooters, and mass shooters are primarily white.[62] Among Black (81.3 percent) and Latino (41.2 percent) individuals, the person most frequently injured was a stranger; for Nonwhite Other, a family member (50.0 percent). The rates of mental health issue(s) reported were highest among white (21.2 percent) individuals who were shot, while Nonwhite Other (33.3 percent) residents had the highest rate of suicidality. The data reflect that mental illness issues were more commonly reported for whites shot by the police, at 21.2 percent, compared to 4.6 percent for Latinos and 3.4 percent for Blacks. Researchers often argue that the excuse of mental illness was often overused as an explanation for criminal offending because there is a large number of US residents diagnosed with mental illness who have not reached a high level of criminal offending.[63] In addition, others have argued that associating extreme violence with unintentional causes for white individuals leads to criminal judgments of leniency.[64]

Black individuals shot had the lowest rate of a criminal record (38.1 percent), followed by white (43.3 percent) residents, Latinos (57.3 percent), and Nonwhite Other (66.7 percent) individuals. Blacks (16.1 percent) and Latinos (13.7 percent) had higher reported gang membership, while white and Nonwhite Other had listed involvement at 0 percent. As gangs have often been created in response to different forms of societal adversity and dangerous neighborhoods, these data reflect the presence of these groups in the city and county of Denver, but by themselves do not justify a shooting.[65]

OFFICERS WHO SHOT

There were significant differences by race and ethnicity identified in the number of officers at the scene, police use of a nonlethal alternative, and the police district for the area of the census tract of the shooting. The median number of officers at the scene was highest among cases where the person shot was white, three (2, 4), while all other racial and ethnic groups had a median of two. This may be reflective of the additional time involved in the shooting of white suspects and the attempt to use nonlethal alternatives, which were used more frequently among whites (15.2 percent), compared to Latinos (12.2 percent) and Blacks (3.1 percent). A nonlethal alternative was not reportedly used at all for Nonwhite Other individuals.

The majority of white (61.5 percent) residents and Black (60.8 percent) persons shot were shot in predominantly white neighborhoods, while the majority of Nonwhite Other (60.0 percent) and Latino (57.7 percent) individuals were shot in predominantly Latino neighborhoods. Among white (30.4 percent) and Latino (39.7 percent) individuals, the Northwest Denver area was where they were most often shot, while Blacks (43.8 percent) were most commonly shot in the Central Denver area and Nonwhite Other (33.3 percent) in Southwest Denver.

Firearms were the objects possessed that were most likely to result in someone's being shot by the police, but the median number of shots fired differed by race and ethnicity. Possession or use of a firearm resulted in a median number of five shots fired by an officer, and this included a median number of four shots toward whites, 2.5 for Blacks, and five for both Latinos and for Nonwhite Other; however, these differences were not statistically significant. When the weapon was described as a vehicle, the shooting resulted in the highest number of bullets fired by officers, with a median of eight shots; these also differed, but not statistically significantly, by race and ethnicity, with whites encountering 14.5 shots, Blacks 8.5, and Latinos three.[66] An example of when an excessive number of bullets were fired toward a white suspect in a vehicle is the following case study: On Friday, April 18, 2003, twenty-year-old Shaun Gilman pointed a red beam at a 7-11 store clerk at 2:53 AM. The clerk called 911. A police officer found the suspect's vehicle a short distance from the 7-11 store and made a stop. The sole officer approached the Jeep and observed a white male occupant behind the steering wheel. The driver, Shaun, put the vehicle in reverse, drove toward the officer at a high rate of speed, slammed into the officer's car, and drove away. The officer called dispatch at 3:08 AM reporting this incident. The Jeep was later located at 3:12 AM stuck on a fire hydrant in Capitol Hill (77 percent white, 11 percent Latino, and 9 percent Black, with a 26 percent rate of poverty). In total, there were twelve shootings in Capitol Hill, making it one of the top five neighborhoods for police to use deadly force. Officers began ordering the driver to surrender. Shaun appeared to hold several objects and point them toward officers. He flipped officers off with his middle finger as they spoke to him through a public address system. Shaun continued revving the Jeep engine, attempting to free the lodged vehicle. Police officers reported thinking Shaun had fired a shot toward officers at 3:35 AM when eight officers, males and females, fired fifty bullets, hitting him an estimated sixteen times.[67] After assessing the scene, police officers discovered that the weapon was a pistol-grip crossbow, which was mistaken for a gun. Hospital staff pronounced Shaun dead at 4:15 AM. He had both acetone and THC in his system. The DA, Bill Ritter, stated that officers tried for twenty-three minutes to resolve the confrontation peacefully and that the number of shots fired ceased immediately once the perceived threat was neutralized. Mr. Ritter concludes:

It is tragic that Shaun Gilman by his conduct caused the officers to take his life. It is also unfortunate that his parents, family, and friends, who knew him as a different person in better times, have had this tragedy visited upon their lives. Unfortunately, these officers encountered Shaun Gilman at a time when he was exposing citizens and the officers to great danger. . . . Here, the officers were patient and made significant efforts to conclude the encounter peacefully. Tragically, for reasons known only to Shaun Gilman, during the entire episode he never once showed any sign of compliance or a desire for a peaceful conclusion. To the contrary, he seemed intent on forcing this result.[68]

Shaun Gilman's family questioned the police response to their bipolar son and the number of shots fired.[69] They reported that when he was off his medication, his behavior changed and that he had only recently moved out and into his own home. The family argued that police officers needed better training when encountering individuals with mental illness. The DA countered that the high number of shots fired at Shaun was because he had covered the windows of his Jeep, which had obstructed officers' view into the car. The officers also found it difficult to determine whether he had been hit by the bullets, since he was in a seated position. The high number of shots was also explained by the action of eight officers firing their weapons at the same time.

Although there were more officers present when a white suspect was shot (three) compared to Blacks, Latinos, and Nonwhite Other (two), it was primarily only one officer who fired their weapon. The authority and deference given to the lone officer's description of events left family members and friends searching for answers. For example, on Wednesday, May 25, 2005, at 1:30 AM, thirty-one-year-old Harrison Owens allegedly assaulted and robbed a man in Capitol Hill; the man fled toward a police car asking for help. The white male policeman, Officer Michael Wyatt, with eight years of experience, observed the bloodied individual run toward him. The robbery victim reported that a Black man with a white shirt had assaulted him and had a gun. The officer exited his patrol car and approached Mr. Owens, who started running away. Officer Wyatt ran after Mr. Owens down a dark alley. He shouted, "Drop the gun" and "Show me your hands." As Mr. Owens ran, he allegedly pointed a gun back toward the officer, who fired one shot, hitting Mr. Owens in the middle right side of his back near the shoulder blade. Mr. Owens fell face down, with a fully loaded .44-caliber revolver near his hand. The autopsy documented a blood alcohol level of 0.161 in addition to meth and cannabinoids in his system. According to news reports, Mr. Owens had previously served five years in prison; several witnesses to the lead-up to the shooting corroborated the officer's testimony.[70] The media reported that the family disputed the allegation of Mr. Owens's trying to shoot a cop and said he was overall a good man, a father of three children, and would give the shirt off his back to help someone. At least seventy family members and friends held a candlelight vigil in his honor.[71] The DA, Mitch Morrissey, found the shooting justified by physical evidence that supported a bullet trajectory consistent with someone pointing a gun behind them. The manager of safety also found that the officer had acted appropriately. However, family members and members of the Black community questioned the officer's version of events because the shooting had occurred in a dark alley without any eyewitnesses or video footage. The officer's claim of threat superseded that of the family of Harrison Owens, making this case was empirically impossible to disprove as long as the officer reported his statement of what occurred to be the truth. Although most officers will never be involved in an officer-involved shooting, this was Officer Michael Wyatt's second shooting in five years. As of 2014, he had been promoted to lieutenant, and in 2021, he participated in a recruitment video describing himself as a formerly closeted gay man who was now able to be openly gay in a more progressive police department.[72] Officer Wyatt thus raises the questions of whether any type of background (race, ethnicity, gender, sexuality, political beliefs, etc.) was less prone to use deadly force when a threat was perceived and of how progressive a police department could feasibly become in refraining from shooting and injuring or killing its citizenry.

Officers' perceived noncompliance to verbal directives increased the chances for Blacks to be shot by law enforcement. For example, on Monday, October 17, 1983, fourteen-year-old William Harper was running from a police officer when the officer shot him in the Five Points neighborhood.[73] The Five Points neighborhood has been affected by gentrification: It was mostly white in 2020 but has historically been a Black and then later a mixed Black and Latino neighborhood with above-average poverty levels. In 1980, the Five Points neighborhood was 64 percent Black,

12 percent Latino, and 20 percent white, with 40 percent of the residents living in poverty. In thirty-eight of the years covered by our study, Five Points has led the city in the highest number of officer-involved shootings (n=22). William, a Black male, along with two friends, reportedly robbed an elderly woman walking with the aid of a cane around 6:15 PM. As they stole her purse, she fell to the ground and was dragged a short distance. A witness alerted a white male policeman with fifteen years of experience, Officer James Tavenner, who began a foot chase. He yelled, "Freeze," "Stop," and "Don't go over the fence or I'll shoot." William allegedly ignored the officer's commands, and the officer shot him in the lower right calf. William did not possess a weapon; the perceived knife may have actually been an Afro-style pick, stated DA Norm Early. William reported the officer saying, "Freeze or I'll blow your head off," and then saying, "Don't think I'm playing," as William continued to walk away. DA Early, who was also Black, stated:

> Based on these and other facts developed in the investigation, we clearly could not disprove beyond a reasonable doubt the "affirmative defense" available to Officer Tavenner under Colorado law. Therefore, no criminal charges are fileable against Officer Tavenner for his conduct in wounding William Harper. At the time of this incident, William Harper had had 18 police contacts in a two-year period and was wanted on arrest warrants for two burglaries and first degree sexual assaults.[74]

It was unknown what challenges in life were exacerbated by this shooting experience, but it appears that William continued to have legal difficulties. In 2020, William was fifty years of age and serving a prison sentence for several different charges acquired in 2006, 2009, and 2018. He was scheduled for a parole hearing in 2021 and was no longer found in the Colorado Department of Corrections inmate search locator in 2023.

Another distinguishing feature of the shootings involving Latinos and Blacks, based upon a review of case studies, was that the officer(s) reported unintentionally firing their weapon. For example, on Thursday, March 25, 1993, around midnight, seventeen-year-old Louis Melendez was with some friends.[75] An officer heard shots fired when he observed several vehicles leaving an area in the Sunnyside neighborhood (63 percent Latino and 33 percent white, with a 22 percent level of poverty). The officer followed a Nissan truck, and two additional patrol cars joined the chase. The officers reported that the suspects in the Nissan truck became stuck when it rammed a police car. The officers exited their vehicles with their guns drawn. They removed three individuals from the front cab and had them lie face down on the ground. They ordered two passengers in the back of the truck to exit the vehicle. Police officers reported that both individuals in the back were nonresponsive to orders, so a Latino officer with five years of experience reached into the bed of the truck to force one of the occupants out with his left hand. During the process, he struck his right elbow on something and fired a shot. None of the officers knew whose gun had fired, but it was later determined that the bullet had penetrated through the left rear of Louis's head. Louis's blood alcohol was 0.18; the police officers removed several guns from the truck. The individuals in the truck reported a desire to seek revenge for a recently shot friend. The DA, Norm Early, stated the following:

> The facts developed in the investigation of this incident support the conclusion that the non-life-threatening injury to Melendez was a result of an unintended discharge of Officer Rubio's service revolver following a sharp blow to his right elbow. Officer Rubio and the other officers involved in this confrontation were clearly justified in approaching the Nissan truck with their weapons drawn. The occupants of the truck were suspected of being involved in a shooting that had just occurred, had recklessly eluded the pursuing officers, and had rammed one of the patrol cars prior to coming to a stop. . . . It is clear that Officer Rubio did not intend to fire his weapon or injure Melendez. Moreover, he did not even know that his gun had discharged until all of the officers were checking their weapons and he found that one of the bullets in his gun had been fired. These are very dangerous encounters that officers are forced to engage in with violent offenders who refuse to cooperate and submit to lawful arrest. Had Melendez complied with the lawful commands of Officer Rubio and the other officers, this unintended discharge could have been averted.[76]

More than likely delirious, Louis initially reported the injury had been caused by his hitting his head on the floor as the bullet fired traveled three inches between his skin and skull. He was treated and released at the hospital. Officer Rubio's gun was a larger-caliber firearm (.357 revolver), which made it surprising that he did not know whether the bullet fired was from his gun. The DA stated that when examined, Officer Rubio had "a significant bruise and abrasion" to his right elbow, consistent with his statement that he had struck his right elbow on something; he was thus not criminally liable.

POST-SHOOTING OUTCOMES

The rates of a lawsuit settlement, as achieved or attempted, statistically significantly differed by race and ethnicity. Rates of achieving a lawsuit were lowest for white (5.7 percent) and Black (8.6 percent) persons shot compared to Latinos (13.2 percent) and Nonwhite Other (16.7 percent). As the egregiousness of police shootings did not differ by race and ethnicity, it was unclear, based upon the small number of successful lawsuits, why Latino and Nonwhite Other families were more successful. In terms of attempting a lawsuit but having it dismissed, six cases (5 percent) were reported for Latinos, but none were listed for the other racial and ethnic groups.

⎯⎯ ✸ ⎯⎯

The sociologist Paul Takagi commented nearly fifty years ago that officers had one trigger finger for whites and another for Blacks, and the findings presented in this chapter support such a conclusion.[77] Black and Latino residents were shot, injured, and killed at higher rates compared to whites. The Nonwhite Other option for race and ethnicity includes Asians, Native Americans, and multiracial persons: These persons had also been shot by law enforcement but less frequently compared to their rate in the general population. The epidemiologists Elle Lett and colleagues questioned whether the lower number of Asians shot by the police complicated being able to claim racism as the explanation for these racial disparities.[78] Based upon our reviews of these cases and historical data, we fall in line with the belief that each racial and ethnic group encounters its own unique forms of racialized oppression and that these can vary by time and place. Since the Asian population was overall very small in Denver, we would need to study a location with a higher concentration of Asians.[79] The same issue applies to Native Americans, who have been described as having the highest rates of police shootings yet are the smallest population group.[80] The largest racial and ethnic minority groups currently in Denver, Blacks and Latinos, have experienced the brunt of police shootings. It is also clear that all residents, even those of the majority racial group, whites, experience the risk of being shot by law enforcement. This understanding is reflective of a public health risk for all residents of the United States, but one that is particularly dangerous for Black and Latino men.

The findings from our data indicate that Blacks were shot at a younger median age (twenty-two), less likely to be under the influence of alcohol and drugs, and not more likely than any other racial or ethnic group to have victimized someone before being shot. Nevertheless, when encountered by a law enforcement officer, they were shot more quickly (three minutes) and less likely to have a nonlethal weapon used on them first. Blacks were more likely to be shot in white neighborhoods and primarily by one police officer.

Latinos, on the other hand, had the largest numerical number of shootings, but at a lower rate of overrepresentation compared to Blacks (3.9 times greater compared to 3.0 times greater for Latinos than white males). Latinos were between the shooting age of Blacks and whites (twenty-eight) and had a higher proportion of foreign born. Comparable to whites, Latinos had a similar percentage under the influence of alcohol or drugs, similar time difference between police arrival and shooting (five minutes), and similar reported suicidal tendencies. Latinos were more likely to be shot in a Latino neighborhood and to primarily have a conflict with a stranger that led to the police response.

White suspects who were shot were primarily older on average (thirty-six), with a high proportion on alcohol or drugs (60.9 percent). The median time between law enforcement arrival and the shooting of a white suspect was five minutes, and the encounter was primarily based on being wanted for something or for creating a disturbance. Whites were shot in primarily white neighborhoods with higher levels of poverty. When victimizing someone, whites were more likely to have victimized a police officer, a partner, or a spouse. They were more likely to be considered as having mental health problems and being suicidal. They were also more likely to encounter a nonlethal alternative before being shot.

Combined, the patterns of racial and ethnic differences can help policy makers and institutional leaders understand what factors heighten the chances for officers to use a firearm when responding to perceived and observed behaviors. The data also highlights the systemic nature of racism in US society and how altering this structural foundation is exceedingly difficult because it maintains settler-colonial interests.

4

TYPES OF SHOOTINGS

Problematic, Questionable, and Less Controversial

I t is hard to imagine that twenty-year-old Steven Gant could have realized the danger he was about to encounter on September 1, 1992, with a Denver police officer who had previously threatened his life.[1] Steven is six foot one, weighs 189 pounds, and is Black.[2] His mother and father both work in law enforcement as sheriff's deputies, one parent in Denver and the other in nearby Adams County.[3] Steven is becoming independent and finding his way in life. Some say he began having legal problems in high school when his parents were divorcing. As an adult, he has been arrested four times, and in one of these incidents, he served 174 days in the Denver County Jail for carrying a concealed firearm.[4] In one of these arrests, he encountered a Denver police officer named Michael Blake, who used physical force that required Steven to visit the hospital for a broken wrist. One newspaper account states the officer told his mother that if he continued hanging out with the wrong people in dangerous places, "It could eventually lead to him getting shot."[5] Steven's mother, a Denver sheriff's deputy, became distraught after hearing this. According to official Denver Police Department records, law enforcement officials recall that Officer Blake told her son, "If I ever see you in Capitol Hill again, I'll shoot you." Three days after his arrest, Steven filed a complaint with the police internal affairs bureau against Officer Blake for excessive force.[6]

Steven has a new girlfriend, and for the past two months, the relationship has been contentious. They live in Capitol Hill, a primarily white neighborhood in the middle of downtown Denver. Rumors suggest she may be selling drugs from her apartment, given the amount of pedestrian traffic and visits that occur even when Steven is not present. The relationship is falling apart, and he wants to collect his items and leave. She doesn't realize it then, but she is pregnant with his baby. Steven and his girlfriend have a verbal argument that escalates into his kicking in the bathroom door. A neighbor overhears the dispute and calls the police at 9:21 AM. The call that goes out to dispatch is a domestic violence call, for which Officer Blake responds quickly and arrives at the scene six minutes later. When Officer Blake arrives, he talks with the person who called the police and then the girlfriend. He then goes and looks for the suspect, whom he sees and states was approaching him. Once he recognizes who it is, he attempts to grab Steven's arm to make an arrest, but allegedly, Steven pushes him off with a forearm, hitting Officer Blake. Steven states he is just grabbing his stuff and takes off running.

Officer Blake follows in pursuit; he advises dispatch that he knows Steven Gant and notifies others that Steven has a criminal record for felony assault and carrying a weapon. He reports that officers must be careful because Steven will resist arrest.[7] Officer Michael Blake, a white male officer who lists his height as five foot eight and weighs 160 pounds, mentions that he has encountered a six foot three, 185-pound Steven in the stairwell.[8] The weight and height difference between the two individuals are mentioned as a factor influencing the officer's decision to feel threatened for his physical safety. Steven, only wearing gym shorts and sneakers and carrying a handful of clothes, possesses no weapon. At least five witnesses overhear Steven plead for his life before Officer Blake fires one bullet from his .45-caliber handgun at the center of Steven's chest, above the level of the left nipple and left of the midline, hitting a major artery. Officer Blake reported that Steven said he would shoot and made a threatening move toward the officer's gun. Auditory witnesses only describe hearing a man's voice stating, "Don't shoot me! Don't shoot me! Don't shoot me!"[9] Another auditory witness reports someone saying, "Oh God, I've been shot. I didn't do anything." After the shooting, a witness visually sees Officer Michael Blake emerging from the stairwell, stating, "I shot him. I can't believe I shot him. Stupid little fucker." A sergeant arriving at the scene asked Officer Blake whether he was okay. Officer Blake allegedly stated, "That son of a bitch. I can't believe it. That son of bitch made me."[10] The autopsy found Steven died because of a gunshot wound to his chest. His body was described as a "normally developed, muscular, apparently well-nourished black man" with toxicology results indicating nicotine and THC in his system.[11]

Steven's father reports having hope that the system he worked for would reach an accurate decision. He had been a sergeant in the US Air Force and served in Vietnam before working in corrections. Steven's mother was beginning to question her trust in law when she shared the sentiment, "FOR 15 YEARS . . . I put all my faith in this system. Now I've lost that faith. There's a man out there on the street who shot my son and because he wears a blue uniform, he's free. I lock people up for less than that every day."[12] The DA, Norm Early, who is also Black, reluctantly takes the case before a grand jury because of what he describes as "many factual contradictions" that pressure him not to make an individual decision on whether to pursue criminal charges.[13] The grand jury agrees that this incident should be brought to trial. Thus, the DA indicts Officer Blake on second-degree-murder charges.[14] Officer Blake is the first officer in Denver to be indicted on criminal charges while in the line of duty in fifteen years. The previous case was Officer David Neil, who shot and killed Arthur Espinoza in 1977 (see chapter 1). However, by the time the case went to trial in December 1993, Norm Early was no longer the Denver district attorney. Thus the job of prosecution went to DA Bill Ritter Jr. Similar to the trial in 1977, the Steven Gant case resulted in the jury finding Officer Blake not guilty of second-degree murder. The lesser charge of third-degree criminally negligent homicide is also blocked by one juror, who refused to convict, resulting in a mistrial.[15] The juror is described as a sixty-year-old male state worker who wouldn't follow the judge's instructions.[16] DA Bill Ritter decides that he will not retry the case, given the perception that another jury might reach the same decision. According to the *Denver Post*, Mr. Ritter stated: "Basically, we looked at the evidence we presented to the jury and the jury's verdicts, and we have no reason to expect that the results would improve on retrial. . . . Given the result, it's our belief that we would not be able to convince a reasonable jury beyond a reasonable doubt that the defendant was guilty of criminally negligent homicide."[17]

This was the DA's decision, despite all the testimony regarding the death threat made by Officer Blake, witnesses describing Steven saying

"Don't shoot," the lack of a weapon, the behavior of Officer Blake after the shooting, and a statement reported to officers that Officer Blake felt inadequate as an officer for not having fired his weapon during two previous shootings. This information was insufficient for a unanimous jury of twelve citizens to find the officer guilty. The mother and girlfriend filed a lawsuit against the city and county in 1993, but it was converted into a lawsuit only against Officer Blake, and the recipient named was Steven's daughter. As the case progressed, both sides agreed to an undisclosed settlement.[18] Officer Blake returned to the Denver Police Department and maintained his career in law enforcement until retiring in September 1999. Steven's father passed away several years after the death of his oldest son at the age of forty-eight, and they are buried near each other in Denver's Fort Logan National Cemetery. Steven's mother also left her position with the Denver County Jail. In 2023, Steven's daughter was listed as thirty years of age.[19]

Based upon the reported evidence, Steven Gant was wrongfully killed by Officer Michael Blake, but the one criminal indictment for this charge resulted in a verdict of not guilty by one member of the jury, thus resulting in a mistrial. Based on media reporting, there were many questions regarding who gets shot by the police and why. Most official news reporting mirrors the police department in blaming the individual shot, and although newspapers may occasionally include contradictory information compared to the officers' story, there was no official version that legally supported a narrative that the officers' behavior existed outside of the law. It was primarily the individuals shot whose lives were scrutinized. In the review of all the police shootings, it was concluded that most law enforcement shootings were questionable.[20] Shootings range along a continuum of different types. On one end, they are problematic, in the middle, they are questionable, and on the other end, they are less controversial. There can be family members and friends of individuals shot in any of these three categories who see a particular shooting as wrongful; at the same time, there can be officers and supporters who consider every shooting justified. The purpose of this chapter is to demonstrate how complicated law enforcement shootings are, given that not all are of the same type.

First, attention will be devoted to problematic shootings before providing an overview of questionable shootings and then less controversial ones. Ten cases that are representative of the overall sixty-two problematic shootings will be expanded to develop a narrative of how district attorneys and police departments attempted to mediate pressures from community members demanding justice.

PROBLEMATIC SHOOTINGS

From 1983 to 2020, there were a total of 298 officer-involved shootings in the geographic area of Denver, Colorado. Four different Denver district attorneys considered almost all (98.7 percent) of the officer-involved shootings legally justified. The DA filed criminal charges in one officer-involved shooting because of a grand jury decision (Steven Gant), one shooting was reviewed by a grand jury, but no criminal charges were pursued (Frank Lobato), and two off-duty shootings involving intoxicated police officers resulted in criminal charges. Despite the legal stronghold of the Denver district attorney almost never filing criminal charges against an officer, shootings were often interwoven with questionable circumstances and competing arguments that often resulted in community members' desiring a higher expectation of "justice" than what was provided by the law. Based upon the review of each case, 21 percent of police shootings were identified as problematic. Each of the sixty-two individuals shot by the police has a story that seriously questions why they were shot by a law enforcement officer. At this point in Denver's history, there have been several controversial police shootings and police-caused deaths (see chapter 2). The individuals shot under problematic circumstances meet a similar script in terms of age, race, ethnicity, sex, and particular sections of the city, and the incidents cover different time periods. On average, there were twelve to nineteen problematic shootings during each decade.[21]

Problematic shootings were more likely to include questionable officer tactics, a higher number of shots fired, and more haste in determining whether to shoot. Fifty percent of problematic shootings occurred with individuals who did not possess a weapon or were carrying a nonlethal or harmless object (e.g., cell phone, lighter, mace, nail clippers, soda can, or stick) but with the police officers describing their behavior with these objects as potentially deadly. Police officers expressed fearing the suspect was reaching for a weapon, acting aggressively, or attempting to gain control of the officer's gun. An equal proportion of problematic police shootings resulted in someone being wounded (50.0 percent) or dying (50.0 percent). A higher proportion of these shootings resulted in a law-suit (27.4 percent) and criminal charges against the officer (12.9 percent), but based on the information presented, these figures could have easily been much higher. Based on community claims and media coverage, there was not one single characteristic that led to protests over a police shooting. Instead, it was the intertwining of several key factors, such as lack of criminal participation by individual suspects and coincidingly questionable officer decision making.

INNOCENCE

In the United States, determining guilt is an outcome of an adversarial process. Legally, the saying is "innocent until proven guilty in a court of law." However, a key feature of officer-involved shootings is claiming sus-pect criminality.[22] Studies on law enforcement have found that officers often justify the need to control suspects with force, and occasionally, this takes the form of lying to ensure a higher chance of conviction or to vali-date the accounts made by fellow officers.[23] In a national study conducted on 925 randomly selected officers, the criminologist David Weisburd and colleagues found that while most officers no longer report accepting the code of silence (e.g., remaining silent after observing officer misconduct), one-quarter (24.9 percent) believed it was not worth alerting authorities if wrongdoing was observed, and nearly two-thirds (67.4 percent) believed it would make their fellow officers treat them negatively.[24] For these rea-sons, slightly more than half (52.4 percent) of officers reported not offi-cially acknowledging wrongdoing when it was observed. In the city and county of Denver, district attorneys and law enforcement officers regu-larly argued that an officer-involved shooting occurred not only because of illegal behavior but also because the suspect represented a significant deadly threat to others. Several shootings that caused outrage and encountered disputes involved questions regarding whether the individual shot was involved in criminal activity and over how the officer determined this individual to be a threat. Community protests and media coverage often pushed public officials to admit that officers may have reached the wrong conclusion regarding the perception of both criminality and whether the suspect posed a deadly threat. Depending on the degree of problematic and conflicting information, district attorneys, mayors, and managers of safety were pushed to reevaluate how to justify such situations. Video footage has become a key tool in validating or disputing such claims, but viewed in isolation, it could be manipulated in a way to support officer assertions.[25]

Highlighting the lack of criminal involvement in many officer-involved shootings was a statement occasionally reported by officers: "I thought he had a gun." In popular media depictions, individuals shot by law enforcement officers were in possession of dangerous weapons and causing public harm. In Denver, slightly more than half (57 percent) of the 298 shooting suspects possessed a firearm, but in 50 percent of the controversial cases in Denver, the victims were not holding a weapon. In addition, based on all shooting cases, only eight cases (2.7 percent) involved shootings that occurred after a suspect killed someone either earlier or in the presence of an officer. Moreover, whereas 75.2 percent of all shooting suspects had not injured someone before being shot, this was the case for 88.7 percent of the problematic shootings. The victimization that did occur was primarily in the form of a physical assault.[26] Psychologists have found from a number of virtual studies that Blacks and whites were more likely to perceive Blacks as possessing a firearm, followed by Latinos, even when such a weapon did not exist.[27] These outcomes were significantly more pronounced when the decision to shoot was made quickly. Despite the police perception of a minority group's gun possession, firearms research indicates that owning a gun is more likely for middle-aged white males.[28] These racialized perceptions of gun possession were not based on data or facts but on stereotypes.

Sixty-three-year-old Frank Lobato met both criteria of neither participating in criminal activity nor possessing a weapon. On July 11, 2004, Mr. Lobato was shot to death for holding possibly no more than a soda can.[29] On Sunday evening around 7:00 PM, officers received a 911 call from a woman stating she had been assaulted and held against her will by her forty-two-year-old boyfriend, who was five foot eleven and weighed 290 pounds.[30] She snuck out of her apartment while the boyfriend was passed out on the couch and ran to a nearby McDonald's to make a call for help. Denver police officers gathered information about the suspect, and they were notified that an elderly uncle, Frank Lobato, also lived in the apartment. When officers arrived at the apartment at 8:07 PM and knocked on the front and back doors, there was no answer. A young boy told the officers that the woman's boyfriend had jumped out of the second-floor window and left the scene. The officers didn't think the boy's story was logical, since the man could have easily walked out either door. After obtaining a ladder from the fire department, the officers entered the second floor of the apartment at 8:26 PM. The officers began checking rooms with flashlights and guns drawn. When they opened a bedroom door, the lead officer, Ranjan Ford, reported someone bolting up from bed holding a blanket and a shiny object in his right hand, stating, "What the fuck?" Startled and reporting he perceived a gun, Officer Ford fired one shot, hitting Mr. Lobato in the chest. Dispatch was notified at 8:45 PM, and Mr. Lobato arrived at the hospital at 9:03 PM and was declared deceased two minutes later.[31] When examining the bedroom, investigators did not find a weapon, only a soda can and some drug paraphernalia containing opium.

The case encountered community outrage and media attention. District Attorney Bill Ritter brought the case before a grand jury; nine jurors were not convinced the officer was criminally liable. For this reason, the DA did not believe he could establish guilt beyond a reasonable doubt before twelve jurors in a criminal trial. As mentioned earlier in the chapter, Bill Ritter did not believe in criminally charging Michael Blake again and, possibly, as he was not originally the prosecutor at the time the grand jury brought charges in the shooting of Steven Gant. However, the manager of safety issued a ninety-day suspension for Officer Ford because he did not believe there was enough evidence for the officer to conclude an imminent threat was present.[32] The policy of comparative discipline prevented a more harsh punishment, and the consequence was reduced to a fifty-day suspension.[33] In controversial cases, the media often pursued information regarding the lives of both the police officer and especially the individual shot. Mr. Lobato was described as a heroin and cocaine addict who lived on disability payments. He grew up in east Denver, lived in California for some time, went to prison, had a lengthy criminal record, and often was homeless in the later years of his life. He was the father of four children, who lived in California. A reporter wrote about how Mr. Lobato previously had violated his probation and was sentenced to three years of intensive supervision at the Salvation Army Adult Rehabilitation Center; he was not supposed to be in the home of his nephew.[34] Despite these negative portrayals, community activists continued to emphasize the harmlessness of an elderly and disabled man lying in his bed without a weapon. Protests and vigils were held in Mr. Lobato's memory and during demonstrations against police brutality. Officer Ford's background was also questioned. He joined the Jasper Police Department (Texas) in 1992 and moved up the ranks. In 2001, he became a member of the Denver Police Department. He was divorced and had allegedly threatened his ex-wife's boyfriend. A woman he dated claimed Officer Ford was violent, aggressive, trigger-happy, and obsessive.[35] A settlement of $900,000 guaranteed the case did not go to trial in civil court.[36] Many community members perceived this as a criminal case, yet the officer did not face legal consequences; instead, Officer Ranjan Ford later moved up the ranks to become a detective and continued working in the Denver Police Department. There were news reports of his struggles with alcohol but never another officer-involved shooting. He died at the age of forty-eight in March 2020.[37]

No-knock search warrants became controversial when based on inaccurate information. On September 29, 1999, three officers (Captain Vince DiManna and officers Mark Haney and Ken Overman) shot and killed forty-five-year-old Ismael Mena for living in a duplex wrongfully identified as a location where drugs were being distributed.[38] Ismael was working the night shift at the Coca-Cola factory and was more than likely asleep when the no-knock raid began at 1:47 PM. Mr. Mena, a father of nine children, had been sending money to his family in Guadalajara, Mexico, by working in various states over the years on a temporary worker visa. He had only lived in the Denver duplex for about a month when officers received a tip from a confidential informant that crack was being sold from the residence. As officers entered the duplex, they arrested a man downstairs and reportedly observed Mr. Mena coming out from his upstairs room with a gun. Officers responded by shooting eight times. A news station later received a tip about officers attempting to cover up the fact that police officers had raided the wrong house.[39] Mr. Mena did not have any drugs in his system, and there were no drugs found in the home.[40]

In response to this shooting, a community group named the Justice for Mena Committee was organized. The Mexican consulate general requested a federal investigation, and the FBI initiated a criminal civil rights investigation.[41] The American Civil Liberties Union challenged the reasoning behind the initial search warrant. Richard and Samantha, both middle-aged community activists and observers of the police since the late 1990s, stated there were several problems with the Mena case that they often couldn't get public officials to admit:

> [Richard] They claim that Ismael Mena fired at them, but we don't believe that really happened. [Why is that?] Well, the gun that they had was a World War II German 22 revolver and it wasn't the firing pin that was broken but the pin that holds the revolver in place. When you pull the trigger the bullet advances and the revolver turns. When the hammer falls it strikes the bullet and fires it through the barrel. This gun you had to manually align the revolver with the barrel so the hammer would actually fire the gun correctly. If Mena had fired at the police three times before they opened [the door] and then fired twice more after they had shot him four times. I don't believe he [Ismael] had the time. Like really, he had been shot very seriously when he sat up and must have returned fire when the police went into his bedroom and finished him off. And we don't believe that he did that. We believe that gun was dropped. I think the police had that gun as a gun to drop. [Samantha continues] The original newspaper stories that reported the Mena killings, the stories published on September 30 of 1999, said that Mena was standing at the top of the stairs in a three point stance shooting. And actually, it later came out that he had never left his bedroom. And they shot him through the door so from the very beginning the police used a story that would justify killing this man but none of that story was really true. [Richard] In fact, over and over again we were able to have stories that the police gave discredited.

A retired FBI agent who investigated the case supported the claim that officers used a "throw down gun" to make it look as if Mr. Mena was at fault and that police had also considered planting drugs, but a federal judge dismissed the lawsuit.[42] The officer responsible for the raid, Joe Bini, pled guilty to a reduced misdemeanor charge for official misconduct.[43]

A twenty-year veteran reported to internal affairs that senior officers had encouraged her to fabricate evidence.[44] A community leader from the Justice for Mena Committee, Leroy Lemos, described the crime scene evidence that concluded the police had moved the body. The mayor of Denver, Wellington Webb, wanted to overhaul the police department, which he described as a "good old buddy system," and pursued finding a new police chief. The mayor asked the police chief to resign and the manager of safety to be replaced. The city paid $400,000 in damages in a settlement to the Mena family.[45] Officer Bini, who later retired in 2008 from the police department while under criminal investigation, was subsequently arrested for child enticement and unlawful sexual contact.[46] The Ismael Mena case was controversial, but most of the legal attention was focused on how the warrant was obtained and reports of trying to cover up a raid that occurred at the wrong address. Captain DiManna retired around 2006 after leading the intelligence bureau involved in the "Spy Files" debacle. Officers Mark Haney and Ken Overman both rose in the ranks and became detectives. Overman retired in January 2005 and Haney in July 2018.

The shooting of twenty-five-year-old Lelani Lucero, a Latina, shared many similarities with the Ismael Mena case.[47] On February 1, 1983, at approximately 9:15 PM, plain-clothed officers attempted to execute an immediate-entry search warrant, based on a first-time confidential informant, for the residence of a man named George Jones. Juan Lucero, Lelani's husband, observed several men outside their home with guns drawn attempting to enter. Unknown to officers, this was not the residence of George Jones. Juan didn't know that the plain-clothes individuals outside were police officers, and he attempted to prevent the armed men from entering his home. The DA seemed unclear who fired the first shot, but gunfire was exchanged. Glass hit one of the officers in the eye, and fellow officers believed he had been shot. Juan took cover as bullets were fired into his home; Lelani was struck in the buttocks while she took cover with the children. Juan fired three rounds from his .22 revolver, and the officers fired thirteen shots. The front entry team entered the residence in uniform, and everyone seemed to realize their mistaken perceptions. Juan, seeing uniformed police officers, dropped the gun and was placed in handcuffs. DA Norman S. Early stated: "After a complete and thorough review of the investigation of this case, I conclude that no criminal charges are fileable against Detective Marc Vasquez or Officer Kenneth Chavez for their conduct in this incident. Given all the facts and circumstances, the officers clearly had a right to return the fire. The fact that they were executing a search warrant that was based on the false information given them by the informant has no bearing on their right to return fire."[48]

Mr. Early outlined six reasons why Juan may have believed a robbery was in progress including (1) closeness in time between shots and the police identification announcement, (2) officers in street clothes, (3) the presence of a wife and children to protect, (4) the fact Juan was not subject to a search warrant, (5) the fact Juan did not shoot at the front entry officers, and (6) the statement of Juan's nine-year-old son that someone was attempting to rob them. The DA did not file criminal charges against Juan and encouraged greater caution to law enforcement officers when initiating arrest or search warrants where intrusion into a residence was required. The Lucero family filed a lawsuit; it is unclear whether they obtained a settlement.

Officers' perceptions at the time they fired their weapons did not always corroborate with the physical evidence or with witness testimony. Antonio Reyes-Rojas, seventeen, was preparing to celebrate the 1998 New Year by watching his friends fire a rifle, a shotgun, and a handgun into the air.[49] Upon hearing shots fired before midnight, Officer Ken Chavez responded to the scene and reported seeing an individual pointing a gun at him; the officer fired two shots. Antonio was hit once in the buttocks as he was walking back into the house. He reported never seeing or hearing the officer or firing a gun. Physical evidence and witness testimony conflicted with the officers' claims. Bill Ritter, the district attorney, did not find corroborating evidence to support Officer Chavez. However, the DA concluded that no criminal charges were going to be filed because the case couldn't be proven beyond a reasonable doubt. The unarmed Antonio accepted a $30,000 settlement along with paid medical expenses for being shot in the buttocks with the bullet exiting near his groin. Officer Ken Chavez, a twenty-year veteran, had been involved in several other police shootings, in 1977, 1980, 1983 (Lelani), and 1996. His career will also be featured in chapter 5. Ken Chavez retired as a lieutenant for the Denver Police Department in 2021.

Finally, guilt is difficult to uphold as an argument when the wrong person is hit by officer bullets. On July 2, 2010, Diamond Demmer, a twenty-nine-year-old Black female, was leaving a club at 1:58 AM and attempting to walk to her vehicle when a fight broke out. She attempted to stay away from a confrontation and took a different route. In the Arby's drive-thru lane, a man began firing a handgun into the sky. Officers were already on the scene, having earlier broken up a fight, when they observed a man in a 2003 GMC Yukon firing a gun. One officer began firing pepper balls; these were ineffective. He then fired three shots from his .45-caliber handgun. Another officer, Robert Fitzgibbons, fired five shots from a .223-caliber AR-15 rifle. None of the bullets hit Shead, who later reported he was firing shots in the air to scare off a potential assailant. However, as Diamond stepped from behind an Arby's restaurant building, she was struck in the left leg and lower torso by bullet fragments and then again in the right leg and lower torso. It was later determined that Officer Fitzgibbons was using unauthorized military tracer bullets that had a greater chance of fragmenting and penetrating. Despite Diamond not being the intended target, District Attorney Mitchell Morrissey stated the totality of facts gave the officers the right to shoot: "The fact that an uninvolved person was injured by bullet fragments from two of Officer Fitzgibbons' rounds is an unintended and very unfortunate outcome, but does not change the officers' justification for firing the shots at Shead. Therefore, no criminal charges are fileable against either officer for his conduct in this incident."[50]

Despite the DA not finding fault in the officer's authority to use deadly force, the manager of safety terminated the officer for using non-department-issued ammunition. Officer Fitzgibbons, forty-one, was an Iraq war veteran and sniper. He appealed the decision, but it was upheld by the Denver Civil Service Commission.[51] It was unclear whether he joined another law enforcement agency. Diamond filed a $40,000 lawsuit.[52] The police had shot at least eight other individuals who were not the intended target, but none of these incidents resulted in a separate DA decision letter.

Law enforcement and the DA were not always successful in convincing the public of a suspect's guilt. Community members challenged public officials' claims when the individuals were unarmed, mistakenly identified, or shot unintentionally. In these cases, there was not determined to be criminal wrongdoing in the shooting itself but rather a violation of department procedures. Officer Ranjan Ford was suspended for fifty days for killing Mr. Lobato, Officer Bini received a misdemeanor charge for obtaining an incorrect search warrant that resulted in the killing of Mr. Mena, and Officer Robert Fitzgibbons was fired for departmental violations in the unintentional shooting that resulted in the wounding of Diamond. These decisions to impose such discipline occurred after months of community protest and legal challenges from public defenders. Officer discipline and lawsuits acknowledged an error in outcomes, but this did not result in any revisions to the law granting officer authority for making such decisions.

SCRUTINIZING OFF-DUTY AND "MOONLIGHTING" OFFICER DECISION MAKING

At least 9.7 percent of problematic police shootings involved officers encountering situations while off duty or while working second jobs as private security. The criminologist James Fyfe has questioned whether off-duty officers should be allowed to carry their firearms, as many situations that individuals encounter may create violence where only potential violence exists.[53] The criminologist Michael White's study of officer-involved shootings in Philadelphia from 1970 to 1978 and 1987 to 1992 found off-duty shootings were more likely to occur in bars or social clubs; this mirrored Fyfe's earlier findings that such cases were more likely than on-duty shootings to receive departmental discipline.[54] However, during this current era of mass shootings, there has become greater encouragement to support the rationale of a "good guy with a gun" as being important to reduce any potential harm.[55] Based upon the data reviewed, the following is an example of how off-duty shootings become intertwined with problematic cases.

In Denver, police officers often worked additional jobs as security guards to supplement their incomes. On Sunday, November 8, 1992, at 10:45 PM, two uniformed officers were arriving at their off-duty job when they heard gunshots. The officers hopped into their personal vehicle to see where the shots were coming from. They noticed two men with cowboy hats and another man walking suspiciously. The officers called dispatch at 10:55 PM, saying shots had been fired and that they were pursuing the suspect. Detective Dennis Chavez and Officer Vince Lombardi yelled,

"Hey you! Police!" and the man began to run and reach into his waistband. The officers began to chase him, and they noticed a small handgun fall on the sidewalk. According to officers, rather than leave the gun there, the suspect picked it back up and started turning his right hand toward the officers. One officer fired five shots; the other officer shot twice. The officers reported the shooting at 10:59 PM and requested an ambulance. Miguel Ochoa, twenty-four years of age, was pronounced dead at 5:18 AM.[56] He had been shot in the upper back right of the midline. The second shot hit Miguel in the lower back. His blood alcohol was .226. Investigators found four .25-caliber shell casings at the scene where they had originally heard shots and one live round in the gun. One witness didn't see anything in his hand, but the DA stated the reason for this was because the Raven .25-caliber semiautomatic pistol was a very small gun, which allowed officers to have a better view of Miguel's hands. The DA, Norman S. Early, concluded:

> Under the facts and circumstances of this case and all applicable Colorado law, Detective Chavez and Officer Lombardi were legally justified in using deadly physical force, to defend themselves, to protect others in the area of the incident, and to neutralize the clear risk to life presented by a man who had fired at least four rounds at targets unknown in the middle of the city, and subsequently, while attempting to elude police dropped and then intentionally picked up a loaded gun in the presence of officers who were ordering him to stop his actions. . . . The fact that Ochoa was shot in the back is of no consequence under the circumstances of this encounter. . . . Those who violate the law with guns and needlessly endanger our citizens and police officers need to know that police officers are not mind-readers and will act on the threat they perceive, whether or not that is what is in the suspect's mind. In the real world of police work, delay can mean death.[57]

Mr. Early claimed this was a violent conclusion to mixing guns with alcohol. The family sued the city and county of Denver. Miguel was a native of Chihuahua, Mexico, and had been working as a roofer in the United States for the last five years. A witness reported seeing a man running down a dark alley and the police officers telling him to stop. The witness then heard shots and observed the man pulling his arms down behind his back as though he was putting a gun in his waistband, but the witness did not see a gun. Another witness reported seeing a truck chase a man. A final witness reported hearing three or four shots and then six shots. The physical evidence suggested Miguel's hands were not bagged at the morgue, and when a gunshot residue test was done, there were no prints found on the .25-caliber gun. It was unclear whether the officers ever encountered any disciplinary action or if a settlement was reached for the lawsuit. Detective Dennis Chavez rose in rank to become a lieutenant and retired in 2016. Officer Vince Lombardi is now a sergeant and was still employed as a law enforcement officer as of 2023.

Another case on December 22, 1996, involved an off-duty officer who had just finished his work shift. Thirty-year-old Manuel Moreno Delgado left a Christmas work party where he worked as a supervisor to drive home in his 1989 four-door Toyota. An immigrant from El Salvador, Mr. Delgado had moved to Colorado in 1995 in search of a better life. He worked two jobs while supporting his wife and two sons, ages six years and eleven months. While driving, Mr. Delgado became involved in a dispute with another driver around 2:00 AM. Unknown to Mr. Delgado, the other vehicle was being driven by an off-duty Denver Police Department officer, Michael Pace, who had gotten off work from the Gang Unit and was driving home in his personal truck. Officer Pace stated that Mr. Delgado had cut him off by speeding up and then slowing down to prevent his entry into the turning lane. According to his statement, Officer Pace rolled down his window and saw Mr. Delgado holding a pistol in his hand and threatening him. Officer Pace responded by firing his .45-caliber handgun six times. Mr. Delgado was killed in his vehicle; an unloaded .25-caliber Phoenix Arms Raven was found between his legs. His blood alcohol was .186. The DA, Bill Ritter, stated:

> There is no evidence to indicate that Officer Pace's account of the fatal shooting of Mr. Moreno-Delgado is inaccurate in any substantial way or to indicate that it could be proved beyond a reasonable doubt that his conduct was unreasonable, and therefore it would be inappropriate to file criminal charges against him with regard to this homicide. When aggressors have guns, unlike other types of weapons, there are very few options available to the officer or citizen who is confronted by them. Lesser degrees of force are generally not available. It is certainly reasonable for them to assume, absent specific evidence to the contrary, that the gun is

loaded and operational. It would be a life and death gamble to assume otherwise. . . . Citizens who are armed with firearms, and produce them in a confrontational, threatening or menacing manner, subject themselves to a lethal response. . . . Police officers and citizens have the right to protect themselves. . . . Finally, this situation demonstrates another negative byproduct of the massive presence of handguns in our community and the deadly consequences of the misuse of those weapons.[58]

The Public Safety Review Commission heard testimony in 2001 that Pace may have lied.[59] A forensic expert concluded in 2001 that Pace should be disciplined and that Mr. Delgado was not raising a gun as contended. Numerous problems at the crime scene were found, including where the gun was found, glass shards under the gun, and the position of Mr. Delgado's head when he was shot.[60] Bullets hit Mr. Delgado above his right ear, the back of the head, and his left shoulder. The media reported Manuel's widow stating that he never lost his temper, handled stressful situations well, and was not known to have possessed a gun. His wife was unaware he owned a gun. There were no traces of any drug other than alcohol in his system.[61] The family sued the city and county and received a $75,000 settlement. Officer Pace never received any disciplinary action. The cases of Miguel and Mr. Delgado were similar in several ways. They were both immigrants shot under questionable circumstances by allegedly pointing small-caliber guns at officers. Both cases were considered legally justifiable, and there were no records of departmental discipline for either officer.

An additional problematic case involving off-duty officers was the shooting death of Jeff Truax and wounding of John Ferguson, which resulted in the formation of the Erickson Commission.[62] On March 20, 1996, around 1:45 AM, Jeff Truax, twenty-five years of age, and John Ferguson, twenty-two years of age, both white males, along with two additional friends, became involved in a fight with two individuals with Spanish surnames. Someone said they were going to grab a gun as Jeff and his friends hurried to their vehicle. Once three of the men were in Jeff's car preparing to leave, two off-duty officers, Kenneth Chavez and Andrew Clarry, were alerted to the fight and attempted to stop Jeff's vehicle.[63] Jeff quickly reversed his vehicle, and it was unclear whether he had heard officers shouting orders, but as he did so, he backed into one of the officers, who fell into the back window of the car, which broke under the weight of the officer and the force of the vehicle while reversing. Officer Clarry immediately began firing, and Officer Chavez, fearing for his partner's life, also began firing at the driver. The officers fired a total of twenty-five shots into the vehicle, hitting Jeff seven times and John twice (once in the right elbow and once in the thigh). Friends reported that there were a bunch of guys throwing bottles at Jeff and that they were simply trying to leave the conflict. Fifty individuals gathered at the scene to hold a candlelight vigil.[64] Both families filed lawsuits; Jeff's family received $250,000, and John's received $75,000. The autopsy of Jeff indicated that his blood alcohol level was .170 percent and that he had suffered multiple gunshot wounds. News reports stated Jeff had two previous criminal charges of assault, but friends described him as a stocky outgoing guy who enjoyed sports.[65] Officer Kenneth Chavez was primarily featured in the news media for his previous shootings during his career, including the shootings of Lelani and Antonio featured in this chapter, but he continued to move up the ranks to become a lieutenant. He utilized his previous training in the US Army Special Forces to guide his police department tactics. Officer Andrew Clarry, a former Marine, also moved up the ranks and eventually became a lieutenant but was not involved in any additional shootings in the city and county of Denver.

Two shootings by off-duty officers did result in criminal charges. The first incident involved a rookie off-duty officer in plain clothes hanging out at a bar with two other off-duty officers in southeast Denver. On June 8, 1983, twenty-eight-year-old Officer Gary Brooke, a white male, and his fellow officers were attempting to escort several women home when they were confronted by three men in the bar's parking lot. At some point during the fight that ensued, Officer Brooke pulled out his Walther PPK .380, and there may have been an attempt to grab the firearm. Once Officer Brooke secured the firearm, the three men fled toward their new BMW vehicle. Officer Brooke fired eight shots, emptying the clip. Bullets shattered the back window and entered the vehicle. One bullet hit nineteen-year-old Thomas Jackson, a white male, in the leg as he ran to get into the passenger side of the vehicle. A Denver police dispatcher received a call from an officer calling for help, and on the police radio, it was aired that there had been shots fired. As Denver police officers began to arrive, they were assisted by an officer working off duty at a nearby establishment. When Officer Brooke initially spoke with the arriving officers, he said, "These guys jumped me and one of them got my gun out of my belt and fired some shots, I got the gun back and it's in the truck." The two other officers, when questioned, stated there had been a fight and that shots had been fired but that they didn't see who did the shooting. As more witnesses began to give statements, one of the officer's stories changed. Officer Brooke was brought in to give a formal statement. He was not in uniform and intoxicated and was advised by his attorney not to say anything. Thomas originally refused to talk to the police but did so later, in the presence of an attorney. His wound was considered life threatening by a physician, but he survived. Officer Brooke later pleaded guilty to felony assault and was fired by the police department. There is no record regarding the consequences.

The second off-duty case in which an officer was criminally charged involved an FBI officer, thirty-year-old Chase Bishop, a white male, who was at a bar showing off some dance moves. As he does a backflip, his gun falls to the ground. When the agent picks up the gun, he accidentally pulls the trigger, firing a bullet that hits a man sitting at the bar's picnic tables.[66] The man shot and wounded was twenty-four-year-old Tom Reddington (a white male). His attorney stated that the gunshot hit a main artery. The FBI agent was charged, fired, and pled guilty to a misdemeanor assault, resulting in two years of unsupervised probation.[67] The DA pursued charges, but this shooting incident was not included on the DA page of officer-involved shootings.[68]

FINDINGS BY TYPE OF SHOOTING: PROBLEMATIC, QUESTIONABLE, AND LESS CONTROVERSIAL CASES

The shootings outlined in this chapter have primarily focused on those categorized as problematic. However, there were shootings that were also questionable and less controversial. Most of the shootings presented in this book were considered questionable (48.3 percent), as some of the decision making or interactions were evaluated. If things had gone a different (and plausible, under the circumstances) way, the use of force might have been averted. There were also some shootings for which, based upon what was reported and from the information available, alternative, less violent outcomes were harder to plausibly imagine; these shootings were categorized as less controversial (30.9 percent). To provide some contrast, the following are results comparing all measures against the type of shooting, which includes problematic, questionable, and less controversial cases.[69]

Based on the *sociodemographic characteristics* of the person shot, the median age differed by type of shooting (*p*-value=0.023). The median age was lowest for problematic cases (median 24.5 years old; Q1: 19.8, Q3: 34.3) while similar for questionable (median 29.5 years old; Q1: 22.8, Q3: 38.0) and less controversial (median 30.0 years old; Q1: 23.0, Q3: 38.0) cases. In addition, the sex of the person shot differed by type of shooting (*p*-value=0.038). The percentage of women was highest for problematic (11.3 percent) cases, compared to questionable (3.5 percent) or less controversial (2.2 percent) cases.

The rates for *alcohol or drug use* at the time of the shooting did not differ significantly between different types of shootings. Thus, the use of a substance by an individual was not the key factor influencing the decision making used by the officer in determining how to respond to the incident.

Based on *shooting-related measures*, the day of the week differed by type of shooting (*p*-value=0.004). Most problematic cases happened on Wednesdays (27.4 percent); less controversial cases happened mostly on Saturdays (27.2 percent). The rate per day of questionable cases strictly increased during the week from Monday to Sunday: Monday (10.4 percent), Tuesday (11.8 percent), Wednesday (12.5 percent), Thursday (12.5 percent), Friday (16.7 percent), Saturday (17.4 percent), and Sunday (18.8 percent). Calls to 911 or community-initiated requests for police presence were less common for problematic (37.1 percent) cases compared to questionable (51.4 percent) and less controversial (63.0 percent) cases (*p*-value=0.007). The reason for action, or the issue the officer was responding to in order to enter the scene or approach the suspect, differed by type of shooting (*p*-value=0.015). Problematic (45.9 percent) and questionable (29.9 percent) cases most often involved a suspect as the reason for action compared to less controversial (27.2 percent) cases, which most often involved a gun incident (*p*-value=0.015) as the issue the officer was responding to. Rates of high poverty levels are higher for problematic (64.5 percent) cases compared to questionable (47.6 percent) and less controversial (42.4 percent) cases (p-value=0.037).

Incident-related factors that significantly differed by type of shooting include the seriousness of the offense (p-value<0.001), possible offense type (p-value<0.001), suspect behavior when shot (p-value<0.001), location on the body of bullets (p-value=0.029), and victimization of another individual (p-value<0.001). In terms of the seriousness of the offense, a felony was the most common type of shooting, but the rate was lowest for problematic (43.5 percent) cases and highest for less controversial (89.1 percent) cases; the percentage of cases involving a felony increased as the severity of the type of shooting decreased from problematic, questionable, then less controversial. Similarly for possible offense types, interpersonal violence was most common across all types of shooting, but the rate was lowest for problematic (40.3 percent) cases and highest for less controversial (80.4 percent) cases; the percent of cases involving interpersonal violence increased as the severity of the type of shooting decreased. The suspect's behavior when shot was a perceived threat for most problematic (51.6 percent) cases and an active threat for most questionable (58.3 percent) and less controversial (82.6 percent) cases. In terms of the location of the body where bullets hit, multiple locations were most common across all types of shooting, but the rate was lowest for problematic (36.8 percent) cases and highest for less controversial (53.8 percent) cases; the percentage of cases involving bullets hitting multiple locations on the body increased as the severity of the type of shooting decreased. The rate of victimization of another individual increased as the severity of the type of shooting decreased; the rate was lowest for problematic (11.3 percent) cases followed by questionable (18.1 percent) and less controversial (44.6 percent) cases.

The *post-shooting characteristic* that significantly differed by type of shooting was the weapon used by the person shot. Those considered problematic cases were most commonly where the shooting victim did not have a weapon (41.9 percent) or had a gun (35.5 percent). A gun was most common for questionable (55.6 percent) and less controversial (73.9 percent) cases.

The median number of *officers who shot* differed by type of shooting (p-value=0.015). The median number of years on the force was the same for all three types (median 1.0 times; Q1: 1.0, Q3: 2.0); however, the maximum number of shots fired was highest for questionable (max: 8 shots) cases followed by less controversial (max: 7 shots) and problematic cases (max: 4 shots). The median number of times the suspect was hit by bullets differed by type of shooting (p-value=0.047). The median number of years on the force was lowest for problematic cases (median 1.0 times; Q1: 1.0, Q3: 1.0) while similar for questionable (median 2.0 times; Q1: 1.0, Q3: 4.0) and less controversial (median 2.0 times; Q1: 1.0, Q3: 4.0) cases. The rate of any officer injured during a shooting increased as the severity of the type of shooting decreased (p-value=0.001). Another officer was injured in 6.5 percent of the problematic cases, 14.6 percent of the questionable cases, and 28.3 percent of the less controversial cases. The type of officer injury differed by type of shooting (p-value=0.039). Those considered problematic cases were most commonly not a result of a vehicle (40.0 percent) or a physical (40.0 percent) injury. A vehicle injury was most common for questionable (45.5 percent) cases, and a bullet injury was most common for less controversial (53.8 percent) cases. Police districts for the area of the census tract of the shooting differed by type of shooting (p-value=0.010). Of the problematic cases, most (35.5 percent) were in central Denver; the questionable (27.1 percent) and less controversial (29.3 percent) cases were most in northwest Denver.

Based on the *sociodemographic characteristics of the officer who shot,* the median number of years on the force differed by type of shooting (p-value=0.016). The median number of years on the force was highest for less controversial cases (median 8.5 years; Q1: 4.8, Q3: 14.3) and lowest for problematic cases (median 4.00 years; Q1: 3.5, Q3: 6.0).

Based on the *postshooting outcomes,* the rate of dispute between accounts decreased as the severity of the type of shooting decreased (p-value<0.001). There was a dispute between accounts for the majority of problematic (67.7 percent) cases; the disputes were less common for questionable (41.0 percent) and less controversial (6.5 percent) cases. The proportion of cases in which the person shot was eligible for the death penalty differed by type of shooting (p-value=0.002). None (0.0 percent) of the problematic cases were eligible for the death penalty; 1.4 percent of questionable cases and 8.7 percent of less controversial cases were. The proportion of cases in which the DA filed charges differed by type of shooting (p-value=0.025). The DA filed charges for none (0.0 percent) of the questionable cases while doing so for 4.8 percent of problematic cases and 1.1 percent of less controversial cases. The proportion of cases in which there was a lawsuit settlement differed by type of shooting (p-value<0.001). Lawsuit settlements were achieved for none of the less controversial (0.0 percent) cases but were for 27.8 percent of problematic cases and 8.4 percent of questionable cases.

The officer-involved shootings presented in this chapter injured or killed the individuals shot, causing heartache and grief for family and friends. In problematic shootings, the individuals shot are *victims* of state violence. Half of the individuals who were found involved in a problematic shooting survived their injuries; the other half were murdered. Questionable shootings could also factor into these forms of evaluation because nondeadly alternatives could have produced a more humane outcome. For less controversial shootings, it was more difficult not to attribute at least some shared blame to the behaviors exhibited by the person shot and the carrying or use of weapons, which negatively affected the interactions with law enforcement. Based on this assessment, we find that since 21 percent of shootings were categorized as problematic and 48 percent as questionable, it is more accurate to describe the individuals shot by the police as victims. They are encountering discretionary violence at the hands of law enforcement officers. As a higher proportion of officers and others were injured in less controversial cases, attributing victim status can be more difficult. Nevertheless, we disagree with the Bureau of Justice Statistics blanket statement of describing those shot and killed by law enforcement as "felons justifiably killed by police."[70]

The imagery of violence to physical bodies brings to mind a video recording of Oscar Zeta Acosta reading a chapter from his book *The Revolt of the Cockroach People*.[71] In chapter 8, Acosta describes his role as an attorney on behalf of a family attempting to learn the cause of death of their son from members of the sheriff's office. The autopsy report reflected the level of physical violence performed on the body in an attempt to find scientific evidence for the cause of death. Observing the cutting of the victim's body weighed heavy on Acosta's soul. Acosta describes his feelings after observing the autopsy:

And when it is done, there is no more Robert [the name of the victim].
Oh, sure, they put the head back in place. They sew it up as best they can.
But there is no part of the body that I have not ordered chopped. I, who
am so good and deserving of love. Yes, me, the big *chingón*! I, Mr. Buffalo Z. Brown. Me, I ordered those white men to cut up the brown body
of that Chicano boy, just another expendable Cockroach. Forgive me,
Robert, for the sake of the living brown. Forgive me and forgive me and
forgive me. I am no worse off than you. For the rest of my born days, I
will suffer the knowledge of your death and your second death and your
ashes to my ashes, your dust to my dust . . . Goodbye, *ese*. Viva La Raza![72]

Our reading of all this pain and suffering, having studied this topic for
decades, has also taken a toll on the authors. It is with reference to this
witness to gun violence that we quote Acosta here.

A common argument in death penalty research was whether one innocent person put to death was enough to question the entire system. Thus,
if any individual can be executed wrongfully, how can we be entirely sure
that our system is fair and just? Police shootings reflect a similar pattern
in that a sizeable number of police shootings were problematic and the
majority of them were questionable. No one should be shot by a law
enforcement officer because officers attempted to enter the wrong home
or because the officer missed the intended target. Young men similar to
Steven Gant shouldn't be required to beg officers not to shoot and experience double victimization when the perpetrator is absolved of wrongdoing. There are many instances that warrant that the officers be made
accountable.

There are shootings for which law enforcement has had to respond with
firearms to stop a threat; however, the proportion of these shootings is
small, but they continue to serve as the framework and justification for
which all shootings become condoned.

5

LAW ENFORCEMENT OFFICERS AND THE PRISTINE FOURTEEN

Efforts to understand officer decision making have often taken into account the characteristics of the officers and the sociodemographic features of the communities in which they interact. As early as 1880, Black residents in Denver petitioned to have a Black officer on the force. Criticisms regarding the lack of Black and Latino officers, along with the barriers to career advancement, were of central importance during the 1960s and continued to be a topic of contestation thereafter.[1] According to the most recently obtained data (June 2020), the Denver Police Department's 1,609 officers and recruits were 64.9 percent white, 21.5 percent Latino, 8.8 percent Black, 2.7 percent Asian, and 0.9 percent Native American. Female officers and recruits represented 14.4 percent of the force. Compared to the county's demographics, whites were overrepresented as police officers, whereas Blacks and Latinos were underrepresented. Female officers were the most underrepresented. An interview with a leader of Denver's Gang Unit was reflective of these concerns regarding the importance of adequate demographic representation.[2] The middle-aged Latino officer stated: "I think that, ugh you as you can see, by having Latinos in the gang unit, we are more sensitive to things, and I like the gang unit to reflect what the city is. I don't fully feel comfortable if I had nothing but blonde hair, blue-eyed males here in the neighborhood because then I would think we would look more like an occupying force, and so our goal is to really reflect the community, and so our goal is to keep a diverse unit because we understand."

Durán inquired about claims of harassment by members of minority communities. The officer responded:

> Right, and I can show you a couple of stats that are not in here, that will show you why, why minorities feel like they are targeted more than Anglos. I will show you why. We have it just right out in front us: where the crimes are being committed. And so, shame on us for, you know just because you live in the inner city, just because you are Latino, just because you are Black doesn't mean you have to be harassed by gang members, doesn't mean you have to live in fear, doesn't mean you have to suffer hearing gunshots every night outside your house. No. So those are the areas that we work, and that's what we do. I don't know how many times do you hear people, and Anglos say, "Don't go down there, that's a bad neighborhood. Why should those people have to live in those bad neighborhoods?" So, we are trying to make it safe for them, that's what we are about.

And with that response Durán agreed. Durán had previously worked in child and family services, juvenile probation, and youth corrections, and he was usually the only Chicano employee, let alone one of the only employees with incarcerated family members and friends coming from a background where his life could have gone down a similar path. Durán pursued occupations in the juvenile justice system to be a mentor and an advocate for marginalized communities. He remembered the individuals he worked alongside. Although a small number of staff members should not have been working in these occupations, the majority were putting forth their best effort and striving to act professionally.[3] Given Durán's interactions with and interviews he conducted with law enforcement officers in Colorado, New Mexico, Tennessee, Texas, and Utah, he cannot make the blanket statement that all officers are bad, nor can he write that the problem with policing is simply a few "bad apples." The challenge is with the structure of policing, its training, its culture, and how the law provides a level of legitimacy to condone a wide range of decision making that only rarely exposes wrongdoing and implements discipline with behavior-changing consequences. Such a perception merges more with seeing policing as a symptom of maintaining the structure of systemic racism and settler colonialism in US society. There are definitely bad actors, but there are also good intentions that sometimes result in mistakes. There are also a small number of crises where it can be hard to see how our current technological capabilities do not require someone to intervene. The problem that remains, however, is that a firearm amplifies existing inequalities. The psychologists Jim Sidanius and colleagues emphasize that law enforcement and the entire criminal justice system are hierarchy-enhancing institutions that tend to favor the socially strong.[4] Utilizing social dominance theory, Sidanius and Pratto suggest "that the law must also be seen as a mechanism by which the rights and privileges of dominant groups are protected and the continued subordination of weaker groups is enforced and maintained."[5] Members of ethnic- and racial-minority groups may be caught in a bind of being socially stigmatized in society but expected to fit into the institution in which they work. The public administration and policy professors Vicky Wilkins and Brian Williams reported the challenges that exist when the structure and processes of an organization develop a level of socialization that supersedes all other identities; those who work as police officers, for example, may only be permitted to represent the blue.[6] Therefore, when the historian Elizabeth Hinton described the escalating number of community rebellions that were triggered by police response, she described how the rotten apple had become the larger systemic problem of a poisoned tree.[7]

A popular policing textbook argues that people often perceive officers as crime fighters, but instead, they are more likely to be focused on peacekeeping, order maintenance, or problem solving.[8] These authors point out that most law enforcement officers will never fire their guns in the line of duty.[9] If shots are fired, not all bullets will hit the suspect, and around half of the suspects will die. This chapter is based on officers who do fire and whose bullets have hit someone, resulting in injury or death. It also includes a qualitative examination of the differing levels of victimization that can occur to law enforcement officers, along with mental health challenges. It features a case study profile of fourteen officers who have engaged in the greatest number of shootings in Denver over a thirty-eight-year period. Finally, the analysis will explore similarities and differences that exist when comparing law enforcement with street gangs.

Officer-involved shootings were primarily focused on the individual shot, who they were, what they did, and what type of moral character they exemplified. The officer(s) who did the shooting were often portrayed as unimportant. Any officer presented with the circumstance that unfolded was provided latitude to make the same reasonable decision, or it hypothetically could result in the officer or a third party becoming seriously physically injured or killed.[10] Such an ideology was reflected in many law enforcement agencies not releasing the name of the officer who shot. In Colorado, the *Gazette* published a news story in 2016 describing the inconsistency among law enforcement agencies within the state for reporting the names of officers involved in shootings.[11] Sometimes, the officers' names were never released. We found that many news agencies included a picture of the person shot by the police but rarely of the officers who did the shooting. Thus, officer-involved shootings were not considered to be based on officers' behavior and perceptions but rather on the actions of the suspect. This is a complete reversal from how homicide offenders are traditionally portrayed.[12] This chapter will challenge that assumption and assert that the lives of the suspect and the officer become intertwined into existing structural inequalities that heighten the chances for certain individuals to be shot and for particular officers to use their firearms.

The sociologist Erving Goffman reported that individuals attempt to control what type of impressions they have upon others.[13] First impressions are crucial in setting the scene for an entire encounter, unless some type of information could be used to contradict, discredit, or throw off this projection of self. By wearing a uniform, police officers become representatives of law enforcement, whereas the individuals they encounter come from a variety of backgrounds. However, as the criminal justice system focuses primarily upon street crime, such a structure places law enforcement officers in a greater number of encounters with individuals living in higher levels of poverty or in communities with greater socioeconomic inequality.[14] In addition, the status of the individual, particularly as a racial or ethnic minority, serves as a "master status," influencing how the officer will interact with this individual.[15] Goffman reported that performances were similar to a stage; there is a front region that we observe and a back region that we do not see.[16] Most of the performances intended for and projected to others occur in a front-region setting that also designates the officer as a member of a team of legitimatized authority. Law enforcement officers internalize an identity to utilize the perceptions they are making to make decisions regarding how to proceed with an encounter. As a member of law enforcement, as a team, officers use their discretion to dominate interpersonal interactions.

The data for chapter 5 goes beyond the data acquired from other chapters by including two additional sources. First, Durán and his research assistants compiled all publicly available news and internet search engine information on each officer. Second, a Colorado Open Records Act (CORA) was filed for the officers with the highest number of shootings with the Denver Police Department.[17] The goal was to examine why law enforcement officers engage in violence and identify what characteristics are shared between those who had the most frequent shootings.

LAW ENFORCEMENT OFFICERS KILLED

Historically, as employees of an occupation that upholds the powers of the state, law enforcement officers face physical and emotional risks.[18] The police researcher Herman Goldstein reported that police were an anomaly in a free society because they had a function to assert authority along with an obligation to ensure, by maintaining order, that constitutional protections are upheld.[19] Nevertheless, the discretion to intervene in encounters and assert authority via the use of force often placed law enforcement officers in an adversarial role. The first officer shot and killed in Denver was Deputy City Marshal James C. Ritchey, on February 3, 1862.[20] He was off duty at the time and walking with a woman when some men made some offensive remarks. Marshal Ritchey threatened to arrest the men; a fight ensued, and Ritchey was shot in the stomach. He died the following day. Over a century, killings of officers have occurred during ambushes,[21] burglaries,[22] domestic disputes,[23] employee termination proceedings,[24] occupational and environmental hazards,[25] and robberies, along with attempted arrests of soldiers, officers, and barricaded suspects.[26] There were also accidental killings of fellow officers with firearms.[27]

One officer who was killed by a fellow law enforcement officer in the police shooting database was the homicide of Deputy Sheriff "Tony" Silva. The district attorney's decision letter stated that on February 3, 1993, thirty-year-old Deputy Sheriff Silva and his thirty-year-old partner Deputy Sheriff John Cordova were transporting a prisoner to the City Jail at 2 AM.[28] As they dropped off the prisoner at the jail, they had to leave their .357 Magnum revolvers at the control center. Upon leaving, Deputy Sheriff Cordova asked Deputy Sheriff Silva to grab his firearm. After joking around, Silva handed the gun to Cordova, but when he did so, the cylinder was out, and when Cordova went to snap it into place, his grip tightened. Cordova's finger pulled the trigger, and the gun discharged. The barrel was pointed toward Silva, and the bullet struck his chest. Cordova cried as he encouraged his partner of five years and close friend to "Hang on buddy, please don't go."[29] Cordova was taken to the hospital as it was believed that he was going into shock. Although no one visually saw the shooting, the DA stated the statements were consistent with the physical evidence. The DA described this incident as "very sad and tragic" and that the one thing this case indicated was the importance of heightened "awareness of the potential danger associated with the handling of firearms."[30] The funeral description includes language reflective of the tremendous loss of a husband, father, son, brother, and friend.[31] Deputy Sheriff Silva grew up in west Denver, played football, wrestled in high school, and was part of a breakdancing crew.[32] His Legacy.com memorial website highlighted the continued sadness for the loss of Mr. Silva felt by his family and friends.[33]

Along with FBI data collection, the website *Officer Down* has recorded every officer's death around the country.[34] For the Denver Police Department, the website lists seventy-four line-of-duty deaths from 1862 to 2020, an average of 0.46 deaths per year (162 years between 1858 to 2020).[35] Nearly 72 percent (71.6 percent) of these deaths were a result of the use of firearms. Twelve deaths occurred during the timeframe of the data analyzed for this book, 1983 to 2020, for a rate of 0.32 deaths per year, which was lower than the average number of residents shot and killed by the police per year, 3.90. Thus, the number of officers killed was twelve times lower than the number of residents killed. Nationally, according to the US Bureau of Labor Statistics, law enforcement had a higher fatality injury rate (13.7 per 100,000 in 2018) for full-time equivalent workers, compared to 3.5 per 100,000 for all other occupations.[36] The reasons for death varied, ranging from violence to transportation incidents and other injuries including falls, slips, and trips. Killings of law enforcement officers have continued to decrease, as efforts to improve officer safety have increased.[37] From 1976 to 1998, seventy-nine officers were feloniously killed per year, on average. Of law enforcement officers killed in the line of duty (n=1,820), 92 percent were killed with firearms, particularly handguns. From 2001 to 2010, the US Department of Justice found that 7 percent of deaths were caused by vehicles and less than 1 percent by knives.[38] According to the data reported to the FBI in 2019, there were forty-eight felonious killings and forty-one additional accidental deaths.[39] After the COVID-19 pandemic, it appeared that officers were at a slightly increased risk of violence, with seventy-three felonious deaths in 2021, sixty-one in 2022, sixty in 2023, and sixty-four in 2024.[40] In addition, many officers became sick with the virus, which pushed many law enforcement agencies to institute vaccination policies. Despite a higher level of risk compared to all other occupations, law enforcement continues to be a safer job than many other kinds of work, including airplane pilot, construction labor, electric power installer, farmer, fisherman, roofer, structural metal worker, taxi driver, timber cutter, and truck driver.[41] This, however, does not mean that officers perceive their occupation to be safe.[42]

The criminologist Caitlin Lynch, a former police officer and current academic professor, described how the police academy and police departments' repeated emphasis upon a "Survival Creed" has resulted in officers living in constant fear despite the overall rare occurrence of physical injury or death to any particular law enforcement officer.[43] The development of these fears has resulted in unchecked aggression and violence that, at its most troubling aspect, was racialized. Lynch reported that the majority of in-line-of-duty deaths were the result of duty-related illness or accidents. Still, even these occurrences make it difficult for officers to discern between actual and perceived dangers. Moreover, Lynch emphasized how the Blue Lives Matter countermovement co-opted Black Lives Matter by provoking public fear regarding a perceived war on cops to justify a police subculture's entitlement to use violence. The sociologist Michael Sierra-Arévalo agreed that police officers' pervasive preoccupation with violence and officer safety despite decreasing fatal injuries has resulted in a culture he called the "danger imperative."[44] The danger imperative describes how officers are socialized to anticipate violence and harm to self in every encounter. Such socialization begins in the police academy, where examples are given of real-life officer encounters that have "gone bad" and where policy-compliant tactics that favor officer-enhanced coercion at the expense of the residents for whom they interact are taught. Such a culture overlaps with a warrior mentality wherein officers need to be aggressive to maintain control over suspects. According to the sociologist William Waegel, one of the justifications for officer-involved shootings given by the police was that it was better to be judged by twelve than carried by six.[45] Hence, the only way to stop violent actors requires officer counterviolence.

It was difficult to predict whether an officer or a third-party injury or death would have occurred had the officer not responded with deadly force. District attorney decision letters often reported how the officer may have saved lives, but based on the information acquired for this study, most circumstances may have, in fact, created an outcome of death or injury, whereas an alternative response could have resulted in a more humane outcome. In most instances, the use of deadly force was *not* a result of a police officer responding to an actual injury of an officer or a third person but in response to a *perceived* danger to themselves or others.

OFFICERS WHO SHOT

Before outlining the characteristics of the officers who shot, it is important to note that the shootings included up to this point in the book were focused on the geographic area of Denver, Colorado. Thus, officer-involved shootings go beyond the Denver Police Department, which accounts for 87.6 percent of the cases, but also includes other agencies such as the Federal Bureau of Investigation, Colorado State Parole, Colorado State Patrol, Transit Security, and US Immigration and Customs Enforcement, along with nearby police departments and sheriff officers. These shootings by other agencies also ran the continuum from problematic (16.2 percent) to questionable (56.8 percent) and less controversial (27.0 percent).

When a law enforcement shooting occurred, the median (Q1, Q3) number of officers on the scene was two (1, 4). In one case, forty-five officers arrived at the scene in an attempt to get an armed suspect who had shot his wife and neighbor to surrender.[46] He threatened officers not to intervene by taking two hostages, possessing an arsenal of weapons, and using propane tanks as explosives. Once a long gun was brought to the scene, the officer was cleared to take the shot. The officer fired one shot from a Colt AR-15 .223 caliber rifle, and the suspect was disabled and subsequently arrested. The suspect, Daniel Abeyta, thirty-one years of age, received a forty-eight-year prison sentence after his court hearing. Durán and Loza categorized this shooting as less controversial, and no criminal charges were filed against the officer. However, Mr. Abeyta's mother stated that her son was not a "monster" and that she thought the decision "unfair."[47] A friend of Mr. Abeyta shared that he thought the relationship between Mr. Abeyta and his wife had ended and that he had "lost it." Thus, when a female neighbor came to help his wife, they were both shot. The wife survived the shooting to her ankle, but the forty-seven-year-old neighbor, Sandy Roskilly, was killed.[48] Adding to the pain of Ms. Roskilly's family was that they were also evicted from the Denver Housing Authority unit where the woman had lived with her seventy-year-old mother and eighteen-year-old autistic son for the past ten years.[49] The housing authority stated the eviction was required by federal rules because Ms. Roskilly was the one who had signed the lease. News reporters discovered that Mr. Abeyta and his estranged wife had a very problematic relationship.[50] In 2003, his wife, who was sixteen years old at the time, was arrested for attacking Mr. Abeyta with a knife and a wrench after also attacking a woman he was dating. In 2007, he threatened his wife with a knife, violated a protective order, and received another charge of criminal mischief, which was dismissed in 2009 because of the ex-wife's noncooperation. Mr. Abeyta's family told police that he was a veteran suffering from post-traumatic stress disorder.[51] Mr. Abeyta testified at court that he had lost his job of thirteen years with the city, his wife was kicking him out, and she told him to go kill himself.[52] He reported that he couldn't kill himself and hoped the police would kill him instead. He testified that he did not intend to shoot and kill Ms. Roskilly.

The median (Q1, Q3) number of officers who shot during an encounter was one (1, 2), and the number of shots fired was four (2, 9.5), of which an average of two bullets (1, 4) hit the suspect. In 10.7 percent of the cases, there were attempts to use nonlethal alternatives, and these weapons primarily included Tasers (40.6 percent) followed by mace (15.6 percent) or a 40 mm launch grenade (15.6 percent). Bivariate statistics indicate significant age group differences in nonlethal alternatives used.

Officers did not use a nonlethal alternative when the person who was shot was a youth (0 percent). There were twenty-five individuals shot under the age of eighteen, and based on the descriptions for each case, it was unclear why officers did not attempt to use nonlethal force in any of these cases. Guns were present in 40 percent of these shootings; 28 percent of the youth under the age of eighteen did not possess a weapon. In two of the shootings involving a juvenile with a knife, even the witnesses thought police should have used a Taser. For the other age groups, nonlethal force was used 6.1 percent of the time for those aged 18 to 27, 10.3 percent for 28 to 37, 25.5 percent for 38 to 47, and 16.0 percent for 48 years and older. After the shooting death of fifteen-year-old Paul Childs in 2003, Mayor John Hickenlooper required the Denver Police Department to equip more officers with nonlethal equipment.[53] However, nonlethal devices can also be deadly. Shortly after this policy change, a man in his forties died from being shot with a Taser after reportedly fighting with officers.

Nationwide, it is estimated that Tasers have resulted in more than 1,005 deaths, most occurring since 2000.[54] Reuters developed a six-part study based upon what it states is the "most comprehensive public accounting to date of deaths and litigation that followed police use of Tasers." They document numerous encounters where family members call the police for help, only to watch a loved one die at the hands of the police. The Taser was developed in 1970, copyrighted in 1993, and mass produced by December 1999. An increasingly significant number of law enforcement agencies adopted the devices and with that came lawsuits regarding the negative outcomes that resulted from how it was being used and on whom it was being used. Although Tasers were considered less deadly than firearms, it was unclear by how much, according to the researchers interviewed by Reuters. The electric jolt causes intense pain, to the point that individuals cannot move and often drop to the ground or experience paralysis. The level of electrical current can vary depending on the type of Taser used, how long it has been charged for, and where and how many times the person is hit, along with the duration of contact with the device. There was no available data indicating the level of frequency of use involving a Taser in Denver, but when Mayor Hickenlooper adopted this tool as an alternative to firearms, his belief was that it could reduce deaths. The data indicates that there can be—and has been—injury and death resulting from law enforcement officers using this device.

Police officers occasionally work off duty and in uniform at nightclubs, banks, or other establishments to supplement their income. In 7.7 percent of the Denver shooting cases, at least one officer was off duty. These twenty-three shootings involving off-duty officers ranged from problematic (22 percent) to questionable (43 percent) and less controversial (35 percent). The Denver Police Department policy allowed officers to work an additional twenty-four hours per week off duty.[55] Since the 1980s, there has been an increase in the number of policies limiting the total amount of off-duty hours and the expected behavior while working at a secondary employer. Moonlighting practices, in other words, working a second job, received mixed reviews; police officers argued it saved taxpayers money by allowing private companies to share the cost while providing additional security.[56] Critics argued that the practice overworked police officers and increased the exposure of the city and county to lawsuits.[57] A *Rocky Mountain News* story in 2003 reported that nearly seven out of eight officers in the Denver Police Department had worked a second job at some point in the last four years. Moonlighting met with public controversy when it was discovered that an officer was working a second job at the same time he was on the clock for his city position and that such a practice may be more prevalent than reported.[58] However, there were no mechanisms in place to collect data on secondary employment to understand how often this occurs. Banks and nightclubs accounted for most of the extra-duty shifts; serving as security at sporting events was also common.

The suspect in each shooting incident was not likely to injure an officer. In other words, 82.3 percent of officers were not injured by the shooting suspect. The 17.7 percent of incidents that involved an injury to a police officer were primarily caused by either a bullet (39.6 percent) or a vehicle (26.4 percent). Three officers were killed in an incident where a suspect was also shot. Two of these deaths were caused by firearms (Patrick Pollock and James Wier), and one death was caused with a vehicle (Robert Wallis).[59] These three deaths all happened within fourteen months, between 1986 and 1988. Since then, an officer-involved shooting incident has not included an officer who has been killed. This does not mean, however, that there were no close calls.

For example, in 2015, Officer Antonio "Tony" Lopez was on patrol in north Denver driving an unmarked narcotics vehicle when he noticed an SUV traveling in the other direction with a badly damaged front windshield around 11:20 AM.[60] Officer Lopez made a U-turn and reported seeing the SUV make a lane change without a turn signal.[61] He activated his emergency lights. The SUV pulled into a liquor store; when the driver got out, he confronted the officer, saying, "What?" The man then began shooting a 7.62-caliber MAK-90 semiautomatic rifle, a variant of the AK-47, toward the officer. The first bullet struck Officer Lopez, who was wearing a ballistic vest, in the chest. The second bullet hit him in the left arm, the third shot in the left leg, the fourth shot in the left thigh, and two additional bullet injuries followed. Officer Lopez took cover behind his police vehicle, looked underneath it to view the assailant's legs, and fired several shots. The man stumbled, then got into his SUV and drove away. A thirty-six-year-old man named Jason Woods was arrested a short distance later and treated for a gunshot wound to his left ankle. After being criminally charged and found guilty, Mr. Woods was sentenced to fifty-two years in prison for shooting Officer Lopez six times.[62] Mr. Woods was aware there was a warrant out for his arrest for a tattoo machine robbery and reported a desire to not go back to prison. Mr. Woods had a criminal record in Colorado, Illinois, and Louisiana. Officer Lopez, the son of a Denver police officer of Cuban ancestry, was recognized as a hero; after several surgeries, he was able to walk again and spend time with his wife and infant son.[63]

Based upon the sociodemographic characteristics of the officers who shot, a total of 394 law enforcement officers participated in shooting someone in Denver between 1983 to 2020.[64] Of these officers, the majority were male (95.9 percent). The race/ethnicity for most officers was white (75.0 percent), followed by Latino officers (19.0 percent) and Black officers (5.0 percent). The median (Q1, Q3) number of years on the force was seven (4, 13) years. At least fifty-seven officers engaged in two or more shootings, and fourteen officers were involved in three or more shootings.[65] There were no significant bivariate associations for the sociodemographic characteristics of the officers who shot by age, sex, race/ethnicity, and foreign-born status. These results are found in tables A2.2–A2.5.

There were significant sex differences in the number of shots fired. A median (Q1, Q3) of four (1, 9) shots were fired by law enforcement officers toward males and 10.5 (2.8, 19.8) shots toward females. As the shooting of females was rarer (a total of fourteen cases), the reasons why mostly male officers perceived the person's behavior as a threat raised many questions. For example, 35.7 percent of these cases involved a female with a firearm, whereas at the same time, in 35.7 percent of the cases, there was no weapon possessed, and the female was not necessarily the intended target. The other weapons included vehicles (21.4 percent) or a knife (7.1 percent). This should not discount, however, the ability of male officers to respond with deadly force when a gun was fired in the direction of officers. For example, Denver Police Department officers Ismael Lopez, six years on the force, and Brandon Reyes, four years on the force, were on patrol in separate vehicles and stopped at a 7–11 store around 11:30 PM to take a break.[66] When they arrived, Officer Lopez noticed a vehicle wanted for eluding the police.[67] A man was seen putting air in one of the tires; Officer Lopez went to investigate. He patted down the male, found a syringe in his pocket, and then placed him in handcuffs. The female driver, thirty-one-year-old Jamie Fernandez, was told to stay in the car, but instead she got out and started to run. The officers yelled out for her to stop; she pulled a small gun out from her purse and fired a shot in the vicinity of the officers. The two officers responded by firing thirty shots and hitting her sixteen times.[68] The total amount of time between Ms. Fernandez's shot and the shots fired by officers was approximately nineteen seconds. The release of the bodycam and store camera videos did little to alleviate the concerns as to why there were so many shots fired. The police officers reported they stopped firing once the gun fell from her hand. Two shell casings were found near Ms. Fernandez's gun. Her purse contained a bottle of alcohol, two baggies of a suspected controlled substance, and another gun magazine fully loaded. Friends and family mourned her death. Ms. Fernandez, a Latina, was killed by two Latino officers. This shooting was categorized as questionable given the reason for the stop and the number of shots fired, especially after Ms. Fernandez's level of threat was contained.

Several studies have assessed whether there was a relationship between the race/ethnicity of an officer versus the race/ethnicity of the person shot. Nevertheless, answering this question can be more complicated than researchers may understand, as reflected in earlier policing studies concluding that the disparity in officer-involved shootings between Blacks and whites was unexplainable or simply the fault of Black residents. One study that had to be retracted for mathematical and logical errors involved a team of psychologists led by David Johnson. These researchers compiled a list of fatal officer-involved shootings using the *Washington Post* and *Guardian* databases.[69] After obtaining a list of shootings, they reached out to 684 police departments, requesting demographic information on officers, and then used other publicly available information to obtain complete information on 72 percent of the shootings and at least partial information in 96 percent of the cases. The authors wanted to predict the race of the person shot from the characteristics of the officer, civilian, and county, using multinomial regression. They argued that rather than using the population as a benchmark for comparison, a better marker was violent crime. The authors explained that they opted to use prediction models because comparing rates to a benchmark would mean that different racial groups have equal experiences in situations that resulted in fatal shootings by police. They found that the race and ethnicity of the person shot were associated with the officer's race and ethnicity: Black officers were more likely to fatally shoot a person who was Black (OR: 1.23, 95% CI: 1.03, 1.48), compared to a person who was white. Officers who were Hispanic were more likely to shoot people who were Hispanic (OR: 1.84, 95% CI: 1.54, 2.20) or Black (OR: 1.29, 95% CI: 1.07, 1.56), compared to white. Based on this model, they reported: "We find no evidence of anti-Black or anti-Hispanic disparities across shootings, and White officers are no more likely to shoot minority civilians than non-White officers. Instead race-specific crime strongly predicts civilian race. This suggests that increasing diversity among officers by itself is unlikely to reduce racial disparity in police shootings."[70]

Johnson and colleagues reported that race-specific crime was found to explain 44 percent of the variance in the race of the person fatally shot. Shortly after the publication of this article, two researchers, Dean Knox and Jonathan Mummolo, challenged the findings based on data limitations used for the comparison, mathematical errors, and logical fallacies.[71] Despite the authors' retraction of the article, its publication and continued presence in a prestigious journal, the *Proceedings of the National Academy of Sciences* (PNAS), has deceptively contributed to shaping the argument about how racial bias in policing may not exist; the article was even cited in congressional testimony. In addition, we found that violent crime was not the best indicator, given racial and ethnic inequality, and rates of violent crime do not always mirror individual cases. We were disturbed by the findings reported by Johnson and colleagues but want to highlight how it has perpetuated the longstanding white habitus that continues to be a challenge in academia.[72] Policing research is often reflective of this dismissal of systematic racism in policing, and such a dismissal provides cover for policy makers to avoid advocating for change.

A research study that goes beyond datasets of convenience was developed by the economist Bocar Ba and several of his political science colleagues.[73] They explored whether the race and gender of police officers affect policing behaviors using data collected by submitting open-record requests to the Chicago Police's human resources department as well as the Illinois Office of the Attorney General for a three-year period (2016 to 2019).[74] These data contained sociodemographic characteristics, including race, gender, language skill, daily shift assignments, and appointment date, along with behavior such as stops, arrests, and uses of force. These demographic profiles of the officers were compared to a specific combination of month/year, day of the week, shift time, and assigned "beat" (MDSBs). These MDSBs were compared across officers. These differences were estimated using ordinary least squares with MDSBs as fixed effects. The researchers found that Black officers made fewer stops, fewer arrests, and had fewer instances of use of force than their white counterparts. The same was true for Hispanic officers, although more modestly. However, Hispanic officers displayed rates of stops, arrests, and use of force with Hispanic civilians comparable to those of white officers. The researchers believed more fine-grained data and analysis of this ethnic group was needed to comprehend these results. Differences in female officers compared to male officers were also found; however, they were smaller in magnitude. Female officers made fewer total arrests and fewer arrests of Black civilians. Female officers also used force less than males overall and fewer times against Black civilians. The authors concluded that despite different patrol assignments, increased diversity narrows the disparity gaps, particularly for Black civilians, which can contribute to changing departmental norms.

THE PRISTINE FOURTEEN

Fourteen Denver Police Department officers stand out in the city and county of Denver as having three or more instances of shooting someone, whether on duty or off duty. In attempting to determine patterns, these fourteen officers will receive additional attention in an effort to learn what characteristics they share and what type of community response they have received.

Of the fourteen officers, some received a lot of media coverage over the years, others almost nothing. The fourteen officers, in alphabetical order by surname, along with what year they attended the academy and unique identifier, include Scott Blatnick (1992; 07), Ken Chavez (1979; 05), Sean Cronin (2005; 099), Pete Diaz (1967; 22), Vincent Gavito (1986; 68), Scott Hartvigson (1990; 13), Vince Lombardi (1989; 31), Jeff Motz (1993; 14), Rich Mumford (1973; 88), Ken Overman (1972; 84), Joe Rodarte (1990; 04), Robert Silvas (1977; 22), Rufino Trujillo (1982; 88), and Larry Valencia (1982; 89). All fourteen were male; seven officers were white and seven Latino. None of the Pristine Fourteen were Black; only one Black officer had more than two shootings.[75] Combined, these fourteen officers account for fifty-eight shootings (19.5 percent) involving twenty-nine homicides, twenty-three injuries, and six cases where the shots fired did not hit someone. Criminological studies have often found a small percentage of offenders account for the majority of offenses—these are termed "chronic offenders" or "career criminals"—and the same trend appears true for officers who participate in shootings.[76] What follows is an overview of several of these officers.

Officer Ken Chavez was born and raised in Denver and came from a military family with origins in Trinidad, Colorado, a community that dates back to when this area of the United States was a territory of Spain.[77] His original hope was to join the Air Force, but because of his eyesight, he was ineligible. Instead, he joined the Denver Police Department in 1979 at the age of twenty-two. Alongside policing, he also served in the Colorado Army National Guard and rose to the rank of lieutenant colonel. As a police officer, he served in many roles, including the gang bureau, and also worked as a homicide detective and school resource officer. Two news stories described his active personality. On a Friday around 11 PM in 1991, he was leaving a grocery store, but when he came outside, his 1984 black Chevrolet Trans Am was gone.[78] He went home, filed a report with the police department, and then grabbed a police radio, a firearm, and a baseball bat, then drove off in his other vehicle to look for his stolen Trans Am. He suspected that the thieves were gang members, as he was working in the gang unit at the time. As he drove into a low-income housing community in west Denver, he found the car and confronted the driver and four passengers. The young men took off running. As they ran, Officer Ken Chavez called them "wimps." Fellow officers were surprised by how determined Officer Chavez was to find his stolen car and were amazed that he did. In another news story, he was playing in a pick-up basketball game with his fifteen-year-old son in 1995.[79] The game got heated, and someone sucker punched him in the temple, but instead of fighting, Officer Chavez arrested the person he suspected of hitting him: a twenty-nine-year-old man who was an engineering manager at Lockheed Martin. As the case went to court, there was some criticism as to why this case resulted in criminal charges rather than being settled on the basketball court. In the end, the jury was unsure beyond a reasonable doubt whether the manager was the one who hit the officer.[80] Witnesses on behalf of the manager stated that Chavez had been "getting in people's face and talking trash" before the incident occurred and called his teammate a "wimp" before his teammate left the game in frustration. The twenty-nine-year-old substitute player, the manager, said he simply fell during play, but then, when he attempted to leave, Officer Chavez flashed a badge in his face and arrested him. After the verdict was rendered, the manager stated it was frightening to think of Officer Chavez out in public with a gun.

Despite these instances of increased public attention, Officer Chavez excelled in his military and academic roles, receiving accolades. As a National Guardsman he was deployed to Afghanistan during Operation Enduring Freedom (sometime between 2001 and 2014) and also deployed to Iraq during Operation Iraqi Freedom (sometime between 2003 and 2011). He reports that he was trained in special forces. Educationally, he earned a bachelor's degree in criminal justice from Metropolitan State University, a master's certificate in Professional Homeland Security from the University of Denver, and another master's in strategic studies from the US Army War College.[81] He received numerous medals from both the Denver Police Department and the Colorado National Guard.[82] He was also a member of the National Latino Police Officers Association.

Officer Ken Chavez was involved in at least six separate shooting incidents. The shootings ranged from questionable to problematic, but he continued to move up the ranks. For the shooting and death of Jeff Truax in 1996, he did receive criticism. Both officers with military experience working off duty as security were not criminally charged but did receive a written reprimand (see chapter 4). This shooting also resulted in the Erickson Commission being formed to investigate the use-of-force policy in Denver and how it compared to several other similarly sized police departments around the country. In an interview with the *Fort Lupton Press*, Officer Chavez stated: "I was very proud of my 42 years of service with the Denver Police Department and I felt I made a difference to solve a lot of crimes and put a lot of bad people away that should not be out there victimizing people."[83] The newspaper stated that in his retirement he was raising horses and was a collector of antique twentieth-century military firearms. Ken Chavez did not stay retired long: He accepted a position as interim police chief for the Leadville Police Department, then became chief of the Severance Police Department in 2023.[84]

Although Chief Ken Chavez had a high number of shootings, the officer who had the greatest number of shooting incidents in Denver was Sergeant Bob Silvas. He joined the Denver Police Department (DPD) in 1977 and retired in 2013. In his thirty-six years with DPD, he was involved in ten separate shooting incidents, across which eight individuals were shot and five killed. His first shooting occurred two years after he graduated from the academy. At least seven of the ten individuals he shot at were either Black or Latino.[85] Officer Silvas's shootings run the continuum from problematic to questionable to and less controversial. The shootings he was criticized the most for were the shootings and deaths of eighteen-year-old Gregory Smith in 2002 and sixteen-year-old Joseph Rodriguez in 1979. In that 1979 case, the defense attorney was so confident after reviewing the evidence that Officer Silvas had murdered this child in cold blood that he wrote the mayor in the mid-1980s that Officer Bob Silvas should be fired before he kills again.[86] The attorney was correct in his analysis: Officer Silvas had nine additional shooting incidents.

When analyzed as an outlier among officers, Officer Silvas was also described as the type of officer you want with you if you run into any problems. A *Rocky Mountain News* story reported that Officer Silvas's attorney reported, "Bob is one of the most highly decorated officers in the department. . . . When you want to send a cop, you send Bob. I don't think there is anybody better."[87] His ex-wife, who too had been a law enforcement officer, called him a "ragingly violent psychopath." According to the *Rocky Mountain News* examination of court records, she accused Silvas of trying to kill her in 1984. When he remarried, his second wife, also a Denver police officer, stood by his bedside after he was shot in a shooting incident. They, too, divorced after having a child together. He was awarded the Purple Heart for getting shot while attempting to stop two men wanted for robberies.[88] One of the two men was later killed by police in a nearby alley. Despite remaining a sergeant and not rising further up the ranks, he received more than forty commendations and was awarded the highest honor (the Medal of Valor) three times. He was sued at least four times for excessive force and received eleven citizen complaints by 1999; these were not sustained, given a lack of evidence. A LinkedIn page with a person named Robert Silvas, who had been a member of DPD from 1977 to 2013, now lists their job as a lab technician supervisor for the Littleton Police Department in Colorado.

Of the Pristine Fourteen officers, many of these shootings span a career of twenty to forty years, but one officer, Scott Blatnick, who joined the police department in 1992, had three separate shooting incidents in one year alone, 1995. In one of the shootings, the shooting and death of thirty-year-old Benny Atencio, there was pressure for criminal charges, and a lawsuit was filed.[89] The mother reported calling the police for help, but instead of receiving help, her son was murdered. The Public Safety Review Commission determined the shooting was an unnecessary use of force. However, when it was presented to the chief of police, David Michaud, he rejected the recommendation, and it was sent to the public safety manager for a final determination.[90] The *Denver Post* reported that although the shootings of civilians stopped, the behaviors that resulted in disciplinary action had escalated.[91] In 1996, he was accused of pushing a woman to the ground during the arrest of her husband and then lying about it. He received a five-day suspension. In 1997, he pleaded guilty to disturbing the peace for causing a "ruckus" at a fellow officer's home, and as a result, he received a year of probation. In 1998, he received two oral reprimands for using excessive force. All of these escalating violations possibly led to his leaving the Denver Police Department in 2002 after ten years of service. Based on the CORA request, Officer Blatnick received thirty-four commendations, including some of DPD's highest awards, including the Medal of Valor (three times), Service Cross (three times), and Merit Award (two times).[92] It is unknown whether he now works for another law enforcement agency or has retired.

Another officer, Sean Cronin, who had three shootings, never encountered criminal charges from the district attorney's office, but in 2021, when he failed to get vaccinated against COVID-19, he was terminated.[93] The website *Officer Down* lists 496 officers who died that year from the COVID-19 pandemic.[94] Thus, his shooting individuals was not a violation, but his failure to comply with the new health policy had consequences. All three of his shootings were questionable, and all three persons shot died as a result of Sean Cronin's decision making. One of these shootings also included a mother's call for help that resulted in a fight with officers and the killing of a young man for attempting to grab and fire an officer's gun.[95]

Officer Rufino Trujillo is another of the fourteen officers who stand out, but less in regard to his shootings and more because of his advocacy later in his career as the Colorado president of the National Latino Peace Officers Association (NLPOA). He joined the Denver Police Department in 1982. He engaged in four shootings during his thirty-one years with the police department. Each of the three suspects he shot was wounded, and the cases were categorized as less controversial. The fourth shooting did not result in the suspect being hit. In his position as leader of the Colorado NLPOA, he was involved in a lawsuit against the Denver Police Department for discrimination against Latinos in regard to hiring, promotion, and discipline.[96] He reported how the number of Latino officers was not representative of the demographics of the city and how Latino officers encountered many obstacles to career advancement. He even sent a formal request to the US Department of Justice to have a gang unit officer who was white be investigated for jumping up and down on a Latino teenager's back while they were in handcuffs.[97] The teen was sent to the intensive care unit with a lacerated liver and broken ribs. The officer, Charles Porter, was criminally charged but acquitted by a jury.[98] In 2010, the manager of safety fired Charles Porter, along with two officers who were present at the time for failing to report.[99] Officer Porter appealed the decision, but the Civil Service Commission upheld it.[100] The city paid $885,000 to settle the lawsuit. Nevertheless, Officer Trujillo was a staunch supporter of officers' having the option to use a firearm when perceiving danger and criticized the punishment given to James Turney for the controversial shooting involving Paul Childs. In an interview with the *Rocky Mountain News*, he stated he had respect for life, "But we have a right to survive just like anyone else. . . . When I signed on with the police department, it was to work for them, not to die for them." In his career, he rose to the level of detective. Rufino Trujillo passed away on September 28, 2024, at the age of seventy-two.[101] His obituary reported that he had served in the US Army from 1976 to 1981.

In total, these fourteen officers accumulated 430 commendations, an average of 30.7 per officer. Some of the Denver Police Department's highest medals, such as the Medal of Honor, Medal of Valor, Distinguished Service Cross, Purple Heart Award, Superior Tactics and Response Award, and Police Merit Award, have been given to these officers. These officers had also acquired 112 separate complaints from a combination of citizen, internal, and scheduled disciplinary infractions. There was only one shooting that resulted in any disciplinary action among the fourteen officers (Chavez); they were more likely to be awarded a medal. Thus, rather than being ostracized, these officers were more likely to be commended and placed on a pedestal: to be pristine. Shootings were not career ending; the biggest consequence resulted from an officer refusing to be vaccinated, which resulted in his termination. All other forms of indiscretion were outweighed by the commendations. Only two of these fourteen officers appeared to have a military background (Chavez and Trujillo); several had worked in gang units and tactical units.

In an attempt to understand why some officers were more violent than others, the *Denver Post* ran a story focusing on a 1986 police academy called "The Animals."[102] The reporter, David Migoya, stated that during the mid-1980s, Denver was having difficulties with crime and homicides and that residents wanted more aggressive law enforcement officers. It was the 1986 Denver Police Academy, consisting of forty recruits, that received this nickname given its collective size, strength, and attitude. Migoya reported how this academy had the highest number of shooting incidents. It was also an academy year that included a physical agility test along with an effort devoted toward eleven weeks at the academy and then eleven weeks of field training known as "street survival." Migoya stated: "The class included bodybuilders, football players, karate experts, gymnasts, competitive firearms experts, and civilian and military police officers."[103] One noted difference was that in that year, there was also a higher number of officer deaths both in the state of Colorado and in Denver. Officers were donating blood and also placing black tape on their badges to honor the dead officers. The thirty-seven officers who successfully completed the academy considered themselves not bullies but rather "sheepdogs looking over the herd."[104] The *Denver Post* found that fourteen of these thirty-seven officers had been involved in the wounding or killing of fourteen residents, of whom thirteen died as a result of gunfire. The next highest was the 1995 academy class, with eight shooting incidents.

MENTAL HEALTH AMONG POLICE OFFICERS

Not only do police officers respond to mental health situations, but they themselves may bring their personal mental health issues to a scene. Research documents that officers experience chronic exposure to trauma, increasing their risk for post-traumatic stress disorder (PTSD), depression, anxiety, and substance use and increasing their need for mental health interventions.[105] One local study found that among 434 patrol officers in Dallas–Fort Worth, Texas, 26 percent had positive screening results for current mental illness symptoms, including depression, anxiety, posttraumatic stress disorder (PTSD), and suicidal ideation or self-harm; 17 percent had sought mental health care services in the year; and 12 percent had a lifetime mental health diagnosis.[106]

Not only were there challenges in diagnosing mental health outcomes among police officers, but as with the general population, there were challenges with seeking treatment for these outcomes, including anxiety, depression, and PTSD. Multidisciplinary Association for Psychedelic Studies (MAPS) has taken the lead in developing treatments for mental health outcomes using psychedelics, including methylenedioxymethamphetamine (MDMA)-assisted psychotherapy for veterans and police officers.[107] Clinical trials have begun to assess the impact of methylenedioxymethamphetamine (MDMA)-assisted psychotherapy with psychotherapy for post-traumatic stress disorder (PTSD) in various populations, including police officers.[108]

Traditional responses to stress and anxiety have primarily involved various forms of self-medication. Law enforcement coping mechanisms have included increased alcohol use, which can result in health, legal, and marital problems.[109] Attempts to become stronger have encouraged some officers to use steroids.[110] The magnification of these poor coping mechanisms can also result in suicide.[111]

COMPARING LAW ENFORCEMENT TO STREET GANGS

Several researchers have noted that individuals involved with street gangs and disadvantaged communities have often labeled members of law enforcement as gangs.[112] For example, in one of Durán's interviews for his dissertation, a respondent reported that "if they actually took the time to document this stuff [abuse of community members], we would actually see the Denver Police is putting in more work than anybody. They function as a gang."[113] Since most of Durán's scholarship has focused on street gangs and the bonding that forms between marginalized individuals attempting to survive along with helping family members and friends cope in difficult social environments, Durán found it important to speak to these claims.[114]

Although levels of culture, solidarity, and response to perceived threats were similar, there were also some very important differences. First, obtaining employment in law enforcement requires meeting some basic professional requirements. Second, working for a law enforcement agency is a paid occupation with benefits and opportunities for career advancement. Third, the occupation is part of an institution that will last beyond any one individual. Fourth, the decision making of law enforcement officers in the form of discretion is legally protected. Fifth, law enforcement is part of a larger carceral apparatus wherein punishment is multifaceted and occurs on multiple levels. Street gangs, on the other hand, attempt to maintain strength and control in a smaller social world in which they live that does not necessarily include economic resources, power, or the entrustment to support individual decision making. If the image of a "gang" is the personification of power, then yes, law enforcement and the military are organizations that are on a scale much bigger than gangs because they are legitimized, whereas street gangs are primarily composed of marginalized individuals and groups who are targeted by the state and thus positioned to not have any type of social power in society. Thus, when Officer Ken Chavez called gang members "wimps," he could do so because he had the law on his side, whereas gang members have only state destruction. Chavez can behave like a predator and can do so legally.[115]

This chapter highlights how both the lives of the suspect and the officers were intertwined. The person encountering the state faced the greatest level of danger, for their killing or injuries could be legally justified. Such interactions enter a structural arrangement not necessarily chosen by either party, but there were characteristics of who was shot more frequently along with who engaged in the most shootings. In most of these circumstances, we have a white male officer killing or injuring Black and Brown residents. However, the officers who had the greatest number of shootings, three or more during their careers, were primarily white officers and Latino officers, and they, too, were primarily shooting Black and Brown residents. These officers also received positive recognition for their decision making and little to no discipline, hence their nickname here, the Pristine Fourteen. The Latino officers exemplify the saying, "All my skinfolk ain't kinfolk."[116] Nevertheless, when minority officers shoot someone who is white, it can heighten the societal critique (e.g., the Erickson Commission). Although law enforcement is not one of the most dangerous occupations, it is heavily influenced by a culture that ingrains fear and the constant potential threat of danger in an attempt to keep officers one step ahead of the residents they encounter in daily interactions.

6

A PUBLIC HEALTH PROBLEM FOR THE UNITED STATES

Places, Practices, and Policies

Today is June 2, 2022, and I'm (Durán) in Uvalde, Texas, at Robb Elementary School, with my wife and seventh-grade daughter. A week earlier, a young Latino man, eighteen years old, entered the school and murdered nineteen fourth-grade children and two teachers with an AR-15-style rifle before law enforcement officers killed him.[1] Before driving four hours to get to Uvalde from Bryan, Texas, I found it difficult to look at a picture of my daughter on our fridge, smiling really big and holding a sign stating: "I am heading to 4th grade." I couldn't imagine losing her at nine or ten years old. All I felt in my heart was incredible sadness and pain for the families and how horrible it was for someone to target young children and teachers. It took law enforcement between seventy-three to eighty minutes to resolve this incident, from the time they arrived at the school to the time they killed the shooter.[2] The focus of this chapter will be to expand the study of officer-involved shootings beyond the city and county of Denver and to highlight the contradiction of a shooting in the small town of Uvalde compared to most police shootings across the country.

Examining the shooting incident in Uvalde is vital because as long as issues such as Uvalde can occur, public officials will resist limiting officer decision making to use deadly force and thus leave police shootings as an unaddressed public health problem. Throughout the day on May 24, 2022, as the news media agencies of CNN, MSNBC, Telemundo, Univision, and statewide reporters descended into the community of Uvalde, the central issue that developed was the ever-changing official version of events. The question became: Why did it take law enforcement so long to enter the classroom to stop the shooter? Even on the news, family members were seen attempting to gain access to the school to rescue their children while armed officers held them back. An investigative committee determined that 376 law enforcement officers from twenty-three agencies were at the scene.[3] They were divided into different tasks, including crowd control, rescuing children in other classrooms, and developing a strategy for stopping the shooter. Most of the news coverage reported did not focus on the individual shooter to prevent the notoriety that he desired and to reduce the likelihood of copycat events.[4] Nevertheless, along with the sadness I feel for the families and children, as a criminologist, I needed to process who this shooter was and how to prevent something like this from ever happening again. Thus it was not just nineteen children and two teachers murdered but also the gunman. Not twenty-one deaths but twenty-two.

According to the timeline of events, minutes before the shooting at the school occurred, the shooter shot his grandmother in the face. She was taken to the hospital, and after many surgeries, she survived her critical wound.[5] It was reported in the news that no funeral home in the local area wanted to accept the body of the shooter.[6] It was later reported that his autopsy was sealed, so it is unknown how many times he was shot by law enforcement officers.[7] The investigative committee, created to provide greater clarity, has provided the most thorough background on the shooter.[8] The report outlined his difficult childhood along with the lack of access to needed educational and social services when he was growing up. All of these life challenges and unmet needs coalesced into his preparations to shoot up a school, and nobody positioned themselves to intervene before this day transpired.[9]

The primary data-gathering tool I use as a criminologist is ethnography.[10] Visiting the community of Uvalde with my physical presence is how I observe and make sense of information. In preparation for my site visit, I created a list of places to examine. My first observation after arriving was the memorial created by the community to honor the victims at Robb Elementary. I wanted to honor and pay my respects to the individuals whose lives were taken too soon. Each member of my family brought a rosary to leave next to one of the markers representing a victim.[11] I then walked around the perimeter of the school and first visited the location where the shooter rammed into a metal gate with a truck and drove into a ditch. It had been reported that the shooter did not know how to drive; thus, driving from his grandparents' home to the school was extremely difficult for him. To do what he was planning required that he reach his destination quickly, and after shooting his grandmother, he couldn't get to the school quickly enough on foot while carrying his firearms. He needed a vehicle. After the crash, he may have been injured, concussed, or confused; he left a bag of fully loaded bullet magazines and his second AR-15-style rifle behind in the truck. I look at the five-foot chain-link fence the shooter jumped over to gain access to the school.

As I continued to walk the perimeter of the school, I started a conversation with a Texas State Patrol officer stationed along the perimeter as extra security. It felt like the right thing to do. He inquires whether I am with the media, and I respond that I am a researcher from Texas A&M University. He tells me he had been stationed along the Texas-Mexico border, but after this incident, he was brought here. We discuss the tragedy of the event. So much of the scene of the shooting, where the shooter lived, and the community do not make sense to me. Why did this incident occur here?[12]

Determined to find answers, the media reports how family and friends describe the shooter as having a troubled life.[13] He was reportedly picked on for having a speech impediment and for having to wear the same clothes every day because he was poor. He quit attending high school, and his poor social skills made it difficult to keep a job.[14] For the past two months, he had been living with his grandparents after having an argument with his mother. At the age of eighteen, in the state of Texas, along with many other states, he was legally able to purchase two rifles.[15] The shooter tried acquiring a firearm sooner, but no one would purchase one on his behalf.[16]

My family and I walked into the store in Uvalde where the guns were purchased. A sign near the gun shop states that one section of the store is temporarily closed because of the recent tragedy, "out of respect for the families." The upper walls of the gun shop display various hunting trophies, such as bear, bison, cheetah, deer, elk, turkey, and warthog. This one-stop shop for hunting gear also contained a BBQ restaurant, where at least a dozen patrons were eating. Despite Uvalde being 72 percent Latino, this store's customers, at the time I visited, were probably 85 percent white.[17] It is sad to think that it is not just the hunted animals but also humans that are affected by these weapons. The animals on the wall are modeled as trophies, whereas deceased humans are hidden from our consciousness in burial. One section of the store includes a section of signs for sale, and they include the following statements: "KEEP CALM AND CARRY," "I Pledge to Vote Against and Actively Oppose any POLITI-CIAN who supports GUN CONTROL," and "BAN IDIOTS NOT GUNS 'MERICA." And with such messages and political support, we are caught in the conundrum of gun violence remaining a lingering public health problem for residents and law enforcement.

The tragic incident at Robb Elementary School on May 24, 2022, taught me that in our gun culture society, a method needs to exist to stop people from shooting others, but who is capable of accomplishing such a task, and how can this be accomplished without causing additional harm?[18] The shooting incident in Uvalde was a contradiction compared to most of the police shootings described in this book. First, most shootings by law enforcement are not in response to a homicide, let alone four or more individuals who have been shot. In our review of shootings, the closest single case would be the incident involving the shooting of Michael Julius Ford by Denver police officers in 2006.[19] In July of that year, twenty-two-year-old Michael, a Black man, entered a Safeway warehouse where he was an employee and killed one worker and injured five others, including a police officer attempting to stop him.[20] Police were held back as Michael set various fires in the warehouse. It took officers seventy minutes to stop the shooter, given the size of the warehouse, the fires Michael had set, and the gunshots. Michael was armed with one six-shot Ruger .357-caliber revolver. He had fired sixteen shots and had a pocket full of bullets. In comparison, the Uvalde shooter had two AR-15-style rifles and fifty-eight thirty-round magazines. He possessed over 1,600 bullets and had fired more than one hundred rounds. In contrast to law enforcement officers in Uvalde considering this a "barricaded subject," Denver police officers responded to Michael's incident as an "active shooter." This designation was created in response to altered police tactics after the murders at Columbine High School. Over 150 law enforcement officers were present at the scene in Denver. Both Michael and the Uvalde shooter were described as quiet and not having criminal records or a known mental health diagnosis, thus ruling out the official labeling arguments of "bad guys with guns" or "mass shooters with mental health problems" because, at the time, these shooters weren't considered to be in either category.

The characteristics of the individuals shot by police were similar in that they both were young ethnic- or racial-minority males between the ages of eighteen and twenty-two. However, according to the mass shooter database compiled by the magazine *Mother Jones*, between 1982 and April 2023, most mass shooters were white (57.6 percent) and male (95 percent),[21] characteristics more likely represented in domestic and lone-wolf terrorist activities.[22] As reported earlier, whites were also more likely to own guns, but despite these patterns, Blacks, Latinos, and Native Americans continue to be shot at and killed at higher rates by law enforcement.[23] The amount of time required to resolve both of these active-shooter cases was rare. In Denver, for example, based on thirty-eight years of police shootings, the average time between an officer being alerted to a problem and a person being shot was five minutes.[24]

Reconciling the contradictions between different types of shootings was important in developing a more nuanced understanding of the police use of force, and to do so often required broadening the number of locations examined. For most of this book, Denver, Colorado, has served as the foundation for understanding officer-involved shootings. It has served this role because the data obtained and time investment, despite limitations, was far superior to what was acquired in other communities. However, Durán, along with his students, attempted to discover patterns involving officer-involved shootings in New Mexico, Texas, and Utah while at New Mexico State University (2006 to 2014) and then in different areas of the South after moving to the University of Tennessee (2014 to 2018). This work began before datasets from *Fatal Encounters, Fatal Force*, and *Mapping Police Violence* were available.[25] This chapter provides an overview of nationwide data-collection efforts and particular patterns from different geographic regions, including the Rocky Mountains, Borderlands, and the South. Emphasis will be placed on describing general patterns, points of interest, comparisons, and an acknowledgment of contextual differences. Such a model, often described in sociology as "comparative-historical," seeks to provide increased insight into how issues relate to other geographic locations or groups. Previously, Durán had participated in a study of disproportionate minority contact, where the first task for researchers was to assess whether or not youth of color were overrepresented in the juvenile justice system.[26] After determining rates along each decision point, then researchers could seek to discover why disparities existed and then what to do reduce these imbalances. For officer-involved shootings, we share a similar sentiment in terms of gaining greater clarity on this topic, with the goal of developing solutions.

NATIONAL DATA

Data is necessary to determine health disparities and other patterns of health outcomes among populations. Health outcomes include mortality and cause of mortality. Currently, mortality databases and reporting systems in the United States list homicide as a cause of death but do not indicate who caused the death.[27] The social epidemiologist Nancy Krieger and colleagues called for public health agencies to include law-enforcement-related deaths to be included as a notifiable condition, given that it was a more common cause of death compared to some of the existing notifiable diseases in some 122 cities with populations of more than 100,000.[28] Surveillance and monitoring or timely and routine data collecting on law-enforcement-related deaths allow for an objective assessment of the impact at the city, county, state, or national population levels. Moreover, being able to see how these relate to practices and policies of law enforcement agencies and agents is a necessary step in creating a system for accountability. Krieger and colleagues emphasized that the United States should not need to rely on a UK newspaper website (the *Guardian*) to report police violence; US public health agencies could begin reporting this information in a timely matter.

Unfortunately, no US-based governmental agency or federal legislation has systematically documented or resolved the issue of reporting police shootings. Thus, the current sources of data for police violence as a result of police shootings involving mortality include public sources of gathered data, including the websites *Fatal Encounters, The Counted, Fatal Force,* and *Mapping Police Violence.*[29] These can be used as a starting point to build a dataset for a city, county, state, or region of interest, along with national analyses. These data will be utilized to supplement the statewide and county patterns outlined in this chapter.

Fatal Encounters is a database based on a large project with a multi-disciplinary team at the University of Southern California.[30] It was based on the premise that police violence information should be publicly available. Thus, researchers have donated their time and energy and request donations from the public to continue this project until the federal government or state agencies can enact a policy to collect these data officially. The database contains the name, age, race, and sex of the person shot as well as the date of the incident, address location, city, county, state, and the law enforcement agency involved in the shooting.[31] The type of force and the cause of death were also listed. The website contains a dashboard that one can use to explore the site or download CSV files. The most significant benefit of *Fatal Encounters* was its breadth (nationwide), its timeframe (2000 to 2021), its inclusion of deaths at the hands of law enforcement (all forms), and its accessibility (it was free to use and download data from). There were also brief descriptions and supporting document links to check original reporting sources.

The Counted database was started in 2015 by the *Guardian*, a UK-based newspaper, in an attempt to provide a record of the number of people killed by law enforcement in the United States.[32] This was done as a response to the police shooting of Michael Brown in Ferguson, Missouri, in 2014. The online database only recorded data between January 1, 2015, and December 31, 2016. The *Guardian* shares data on the website using police reports and witness statements; it also gathers information from news outlets, research groups, and other open-source sites. The database contains the name and pictures of the person shot, as well as the age, race or ethnicity, and sex, and it indicates whether the person shot was armed or unarmed and the classification of the incident (e.g., whether it was a gunshot, Taser, etc.). The database can be sorted by various measures within the site, and there is a link to download the dataset. It was unclear why the newspaper ended these data-collection efforts, but it is clear that their efforts helped bring national and global attention to the issue. In a current news report regarding police violence, they cited data from

Mapping Police Violence; perhaps the *Guardian* has deferred to this source as taking a lead role.

Fatal Force is a website that provides a variety of graphs and tables that summarize some of the data; it also provides a map plotting each location of a deadly shooting.[33] The website can be searched by various measures such as age, race, sex, state, and whether the shooting suspect had a mental illness or a weapon, as well as whether the officer had a body camera on. The data can be downloaded straight from the website. The benefits of this website are that it focuses specifically on police shootings and that it was the most updated to the present time, with a timeframe from 2015 to 2023. They, too, include a link to their data source.

Mapping Police Violence is a website that compiles data from *Fatal Encounters*, *Fatal Force*, official government data sources, and Google news alerts.[34] The database contains measures including name, age, race or ethnicity, sex, date of the event, the street address where the event occurred, and whether a firearm was used in the incident, among other variables. A total of 11,777 records of individuals killed by law enforcement exists in the database, which can be downloaded in its entirety and covers the years from April 2012 to June 2023.

Last, we point out that there has been some expressed enthusiasm regarding the Centers for Disease Control and Prevention's (CDC) National Violent Death Reporting System (NVDRS). NVDRS is the only state-based surveillance system that includes the "who, when, where, why, and how" for violent deaths.[35] A study conducted by the medical researchers Andrew Conner and colleagues compared NVDRS against open-source databases and found a high level of consistency.[36] The authors of this study cross-linked data sets from *Fatal Encounters*, *Mapping Police Violence*, *Gun Violence Archive*, *The Counted*, and *Fatal Force* for the year 2015. The researchers concluded that NVDRS was a comprehensive way to analyze fatal shootings of civilians by law enforcement officers. Still, the data will become better when the data set expands beyond the current twenty-seven states to include all fifty states.[37] Nevertheless, despite the advantages of NVDRS compared to other official sources, such as supplementary homicide reports or the National Vital Statistics System, the authors found that some open-source datasets identify more officer-involved shootings in real time, as there was an eighteen-month lag between when a shooting occurs and the data becomes available; this lag occurs because a coroner's report is included in the analysis. The states listed as available for this book include Colorado, New Mexico, and Utah, but as of 2015, it did not include Tennessee or Texas. Unfortunately, gaining access to these data required submitting an application and seeking approval, which was not provided to the authors at the time of this book's publication. Fortunately, researchers have found consistency between the public source data and the NVDRS data for Denver, Colorado, from 2015 to 2019.[38]

One major obstacle encountered in every city and county Durán studied after Denver was that decision letters and DA records on officer-involved shootings were almost entirely not made publicly available. Instead, Durán and his students had to rely on newspaper records through *Newsbank Access World News*, local newspapers, and internet searches of official agencies to put together a timeline of shootings. Now that data is available from additional sources (i.e., *Fatal Encounters*, *Fatal Force*, *The Counted*, and *Mapping Police Violence*), they will be reviewed and incorporated when relevant to ensure increased accuracy for the years between 2000 and 2020.

In contrast to the lack of data on officer-involved shootings, the Death Penalty Information Center provides great insight into the number of executions in the United States.[39] For example, from 2000 to 2020 there have been 931 executions, for an average of forty-four killings per year. These numbers differ significantly from estimates of around one thousand officer-involved shooting deaths per year; this means that during the same timeframe, there were 21,000 officer-involved killings. The typical way we think about a punishment of death at the hands of the state is the death sentence, which is handed down at the end of a jury trial; we can see here that there is a much more frequent form of death at the hands of the state, one that takes place extra- or prejudicially: the officer-involved shooting incident.

REGIONAL DIFFERENCES

Each community has its own localized history. States vary in terms of climate, demographics, geography, and politics. As a methodological base,

Durán has always utilized ethnography to learn as much as possible about each county.[40] In addition, archival and primary documents were important for describing the contextual past. Moving to different states and regions of the country pushed Durán to gather and include more observations in his dataset, based on comparisons. As officer-involved shootings occur in different geographic contexts, characteristics can be quantified and coded to yield analyses that reflect the distinct issues encountered by residents living in these social environments. Contributing to the discussion regarding how patterns of officer-involved shootings differ by geographic areas were two journalists, Joel Garreau, from the *Washington Post*, and Colin Woodard, from many news outlets but most recently *Politico*.[41] These writers stand out in terms of describing regional, environmental, and social differences in the United States. Garreau stated that while there may be fifty states and three countries in North America, the continent really comprised nine nations, each living in a different reality. Woodard agreed that there has never been one America, but rather than nine nations, he argued that there were eleven nations, each with their own regional culture. These journalistic insights will be merged with ethnographic observations. For comparability to the Denver study, the years between 2000 and 2020 were selected.[42] Our focus centers on counties as the region of observation. These were the areas reviewed by district attorneys, and they often highlight greater community racial and economic variation in comparison to cities. Counties often include urban and rural geographies and allow for the inclusion of white flight to the suburbs along with inner-city gentrification patterns.

ROCKY MOUNTAIN REGION

The geographical area we will be referring to as the Rocky Mountain region is defined by its large mountain ranges and was described as the "Empty Quarter" by Joel Garreau and the "Far West" by Colin Woodard. Garreau described the Empty Quarter as the area perceived as the "West," where values and ideas date back to the frontier and where early settlers had to learn to make use of the land.[43] Woodard described the Far West as an area of the country where geography and climate made it difficult to establish the same farming and lifestyle techniques that were employed in the eastern nation of "Greater Appalachia."[44] Woodard emphasized how federal control of the land, as it became incorporated into the United States, shaped residents in the Far West to push for increased local decision making, inculcating a culture of individualism and a level of hostility toward authority.

COLORADO: DENVER COUNTY

As most of this book's focus has been on the data collected in Denver, Colorado, but this is just one city and county in a state of 5.84 million people as of July 1, 2022.[45] The state has 103,637 land square miles, for which the population was 55.7 per square mile. The five most populated counties in the state (along with its most populated city in parentheses) are El Paso (Colorado Springs), Denver (Denver), Arapahoe (Aurora), Jefferson (Lakewood), and Adams (Thornton). The cities with larger populations have their own police departments; many of the rural communities are patrolled by county sheriff's offices. According to the 270toWin website, Colorado has voted primarily Republican for the presidential election from 1920 to 2004 but has voted with Democrats up to 2024.

Based on 2016 data, the *Guardian* ranked Colorado as having the ninth-highest rate in the country for deaths at the hands of law enforcement (.59 per 100,000). Based on data acquired from *Fatal Encounters* and cross-listed with *Fatal Force* for the years between 2000 and 2020, there were determined to be 474 records of individuals who had been shot and killed by law enforcement officers.[46] The rate of killings compared to Colorado's population was .43 per 100,000 over a twenty-year period, with the highest years continuing each year after 2016. The number of shootings was highest in 2018, in which forty-six individuals were shot and killed by law enforcement officers, resulting in a rate of .83 per 100,000. During the timeframe between 2000 and 2020, Colorado did not execute any of its prisoners on death row and decided to abolish the death penalty in 2020, following a recognition that the penalty could not be administrated equitably in the state.[47] Thus, death at the hands of the state was not ever occurring after an adversarial court process but, instead, taking place before an individual had been arrested and thus afforded fewer constitutional protections. In 2015, the Colorado state legislature passed a senate bill (SB 15-217) to force police agencies to report whenever a law enforcement officer fired a gun at a person.[48] This legislation was repealed, and data collection ended on June 30, 2020.[49] However, it appears that a new senate bill (SB 20-217) will ensure that all peace officers will continue to report these data to the Division of Criminal Justice beginning January 1, 2023.[50]

Based on data availability in these other geographical areas, the time-frame is limited to 2000 and 2020 for comparability purposes. Denver had 152 shootings at a rate of 1.15 shootings per 100,000 residents, and 56.6 percent (n=86) of the shootings resulted in death at a rate of .69 per 100,000 residents. Based on the five US counties studied in this chapter, Denver ranked second highest for its shooting rate and for its death rate. As of 2023, three years past the timeframe for the data analyzed and presented in this book, officer-involved shootings continue to occur in Denver. The district attorney data indicate there were seven shootings in 2021, five in 2022, and nine in 2023.[51] Based upon trend data outlined over thirty-eight years, there appeared to be a slight decrease in the rate since 1980 and 1990 but probably not on a scale from 2000 to the present significant enough

TABLE 6.1. Law Enforcement Shootings in Select US States Between 2000 and 2020

Area: State and county	Population average	Shooting count	Shooting deaths count	Shooting rate (per 100,000)	Death rate (per 100,000)
Colorado	5,068,598	N/A	474	N/A	.43
Denver	622,209	152	86	1.15	.69
Utah	2,782,590	N/A	183	N/A	.30
Weber	232,039	39	26	.78	.52
New Mexico	2,018,674	N/A	271	N/A	.63
Doña Ana	203,957	54	37	1.22	.84
Texas	25,266,083	N/A	1,474	N/A	.27
El Paso	790,406	66	43	.38	.25
Tennessee	6,351,072	N/A	401	N/A	.30
Knox	433,834	56	35	.62	.38

Note: Locations are listed in the order they were discussed.

to remove Denver from the list of the nation's leading cities and counties with officer-involved shootings.

UTAH: WEBER COUNTY

The State of Utah's unique history was based primarily on the religious influence of the Church of Latter-Day Saints, who fled to the state from persecution elsewhere.[52] The geographic region is scenic with mountains, lakes, green vegetation, and also areas with extreme deserts. The state experiences all four seasons—fall, winter, spring, and summer. As of July 1, 2022, Utah had a population estimate of 3.38 million residents within 82,377 square miles, or 39.7 persons per square mile.[53] The five most populated counties in the state (with its most populated city highlighted in parentheses) are Salt Lake (Salt Lake City), Utah (Provo), Davis (Layton), Weber (Ogden), and Washington (St. George). According to the 270toWin website, Utah has voted Democrat when Franklin D. Roosevelt (1932–1944), Harry S. Truman (1948), and Lyndon B. Johnson (1964) ran for president but has voted for Republican candidates from 1968 to 2024.

In 2016, the *Guardian* ranked Utah as having the thirty-fourth highest rate of deaths at the hands of law enforcement in the country, at a rate of .27 homicides per 100,000. Despite a one-year lower ranking for the United States, it was high in comparison to the number of homicides that occur in the state. The *Salt Lake Tribune* published a news article in 2014 titled "Killings by Utah Police Outpacing Gang, Drug, Child-Abuse Homicides."[54] The journalist reviewed nearly three hundred homicides from 2010 to 2014 and found the use of force by police officers was the second most common way, after intimate partner violence, for Utahns to kill one another. Almost all of the shooting deaths had been considered legally justified. The journalist interviewed several sources to discover why law enforcement officers in Utah killed so many people; the explanations ranged from a violent society, training, and a lack of civilian oversight. Despite this news report, it did not appear there was any legislation passed to collect data on shootings or to limit law enforcement powers. Based on the *Fatal Encounters* data reviewed to determine Utah averages from 2000 to 2020, there were 183 police shooting deaths, for a rate of .30 per 100,000. This rate was similar to the rate in the state of Tennessee, higher than Texas, and lower than Colorado and New Mexico. According to the Death Penalty Information Center, Utah has executed one individual from 2000 to 2020.

To provide a context for Utah, it is important to highlight that Durán grew up in Salt Lake County (Midvale) and that his transformative years between the ages of twelve and twenty-four were in Weber County, Utah (Huntsville and Ogden). The geographic area was part of a metropolitan belt known as the Wasatch Front, which combined cities and suburbs of around two million residents. It stretches from Santaquin in the south, Salt Lake City in the center, and Logan in the north. Durán's previous research in Weber County and the state of Utah found historical problems involving racial and ethnic discrimination and disparities that highlight structural inequalities.[55] Much of this was reflected in disproportionate minority contact for juveniles at the point of arrest, a lack of racial and ethnic representation, and disproportionately higher rates of incarcerations for Blacks and Latinos compared to whites. As of July 2022, the population of Weber County included 269,561 residents, which were 75 percent white, 19 percent Latino, 2 percent Black, and 2 percent Asian.[56] The Latino population has been the fastest growing. For example, in 2000 Latinos were 13 percent of the population whereas the white population was at 83 percent.

From 2000 to 2020, there were thirty-nine officer-involved shootings in Weber County, of which 67 percent (n=26) resulted in death. All the shootings were of males. Based on various assessments, at least 67 percent of the individuals shot were white, 26 percent were Latino, and 3 percent were Black; the racial and ethnic identity of 5 percent of individuals shot could not be determined. Compared to the population, these numbers seem to highlight that whites were shot less frequently, followed by Latinos, then Blacks, who were shot more frequently. One benefit available in Weber County was that as of 2020, the district attorney began providing body-cam footage and force investigation team reports somewhat similar to the DA officer-involved decision letters used in Denver.[57]

Contrary to many law enforcement agencies around the nation being criticized for shooting Black residents, the low proportion of Blacks living in Weber County and in the state of Utah more generally reduced this level of condemnation. Despite a higher proportion of Latino residents who were shot by the police, these shootings did not generate a heightened level of attention or denunciation. The shootings that did generate disapproval were those in which officers shot white residents. For example, one officer-involved shooting that generated a tremendous amount of debate was of a thirty-seven-year-old white military veteran named Matthew Stewart. On January 4, 2012, Mr. Stewart encountered a "knock and announce" drug raid by the Weber-Morgan Narcotics Strike Force at his home.[58] It was reported that during the raid, Mr. Stewart shot and killed one officer (Officer Jared Francom) and injured five other officers before he was shot twice and arrested. He reported to a newspaper that he had just woken up from sleep to begin working a graveyard shift when plainclothes men armed with guns began firing at him.[59] He didn't hear the men announce themselves as police serving a search warrant. Fearing for his life and thinking he was being robbed, Mr. Stewart fired back in self-defense. After being arrested, police discovered sixteen marijuana plants growing in his basement. The outcome of the incident made many residents question the chosen strategy to fight a "war on drugs" utilizing SWAT tactics. Unfortunately, the legal debate was never reached, as Mr. Stewart committed suicide in his jail cell 506 days after his arrest.[60] It was unclear why Mr. Stewart committed suicide; family members were shocked to hear the news.[61] Earlier reports described his difficulty adjusting to life with a colostomy bag, which he needed after being shot in the stomach; never-ending pain in his leg from a bullet wound; and frustration regarding his legal defense.

A couple of years later, a documentary titled *Peace Officer* featured a retired law enforcement officer, William "Dub" Lawrence, who questioned the official account of the Matthew Stewart shooting based on his forty-five years as an investigator and his analysis of the crime scene. Mr. Lawrence, who had at one time been elected sheriff of Davis County, determined that officers had probably fired first and that one or more officers may have actually been shot by friendly fire (a shooting by a fellow officer).[62] The retired officer, Mr. Lawrence, felt a sense of guilt: He was one of the officers who brought the SWAT unit to Utah based on what he had learned from the Los Angeles Police Department. He believed a SWAT unit had also wrongfully killed his son-in-law despite being found legally justified based on his analysis of the crime scene. Five years after the shooting incident in 2012, Mr. Stewart's mother was still trying to clear her son's name and was finding solace among other victims of police violence.[63] Officer Francom's wife, children, and fellow officers continued to mourn his death; the city named its public safety center after him.[64]

The police department spokeswoman reported steps to ensure that a tragedy like this would not happen again by improving departmental equipment, training, and tactics.[65]

This case, along with the incidents involving white suspects, highlights the concept of "interest convergence," developed by the legal scholar Derrick Bell.[66] Bell posits that given the racial hierarchy in the United States, changes in practices will occur when they benefit whites. Thus, if the white community experiences the negative impact of officer-involved shootings, greater rules and regulations will develop to control law enforcement discretion. In this manner, the statewide review seemed more critical and policy oriented. The officer-involved shooting incident of Matthew Stewart is not the only questionable shooting that has occurred in Weber County. There were additional shootings where family members disputed officer decision making and even some shootings where officer body camera footage made the shooting look worse.[67] Utah, as a state and as highlighted by Weber County, demonstrated that officer-involved shootings were a significant cause of loss of life, second only to domestic violence. It also highlighted that despite the disproportionate killing of Latinos, it was primarily the problematic and questionable killings of white residents that drew criticism. Despite interest convergence in which whites were negatively affected, these shootings have not resulted in greater transparency or new limits to law enforcement powers. Based on the shooting and death rates from 2000 to 2020, the years between 2017 and 2020 were Utah's highest in a four-year period (n=15 shootings, whereas other four-year increments ranged from one to nine). According to the Weber County Attorney's website, the number of shootings remained elevated: There were three reported shootings in 2021, one in 2022, and six in 2023.[68]

THE BORDERLANDS

The journalists Joel Garreau and Colin Woodard both acknowledged the influence of Mexico and Spain on the border region of the United States and Mexico. Garreau labeled this nation of the United States as "Mex-America" because of the high population of Mexican Americans, use of the Spanish language, and cultural influences.[69] Its geographic reach extended from Los Angeles to Tucson, San Antonio, and Houston. Garreau reported a belief that MexAmerica may be the most misunderstood of the Nine Nations because of a lack of clarity regarding how many Hispanics, documented and undocumented, live in the area. He also noted the Anglo level of prejudice toward Hispanics, which are considered "as one undifferentiated mass of greasers and wetbacks" despite the heterogeneity that exists among this ethnic/racial group.[70] There has been a long history of racism against Mexican Americans in the Southwest, which tends to be less discussed in national discussions about racism.[71]

Woodard, on the other hand, identified this nation of the United States as "El Norte" because it was one of the oldest Euro-American nations, dating back to the sixteenth century as part of the Spanish empire. The border between both countries, Mexico and the United States, resembled East Germany and West Germany during the Cold War; the militarized, walled border separates two peoples with a common culture. It was also home to a large and growing Hispanic population expected to exert an increasingly greater political and social influence on the United States. In Durán's previous research, he learned that this geographic area was considered the birthplace of Hispanic organizing, which developed into street organizations wherein marginalized youth participated in protective yet divisionary survival strategies that existed alongside state violence.[72] It was also a place where Hispanics could become doctors, lawyers, politicians, professors, and other types of professionals. The communities stretching along the US-Mexico border have some of the lowest rates of homicides in the country. In addition to the public data sources listed earlier, we also found a website devoted to law enforcement shootings on the border titled *Southern Border Communities Coalition*, which brings together networks from the southern border seeking to improve the quality of life of border residents by promoting policies and solutions.[73] One of the links on this website has been keeping track of fatal encounters with US Customs and Border Protection since 2010.[74]

NEW MEXICO: DOÑA ANA COUNTY

New Mexico, nicknamed the Land of Enchantment, was acquired as a territory of the United States after the Treaty of Guadalupe Hidalgo and much later became the forty-seventh state.[75] As a state, New Mexico is distinct as having some of the oldest inhabited communities in the United States, ones existing centuries before European colonization. The state is home to twenty-three Native American tribes consisting of nineteen Pueblos, three Apache tribes, and the Navajo Nation. The early presence of explorers from Spain formed a mixed culture and family that existed before the US westward expansion.[76] Much of the state is rural. As of July 1, 2022, New Mexico had a population estimate of 2.1 million residents in 121,313 land square miles, with a population of 17.5 per square mile. The five most populated counties in the state (with the most populated city in that county highlighted in parentheses) are Bernalillo (Albuquerque), Doña Ana (Las Cruces), Santa Fe (Santa Fe), Sandoval (Rio Rancho), and San Juan (Farmington). According to the 270toWin website, since statehood in 1912, New Mexico has voted for Democrats in seventeen presidential elections and Republicans in twelve elections.

In 2016, the *Guardian* ranked New Mexico as having the second highest rate of deaths at the hands of law enforcement in the country (1.1 per 100,000 residents). This trend has continued, and after the murder of George Floyd, the *Guardian* published an article in 2021 inquiring whether the state was ready to change.[77] As pointed out in this news article, the city of Albuquerque in the county of Bernalillo has received much media coverage for various shootings; it was the city ranked second highest in the nation for fatal police shootings between 2015 and 2021, with a rate between 1.0 and 1.25 per 100,000 residents.[78] Even as early as 2014, the US Department of Justice's Civil Rights Division concluded that the Albuquerque Police Department "engages in a pattern of practice of unconstitutional use of deadly force," which was determined by a review of all fatal shootings by officers between 2009 and 2012.[79] Based on the *Fatal Encounters* data reviewed to determine New Mexico counts from 2000 to 2020, there were 271 shooting deaths, a rate of .63 per 100,000. This was the highest rate for any of the states included in this book and was more than double the rate found in the states of Tennessee, Texas, and Utah. Contrary to other areas around the country seeking to increase transparency, it was reported that after a law enforcement task force turned over their investigative report to the district attorney and the shooting was ruled justified, it was then sealed, preventing the public from reviewing the evidence.[80] According to the Death Penalty Information Center, New

Mexico has executed one resident from 2000 to 2020; in 2009, they became the fifteenth state to abolish the death penalty.

The major difference Durán observed while living (2006 to 2014) and researching Doña Ana County, New Mexico, which includes the city of Las Cruces, was the presence of Hispanic police officers, judges, and a community in which Hispanics were the majority of the population. Many of his college students majored in criminal justice and desired careers in law enforcement.[81] The county population in July 2022 was 223,337 residents, of whom 69 percent were Hispanic, 26 percent white, 3 percent Native American, and 3 percent Black.[82]

From 2000 to 2020, fifty-four individuals were shot by law enforcement officials in Doña Ana County. Sixty-nine percent (n=37) of these shootings resulted in death, and 94 percent of the shootings were of males. Fifty-seven percent of the shootings were of Latinos, 26 percent white, 7 percent Black, 4 percent Native American, and 6 percent unknown. Compared to the county-level population, this indicated Hispanics were shot less frequently, whites comparably, and Blacks and Native Americans more often but less numerically. The shootings in Doña Ana County highlighted the issues pertaining to the state of New Mexico but also as a border state with Mexico, where many different law enforcement agencies are involved in surveillance and security. Border Patrol checkpoints were additional hot spots because individuals unfamiliar with the US-Mexico border can be surprised about what may transpire when passing a federal agent, drug-sniffing dogs, or various types of surveillance equipment. Many of the other descriptive patterns involving an individual with a knife, bat, gun, or vehicle were repeated, resulting in a person getting shot by law enforcement.[83] There were lawsuits in disagreement and police violence that went beyond shootings to also include chokeholds and other controversial practices that were supposedly nonlethal.[84]

At this point of the book, only two officers were criminally charged and found guilty of a shooting. A law enforcement shooting between two off-duty officers stands out in the number of times prosecutors sought to prove guilt but were unsuccessful each time. On October 28, 2014, two Santa Fe County sheriff's officers, Tai Chan, and Jeremy Martin, were on their way back to Santa Fe, New Mexico, after transporting a prisoner to Safford, Arizona, and they spent the night at a hotel in Las Cruces, New Mexico.[85] After transporting the prisoner, they rented a room around

4 PM on a Monday and went to a restaurant-type bar, where they both consumed large amounts of alcohol and watched football. They got into an argument at the restaurant, and the quarrel escalated in their hotel room. Tai fired several rounds from his duty weapon shortly after midnight, hitting Jeremy five times in the back, rear end, and arm as he fled to the elevator.[86] They both were around the same age, twenty-seven and twenty-nine, and both had worked for about three years as Santa Fe County sheriff's deputies. Jeremy had a wife of twelve years and three children. After the shooting, Tai was charged with murder; he pleaded not guilty, claiming the shooting was self-defense.[87]

At his murder trial, Tai testified that Jeremy had threatened to frame him for murder and pointed a gun at him. In self-defense, Tai reported that he grabbed the firearm away from Jeremy and fired ten shots as Jeremy fled.[88] Tai testified that he and Jeremy had had few interactions before this transport and were only placed together because Tai's regular partner could not travel, for medical reasons. Tai told Jeremy at the restaurant that Jeremy was guilty of not saving two individuals in a double homicide because he had not arrived quickly enough, which angered Jeremy. After returning to the hotel, Jeremy punched Tai in the face and threatened to shoot him; Tai got a hold of the gun and started firing. The judge declared the case a mistrial because the jury could not reach a consensus on any of the charges.[89] The case was retried a second time, resulting in another mistrial. The third time the case was retried, the judge dismissed the case and fined the DA for prosecutorial misconduct regarding a report over alleged evidence tampering and violating Tai's right to a speedy trial.[90] In this case, the authors of this book are not attributing guilt to either party but pointing out how difficult it can be for officers to face criminal charges and be found guilty, even when off duty, and when the person shot or killed is also a fellow law enforcement officer.

TEXAS: EL PASO COUNTY

Texas, nicknamed the Lone Star State for its state flag, is the second-largest state in the country (after Alaska), with 268,597 square miles. As of July 1, 2022, Texas had an estimated population of 30.03 million residents, with 111.6 persons per square mile. The five most populated counties in the state (with the most populated city in that county highlighted in parentheses) are Harris (Houston), Dallas (Dallas), Tarrant (Fort Worth), Bexar (San Antonio), and Travis (Austin). Historically, law enforcement officers working for the Border Patrol and Texas Rangers were actively involved in police violence.[91] The historian William Carrigan reported that the highest levels of violence in Texas occurred in southern Texas, where the Texas Rangers often joined Anglo aggression by going on a "brutal binge of retaliation, summarily killing hundreds of Mexicans without due process of law."[92] Acts of violence by Border Patrol and Texas Rangers have been documented by the historians Kelly Lytle Hernández, Monica Muñoz Martinez, and David Romo.[93] According to the 270toWin website, Texas was originally a state in favor of the Democratic Party until the election of Hoover in 1928. Since 1980, this state has favored Republican candidates.

In 2016, the *Guardian* ranked Texas as having the twenty-eighth highest death rate at the hands of law enforcement in the country. Based on data acquired from *Fatal Encounters* and cross-listed with *Fatal Force* for the years between 2000 and 2020, there were 1,474 records of individuals who had been shot and killed by law enforcement officers. The rate of killings compared to Texas's population was .27 per 100,000. Despite such a high number of killings, the large population resulted in this rate being the lowest of the five states explored in this book. According to the Death Penalty Information Center, Texas executed 371 individuals during the time frame between 2000 and 2020.[94] Thus, law enforcement officers were killing residents four times more frequently than even the state with the most significant numerical use of the death penalty.[95] The Texas Justice Initiative (TJI), a nonprofit organization, has collected, analyzed, and published data on officer-involved shootings in Texas from 2016 to 2023. When analyzing data from 2015 to 2018, they found that officers involved in shootings tended to be younger officers, particularly under the age of thirty (33 percent), male (97 percent), and predominantly white (69 percent).[96] These percentages exceeded the age, sex, and racial demographics for all Texas officers. Based on their analysis of data from 2016 to 2019, TJI found that the civilians shot were primarily white (36.3 percent), Hispanic (32.9 percent), or Black (27.8 percent).[97] Males were also more likely to be shot (93.5 percent).[98] That TJI was able to analyze these data came from a law that became effective on September 1, 2015, requiring law enforcement agencies to file a simple report within thirty days of an officer-involved shooting, whether fatal or not. In 2017, the law was amended to impose penalties of up to $1,000 daily for agencies that did not properly file these reports.

In terms of homicides, El Paso has continuously ranked as the lowest or one of the three lowest large cities in the United States compared to other cities its size.[99] As of July 2022, the population in El Paso County, Texas, was 837,918 residents, of whom 82 percent were Hispanic, 12 percent white, 4 percent Black, and 1 percent Native American. During the time frame between 2000 and 2020, El Paso County had sixty-six officer-involved shootings. Sixty-five percent of these shootings resulted in death (n=43), and 96 percent of the shootings were of males. Proportionately, 76 percent of the shootings were of Latinos, 12 percent whites, 2 percent Blacks, and 6 percent unknown. One item that was different for El Paso was that there were seven shootings, shot and/or killed, where the name of the individual was never released.

An officer-involved shooting that highlights issues on the border region includes a shooting by a Border Patrol officer in El Paso who fired a deadly shot into Mexico, killing fifteen-year-old Sergio Adrian Hernandez-Guereca on June 7, 2010. The photograph image of the youth lying in blood while his family members mourned was an ominous reflection of state-sanctioned violence. Video footage shows some of Sergio's friends throwing rocks as they observe a friend getting arrested by the Border Patrol agent Jesus Mesa Jr. Sergio, who was described as a hard-working student, was not one of the rock throwers.[100] A Mexico City newspaper editorial described how racism was on the rise in the United States and outlined numerous instances of attacks by hate groups along with state and national discriminatory practices.[101] Seven months later, the Associated Press reported that Sergio's family had filed a $25 million wrongful death lawsuit, and the news agency seemed to partake in a character assassination as they described several arrests Sergio had encountered before this incident.[102] The Justice Department and federal prosecutors reported insufficient evidence to pursue federal criminal charges against the US Border Patrol agent Jesus Mesa Jr. because Homeland Security policy allowed agents to use lethal force against rock throwers.[103]

The American Civil Liberties Union (ACLU) participated in efforts to alter border patrol policies to hold overzealous law enforcement officers in check. The ACLU described how video footage demonstrated that Sergio and his friends were playing a game where the youth ran across a culvert and touched the fence on the US side and Mexico side.[104] But this footage did not show Sergio throwing rocks, only observing. Shortly after the killing of Michael Brown in Ferguson, Missouri, the news magazine *The New Republic* published a story putting a spotlight on shootings by Customs and Border Protection.[105] The journalist reported how officers from this agency had been involved in killing forty-six people since 2005; almost all were people of color, most were unarmed, and none of the officers were indicted or convicted of a crime. Agents' names had been made public for only sixteen of these forty-six incidents. The author of the article reported that the injustices of those who were primarily foreign born had been ignored and that these murders deserved accountability.

The shooting case eventually went all the way to the US Supreme Court in 2020 to determine whether Sergio's family, including other families, of a person standing in Mexico could sue a federal agent who was on US soil. In a 5–4 opinion, the Supreme Court deferred to Congress to allow lawsuits when law enforcement officials were involved in cross-border incidents, thus denying the victims across the border the right to sue. The majority, under Justice Samuel Alito, argued that Sergio lacked constitutional protection against the use of excessive force because he was in Mexico; to do so would have implications for foreign relations and national security. Justice Ruth Ginsburg dissented along with Justice Breyer, Justice Sotomayor, and Justice Kagan. Justice Ginsburg argued that the precedent of *Bivens* was to deter an officer and thus that it should not matter where the bullet landed.[106] Justice Ginsburg stated, "It scarcely makes sense for a remedy trained on deterring rogue officer conduct to turn upon a happenstance subsequent to the conduct—a bullet landing in one half of a culvert, not the other."[107] Ginsburg noted plaintiff briefs describing the numerous instances where this issue had occurred, along with other forms of complaints regarding Border Patrol activities that have gone unaddressed. Thus, this type of behavior required alteration and redress.

Reviewing cases in El Paso County, it was found that one shooting resulted in a grand jury indictment. It involved the April 29, 2015, killing of Erik Emmanuel Salas by the El Paso Police Department's Officer Mando Kenneth Gomez.[108] Erik, twenty-two years of age, was shot three times in the back at his home when reportedly advancing toward officers with a brake pad in his hands. Officer Gomez was apparently the first on-duty officer indicted for an officer-involved shooting, but he was later acquitted of manslaughter and resumed his duties as a police officer.[109] The El Paso City Council agreed to settle the lawsuit with the family for $1.2 million.[110] Encountering accusations that the El Paso Police Department had been using excessive force with near-impunity, the city formed a task force to reduce racial disparities and improve interactions and also began using a crisis intervention team in 2017 after multiple lawsuits. Despite these efforts to improve police practices, the use of the grand jury in El Paso was critiqued because information was often withheld from the public, limiting transparency. As reflected in the seven shootings for which the name of the shooting suspect was never released, the names of the officers involved were also missing, and this made us very curious as to whether every officer-involved shooting in the county was being reported.[111]

THE SOUTH

The South was a region of the country where slavery was legal from 1776 to 1865.[112] It was a region of the country where Civil War battles occurred to end this practice in the United States. It was a place where, after slavery was ended, the Supreme Court decision of *Plessy v. Ferguson* ensured that a Jim Crow South maintained a segregated society between Blacks and whites.[113] The journalist Joel Garreau identified this region of the country or nation as "Dixie," a place where people identify themselves as "Southerners" to distinguish themselves from the North.[114] Garreau reported: "Long a region identified with stagnation—backward, rural, poor, and racist, a colony of industrialization North, enamored of an allegedly glorious past of dubious authenticity—Dixie is now best described as that forever-underdeveloped North American nation across which the social and economic machine of the late twentieth century has most dramatically swept."[115] Garreau also noted that the South was a place where strangers could wave at you and say hello. It was a place that was direct about its intentions, as reflected in the different civil rights strategies utilized by Martin Luther King Jr. in the South and Malcolm X in the North.

Malcolm X reported that white liberals in the North were more like "foxes," whereas whites in the South were more like "wolves."[116] However, he preferred the South because it was direct, in comparison to the hypocrisy of the North. Malcolm stated: "I'd rather walk among rattlesnakes, whose constant rattle warns me where they are, than among those northern snakes who grin and make you forget you're in a snake pit."[117]

Woodard refers to this region, one of his eleven nations, as "Greater Appalachia" because the land was settled in the early eighteenth century by war-ravaged immigrants from Northern Ireland, northern England, and the Scottish Lowlands. In the United States, writers and journalists often referred to these residents as "rednecks," "hillbillies," "crackers," and "white trash." It was an area that had forged an alliance with the Deep South for a "Dixie" coalition and an identity emerging as the "South" because they had joined forces under the Confederacy to fight the Northern Union during the Civil War. Even the emergence of the Ku Klux Klan was created from this warrior order, part of the Appalachian phenomenon designed around individual salvation and defense of traditional social values. Such an organization spread nationwide, creating a secret society that followed its own laws at the expense of Blacks, Catholics, Jews, and foreigners.

TENNESSEE: KNOX COUNTY

Tennessee exists between the Deep South and Appalachia. Scholars described the state as reflecting three different sections: in the west is the city of Memphis (slavery and more aligned with the Deep South), central is the city of Nashville, and the east includes the city of Knoxville, which attempted to stay neutral during the Civil War. However, the state of Tennessee eradicated Native Americans, maintained slavery for as long as possible, and afterward maintained Jim Crow laws of inequality until the 1954 *Brown v. Board of Education* decision forced the adoption of change. It has been a state that has struggled to write its own history and correct its challenges. As of July 1, 2022, Tennessee had a population estimate of 7.05 million residents in 41,233 square miles, with 167.6 persons per square mile. The five most populated counties in the state (with the most populated city in that county in parentheses) are Shelby (Memphis), Davidson

(Nashville), Knox (Knoxville), Hamilton (Chattanooga), and Rutherford (Murfreesboro). According to the 270toWin website, since statehood in 1796, Tennessee has provided electoral college votes for six different political parties for president but has voted Republican since 2000. The state favored Bill Clinton in 1992 and 1996.

In 2016, the *Guardian* ranked Tennessee as having the nineteenth highest rate of deaths at the hands of law enforcement in the country. Officer-involved shootings hold great significance in Tennessee because the Memphis Police Department shared data with James Fyfe, one of the earliest researchers to study officer-involved shootings. It was also the location for the Supreme Court decision of *Tennessee v. Garner*. However, in Tennessee, there is no law requiring an agency to investigate or report officer-involved shootings. The Tennessee Bureau of Investigation functioned as a fact-finding agency when requested by a district attorney to investigate a shooting.[118] At the conclusion of the investigation, these facts were shared with the district attorney, who then decided whether to file criminal charges. Based on the *Fatal Encounters* data reviewed to determine Tennessee counts from 2000 to 2020, there were 401 shooting deaths, at the rate of .30 per 100,000. This rate was similar to the state of Utah and higher than Texas but lower than Colorado and New Mexico. According to the Death Penalty Information Center, Tennessee has executed thirteen residents from 2000 to 2020.

Knox County, Tennessee, includes the city of Knoxville and the town of Farragut. As of July 2022, the population in Knox County included 494,574 residents, 81 percent white, 9 percent Black, 5 percent Latino, and 3 percent Asian. Despite their small numbers, Blacks were segregated into several neighborhoods. Research on police shootings began after Durán began living and working in Knoxville, Tennessee, between 2014 and 2018.[119] In Knox County, from 2000 to 2020, there were fifty-six officer-involved shootings. Sixty-three percent of these shootings resulted in death (n=35); 96 percent of the shootings were of males. Proportionately, 68 percent of the shootings were white, 27 percent Black, 4 percent Latino, and 2 percent Asian.[120] One helpful aspect of data collection was that the Knoxville Police Department provided a list of all of the officers involved in shootings, including those injured, killed, and not hit. The Knox County Sheriff's Office did not report similar information despite members of their force being actively involved in shootings.

This chapter has featured a range of shootings but probably one shooting that best reflects the ongoing issue of racialized police shootings was the shooting death of a nineteen-year-old Black male named Sean Gillispie. The shooting occurred at a local gas station and convenience store in east Knoxville on May 18, 2003. In 2000, the census tract described the community as 90 percent Black and 9 percent white. A white female store clerk had called 911 at 3 AM, reporting a large crowd, including vehicles and loud stereos, that had become unruly.[121] The store was familiar to the police; it was one of the busiest locations in the city for police calls because its parking lot was a hangout spot after the bars closed in Old City. It was also located between two rival housing projects.[122] Around 3:18 AM, two white police officers, Jason Keck and David Ogle, approached a Chevrolet Caprice at the convenience store and spoke to the driver. Sean was sitting in the back seat, and one of the officers became concerned about his hands. Thinking he had a gun, Officer Keck fired one shot, striking Sean in the chest. Afterward, police did find a gun under the passenger seat, $1,000 in cash in the glove box, and substances believed to be cocaine and marijuana. A week later, more than seventy-five people, including family members, friends, and civil rights organizations, came together to hold a candlelight vigil in front of the Knoxville City-County Building downtown.[123]

Three months after the shooting incident, the DA, Randy Nichols, reported that he had reviewed the shooting and that based on the evidence and the officer's perception of a gun being raised, no criminal charges were to be filed against the officer.[124] The family filed a lawsuit against the city of Knoxville based on the conflicting statements of where the gun was in the car, whether Sean could have had a gun in his hands if it was found under the front passenger seat, and how he could be shot in the chest if hiding a gun.[125] The family asserted that Sean was holding his cell phone, and witnesses at the scene also contested possession of a gun or even a reason why Sean would reach for a gun.[126] In response to the lawsuit, the trial court favored the city, and upon appeal, the trial court decision was upheld.[127] The case of Sean attracted national attention when the National Association for Stock Car Auto Racing (NASCAR) driver Bubba Wallace reported that after the George Floyd incident, his cousin, Sean Gillispie, had been killed by a white police officer.[128] This, along with other incidents, led Mr. Wallace to support Black Lives Matter and protest the use of the Confederate flag at NASCAR races. Because of the negative media attention, NASCAR responded by banning the display of the Confederate flag at racing events.[129]

Black residents in Knox County continued to be shot by police at disproportionate rates compared to their population numbers. A recent shooting of a seventeen-year-old Black male student who was shot and killed in a high school bathroom compounded the disproportionate violence occurring in the Black community of Knoxville.[130] If every officer-involved shooting were considered, including misses, the disproportionate rates by race and ethnicity would be even greater, as several of the officer-involved shootings where officers missed included Black suspects. For example, the Knoxville Police Department reported ten additional incidents where shots were fired but missed the subject. Five of these shooting attempts were of Black males, three of white males, and one involving a white male and white female together. Including these shootings would increase racial disproportionality, and therefore, the inclusion of Knox County sheriff's data to include shootings involving the bullets fired but missed is of high interest.[131]

⸺ ❧ ⸺

The data presented in this chapter highlights that officer-involved shootings in the United States are a public health problem. The coverage of one geographic area, Denver, provided a case study of officer-involved shootings, but to get the full magnitude of the issue requires examining communities across the nation. As the chapter includes five states (Colorado, New Mexico, Tennessee, Texas, and Utah) and three regions of the country, we begin to develop a broader glimpse into local challenges where the law allows law enforcement officials to decide whether to use deadly force that results in a level of punishment that exceeds traditional forms of consequence that occur after someone has been arrested, found guilty, and given the ultimate punishment, the death penalty. However, in these cases, the individuals were never arrested, convicted, or sentenced: They were killed and injured prior to any due process of law. Police firearm violence has a major impact on communities, and leaving this issue unaddressed only perpetuates the fact that this is a nation in which many lack legal protection from state violence.

Of the five counties reviewed, Doña Ana County, New Mexico (Borderlands), had the highest shooting rate and highest death rate, followed by (2) Denver, Colorado (Rocky Mountains); (3) Weber County, Utah (Rocky Mountains); (4) Knox, Tennessee (South); and (5) El Paso, Texas (Borderlands). These states range in presidential political party affiliation from Democratic to Republican, and this affiliation does not appear to influence the policies affecting police use of force as the national law allows it. The Democratic states were primarily against the use of the death penalty whereas the Republican states, especially the state of Texas, used it more frequently. However, none of the states utilize the death penalty at the same rate that they allow law enforcement officials to use discretionary decision making when deciding whether to use deadly force with a firearm.

Another pattern we found when examining different counties was that the proportion of Latino residents shot in Latino communities was lower than the proportion of Latino residents shot in communities where whites are the majority of residents and members of law enforcement agencies. In other words, Black and Latino residents were the most overrepresented as individuals shot or shot most often in white communities. Although there were a high number of Latino officers and the majority of residents who were shot were Latino, the disparity was less extreme. In addition, the whites were also not shot at higher rates but were shot in proportion to the size of their population. Future research must examine these disparities and trends on a larger scale. However, we do find that although, yes, the structure of policing can influence individuals from marginalized groups to participate in such incidents, they do not do so at rates that are more extremely slanted in terms of overrepresentation.

7

ACCOUNTABILITY THROUGH LEGISLATIVE ACTION, INSTITUTIONAL POLICIES, AND RESEARCH

E very community featured in this book, along with a countless number of communities of color not analyzed, has had at least one form of protest, community forum, or organization created to respond to police violence.[1] Despite frustration and advocacy for change, certain incidents forced community residents to the streets and public settings to protest. One change noted by the historian Elizabeth Hinton, who covered Black rebellion from primarily 1968 to 1972, along with some noteworthy cases occurring afterward in Miami, Los Angeles, Cincinnati, and then internationally after the killing of George Floyd, was that there was an increasing number of white residents becoming involved in protesting police violence.[2] A large number of these protests even occurred in cities and suburban communities where whites were the majority. This highlights a possible shift in awareness beyond instances of police violence contained in racially segregated areas where social media and news outlets struggle to disseminate information to other audiences. Such events made me reflect upon a coalition of Black, Brown, Native, Asian, and white residents who joined forces in Denver, Colorado, after the killing of Paul Childs in 2003. Not only was the coalition racially and ethnically diverse, but it also comprised men and women and people of every age.

The coalition, which was never given a formal name, was organized by Ernesto Vigil, a previous leader in the Chicano civil rights organization known as the Crusade for Justice.[3] The coalition met regularly from 2003 to 2005 with representatives who worked with various organizations responding to social problems involving the police and the community. The purpose of the group was to initiate change. The process involved organizing and sharing insight at public forums and with the media, along with scheduling meetings with political representatives in the community. At the grassroots level, none of the members of this coalition were employees of law enforcement or city, county, or federal government; instead, they were individuals living and working in the community.

One open forum of note involving this coalition occurred at Brother Jeff's Cultural Center and Café on Martin Luther King Jr. Day on January 19, 2004.[4] Earlier in the day, residents participated in the annual MLK "Marade," one of the largest in the nation. Kim Muhammad of the *Denver Weekly News* reported on the event.[5] She describes the community forum and efforts to combat police brutality and misconduct by sharing insights from each presenter. Brother Jeff welcomed everyone to his cultural center in the Five Points neighborhood and described the importance of MLK's work and the civil rights struggle. Shortly after, Shareef Aleem, the organizer of Operation Get Turney, described the effort to hold Officer Jim Turney accountable for the shooting death of Paul Childs. Steve Nash of Denver Copwatch spoke next. He described his efforts as a white man to document and bring to light differential policing involving young males of color. He was appreciative of the opportunity to speak about these efforts. Earl Armstrong, the head of the Black and Brown Express, emphasized the importance of more Black men asserting themselves in the effort toward contributing to solutions in the community rather than devoting their energies toward street organizations such as the Crips and the Bloods. Robert Durán spoke next about law enforcement labeling Black and Latino youth as being gang members and how their statistics defy benchmark comparisons to the population. Ernesto Vigil, the Chicano historian, described how such labeling had occurred in the past, and a city councilman named Hiawatha Davis challenged these DPD statistics, resulting in the police department altering its gang membership estimates by half. Toward the end of the forum, Marge Taniwaki, a survivor of Japanese internment camps during World War II, reported her role on the newly appointed police review commission along with

Brother Jeff. She emphasized that they both planned to continue the effort to resolve problematic policing issues. The coalition with no formal name continued to meet and organize. However, members went their separate ways, and sustaining such a group over time without an institutional framework was difficult.[6] The formal police review commission that included Brother Jeff and Ms. Taniwaki, initiated by Mayor Hickenlooper, also disbanded as law enforcement and community members disagreed regarding the necessary reforms.[7]

⸺ ⛁ ⸺

Although this story focused on grassroots organizing to create change, it should not be the responsibility of oppressed communities to enact the reforms necessary to improve a society desiring to become a democracy; rather, it is the duty of that society's leaders, laws, and institutions. The research presented in this book has found that officer-involved shootings are a public health problem that has largely gone unaddressed, but allowing this violence to continue must end. Addressing public health problems in the United States requires interdisciplinary, evidence-based action based on data-driven solutions developed by various institutions.

This chapter will contribute to that effort by outlining various initiatives to alter governmental and institutional practices to address police violence, particularly in the reduction, if not elimination, of the use of firearms. Although research on the "use of force" has increased exponentially since 2014, particularly regarding firearms, the changes are yet to be seen. The analysis we will present will be separated into three parts. Part 1 will focus on solutions to *stop* officer-involved shootings, beginning at the governmental and legislative levels to enact sweeping changes to use-of-force laws. The demand for structural change will then focus on law enforcement agencies and what alterations can be created on an institutional level. We then examine how the survival of the oppressed, the most marginalized in US society, has pushed for greater accountability and much-needed structural alterations to ensure a more humane and just future. Part 2 focuses on current *research gaps*; we will argue that intertwining public health and criminal justice can provide evidence-based solutions to inform policy makers about police violence. Part 3 contributes a social-ecological model that draws upon epidemiological criminology to present a collaborative strategy for future data collection systems. Although we currently do not have data to highlight the efficacy of these recommended changes, we hope the findings from our research and previous studies can help design a path forward.

PART 1

GOVERNMENTAL AND LEGISLATIVE ACCOUNTABILITY

The first level of responsibility lies with the federal government. Its role is to enact legislation to stop the overuse of firearms to respond to perceived noncompliance with law enforcement orders. Historically, such restraint has not been placed on law enforcement by legislators but instead occurs under review from the courts (i.e., a second level of responsibility). At least two use-of-force cases have reached the Supreme Court: *Tennessee v. Garner* (1985) and *Graham v. Connor* (1988). *Tennessee v. Garner* established that a law enforcement officer may not use deadly force unless an officer has "probable cause to believe that the suspect poses a significant threat of death or serious physical injury to the officer or others."[8] The justices ruled that the killing of a fleeing suspect is a seizure that must be reasonable under the Fourth Amendment. Determining what that reasonableness should look like was established in *Graham v. Connor*.[9] In that case, the justices argued that the Fourth Amendment's "objective reasonableness" standard could be analyzed to determine whether an incident involved excessive force. The justices argued: "The 'reasonableness' of a particular use of force must be judged from the perspective of a reasonable officer on the scene, and its calculus must embody an allowance for the fact that police officers are often forced to make split-second decisions about the amount of force necessary in a particular situation."[10]

Disregarded in both US Supreme Court cases was whether such actions violated the Fourteenth Amendment's equal protection under the law or the Eighth Amendment's guidance against cruel and unusual punishment.[11] Edward Garner's father attempted to argue that the Fourteenth Amendment had been violated because most of the individuals shot under similar circumstances in Memphis were Black.[12] Such a dismissal from remedying racial inequality was reflected in the US Supreme Court case of *McClesky v. Kemp*, where the majority of justices ruled that statistical evidence of racial discrimination was not enough to invalidate the use of the death penalty. Doing so could open a Pandora's Box after which all criminal justice decision making could be ruled unconstitutional.[13] In *Graham v. Connor*, the Supreme Court maintained that cruel and unusual punishment was not applicable because such a standard only applies after the state complies with guarantees that occur after criminal prosecutions. Such a conclusion was reached despite most state-sanctioned deaths occurring at the front end of the criminal justice system rather than at the end. Thus, no legal restraint was provided.

Legal scholars have often argued that the law continues to serve the interests of the dominant classes.[14] The sociologist and legal scholar Wendy Moore analyzed several landmark US Supreme Court cases to highlight how the court's commitment to precedent has only maintained racial oppression.[15] She stated that the disconnect between formal legal equality and structural reality ignores how historical legal precedent continues to reproduce white privilege, power, and wealth.

In relation to the limits of law, existing federal policies often promote police violence, which systematically leads to various public health disparities and inequities.[16] To date, there are no governmental efforts to address settler colonialism in North America; as such, a discussion questions the entire existence of colonial countries such as the United States.[17] There have been efforts to examine both racism and police violence as public health problems.[18] Leading health organizations in the United States acknowledge that racism is a factor in ethnic and health disparities. According to Rahwa Haile and colleagues, in 1951, a Black-led coalition submitted a petition to the United Nations titled "We Charge Genocide" to highlight the many forms of state violence targeted toward Blacks in the United States.[19] In 2020, the authors emphasized how a working group within the United Nations once again focused on the contemporary patterns of police killings of Black people in the United States as reminiscent of the racial terror produced by lynchings of the past. The National Academy of Medicine (NAM), Institute of Medicine (IOM), and National Academies of Sciences, Engineering, and Medicine have made statements and published reports on institutional bias and structural racism affecting the health of BIPOC (Black, Indigenous, and

People of Color) in the United States.[20] They note: "Research and data clearly show that structural racism and the experience of day-to-day racism result in significant and compounding negative health impacts for people of color."[21] Thus, public health scholars favor policies that value life over death by outlining how an improved infrastructure of harm-minimization policies can reduce violence.[22]

Federal and state legislation can also focus on stricter firearm legislation to limit access to firearms. Possession of an actual firearm or a perceived firearm was found to be present in slightly more than half of officer-involved shooting cases; thus, eliminating or reducing this object could help officers perceive and use a less lethal alternative than reaching for a firearm. However, this does not stop the cases where residents have been shot despite being unarmed. Aaron Kivisto from the School of Psychological Sciences at the University of Indianapolis and two other colleagues conducted a cross-sectional, state-level study to evaluate the effect of state-level firearm legislation on rates of fatal police shootings. They analyzed US data from the *Guardian*'s "The Counted" for January 2015 and October 2016. They found that states with firearm legislation had significantly lower rates of fatal police shootings.[23] They also found that states with laws regulating firearms had lower rates of fatal police shootings.[24]

In addition to addressing access to firearms, states can enact legislation to improve data collection on officer use of force. States such as California and Texas have enacted such legislation and imposed consequences for agencies failing to report.[25] The value of data collection in outlining the problem and providing guidance toward solutions will be highlighted in part 2 of this chapter, but such data collection availability and access were often dependent upon laws to ensure it was collected and instituting consequences if it was not reported.

States can also pass legislation to end qualified immunity, which stems from a US Supreme Court decision that grants officers legal protection unless they knowingly violated the law.[26] For example, the state of Colorado passed SB-217, which made law enforcement officers personally liable for 5 percent of a settlement or $25,000, whichever is less.[27] To protect themselves, officers can purchase liability insurance for around $25 a month, and these premiums can be reduced if officers take de-escalation training and do not have incidents of aggressive policing. Such a decision was an attempt to reduce the amount of money that taxpayers should have to pay out from lawsuits for officers' questionable decision making.[28]

One study questioned what level of influence states might be able to have in reducing officer-involved deaths (OID).[29] The authors examined the impact of current federal laws on each state between the years 2013 and 2019 using the data acquired by *Mapping Police Violence*, US Census data, and uniform crime reports. They found that the Supreme Court decisions did not have a consistent effect among states for reducing the rate or number of OID. The authors cautioned that such results did not mean that these laws had no effect but that the impact was more difficult to ascertain, whereas other data indicators, such as state population size and state rates of violent crime, were found to be better predictors. Moreover, they encouraged greater efforts to reduce concentrated disadvantage in communities to decrease levels of violence. They recommended improved data collection because it was unclear whether prosecutors were pursuing disciplinary consequences for police officers. Thus, the existence of laws did not necessarily imply the enforcement of the law.

Additional forms of transparency and review can also occur at the city or county level by creating independent monitors, civilian review boards, and participatory budgeting. For example, the city and county of Denver established the Office of the Independent Monitor (OIM) after the killing of Paul Childs. Based upon data provided by annual reports, the OIM is responsible for monitoring DPD and Denver Sheriff Department investigations involving complaints and ensuring the process is available to all community members. The OIM provides information regarding the number of violations, specification types, and outcomes of closed complaints. In addition, the office provided a paragraph of information for significant disciplinary cases that were closed in the first half of 2023 that resulted in resignations, retirements, and suspensions of ten or more days.[30] The OIM also provides information regarding commendations and critical incidents involving the use of force. Such an office provides greater transparency in complaints and institutes a perception that inappropriate behavior will be addressed.

Establishing and providing authority to civilian review boards have encountered many obstacles, as outlined in this book, in the city and county of Denver. Many have referred to the city of San Francisco as a model where such community involvement in monitoring the police has occurred.[31]

At the city level, there is also the possibility that participatory budgeting may rein in police departments acting out of line. Community-based federal initiatives were developed under the Equal Opportunity Act of 1964 to incorporate citizen participation. Participatory budgeting, a model that was created in Porto Alegre, Brazil, and has since been adopted in seven thousand cities globally, has been seen as emancipatory.[32] Two researchers examined how the killing of George Floyd by law enforcement officers in Minnesota also put pressure on city officials in Austin, Texas, to address policing issues. Participatory budgeting resulted in reducing a small percentage (2.5 percent) of funding to the Austin Police Department. Despite being a small percentage, the amount of the reduction was $11 million dollars.[33] Nevertheless, the Republican governor of Texas responded by passing legislation to prevent such methods of reducing police budgets, and he deployed state police officers to increase patrol activities, thereby countering the community's efforts to alter police practices.[34] Despite these challenges, we must continue to put pressure on public officials to do more to stop police violence.

INSTITUTIONAL ACCOUNTABILITY: LAW ENFORCEMENT

Another key area for stopping police shootings is to address the institutions of law enforcement. Although there have been important and legitimate calls to "defund" or "abolish" the police, most efforts to alter police practices have been based on various forms of reform.[35] Various studies have sought to evaluate whether policies, departmental leadership, organizational culture, training, mental health, and discipline can alter policing. Law enforcement agencies can reform in response to crises, become defunded, or potentially be placed under federal consent decrees.[36] Early warning systems, external evaluations, lawsuits, and increased transparency can aid in these efforts. Policing can be analyzed under the theoretical framework of a racialized organization.[37] Efforts to alter this institution and its organizational capacity have recently begun at the federal level.

For example, under the Obama administration, the first-ever session on reforming the police was instituted, resulting in the report titled "The President's Task Force on 21st Century Policing."[38] The task force provided several recommendations at levels involving the local government, law enforcement, and community where change can be initiated.

In terms of law enforcement policies, a literature review was conducted by the legal scholar and sociologist Osagie Obasogie and coauthor Zachary Newman on police violence, use of force, and public health in the United States.[39] They examined the role of use-of-force policies in legalizing police violence with public health implications using an online database that documents police force policies (n=18) for various cities in the United States. The coding incorporated themes such as reasonableness, basic human life protections, force, de-escalation, alternatives, mental health, intervening in and reporting on fellow officers' use of excessive force, and the need for medical aid. Based on this analysis, Obasogie and Newman reported: "There is generally a lack of substance and depth in conferring guidance, restriction, or description beyond the constitutional bare minimum articulated by the U.S. Supreme Court in *Graham v. Connor* that police use of force must be reasonable."[40]

In conclusion, the two authors determined that police violence was perpetuated and legitimized by use-of-force policies that, in turn, affect community public health.[41] Current policies they found had only provided officers tremendous leeway in using aggression and deadly force, which has resulted in devastating outcomes on minority communities' health. Both researchers encouraged intervention and reform to current policies to design rules to minimize harm along with protecting the "value" and "sanctity of life."

The political scientists Jay Jennings and Meghan Rubado explored whether the collection of agency-level policy data results in a reduction in officer-involved gun deaths.[42] Specifically, they assessed whether (1) community policing training lowers rates of gun deaths by police, whether (2) assigning officers to regular "beats" will also lead to lower gun death rates by police, and whether (3) the policy of requiring a written report when an officer displays or aims their firearm lowers rates of gun deaths. The authors merged data from the *Fatal Encounters* online database, the US Bureau of Justice Law Enforcement Management and Administrative Statistics (LEMAS), and the US Census Bureau's American

Community Survey. A total of 5,141 police-involved deaths from 2000 through 2015 were included. The dependent variable was defined as the number of officer-involved deaths for every 100,000 people in the community served by the police department. The results indicated that agencies that required community-policing training for nonrookie officers and assigning officers to regular beats did not result in lower gun death rates. However, the policy of requiring a written report when an officer displays or aims their firearm did lead to a decrease of 0.322 per 100,000 in the number of fatalities, which was equivalent to a reduction of forty fatalities over a fifteen-year period. The authors speculate that the policy that reduced fatalities discourages police officers from drawing their guns because it would mean having to deal with additional paperwork; this encouraged the development of better "gun drawing" habits.[43] The early critical criminologist Paul Takagi went a major step beyond a policy requiring officers to disclose when they pull a firearm.[44] He suggested the immediate disarming of the police but felt that even such an effort would not eliminate other forms of police brutality. Although it is hard to imagine law enforcement officers without firearms in the United States, several other countries do not arm their police with guns.[45]

Additional policy changes recommended by the Center for Racial Justice at the University of Michigan that are not outlined in this chapter include (1) "restricting or banning chokeholds and strangleholds," (2) "requiring officers to give verbal warnings before using deadly force," (3) "prohibiting shooting at moving vehicles," (4) "requiring that all reasonable alternatives be exhausted before the use of deadly force," (5) "implementing a duty to intervene if another officer is misbehaving," (6) "banning or restricting no-knock warrants," (7) "requiring the use of body cameras," (8) "residency requirements," (9) "racial diversification," and (10) "limiting the transfer of military equipment to law enforcement."[46]

In terms of the impact that policies can have upon a police department, the criminologist Michael White analyzed 982 shootings resulting in injury or death in Philadelphia between 1970 and 1992. He found that implementing a more restrictive police shooting policy was ineffective when police leadership did not enforce any consequences. Thus, informal organizational rules or culture were possibly more important in addressing, from the top down, than policies that look good on paper but are not followed. The study of organizational culture in policing has a long history, but many of these studies highlight perceptions that uphold secrecy, loyalty, and overcoming the potential and imagined dangers of the job. Being socialized into this culture begins in the training academy. According to the Bureau of Justice Statistics of the US Department of Justice, the average length of core basic training was 833 hours, or twenty-one weeks.[47] The information presented was equally divided between stress and nonstress environments, but four times more instruction hours were devoted to firearms skills (seventy-three hours) than to de-escalation techniques (eighteen hours). The criminologist Robin Engel and colleagues from the Center for Police Research and Policy have published most of the reviews of the literature and evaluations of de-escalation training.[48] In one of these studies, Engel and colleagues identified sixty-four de-escalation training evaluations conducted over a forty-year period where the impact of this training was largely unknown. Thus, these researchers encouraged prioritizing this research.[49] By taking her own advice, the second study conducted by these researchers examined the Louisville Metro Police Department, wherein they found that there was a significant reduction in the use of force (28.1 percent), citizen injuries (26.3 percent), and officer injuries (36.0 percent) in the post-training period after officers received de-escalation training.[50]

Nevertheless, de-escalation training may be difficult to implement when agencies and administrators do not endorse or support such a method for responding to police calls. For example, the sociologist Samantha Simon conducted a year-long ethnography with four police departments and conducted forty interviews with law enforcement officers, which led her to conclude that these officers were primarily being trained to perceive themselves as confronting an enemy, namely, men of color, and that violence was a moral necessity to protect themselves.[51] Despite law enforcement agencies' preoccupation with personal victimization and "warrior training,"[52] there is data to suggest that nonstress training geared more toward intervention can reduce suspect and officer injuries.[53] Nevertheless, personal or close peer victimization has been found to increase use of force, and thus is a key period for increased training resources, as is often used in violence-interrupter programs, to ensure officers do not physically act out.[54]

A team of US and international scholars focusing on police-related research was invited to contribute to an urgent issue paper for the British

Psychological Society in 2021 and share their commentaries on the directions for future research for advancing police use of force research and practice.[55] Scholars encouraged changes in policy and practice. One scholar, the criminologist Michael White, asked, "Can training change officer perceptions and use of de-escalation?"[56] White highlighted that there was almost no research on the de-escalation practices of police and instead that most research focuses on the use of force. White reported the results of a 2020 study by the Tempe, Arizona, police department and a research team at Arizona State University indicating that training can change an officer's perceptions and use of de-escalation. A survey was administered to officers seven months before training and then four months after. Those who received the training were less likely to be condescending, more likely to attempt to build rapport, less likely to use imposing body language (including having their hand on their firearm), and more likely to resolve encounters informally with civilians. White noted that de-escalation tactics were already valued at the Tempe Police Department and that this may not be evidence of the training being the sole influence on these promising results. Nonetheless, White recommended further research on de-escalation training as prevention rather than solely focusing on the use of force. Similarly, other scholars included in the urgent issue paper indicated the need for research on police officers' de-escalation approaches and performance under high-stress situations and the process leading up to the use of force.

The psychologist Kimberly Kahn, another member of the urgent issue paper, reported that reducing racial bias was an understudied topic in the use of force training. In addition, Kahn endorses not just training to address bias but also increasing the time spent developing relationships with the diverse communities that they police to reduce stereotypes. Kahn suggests that addressing these implicit biases would be the first step in attempting to bring about institutional changes and systemic reform. Investigators researching implicit bias, largely unconscious or semiconscious, have debated whether this trait can be changed. Explicit biases are claimed and adopted as part of an identity, but implicit biases are often personally unknown. Examples of officers perceiving a suspect of color to be armed when, in fact, they were not reflect this disconnect. The officer thought they were operating on factual information, but implicit biases may have led to an inaccurate assumption. A criminal justice professor,

Lois James, studied how police officers were more likely to associate Black Americans with weapons and found that a lack of sleep heightened these misperceptions.[57] James stated how the results obtained from studying eighty police officers indicated that implicit bias was subject to change. Thus, improving officer health regarding sleep has important implications for improving fairness and equality in police-citizen interactions. Additional psychological studies have included how Black youth were perceived as older (adultification) and angrier when displaying emotion than white children are, which can result in increased negative consequences.[58]

In terms of training skill sets, there is a strong pattern of negative police interactions with individuals having mental health issues, including in those interactions ending in death. Police are not the ideal interlocutors when a person is in a mental health crisis, yet they are often the ones on the scene. Calls for action to defund and reform police receive support from advocates who desire improved policies and procedures to respond to situations involving mental health needs and crises.[59] Too many examples in this book include a loved one calling 911 in an attempt to receive support for a family crisis only to have it result in injury or death. A review of the literature, including eighty-five studies, of which twenty-one were data driven, found that one-quarter of people living with mental disorders have been arrested by police and that 12 percent interacted with police in their process of accessing mental health services.[60] At least one-quarter of all police interactions with persons with serious mental illnesses in the United States end in death, which translates to a sixteen-fold increase in the risk of dying by police compared to other civilians.[61] According to the *Washington Post* database, police officers shot and killed 460 people nationwide in 2015, of which 124 (26.9 percent) were having a mental or emotional crisis, including suicidal intentions or a history of mental illness, as confirmed by family members or police.[62] The Bureau of Justice Assistance outlines models to improve law enforcement response when a person exhibits a mental health outcome including (1) mobile crisis teams (MCTs), (2) crisis intervention teams (CITs), (3) co-responder teams, (4) emergency medical services (EMS)/ambulance-based responses, (5) flagging systems, (6) standalone training packages/de-escalation training, and (7) case management/high utilizer teams (mental health/law enforcement).[63] CITs were a program integrated within police departments to reduce negative interactions and injury by police officers when responding to persons with mental health outcomes.[64] Crisis intervention teams have been integrated with law enforcement for over thirty years in over 2,700 police departments, but there was a lack of evidence-based evaluation of their effectiveness in reducing arrests or shootings of persons with mental health outcomes.[65]

Law enforcement officers were not only responding to mental health issues in the communities in which they worked; they, too, experience higher levels of stress, trauma, and ambiguity regarding how to manage difficult situations. Researchers have been surprised by why more scholars have not identified the mental health of law enforcement officers and how it affects their daily performance on the job as a key area of police reform.[66] The research literature has found that law enforcement officers experience difficulties involving alcohol/drug abuse, suicide, and problematic behaviors in home settings, including domestic violence between partners and children.[67] Many law enforcement officers underreport mental health issues, and current levels of stigma prevent these types of workers from disclosing such information to their employers.[68]

Finally, discipline was a necessary element in correcting wrongful behavior. However, there is much contention regarding whether law enforcement agencies impose discipline and, if and when they do, whether it is effective enough to change behavior. In Denver, many problems revolved around comparative discipline to ensure that current officer misbehavior was never evaluated more seriously than previous wrongdoing. The problem was that in the past, discipline was light, and thus every future violation was treated similarly. There are some patterns regarding which characteristics may predict more difficulty as officers. The sociologists James McElvain and Augustine Kposowa found young males and officers with fewer than ten years on the force were more likely to receive misconduct cases; these officers were also more likely to be investigated later in their careers.[69] However, the law professor Barbara Armacost has reported that most law enforcement agencies view police misconduct as attributable to isolated factual and moral judgments and downplay the influence of a department's organizational culture.[70] If it does occur, accountability primarily targets individuals or the "rotten apple," not the "rotten barrel." Thus, much of the reason that departmental responses were unsuccessful was because they never addressed the endemic organizational issues.

The rare instances where police departments find misconduct and impose discipline can result in the officer finding employment with another law enforcement agency, a term the law professors Ben Grunwald and John Rappaport define as "wandering officers."[71] These legal analysts collected data on 98,000 full-time law enforcement officers employed by one of five hundred agencies in Florida during a thirty-year period. They found that only 3 percent of these law enforcement officers had been fired and that these are often rehired in smaller agencies and agencies in larger communities of color. These same officers were also more likely to be fired again and subjected to "moral character" complaints. The authors of this study noted their concern about the influence these officers may have had on other officers. The main finding we have for this section is that the institution of law enforcement needs to be altered to be more humane and just.

THE PURSUIT OF HUMAN RIGHTS: THE "VISION AND NERVE" OF THE OPPRESSED

Unfortunately, it has been the marginalized in US society who have generally been the most affected by police violence, as with most public health issues or health disparities.[72] If the rich and powerful were disproportionately targeted, it would more likely result in legal and policing alterations (i.e., interest convergence). Nevertheless, the characteristics presumed to suggest the greatest threat to public safety have primarily included the intersection of sex (male), race and ethnicity (Black, Latino, and Native American), the poor, and residents living in socioeconomically disadvantaged communities. Given this disproportionate impact upon marginalized groups, they have been the individuals who have organized to stop abuse and encourage increased humane behavior and civil rights.

These efforts have primarily consisted of organizing social groups to respond to and address community problems toward which law enforcement had turned a blind eye. Over the past century, various organizations have developed in an attempt to make law enforcement activities more accountable and transparent. They have protested, held forums, collaborated with lawyers and researchers, and even conducted their forms of oversight and fact-finding. Some groups operating in Denver were featured in chapter 1, and other notable groups include the Black Panther Party and Crusade for Justice.[73] Contemporary movements have also included organizations such as Copwatch, which oversee police activities through written and video documentation involving police encounters with the community.[74] Defense attorneys have been of value in helping bring lawsuits or efforts to change existing policies. The American Civil Liberties Union has participated in several initiatives.

Coalitions that can go beyond an oppressed group by crossing over toward developing allies, instituting civilian police review, and finding lawyers to pursue legal lawsuits can often create mainstream bridges of change. Strategies of resistance involving Black, Brown, and Native Unity in conjunction with white support have uplifted communities to pursue a sense of humanity and dignity that has often been denied to human beings delegated as expendable: The vision of a social movement.[75] Nevertheless, the sad reality is that such coalitions have often been lacking as each racial and ethnic group has become segregated into separate social worlds. Given this social reality, both nonviolence and self-defense have been required in bringing about change "by any means necessary." In one of Malcolm X's final speeches, he argued that Black residents needed self-defense if the government did not provide protection:

I do not advocate violence. In fact the violence that exists in the United States is the violence that the Negro in America has been a victim of, and I have never advocated our people going out and initiating any acts of aggression against whites indiscriminately. But I do say that the Negro is a continual victim of the violent actions committed by the organized elements like the Ku Klux Klan. And if the United States government has shown itself unwilling or unable to protect us and our lives and our property, I have said that it is time for our people to organize and band together and protect ourselves, to defend ourselves against this violence.[76]

In the governmental effort to oppose civil rights, mass incarceration developed in the mid-1960s during the War on Poverty and accelerated in the early 1970s during the War on Crime. This removed a large number of Black and Brown leaders from carrying on this struggle.[77]

PART 2

PUBLIC HEALTH RESEARCH ON POLICE VIOLENCE

We found a growing representation of police violence as an outcome or risk factor in the public health literature, along with funding opportunities, conference presentations, and calls for action. Regarding the public health literature, most are indexed and cataloged in PubMed by the National Library of Medicine. There were 242 published articles on PubMed with the keyword "police violence" as of May 29, 2024.[78] Before 2014, these included five or fewer publications per year. These increased to ten to twelve per year in 2016–2019, reaching fifty articles published in 2021. Using the keyword "police shootings," forty-nine articles come up.[79] Most of the health research on police shootings and police violence has been since 2016 (n=217 and n=40, respectively).

The National Institutes of Health (NIH) has funded 536 projects that include the term "police violence" since 1985 in the United States as of May 29, 2024.[80] All NIH-funded projects and related publications are posted on their RePORTER site. Before 2007, one to four projects were funded per year. In 2007, there were twenty, then reaching thirty-eight projects funded in 2022 and forty-eight in 2023. The majority of the projects were funded through the National Institute on Drug Abuse (NIDA) (126 projects) and the National Institute on Alcohol Abuse and Alcoholism (NIAAA) (79 projects) with a substance use focus, followed by the National Institute of Child Health and Human Development (NICHD) (62 projects) and National Institute of Mental Health (NIMH) (60 projects). Using the keyword "police shootings," six NIH-funded projects come up.[81] We see a growing commitment from the NIH to document and understand the contributing factors and consequences of police violence. Not all criminologists have been in favor of using the term "police violence" because they argue that in many circumstances, police officers may primarily be reacting to a real threat from someone armed with a dangerous weapon, primarily a firearm.[82] We are in favor of using the term "police violence" because we have found less than one-third of the cases we examined to be less controversial and because weapons, when possessed, were most often never used. In addition, the term "police violence" also links the historical impact that usually exists with departments using force and not encountering a consequence, even when problematic.

POLICE SHOOTINGS VERSUS POLICE VIOLENCE IN THE LITERATURE

As mentioned, the health literature includes 242 published articles on "police violence" indexed in PubMed as of May 29, 2024.[83] When using the keyword "police shootings," the total number of publications is forty-nine.[84] The literature on police shootings, which formed the data presented in this book, was much more limited, although it was the most commonly published type of violence resulting in death. Shootings, we imagine, should also overlap in collaboration with studies on firearm violence. These examples should include the Gun Violence Archive, mass shootings, and mass killings.[85] It is our desire that the recent US surgeon general's emphasis on firearm violence as a public health crisis will aid in these efforts.

The literature on police violence includes police shootings and police use of guns, as well as other weapons, including vehicles, as well as the use of excessive force and physical violence. The literature on police violence is also broader in terms of the outcomes or factors of interest, including infant mortality, mental health outcomes, suicide attempts, suicide by cop, sexual risk, the risk for HIV, community mistrust of police, legislation, structural racism, and human rights.

MISSING MEASURES AND DATA

We can also discuss the intersection of police shootings, gender, and sexual orientation and the lack of data collected or available to establish data-driven associations. In terms of demographic data for the person shot, we did not have information on gender and sexual orientation. We do not know how many sexual and gender minorities, including transgender or gender-nonbinary individuals, were shot by police in Denver between 1983 and 2020. The police have historically criminalized LGBTQ+

populations that exist within communities of color.[86] Also documented are the negative interactions between LGBTQ+ populations and police, which are associated with increased use of drugs.[87] Hence, there was a strong possibility that LGBTQ+ were included in this analysis. There is also limited data in terms of demographic data for the officer who shot.

Contemporary research on Latino interactions with law enforcement lacks the depth of insight of similar research on Blacks or whites, and researchers have questioned this omission.[88] The best explanation offered is the lack of data collection that has separated Latinos from other racial groups. Such a discussion could also be important in determining why Latinos experience a higher number of officer-involved shootings than whites but fewer than Blacks in some settings. In some of these geographic areas, Latinos and not Blacks encountered greater disproportionality in officer-involved shootings compared to whites. There were also discussions regarding whether Latinas/os have been able to mobilize the media the same way as other racial and ethnic groups. *The Latino Media Gap: A Report on the State of Latinos in U.S. Media* found that less than 1 percent of news stories were devoted to Latinos.[89] Most of these news stories focused on crime or illegal immigration, which contributes to negative stereotypes about this population group.[90] It is also of importance when coding for researchers to point out when an individual is of mixed racial and ethnic heritage, such as white and Latino or Black and Latino, which could result in the undercounting of Latinos. More research is required to understand colorism and how dark- and light-skinned individuals may provoke a different reaction from law enforcement officers based on phenotype. Moreover, using surnames to determine ethnicity or race requires further assessment as to whether they mark ancestry, marriage, or adoption.

Native Americans have also primarily been omitted from many studies on the use of force despite being found to be the most overrepresented in comparison to whites and other racial and ethnic groups.[91] Some of these challenges result from the smaller numerical nationwide population, differences that can exist on reservations compared to these locations, and phenotypical variety that may exist in tribally affiliated groups compared to self-identification. Historically, we know Native Americans have been particularly targeted in the United States by genocide and ethnic cleansing.[92] Asian populations are the least affected by police use of deadly force, but the reasons why seem to be unclear. Many researchers have highlighted how there is tremendous heterogeneity in the group identified as Asian regarding income and migration experience. On average, Indians, Filipinos, and Japanese groups have higher median household incomes than Burmese, Nepalese, Hmong, Korean, and Vietnamese residents.[93] Because of historical, exclusionary immigration policies, it has also been primarily Asians with higher levels of education who have immigrated to the United States.[94] We need increased studies on Asian communities and policing to determine how these interactions may differ from other population groups.

To connect gaps in missing measures and data, researchers have repeatedly stressed the creation of a national database to monitor and understand police use of force involving firearms and incidents that result in death.[95] Moreover, there was encouragement to provide penalties or consequences for agencies failing to report in a timely manner. It should be a goal for any city, county, state, or federal system to have the ability to review scientifically gathered data on social patterns.

PART 3

CRIMINAL JUSTICE AND PUBLIC HEALTH: EPIDEMIOLOGICAL CRIMINOLOGY

The complexity of the issue and the intersecting factors contributing to police violence and police shootings were evidenced by the current literature and challenged by the limited surveillance data sources. This collaboration between Durán and Loza in this book allowed for discussions and exploration of future police shooting research from the place where criminal justice and public health intersect, thus contributing to a framework of epidemiological criminology.[96]

For example, future research using public health models and approaches can include or apply the social-ecological model. This approach can be integrated into comprehensive or collaborative research involving interdisciplinary teams. For example, the work presented in this book lives at the intersection of social epidemiology, criminal justice, and sociology. This is not a novel concept, but its application to racialized police shootings and social determinants of police violence is.

The physician and epidemiologist Etienne Krug and colleagues organized the factors associated with physical, sexual, psychological, and deprivation violence into self-inflicted (i.e., suicidal behavior, self-abuse), interpersonal (i.e., family/partner and community), and collective (i.e., social, political, economic) measures.[97] Their report was not created for police violence or police shootings, but if we use their model to categorize these, these would be considered interpersonal physical violence by a stranger in the community. This was vague and not ideal for police shootings. However, based on the published literature, this grouping of measures was similar to the structure suggested in the social-ecological model, which has not yet been used or adapted for police shooting or police violence research.

SOCIAL-ECOLOGICAL MODEL

The social-ecological model describes measures that contribute to the etiology of an outcome organized in multilevel frameworks, including social environments.[98] Early work described these levels as including interpersonal, organizational, community, and public policy in the context of health promotion and public health interventions.[99]

The Centers for Disease Control and Prevention (CDC) share the social-ecological model of health as one of the "Models and Frameworks for the Practice of Community Engagement," recognizing the interaction between measures for cultural and social norms and the health, economic, educational, and social policies that are represented in each of the model's levels.[100] The levels of the CDC's social-ecological model for health include the individual, relationship, community, and societal. For each level, the CDC defines the type of measures that would be collected when assessing violence prevention.[101] These include the following:

Individual: The first level identifies biological and personal history factors that increase the likelihood of becoming a victim or perpetrator of violence. Some of these factors are age, education, income, substance use, or history of abuse. Prevention strategies at this level promote attitudes, beliefs, and behaviors that prevent violence. Specific approaches may include conflict resolution and life-skills training, social-emotional learning, safe dating, and healthy relationship skill programs.

Relationship: The second level examines close relationships that may increase the risk of experiencing violence as a victim or perpetrator. A person's closest social-circle peers, partners, and family members influence their behavior and contribute to their experience. Prevention strategies at this level may include parenting or family-focused prevention programs and mentoring and peer programs designed to strengthen parent-child communication, promote positive peer norms, improve problem-solving skills, and promote healthy relationships.

Community: The third level explores the settings, such as schools, workplaces, and neighborhoods, in which social relationships occur and seeks to identify the characteristics of these settings that are associated with becoming victims or perpetrators of violence. Prevention strategies at this level focus on improving the physical and social environment in these settings (e.g., by creating safe places where people live, learn, work, and play) and by addressing other conditions that give rise to violence in communities (e.g., neighborhood poverty, residential segregation, and instability, high density of alcohol outlets).

Societal: The fourth level looks at the broad societal factors that help create a climate where violence is encouraged or inhibited. These factors include social and cultural norms that support violence as an acceptable way to resolve conflicts. Other large societal factors include the health, economic, educational, and social policies that help maintain economic or social inequalities between social groups. Prevention strategies at this level include efforts to promote societal norms that protect against violence, as well as efforts to strengthen household financial security, education, employment opportunities, and other policies that affect the structural determinants of health.

This structure of organizing measures has been adapted and applied to various health outcomes, including drug use[102] and risk behaviors and prevention of HIV.[103] It has also been applied to violence as a public health issue,[104] including school shootings, gun violence, and the prevention of firearm injury[105] and suicide.[106] The social-ecological model has not yet been applied to police shootings, although it has been applied to police misconduct[107] and police bias in using deadly force.[108]

The sociologists Roger Dunham and Nick Petersen propose the following when generating evidence-based policies for reducing police bias in the use of deadly force while applying the social-ecological model:

> For all officer-involved shootings, data should be collected on (a) officer/ suspect characteristics, (b) social-ecological context, (c) situational circumstances, and (d) incident outcome. Data on basic officer/suspect demographics (e.g., sex, age, and race/ethnicity) and officer occupational characteristics (e.g., rank, number of prior shootings, and administrative complaints) are necessary for understanding the extent to which officer-involved shootings vary across different segments of the population and police force. Geographic identifiers (e.g., state, county, city, and jurisdiction) should also be collected so researchers can better pinpoint social-ecological predictors. Moreover, the database should include information on whether the suspect possessed a weapon or resisted arrest.[109]

These researchers encouraged the acceleration of evidence-based efforts to reduce officer-involved shootings, given the history of racialized policing, and to ensure more equitable practices.

ADAPTATION OF THE SOCIAL-ECOLOGICAL MODEL FOR POLICE SHOOTINGS RESEARCH

Many of the measures collected and presented in tables A2.2–A2.5 fall under several of the levels of the social-ecological model. However, future studies can expand the data collection to include measures that cover the different areas of the model, thus providing a framework for more comprehensive police shootings or police violence research. Based on measures included in the present study and other studies published in the literature, we propose the following application of the social-ecological model for documentation and prevention of police shootings or police violence research. Depending on the circumstances and outcome of the shooting, assessing some of these measures may not be an option. For example, if the person dies because of the shooting, some post-shooting measures will not be assessed. These are presented in table A2.6 (see appendix 2).

The epidemiologist Jordan DeVylder and colleagues call for action, given the overwhelming evidence documented in their public health literature review, within the social determinants and health disparities framework, on the association between police violence and mental health symptoms, physical health conditions, and premature mortality in the United States.[110] These researchers recognize that despite all the possible or potential interdisciplinary research efforts that can address this issue, a "true solution to this issue requires a drastic reformation or replacement of the criminal justice system, as well as addressing the broader context of structural and systemic racism in the USA."[111] Hence, although research brings attention and generates evidence of how police violence is linked to public health disparities and inequities, research alone was not the solution.[112]

Efforts to decolonize various aspects of US society, including education, politics, employment, and the police, have encountered various obstacles. Neglect at the federal, state, and county levels reflects a story of governmental officials not doing enough to stop law enforcement violence. The standard practice has ignored and suppressed data collection on the topic, so the magnitude of the problem was not measured, reported, or disseminated. Community advocacy and support from the media have resulted in data collection that has shined a light on the extent of the problem. Community groups and residents have long been fighting the battle to have their stories told but have encountered little leverage to do anything to change the system.

In this chapter, we have called on public officials to enact legislation stop the use of law enforcement violence on its residents. We have outlined barriers that prevent change in law and in the institution of law enforcement. Thus, as always, we have had to overly rely on marginalized community members for the creation of change, but in so doing they are often targeted and demonized. Thus, we need the support of more white allies who will not accept injustice. Such efforts, we believe, will include the importance of research and merging different academic disciplinary fields to develop solutions.

CONCLUSION

I t is the summer of 2020, and I am (Durán) watching cable news on the TV.[1] There is a report of a white police officer killing a Black man. Such a news report does not create much shock; I have been consistently researching police shootings for nearly two decades—let alone sifting through centuries of documented killings by agents of the state, even going back to lynching—and I have become resigned to their regular occurrence. It is a repeatedly reported fact that police officers kill Black men at a higher rate than they kill white men. Authority figures, along with many academics, find ways to justify these killings and put the blame on individuals or communities while discounting the centuries of settler-colonial violence, which has disproportionately targeted minoritized groups. Later in the evening, I decide to watch the full recording of the incident. My anger grows with each second of the nine-minute YouTube video of the execution of George Floyd. Three officers held down his body. One officer stands guard against anyone trying to intervene. Witnesses plead with the officers to release their restraints on this man and apply aid to preserve his life. The officers remain defiant. I watch in horror. No help is coming to Mr. Floyd. No one will stop this killing, because individuals who enforce the law are enacting the murder.

After watching something like this, I have to work off my anger. Let the burpees begin! Something has to calm me down, physically and mentally. Exercise and boxing have been family traditions; they have helped us fight and survive colonization. A college education provided me with hope. If I become educated, conduct research, and report results, then I can change policies and practices. Reaching middle age has taught me that what have primarily kept my family alive have been strategies of persistence, not my education from predominantly white institutions (PWIs), earning a doctorate, or working at R1 research universities. The tactics that kept my family alive were physical preparedness, prayer, the faith that things can and will improve, and familial support and commitment to always help one another.

The day after the murder of George Floyd, I ask myself, "Now what?" My son and wife are heading to a protest; I stay home. I'm dismayed about whether protests can fix any of these issues.[2] Protests have been occurring for decades, and state violence persists. My wife calls and tells me to at least drive by the protest to where they are standing alongside the street.[3] My daughter and I drive by, honking the car horn to show our support. Demonstrators cheer in appreciation. The next day, there was another protest, and once again, my wife encourages me to come out. I decided to attend and bring my eleven-year-old daughter. I feel uplifted seeing the support from so many others saying that what occurred was wrong. This is the solidarity or collective effervescence that the sociologist Emile Durkheim never imagined for societies designated as being under fatalistic social control.[4] As we stand near the Bryan Police Department, there are Black, Brown, and white residents standing in solidarity. We receive some occasional heckling; someone driving a truck almost runs over some people.[5] My family and I hold a flag stating "Black Lives Matter." The following week, there was another protest. My frustration pushes me to ask myself what more I can do. The primary contribution I believe I can offer as an academic is to finalize the data collection and submit our long-overdue book proposal to Columbia University Press. The data on officer-involved shootings presented in this book needed to be shared, analyzed and worked up into data-driven policy solutions. Research is my favorite activity, but it has no value until it can be disseminated and then cultivated into dialogue to pressure for change to improve lives and social conditions. In many ways, it reflects social science oriented toward social justice rather than detached observation.[6] It is a sociology interested in public health, choosing a side, advocating on behalf of the underdog, and developing liberatory scholarship.[7]

George Floyd's viewing and funeral were to be held in his home city: Houston, Texas. When this information was shared, my wife and I wanted to attend: Bryan, Texas, is only an hour and a half away. We both want to give our final respects and condolences to Mr. Floyd and his family. Thousands of people showed up to his viewing on June 8, 2020.[8] We wait in line to catch a shuttle bus that will take us to a church. We stand sweating in the Houston heat and humidity, wearing facemasks, as it is still during the COVID-19 pandemic. We are in line next to two members of the Buffalo Soldiers MC. The website for the National Association of Buffalo Soldiers and Troopers Motorcycle Club describes the group as promoting the history of African American veterans to be positive role models for youth and support fellow veterans.[9] Once we catch the shuttle and arrive at the church, I notice a large crowd and the media surrounding the Reverend Al Sharpton, civil rights attorney Ben Crump, and other Black leaders as they speak. We walk to stand in another line, where we are ushered through to see the body of Mr. Floyd as he lies in a casket. When I reach the front, I kneel and make the sign of the cross.[10] Rest in Power, Mr. Floyd. We sign the visitor book and catch a shuttle bus back to where we parked.

I feel a sense that we, as a society, have to do something to stop police violence. The protests are everywhere. A social movement develops involving protests, building on its past efforts, and increased emphasis regarding the importance of Black lives to US society. The lead officer, Derek Chauvin, and several of his fellow officers on the scene are subsequently criminally charged, arrested, and convicted. I think to myself that a chokehold restraint for nine minutes evoked a public response different from the kind often evoked after an officer-involved shooting. A bullet enters a body very quickly; it's less "hands-on" and less likely to result in criminal charges. Either way, video footage may be crucial in showing and providing evidence for when an encounter is particularly problematic.[11] For such a long time, officers simply needed to claim resisting arrest or that the officer feared for their life, and a district attorney would not file criminal charges.[12] The law's granting of the authority to take life as part of a job offers the reassurance that most of these decisions will have few, if any, negative consequences.

───── ⚬∞⚬ ─────

This book began with the funeral viewing of Michael Grimaldo, who was killed by the police, and it ends with the funeral viewing of George Floyd, who was also murdered by the police. These homicides, both problematic, resulted in different outcomes for the officers involved. Nevertheless, they contrast significantly with the delayed law enforcement response that occurred in Uvalde, Texas. Based on the data we have collected and analyzed, most officer-involved shootings were not in response to incidents such as those that occurred in Uvalde; in fact, only 2 percent of shootings in Denver included a homicide occurring before the suspect was shot. We do recognize, however, that officer-involved shootings exist along a continuum. Most shootings in Denver were questionable (48.3 percent), some were less controversial (30.9 percent), and others were problematic (20.8 percent). No matter what type of shooting, district attorneys rarely filed criminal charges, and law enforcement agencies seldom found departmental policy violations. Caught in this web of state violence were a significant number of United States residents who were injured or killed each year by law enforcement. *Fatal Force* estimates that 1,160 people have been shot or killed by law enforcement in the past twelve months (as of December 2024) and 10,293 people since they began gathering data in 2015, for an average of 1,144 residents per year.[13] Shootings make up the bulk of these fatalities, but other causes of death also occur from Tasers, restraints, and other forms of excessive force. Somewhere along the line, as has been occurring with critiques of the death penalty, was whether the so-called democracy of the United States of America should condone the killing of nearly one thousand or more residents per year and not provide any transparent data collection or restraint upon authority figures.[14] The Constitution was predicated on the notion of innocent until proven guilty in a court of law, and a homicide at the front end of the system by a law enforcement officer defies that protection.

In the early 1900s, when Ida B. Wells and W. E. B. Du Bois questioned the legitimacy of lynching, it was an accepted extralegal event. Often, hundreds of men, women, and children gathered to watch such a spectacle.[15] Wells and Du Bois demonstrated how data collection could inform and increase public awareness and understanding of lynching and help lead the opposition to these controversial actions. The collected data on lynching established that a higher proportion of Blacks were denied a finding of guilt or innocence in a court of law or a reasonable punishment for the alleged offense.[16] They too were denied due process of law. In the post–civil rights era, officer-involved shootings are the new form of lynching in communities across the country. The *Washington Post*, *Fatal Encounters*, and *Mapping Police Violence* databases remind us of the ongoing body count. However, to much surprise to the state was how the George Floyd protests took on an international call to eradicate societal racism and bring increased attention to ongoing issues of racial inequality in the United States.[17]

Most district attorneys have been less than progressive, generally upholding the laws that do not question officer decision making. Even if a DA does take a case before a grand jury, usually motivated by an attempt to reduce external criticism, they could sway the outcome to one of not filing charges and thereby absolve themselves from blame and accountability. And even if charges are filed, finding twelve jurors that will find an officer guilty beyond a reasonable doubt was difficult. Even the Steven Gant case in Denver, in which the unarmed victim was heard pleading for the officer not to shoot, was unable to meet the lower-degree threshold of negligent homicide because one of the twelve jurors refused to convict. In presenting 298 shootings from Denver, only three law enforcement officers were criminally charged. Two of the three were found guilty, and both were off duty at the time. Seven cases resulted in disciplinary charges from the law enforcement agency. These numbers mirror the lack of criminal charges against law enforcement officers in New Mexico, Tennessee, Texas, and Utah. In the counties examined in these states between 2000 and 2020, there were a total of 215 shootings, for which only one officer was criminally charged; he was not convicted. Legal or disciplinary consequences seemed to have little weight; most terminated officers were often reinstated or rehired by another law enforcement agency.[18]

Evaluating law enforcement officers' decisions to use deadly force was important in comparison to the data available on the actions of the suspect, the type of incident, the context of where the shooting occurred, and the characteristics of the suspect. The individual and officers' uncertainties will be forever intertwined. The consequences for residents consisted of injury or death. Surviving bullet wounds could cause debilitating, lifelong disabilities. There were apologies if the person shot was not the intended target or shot by accident. Some individuals shot will be criminally convicted for the acts that led to a law enforcement response. They may serve years incarcerated, others decades, and some for the remainder of their life. The pain felt by individuals who survive an officer-involved shooting, along with the lives of their family and friends, are forever altered. The families affected by the shooting of a member of the family continue life with the absence of mostly fathers, sons, brothers, and uncles.[19] Family members, including mothers, grandmothers, wives, and sisters, are forced to pressure authorities to do something, anything, to address the shooting of their loved one.[20] The communities where these shootings occur become graveyards of violence, whether enacted by the state or interpersonally. Certain sections of society become disproportionately affected.[21]

The criminologist David Klinger reports that officers also feel a sense of psychological impact; their choices to shoot play repeatedly in their heads.[22] Most officers were probably not receiving needed therapy or stress mediation when they or fellow officers were exposed to potentially violent circumstances.[23] The impact upon an officer can be hard to read when a policing culture includes statements and jokes made by some officers that disregard life and possibly reflect an interest in hurting undesirable or marginalized individuals.[24] Most officers, however, do not participate in an officer shooting, and nearly one-third of these shootings were less controversial, where their actions arguably could have protected a life or even lives. Some officers do seem to uphold an ideal of "protect and serve," and it can be hard to know whether a hierarchy-enhancing institution, as outlined by social dominance theory, can include a continuum of officers with different patterns of behavior and personal beliefs than the organizational culture.[25] For example, imagine William "Dub" Lawrence, the retired Davis County, Utah, sheriff, calling out the discrepancies in police shootings or Serpico bringing down crooked cops in New York City.

Officer-involved shootings are not random or based strictly on an equal level of perceived threat. Structural characteristics such as age, gender, race and ethnicity, and location cause certain individuals to experience a higher risk for an encounter with a more aggressive use of force by law enforcement officials. Patricia Hill Collins and others emphasize that the theoretical concept of intersectionality remains key in recognizing the social-structural arrangements of power.[26] Second, firearms are the object perceived as the greatest threat to safety. This does not mean, however, that the firearms on the scene are always real or are being used in a threatening manner, but rather that the presence of a perceived gun highlights a higher standard of alert. Gun violence does result in the highest proportion of deaths compared to other weapons. It is estimated that eight out of ten US murders in 2021 involved a firearm.[27] Data indicates that despite a higher level of gun ownership among whites, authorities deem firearms particularly threatening when they are in the hands of Black or Latino residents. Research has found firearm violence disproportionately affects Blacks; they have a mortality rate twelve times higher, per capita, than whites.[28] However, since most officer-involved shooting incidents were not in response to a homicide, we may question why greater pressure has not been placed on law enforcement to pursue an alternative resolution. It is somewhat ironic that the object determined the most threatening (i.e., a firearm) is also the object used to challenge that threat (i.e., a firearm), thus producing a similar result: a higher chance of death when used.

THE RACIAL STATE OF EXPENDABILITY

Justice Required adds another level of empirical and theoretical analysis to the framework of racialized social control, and that is on the topic of the racial state of expendability. The ethnic studies scholar John Márquez conducted a historical and cultural analysis of the experiences of Black and Latino residents in Baytown, Texas, to explore shared struggles that maintain Black-Brown solidarity. To describe these experiences, the concept of a racial state of expendability was used to highlight "a fundamental and existential life devaluation, a perpetual susceptibility to obliteration with legal impunity that allows for all other modalities of injustice, including exclusion and exploitation, to occur and endure."[29] Settler-colonial studies have done well describing how indigenous populations and subjugated groups were used for labor and without a position of inclusion in the future vision of the state.[30] Thus, a process was needed to remove "undesirable" populations, and violence was central to maintaining this structure.[31] Mass incarceration incapacitates, deportation removes, and officer-involved shootings eliminate.

We have established that law enforcement officers shoot Blacks and Latinos at a higher rate compared to whites. Black overrepresentation as police homicide "victims" is a fact.[32] Despite traditional criminology and criminal justice claims of victim-precipitated homicide, we need to recognize the reality of such a disparate system as systemic racism.[33] Such data is aligned with a theme outlined by the criminologist Paul Takagi, who reported fifty years ago that law enforcement officers possess two trigger fingers (one for whites and another for Blacks).[34] In addition, the inclusion of Latinos highlights overrepresentation compared to whites but at rates lower than Blacks. Nevertheless, depending on the community, as highlighted in this book, Latinos were the greatest total number of shooting victims for the counties studied in Colorado, New Mexico, and Texas. The ethnic studies scholar John Márquez has advocated for a concept of "foundational blackness" to articulate how Latinos, primarily deemed nonwhite, have experienced forms of oppression that align more with Blacks.[35] The long and difficult history of colonization did not end when regions of the North American continent became territories and then states. The effects of colonization have persisted through the post–civil rights era. In the United States, we must not only remember slavery and the Civil War but also the violent seizure of indigenous lands, the genocide of native people, and the conquest of the Southwest, which was once a territory of Spain and Mexico.[36] A broadened version of history could serve to challenge strongly held ideologies regarding who is native or an immigrant.[37] These data also find that marginalized whites (e.g., those with a lower socioeconomic status, mental illness, having suicidal thoughts, and experiencing alcohol or drug addiction) were also shot by the police. These populations were found to be the majority of individuals experiencing officer-involved shootings in the counties where whites were also the majority of the population, such as the counties examined in Tennessee and Utah, and reflected in nationwide demographics. The killing of many white residents is also challenged and marks points of potential collaboration in solidarity for developing a social movement that challenges violence enacted by the state. Humans living in a democracy should not live with the threat of potential death at the hands of those entrusted to enforce the laws of the state.

DEMANDING A RECKONING

Both critical race and social dominance theorists often argue the law alone cannot change racism.[38] Mari Matsuda, when summarizing the scholarship of critical race theory's founder Derrick Bell, stated Bell described the law as "both a product and a promoter of racism."[39] Note the words of the Fourteenth Amendment: "No State shall make or enforce any law which shall abridge the privileges or immunities of citizens of the United States; nor shall any State deprive any person of life, liberty, or property, without due process of law; nor deny to any person within its jurisdiction the equal protection of the laws." Is this reality or hyperbole? Many have argued that the Thirteenth Amendment adds a loophole in the abolition of slavery. This passage states: "Neither slavery nor involuntary servitude, except as a punishment for a crime whereof the party shall have been duly convicted, shall exist within the United States or any place subject to their jurisdiction."

The slavery clause exempts criminal convictions, but it does not override the right to have a court hearing and jump straight to a forfeiture of life. Thus, law enforcement officers can utilize the presumption of guilt to use a firearm to enact the state's highest level of punishment: death. Officer-involved shootings demonstrate that the law justifies the use of deadly force in all types of shootings, whether these are less controversial, questionable, or problematic.

The traditional framework of blaming "bad apples" was maintained rather than finding fault in the law or limiting the authority of law enforcement officers' discretion to use deadly force. The historian Elizabeth Hinton, when analyzing rebellions that resulted from police violence, stated how community residents concluded that rather than a bad apple, it was a bad apple that had sprung from a "poisoned tree."[40] It is such a tree that has allowed the Pristine Fourteen to continue receiving commendations and rise in rank. We believe that the practice of highly active officers is not limited to Denver. Moreover, the poisoned tree extends to a nation that has used violence as a tool to create and maintain its power.[41]

FUTURE RESEARCH

As researchers, we continue to hope for an independent, evidence-based, research-focused design that operates with the goal of improving public health by reducing gun-related violence and improving relations between law enforcement and marginalized communities.[42] We have advocated on behalf of a social-ecological model. In such an effort, this book contributes one of the most in-depth empirical studies regarding officer-involved shootings ever produced. However, such a study or analysis is far from complete. Much more research is still needed.

We adopted a mixed-method approach of integrating qualitative and quantitative data to examine officer-involved shootings. Denver, Colorado, served as our base for analysis, but we have since branched out to police shootings in New Mexico, Tennessee, Texas, and Utah. This is but a small segment of all counties nationwide, and thus efforts to expand this study into other communities through collaboration are highly desired. The US Census Bureau lists 3,144 counties or county equivalents (parishes, boroughs, independent cities, etc.) in the United States.[43] In addition, unfulfilled data analyses were still desired in each setting. For example, in Denver, Durán and Loza have data on all the addresses where these shootings occurred, and, thus, there is still work we would like to do in collaboration with someone specializing in GIS analysis. Pins on a map are far from the level of analysis needed to highlight officer-involved-shooting concentrations and variations over time.[44] In addition, we also have obtained 150 autopsies that could benefit from the analysis of a medical researcher. Moreover, we have an interest in interviewing family members, friends, and survivors of officer-involved shootings to learn more about the aftermath of these shootings. We also have an interest in interviewing law enforcement officers who have been involved in shootings and maybe even officers who could have used their firearms but chose an alternative form of resolution in order to determine how officers working in the same organization can reach different conclusions in resolving conflict.

In conclusion, the authors of this study wish to repeat: Such a high level of fatal force used upon this nation's residents is counter to democracy and is more reflective of settler colonialism. Just as the state realized that public executions were too controversial of a practice, moving capital punishment behind prison walls, so too is the ongoing public spectacle of officer-involved shootings. Police shootings highlight the minimal threshold needed for which an officer can take an individual's life. Nationwide, the United States has also begun to rethink whether even the punishment of death is justifiable, given all the potential for problematic errors during investigation and trial. In examining the atrocities of the past, several historians' final conclusions are well worth noting. For example, the Black studies professor William King, when outlining the public lynching of Andrew Green in Denver, Colorado, reported, "We must begin to ask *who benefits* from the way things are and *at what social and personal cost to others* does it occur."[45] His second key conclusion was how the journey for Blacks in the United States causes us to reexamine our concept of freedom, given that our society provides disparate opportunities vis-à-vis one's position in the social order rather than upholding a principle of equality. The historian Gary Roberts, when coming to terms with how events such as the Sand Creek Massacre of Indigenous people could occur, pointed to indifference.[46] Moreover, the irony in how the pursuit of freedom, equality, and justice in the United States contains within it a history of brutality and oppression is palpable. Roberts emphasized that acknowledging past errors was an important first step, but doing something different in the future was the harder, second step.

Marginalized population groups should not have to plead for the end of their killing and injury. Despite states of denial, advocacy groups have sought to expose wrongdoing. The Stolen Lives Project provided data on police killings when no national, state, or local agency would cooperate; then these efforts were taken on by media-based, crowdsourced data. Thus, we now have data which the state has failed to produce. In the 1960s and 1970s, civil rights organizations called out injustices and used both nonviolence and self-defense tactics. The Black Lives Matter movement has carried on these efforts, and no backlash should revert these needed changes in US society. In this book, we have outlined solutions we believe are critical in addressing police violence, particularly with the use of firearms. Key among these efforts has been our attempt to gather and analyze the most comprehensive dataset on police shootings. However, it is unfortunate that despite some states passing legislation to provide more transparency, many other states and counties (i.e., Denver County) have reverted to keeping these data closed and no longer available, making it very difficult for citizens and researchers to examine the behavior of the servants of the people. And as long as there is NO JUSTICE, there will be NO PEACE, and those who maintain such a system must be held accountable.[47]

ACKNOWLEDGMENTS

DURÁN

It is never an easy process to write a book, let alone collect the data required to make it happen. This book project began in April 2003 and has continued for the last twenty-two years. It began out of frustration. At the time, I had taken a graduate course on the death penalty at the University of Colorado and was working on my doctorate, studying gangs and the police. All the while, it seemed like people didn't recognize the level of death occurring at the front end of the system: that is, at the hands of the police. After coming to learn more about police shootings in Denver, I realized this lack of scholarly knowledge needed to change.

For the past twenty-two years, there have been a lot of people to acknowledge. First, I'd like to thank my coauthor, Dr. Oralia Loza, for ensuring that the data collected could be used for a purpose beyond my skillset, as I am trained as an ethnographer. Thanks for your patience with time delays, COVID-19 madness, and for walking me through how you analyze the world. It is my view that our collaboration has led us to better understand this topic and work toward data-driven solutions. Much appreciation goes to the Interdisciplinary Research Training Institute (IRTI) (NIH-NIDA R25 DA026401), through the University of Southern California, School of Social Work, for bringing us together to study drug abuse among Latina/o/x populations. I was part of the 2011 cohort, and

Loza was part of the 2007 and 2013 cohorts. The IRTI is led by Professors Avelardo Valdez and Alice Cepeda and has an excellent support crew of participants and members.

In Denver, my support began before my research on police shootings as a doctoral student at the University of Colorado (CU). For my dissertation, I was observing the police and conducting interviews with a wide range of people, including community members, gang members, law enforcement officers in the Denver Police Department (DPD), and attorneys in the district attorney's office (DA). I was extremely appreciative of community activist leaders such as Ernesto Vigil, Denver Copwatch's Steve and Vicki Nash, and Shareef Aleem, who were focused on addressing issues regarding police violence and harassment. These efforts resulted in the creation of my first book, *Gang Life in Two Cities: An Insider's Journey*. The officer-involved shooting described in the introduction to that book made me realize that a more concentrated focus on shootings was necessary.

The opportunity to focus specifically on police shootings began with my first appointment at New Mexico State University (NMSU). As I visited Denver in the summer, I began to visit the district attorney's office to review the investigatory case files. At the Denver DA Office, I'd like to thank Chuck Lepley, who welcomed me to review the files, provided me a space to work, and talked openly about how officer-involved shooting cases were legally analyzed. Afterward it was Lamar Sims, who although not as talkative or interactive, also ensured I had a space to review the case files. My graduate students at NMSU were the first to help me organize and digitize the data. I'm thankful for the contributions from Samantha Slim, Wesley Patterson, and Lisa Wright.

I was then off to the University of Tennessee (UT), where I once again received summer research funding to receive support from two graduate students during different years to help me focus on officer-involved shootings in the southeastern United States. I'd like to thank Maria Bordt and Bethany Nelson. At Texas A&M University (TAMU), my research assistant Jason Campos and student researcher Gilda Prado gathered additional data on specific officers involved in shootings. Much appreciation also goes to Jami Milsap at the Denver Medical Examiner's Office, who expedited my access to autopsies rather than filing one case request per month.

I'd like to thank Columbia University Press for supporting my writing projects over the past decade, especially Eric Schwartz and Alyssa M. Napier for seeing this book move forward. Academics come to realize in their careers that research doesn't count until it can be published and disseminated. In terms of writing support and funding, I'd like to acknowledge an NMSU internal grant, the Texas A&M University's Glasscock Internal Faculty Residential Fellowship, which allowed me a semester off from teaching to write, analyze data, and transition back to life after the global pandemic of COVID-19. Although *Justice Required* is an original manuscript, our analysis has benefited from peer reviews received from prior publications. The ideas included in chapter 3 were originally introduced in *Contemporary Justice Review: Issues in Criminal, Social, and Restorative Justice*. A section of the introduction, chapter 4, and conclusion appeared in *Du Bois Review: Social Science Research on Race* 13, no. 1: 61–83. Chapter 6 was developed from research initially analyzed in *Gringo Injustice: Insider Perspectives on Police, Gangs, and Law*, ed. Alfredo Mirandé (Routledge).

I'd like to thank my academic mentors over the course of my career who have shaped my scholarship and have always been cool with me. In alphabetical order by surname, these scholars are Patti Adler, David Brotherton, Alice Cepeda, Teresa Cordova, John Hagedorn, Aaron Kupchik, Vera Lopez, Ramiro Martinez, Alfredo Mirandé, Joan Moore, Ed Muñoz, Wilson Palacios, Ruth Peterson, Edwardo Portillos, Nancy Rodriguez, Martín Urbina, Avelardo Valdez, James Diego Vigil, and Tom Winfree. In addition, I have much love for my academic homies, who hang out with me at every conference as we represent the LC, DPCC, RDCJN, and PITA. Life in academia is always more fun with friends who understand a similar battle in starting from the bottom and now we are here![1]

Finally, no project is possible without the support of your family. The people who live, celebrate, cry, and die by your side. As usual, my utmost respect and love for my wife, Charlene, who has traveled a road with me that no one knows but her, along with her ride-or-die companionship since we were fifteen and sixteen years old. I love you, Charlene. To our four children, keep making me proud as we challenge generations of exclusion and overcome adversity. To our grandkids, who have endless energy, enthusiasm, and sass and keep making me smile. To the family we have lost, particularly my parents and brother over the last decade and recently my father-in-law (Otis Shroulote Sr.) and mother-in-law (Mary Jane Chavez-Shroulote). We love and miss you. This book is a result of all of the people who have invested in the struggle for transparency, justice, and the resolution of conflict with human dignity and ensuring we hold those in power accountable.

LOZA

Rigorous statistical design and data analyses are expected in the scientific literature. My statistical background and training allow me to collaborate with colleagues in various fields and keep my career fruitful, meaningful, and challenging. As an instructor in public health, I introduce students to health disparities and the appropriate methods to identify these. Taking a step back, I am grateful to my high school education in Decoto, California, at James Logan High School and the Upward Bound Program at Cal State Hayward (now East Bay), by educators who participated in the civil rights movement and exposed me to social justice issues, especially Mireya Cazares, Dorothy Allen, and Wayne Kitchen (RIP 2023). In their own unique way, they each posed the question, "what side of history do you want to be on?" after discussing historical or current events that were difficult to digest. Do you want to be one who forgets their roots? One who is silent in the face of injustice? They guided me to have a social conscience and not ignore it.

Part of my research trajectory has been quantifying and analyzing data on public health issues or invisible populations. For example, I have participated in and led research with people who engage in drug use or sex work on the US-Mexico border and with LGBTQ+ populations in Texas. For me, it is a powerful act to illuminate the data and give voice to the people it represents.

Interdisciplinary Research Training Institute on Hispanic Drug Abuse (IRTI), led by Professors Alvelardo Valdez and Alice Cepeda in 2013, fostered collaboration between early researchers to address significant societal problems.[2] It was clear that we cannot address or document these in a silo or by researchers in only one discipline. Through IRTI, I met Dr. Robert Durán and began to discuss our potential collaboration working with his police shooting data. As a trained statistician with experience as a statistical consultant, I knew I could assist with database management and data analyses as well as other technical aspects of the project. That is not what drew me to the collaboration. Durán's data spoke to a greater issue of social injustices, and I became committed to contributing to getting his data, a labor of love on Durán's part, analyzed and published.

APPENDIX 1

DATA SOURCES AND ANALYSIS

The purpose of this appendix is to provide a brief overview of the data sources and analysis. Durán began focusing on collecting officer-involved shooting data starting in April 2003. At the time, he already had experience observing police officer interactions with community members, conducting interviews with individuals to learn about their experiences with the police, and conducting interviews with law enforcement officers. After the completion of his dissertation in 2006, Durán moved to Las Cruces, New Mexico, where he continued the study of police shootings in Denver, and during several summers, he returned to review shooting incident files held at the district attorney's office. He also began researching shootings in Doña Ana County, New Mexico, and El Paso, Texas. This research overlapped with interviews and observations he was conducting on the US-Mexico border. In 2014, Durán moved to Knoxville, Tennessee, where he began researching police shootings, gangs, and community issues. The summer before moving to Tennessee, he discussed his research hurdles with Oralia Loza, and they decided to collaborate on managing and analyzing these data from Denver. The original focus was to write articles on the topic, but over time, we both realized a bigger project, such as a book, could provide a more comprehensive overview. In 2018, Durán moved to Bryan, Texas, where he continued these research studies by mentoring two Research Experiences for Undergraduates (REU) students as part of their National Science Foundation fellowship. They focused on examining officer-involved shootings in Houston, Texas, and a new project is exploring the counties on the Texas side of the US-Mexico border.

DATA COLLECTION

The overview here focuses on Denver, Colorado, but data collection was replicated to the best of Durán's abilities in Doña Ana County, New Mexico; Knox County, Tennessee; El Paso County, Texas; and Weber County, Utah. Data collection on officer-involved shootings began in 2003 in Denver, Colorado, and continued meticulously until 2023. Research in Utah coincided with the research in Colorado. As Durán moved to different universities, data collection began in those areas (New Mexico and Texas since 2006, Tennessee since 2014).

The approvals to conduct research on human subjects were granted at the University of Colorado for Durán's dissertation. Durán was subsequently approved to conduct research on law enforcement shootings at New Mexico State University and the University of Tennessee. The analysis of the data for Denver, Colorado, was reviewed and deemed exempt by the University of Texas at El Paso IRB (project number: 2307099-1) on March 21, 2025, under the title "Justice Required: Police Shootings as Legalized Violence" for Dr. Oralia Loza. Durán is renewing his IRB exempt status at Texas A&M University.

DENVER DISTRICT ATTORNEY'S OFFICE

Durán's full immersion into this study was initiated by compiling a list of shootings available at the DA's office. The DA in Denver, Colorado, reviews all police-involved shootings to determine legal justification. Denver District Attorney Mitchell R. Morrissey reported, "For more than a quarter century, Denver has had the most open officer-involved shooting protocol in the country."[1] The police shooting files were open to the public for in-person review in the municipal office building. Included in these files were a Homicide Unit investigation conducted by the Denver Police

Department, formal voluntary statements from witnesses and officers, autopsy reports, an overview of crime scene evidence collected, and a decision letter. The file boxes were obtained for me by the assistant district attorney and were somewhat organized by year. The assistant district attorney was a tremendous help in this project as he had been involved in reviewing police shootings in Denver since 1983, apart from a slight leave during the mid-1990s.[2] Durán devoted several forty-hour weeks, over a period of three years, reviewing the complete files at the DA's office. The timeframe focused on the collection of data for all shootings by law enforcement officers within the city and county of Denver, Colorado, between January 1, 1983, and December 31, 2020.

In addition to reviewing files, the first author watched thirty-seven police interview videos at the DA's office of officer-involved shooting incidents from 1988 to 2011. This author took handwritten notes of the accounts on a notepad. Morrissey stated how the use of the videotape interview room has included voluntary sworn statements from officer(s) and witnesses since 1983: "No other major city police department in the nation can make this statement."[3] The researcher originally selected a random sample for review, but because of missing videos in several files, a convenience sample was obtained. Time length in videos ranged from thirty minutes to over four hours. Police department officials conducted individual interviews with the officers involved or present when the shooting occurred, witnesses, and occasionally individuals who had been shot. The interviews were conducted shortly after each shooting.

DENVER DISTRICT ATTORNEY DECISION LETTERS

District attorney reports were obtained from 1983 to 2023 (n=278, or 93.3 percent of cases). These decision letters included a brief summary of the information contained in the complete file held at the DA's office. They ranged in length from two to forty-seven pages. Copies of these letters were made available to me for further review and were valuable in developing a comprehensive database for each shooting. A small number of decision letters (n=21) were not available in the case file or with the assistant DA. The DA did not write letters in five cases where criminal charges were pursued or brought before the grand jury. It is important to note that these reports provided legal justification for shootings and that the DA often condemned the suspect and outlined the reasoning used by the officer(s) to determine whether to use deadly force. Reports often included crime scene photos; pictures of the weapon, if any; and a geographic layout for where the shooting occurred.

MANAGER OF SAFETY REPORTS

Manager of safety reports were obtained on a number of shooting incident cases between 2003 and 2011 (n=22, or 7.4 percent of cases); there was no a central depository for these files. These documents provided insight into the determination as toward whether departmental policies were violated and whether they should result in discipline. Like the DA decision letters, manager of safety public statements provided additional background information for shootings since 2003 that resulted in death. The key themes reviewed were the reasonableness of the officers' tactics, reasonableness of the assessment of the threat, and reasonableness of the choice to use force. These public statements were mostly supportive of officers, but two cases resulted in officers who were disciplined for their behavior.

NEWSPAPERS

All available newspaper coverage regarding these shootings was pursued, utilizing Newsbank from 1988 to 2023 and viewing the years between 1983 to 1988 on microfilm. Newspaper coverage was obtained for 85.6 percent of cases involving an individual shot, which resulted in 1,228 news stories. A separate data collection was conducted on officer backgrounds and news articles, and these have not been counted but most likely mirror those involving individuals shot. Newspaper coverage often provided insight on criminal records and responses by family members or witnesses, and these articles primarily support a law enforcement view of the incident and the decision making regarding why they had to use force, but some stories were more critical or at least questioning. Hirschfield and Simon have a good article reviewing news media legitimacy claims for police shootings.[4] The local newspapers, such as the *Denver Post, Rocky Mountain News,* and *Westword* often competed for who had the best access to in-depth versions of the shootings.[5] Lawyers challenged some of the shootings in court, and the media occasionally shared factual contradictions.

DENVER MEDICAL EXAMINER AUTOPSIES

Durán began requesting autopsies from the Denver medical examiner's office in 2007. Autopsies were obtained for every person killed from 1998 to 2020 and sporadically for cases before this time period (n=109, or 72.7 percent among those who died as a result of the shooting or soon after from suicide). Autopsy records note the body's condition, bullet damage, height, weight, tattoos, and any alcohol or drugs in the system of the person killed.

ADDITIONAL DATA SOURCES

What follows is a list of some additional data sources obtained for each shooting incident, listed in alphabetical order:

Ancestry.com   Search of personal records and family associations.

Colorado Department of Corrections Offender Search   Provides a picture, height, and weight, along with prison sentence and expected parole dates.

Colorado Department of Public Safety Colorado arrest records   These were available for purchase.

Denver Police Department   Records submitted to the DA's office for review. Records also obtained on officers based on the Colorado Open Records Act. The police department also provided demographic data. They also published annual reports that highlighted an overview of the department, demographics, police districts, initiatives, and efforts to reduce crime in the city and county.

Denver Sheriff Department Inmate Search   Internet search provides name, race, height, age, sex, eye color, hair color, booking date, booking number, and offense type.

Google search engine   Used to search for any information relevant to the individual shot and the officers involved.

Gravestones   Such markers include date of birth, date of death, name, and location of burial. Example: Findagrave.com.

Obituaries   These vary depending upon source but primarily include date of birth, date of death, name, family members, background, and location of service.

Public Access to Court Electronic Records (PACER)   Search of court records involving criminal charges and or lawsuit filings.

Social media   Searches for the pages of the individual shot and of the officers involved. Facebook, Instagram, Twitter, etc.

YouTube videos   Occasionally available for bodycam footage, news reporting, or public briefing reports given to the public by the DA's office.

FIELDWORK AND INTERVIEWS

A foundation for my (Durán's) insights regarding policing in Denver, Colorado, and Weber County, Utah, were based upon my ethnographic field observations. I observed more than two hundred police stops from 2002 to 2006 as part of a police observation group, which was given the pseudonym People Observing Police (POP) in *Gang Life in Two Cities*.[6] Walking and interacting with residents also occurred in the highest-concentrated Latino, Black, and white neighborhoods. Based on where I lived, a higher proportion of involvement was in North Denver, West Denver, and downtown. Similar neighborhood fieldwork occurred in Doña Ana County, New Mexico, and El Paso, Texas, from 2006 to 2014. These observations can be found in *The Gang Paradox*.[7] Field observations of neighborhoods and policing occurred in Knox County, Tennessee, from 2014 to 2018, largely influenced by gang expert testimony cases.

Finally, in an effort to develop a broader view of police shootings, Durán conducted semistructured interviews with seven individuals regarding police shootings. Six of these individuals were critical of the police and often some of the most prominent community activists, working on behalf of family members. Another individual, interviewed informally, was one of the key prosecutors in the DA's office for three decades.

MEASURES

Data is not publicly available for all of the measures included in the dataset. Specifically, data on the officers (e.g., badge number, number of years on the force, sex, race/ethnicity, and age) who shot was not always made available or published in any of the sources. Hence, in some cases, the data is missing.

Sociodemographic Characteristics of the Person Shot include age (years), age group (<18, 18–27, 28–37, 38–47, 48+), sex (male, female), race/ethnicity (white, Black, Nonwhite Other, Latino), foreign-born status (yes, no), and living location (Denver, Aurora, Colorado, Outside Colorado).

Measures for Alcohol and Drug Use of the Person Shot include use (yes, no) of any alcohol or drug then, specifically for alcohol, marijuana/THC, cocaine, heroin/opiates, and methamphetamine/amphetamine.

Measures to describe the Shooting Incident include time wave (1983–1990, 1991–2000, 2001–2010, 2011–2020), day of the week of shooting (MTWTFSS), time of day of shooting (morning [6:00 AM to 11:59 AM], afternoon [12:00 PM to 5:59 PM], evening [6:00 PM to 10:59 PM], night [11:00 PM to 5:59 AM]), number of additional people shot (0–3 persons), the time difference between arrival and shooting (minutes), 911, community-initiated engagement (yes, no), and the person who contacted the police (self, family member, partner/spouse, friend, victim, employee, stranger observed, burglar alarm).

Other shooting-related measures include the reason for action based on the issue the officer was responding to enter the scene or approach the suspect (assault, burglary/theft, disturbance, gun incident, homicide, property damage, robbery, suspect, traffic), the location where the person was shot (indoor, outdoor), and shooting location details (public place, living area), as well as the proportion of race/ethnicity >50 percent in the neighborhood where the shooting occurred (white, Latino, Black) and the proportion of poverty in the neighborhood where the shooting occurred (low, medium, high, ghetto).

Incident-Related Factors include the seriousness of the offense (nothing, misdemeanor, felony), possible offense type (nothing, curiosity, interpersonal violence, suicidal/welfare check, property crime, traffic, previous crime), suspect's behavior when shot (active threat, vague threat, perceived threat), and whether the suspect fled from the officer in a different neighborhood (yes, no). For the person shot, the location on the body bullet(s) hit (arm/hand, leg/foot, chest/shoulder/pelvis, head/neck, back/butt, multiple locations), whether they victimized another individual (yes, no), and if so whom (police officer, partner/spouse, family member, stranger, employee).

Post-shooting measures included whether they had a weapon (none, knife, gun, vehicle, other object) and whether they reported (yes, no) a mental health outcome, suicidality, criminal record, previous prison history, and gang membership.

For each case, we have Officer-Related Measures that include the number of officers at the scene, the number who shot, the number of shots fired, and the number of times they hit the suspect. The data also includes if at least one officer was off duty (yes, no) and if any officer used a nonlethal alternative (yes, no) and, if so, what alternative (pepper spray, mace, 40 mm launch, negotiator, friend, Taser, crisis intervention trainee). Additional measures included if any officer was injured during a shooting (yes, no) and if so, the type of injury (bullet injury, vehicle injury, knife injury, physical injury, death). For each shooting, the police district for the area of the census tract (Northwest Denver, Northeast Denver, Southeast Denver, Southwest Denver, Northeast Denver/DIA, Central Denver), law enforcement agency (Denver Police Department, other), and police chief (Whitman, Michaud, White, Coogan, Zavaras, Pazen, Sanchez, Collier, other) were recorded.

Sociodemographic Characteristics for each of the officers who shot include sex (male, female), race/ethnicity (white, Black, Asian, Latino, Multiracial), and number of years on the force. These measures were analyzed differently than the rest, given that more than one officer may have shot at each scene.

Measures for Post-Shooting Outcomes include the outcome for the person shot (wounded, killed), if there was a reported dispute between accounts (yes, no), if the incident resulted in incarceration in jail or prison for the person shot (yes, no), if their case was eligible for the death penalty (yes, no), and if the person shot is currently in Colorado (yes, no, deceased). These measures also include if the district attorney filed charges (yes, no) and the name of the district attorney (Morrissey, Ritter, Early, McCann, other). For each case, data include if there was a lawsuit settlement (no, yes, attempted) and, if so, the settlement amount (dollars). Finally, the shooting incident level of critique (problematic, questionable, less controversial) was assessed.

For each case, it is noted whether the data was sourced from (yes/no) the decision letter, review of the DA file, review of the video, copy of autopsy for those who died because of the shooting or soon after from suicide, or news coverage, and if so, the number of news articles.

DATABASE MANAGEMENT

We first collected the data qualitatively and stored it in Excel. Measures used in this study were coded and imported into SPSS and prepared for analysis. The analytical outcomes were age group, sex, race/ethnicity, and foreign-born status of the person shot. Earlier database management was described in a previously published study by the authors.[8]

Measures for race/ethnicity of the highest proportion in the neighborhood where the shooting occurred, and race/ethnicity greater than 25 percent in the neighborhood where the shooting occurred were created based on the census tract the police officer shot the suspect in using the Geolytics Neighborhood Change Database 1970–2010.

Age was missing for two observations; in both cases, youth were shot. A measure for age category (<18, 18–27, 28–37, 38–47, 48+) was created. The two youths with missing values for age and were grouped with those aged <18 years old in the age category.

A measure for time wave (1983–1990, 1991–2000, 2001–2010, 2011–2020) was created from the year the shooting occurred. All levels are in ten-year intervals except for the first (1983–1990).

There is one instance in which two persons were shot together a total of forty times. For these cases, we do not have data on how many times each person was shot. For these two cases, twenty shots per person were entered in the dataset.

Given that, in some cases, more than one officer shot per suspect, the dataset was modified for the analysis of sociodemographic characteristics for each of the officers who shot. First, we exported the SPSS dataset for the analytical outcomes (age group, sex, race/ethnicity, and foreign-born status of the person shot) and officer measures (age, sex, race/ethnicity, years on the force) into an Excel file. We transformed the data so that each observation represented an officer who shot (up to a total of four sets). The age of the officer was removed, given the low sample size (most were missing values). This data was employee protected and not made available to the author. Data for up to four officers were included in the original dataset; however, more than half of the cases had one or two officers on the scene. Data for the analytical outcomes were repeated for each officer who shot a suspect. So rather than each observation/row representing a person shot, each observation/row represents an officer who shot.

ANALYSIS

The qualitative analysis included reading through all reports and highlighting common themes, entering these data into an Excel file, and then creating overviews for each shooting based on combined data sources. To create a realistic overview of 298 cases, of which 213 included whites, Blacks, or Latinos, computer software randomized all shooting cases by each racial and ethnic group, resulting in twelve cases, or four to five cases per group (see table 4). The cases produced cover a range in the number of years (1983 to 2020), types of incidents, and types of shooting coded as problematic, questionable, or less controversial.

Quantitative analysis included descriptive statistics and bivariate analysis. Descriptive statistics of all measures for the suspect and officer characteristics and contextual factors include sample size (n), frequency and percent for categorical variables and sample size, Q1 (25th percentile), median (50th percentile), and Q3 (75th percentile) continuous variables, given that data for these measures were not normally distributed.

There are four categorical analytical outcomes: age group, sex, race/ethnicity, and foreign-born status of the person shot. For binary outcomes, bivariate associations were determined with Pearson chi-square or Fisher's exact test, as appropriate, for categorical variables and Mann–Whitney U test for continuous variables. For outcomes with more than two levels, bivariate associations were determined with Pearson chi-square or likelihood ratio test, as appropriate, for categorical variables and the Kruskal-Wallis test for continuous variables. For all analyses, significant test results were determined at the alpha level of 0.05.

The author entered all sources of data into SPSS (version 25)[9] and QSR NVivo (version 10)[10] for different forms of analysis. One hundred and fifteen variables were coded in SPSS so that these can be used in quantitative analysis including descriptive statistics and bivariate associations. These included incident characteristics (when, where, why, etc.), suspect characteristics (age, background, gender, race), officer characteristics (years on the force, gender, accompanied by another officer, recognition for shooting), and additional details (criminal records, prison records, disputed shootings, consumption of drugs and alcohol). In order to separate problematic shootings from the broader number of shootings, the author coded each file with a plus and minus ranking that ranged from −9 to +7, with an average of +1.

POST HOC ANALYSES

After the initial analyses were conducted, we conducted several post hoc analyses. The first looked at the changes in the availability of data sources over time. These results are presented in table 6. One of the measures for Shooting Incidents was time wave (1983–1990, 1991–2000, 2001–2010, 2011–2020). For data sources, we had data on whether a decision letter, review of DA file, review of the video, copy of autopsy for those who died as a result of the shooting or soon after from suicide and news coverage were available for the case. Bivariate associations were determined for data source measure with frequency and percentage by time wave intervals and a Pearson chi-square or likelihood ratio test. Significant test results were determined at the alpha level of 0.05.

The second post hoc analysis assessed whether alcohol and drug use were associated with the shooting outcome. These results are presented in table 9. Post-Shooting Outcomes included the outcome for the person shot (wounded, killed). We conducted bivariate analyses of the measures for Alcohol and Drug Use of the Person Shot versus the outcome for the person shot. The measures for alcohol and drug use include any alcohol or drug, alcohol, cocaine, heroin/opiates, marijuana/THC, and meth-amphetamine/amphetamine. Bivariate associations were determined for each drug use measure with frequency and percentage for those wounded and killed and a Pearson chi-square test. Significant test results were determined at the alpha level of 0.05.

Last, we assessed if the proportion of cases in a reported dispute between accounts differed over time. These results have been presented in chapter 2.

METHODOLOGY

The primary methodology utilized in this book was mixed methods. Durán is trained as an ethnographer and utilizes qualitative data collection. Loza is a statistician and utilizes database management to prepare quantitative data for statistical analysis. We found the approach of merging both methodologies together beneficial when analyzing police shootings.

APPENDIX 2

DATA TABLES

TABLE A2.1. Descriptive Statistics for Measures for Person Shot, Officers Who Shot, Shooting-Related Factors for All Police Shooting Cases in Denver, Colorado, 1983–2020 (N=298)

Sociodemographic characteristics of the person shot	N	Frequency (%) median (q1, q3)
Age at time of shooting	296	29 (22, 37)
Age group	298	
<18		25 (8.4%)
18–27		114 (38.3%)
28–37		87 (29.2%)
38–47		47 (15.8%)
48+		25 (8.4%)
Sex	298	
Male		284 (95.3%)
Female		14 (4.7%)
Race/ethnicity	296	
White		92 (31.1%)

(continued)

TABLE A2.1. Descriptive Statistics for Measures for Person Shot, Officers Who Shot, Shooting-Related Factors for All Police Shooting Cases in Denver, Colorado, 1983–2020 (N=298) (*Continued*)

Sociodemographic characteristics of the person shot	N	Frequency (%) median (q1, q3)
Black		64 (21.6%)
Nonwhite other		9 (3%)
Latino		131 (44.3%)
Foreign-born status	**298**	
Foreign born		13 (4.4%)
Where person reportedly lived	**279**	
Denver		139 (49.8%)
Aurora		9 (3.2%)
Colorado		121 (43.4%)
Outside colorado		10 (3.6%)
Alcohol and drug use of the person shot		
Any alcohol or drug	**275**	**152 (55.3%)**
Alcohol	274	98 (35.8%)
Marijuana/thc	274	50 (18.2%)
Cocaine	274	34 (12.4%)
Heroin/opiates	274	12 (4.4%)
Methamphetamine/amphetamine	274	35 (12.8%)
Shooting-related measures		
Time wave	**298**	
1983–1990		65 (21.8%)
1991–2000		83 (27.9%)
2001–2010		63 (21.1%)
2011–2020		87 (29.2%)

Sociodemographic characteristics of the person shot	N	Frequency (%) median (q1, q3)
Day of the week	298	
Monday		38 (12.8%)
Tuesday		39 (13.1%)
Wednesday		47 (15.8%)
Thursday		33 (11.1%)
Friday		43 (14.4%)
Saturday		56 (18.8%)
Sunday		42 (14.1%)
Time of day	295	
Morning (6:00 am to 11:59 am)		26 (8.8%)
Afternoon (12:00 pm to 5:59 pm)		73 (24.7%)
Evening (6:00 pm to 10:59 pm)		85 (28.8%)
Night (11:00 pm to 5:59 am)		111 (37.6%)
Number of other people shot	298	
0		293 (98.3%)
1		4 (1.3%)
3		1 (0.3%)
Time difference between police arrival and shooting (minutes)	209	**5 (2, 13)**
911, community-initiated engagement	298	**155 (52%)**
Who contacted the police?	149	
Self		3 (2%)
Family member		24 (16.1%)
Partner/spouse		22 (14.8%)
Friend		3 (2%)
Victim		24 (16.1%)

(*continued*)

TABLE A2.1. Descriptive Statistics for Measures for Person Shot, Officers Who
Shot, Shooting-Related Factors for All Police Shooting Cases in Denver,
Colorado, 1983–2020 (N=298) (*Continued*)

Sociodemographic characteristics of the person shot	N	Frequency (%) median (q1, q3)
Employee		17 (11.4%)
Stranger observed		55 (36.9%)
Burglar alarm		1 (0.7%)
Officer's reason for action	**297**	
Assault		30 (10.1%)
Burglary/theft		13 (4.4%)
Disturbance		52 (17.5%)
Gun incident		57 (19.2%)
Homicide		4 (1.3%)
Property damage		6 (2%)
Robbery		32 (10.8%)
Suspect		87 (29.3%)
Traffic		16 (5.4%)
Location of person shot	**298**	
Indoors		69 (23.2%)
Outdoors		229 (76.8%)
Shooting location details	**298**	
Public place		178 (59.7%)
Living area		120 (40.3%)
Proportion of race/ethnicity >50% in the neighborhood where shooting occurred	**247**	
White		121 (49%)
Latino		100 (40.5%)
Black		26 (10.5%)

Sociodemographic characteristics of the person shot	N	Frequency (%) median (q1, q3)
Level of poverty in the neighborhood where shooting occurred	297	
Low		34 (11.4%)
Medium		86 (29%)
High		147 (49.5%)
Ghetto		30 (10.1%)
Person shot: seriousness of offense	298	
Nothing		28 (9.4%)
Misdemeanor		56 (18.8%)
Felony		214 (71.8%)
Person shot: possible offense type	298	
Nothing		10 (3.4%)
Curiosity		23 (7.7%)
Interpersonal violence		177 (59.4%)
Suicidal/welfare check		9 (3%)
Property crime		27 (9.1%)
Traffic		24 (8.1%)
Previous crime		28 (9.4%)
Person shot: suspect behavior when shot	298	
Active threat		177 (59.4%)
Vague threat		30 (10.1%)
Perceived threat		91 (30.5%)
Person shot: flee from officer in different neighborhood?	298	**29 (9.7%)**
Person shot: gunshot wound location(s) on body	272	

(continued)

TABLE A2.1. Descriptive Statistics for Measures for Person Shot, Officers Who Shot, Shooting-Related Factors for All Police Shooting Cases in Denver, Colorado, 1983–2020 (N=298) (*Continued*)

Sociodemographic characteristics of the person shot	N	Frequency (%) median (q1, q3)
Arm/hand		17 (6.3%)
Leg/foot		26 (9.6%)
Chest/shoulder/pelvis		61 (22.4%)
Head/neck		28 (10.3%)
Back/butt		20 (7.4%)
Multiple locations		120 (44.1%)
Person shot: victimized another individual	**298**	**74 (24.8%)**
Person shot: injured whom?	**73**	
Police officer		16 (21.9%)
Partner/spouse		14 (19.2%)
Family member		10 (13.7%)
Stranger		31 (42.5%)
Employee		2 (2.7%)
Person shot: post-shooting weapon discovery	**298**	
None		42 (14.1%)
Knife		37 (12.4%)
Gun		170 (57%)
Vehicle		32 (10.7%)
Other object		17 (5.7%)
Mental health reported	**261**	**26 (10%)**
Reported suicidal	**290**	**42 (14.5%)**
Criminal record	**287**	**140 (48.8%)**
Previous prison	**295**	**60 (20.3%)**

Sociodemographic characteristics of the person shot	N	Frequency (%) median (q1, q3)
Reported gang membership	288	27 (9.4%)
Officers		
Number of officers at scene	298	2 (1, 4)
Number of officers who shot	298	1 (1, 2)
Number of shots fired	297	4 (2, 9.5)
Number of times hit suspect	298	2 (1, 4)
At least one officers was off duty	298	23 (7.7%)
Nonlethal alternative used	298	32 (10.7%)
Type of nonlethal alternative	32	
Pepper spray		3 (9.4%)
Mace		5 (15.6%)
40 mm launch		5 (15.6%)
Negotiator		4 (12.5%)
Friend		1 (3.1%)
Taser		13 (40.6%)
Crisis intervention trainee		1 (3.1%)
Any officer: injured during shooting	298	51 (17.1%)
Type of officer injury	53	
Bullet injury		21 (39.6%)
Vehicle injury		14 (26.4%)
Knife injury		6 (11.3%)
Physical injury		9 (17%)
Death		3 (5.7%)
Police district for the area of census tract of shooting	298	
Northwest Denver		84 (28.2%)
Northeast Denver		39 (13.1%)

(*continued*)

TABLE A2.1. Descriptive Statistics for Measures for Person Shot, Officers Who Shot, Shooting-Related Factors for All Police Shooting Cases in Denver, Colorado, 1983–2020 (N=298) (*Continued*)

Sociodemographic characteristics of the person shot	N	Frequency (%) median (q1, q3)
Southeast Denver		35 (11.7%)
Southwest Denver		54 (18.1%)
Northeast Denver/DIA		19 (6.4%)
Central Denver		67 (22.5%)
Law enforcement agency	**298**	
Denver police department		261 (87.6%)
Other		37 (12.4%)
Police chief	**297**	
Whitman		57 (19.2%)
Michaud		56 (18.9%)
White		42 (14.1%)
Coogan		29 (9.8%)
Zavaras		27 (9.1%)
Pazen		23 (7.7%)
Sanchez		12 (4%)
Collier		10 (3.4%)
Other		41 (13.8%)
Sociodemographic characteristics of the officers who shot		
Sex	**473**	
Male		455 (96.2%)
Female		18 (3.8%)
Race/ethnicity	**403**	
White		291 (72.2%)
Black		16 (4%)

Sociodemographic characteristics of the person shot	N	Frequency (%) median (q1, q3)
Asian		2 (0.5%)
Latino		90 (22.3%)
Multiracial		4 (1%)
Number of years on the force	**388**	**7 (4, 13)**
Post-shooting outcomes		
Person shot: outcome	**298**	
Wounded		152 (51%)
Killed		146 (49%)
Reported dispute between accounts	**298**	**107 (35.9%)**
Person shot: death penalty eligible case	**298**	**10 (3.4%)**
Person shot: was in a Colorado prison between 2013–2022	**202**	
No		10 (5%)
Yes		41 (20.3%)
Deceased		151 (74.8%)
DA file charges	**298**	**4 (1.3%)**
District attorney	**298**	
Morrissey		82 (27.5%)
Ritter		85 (28.5%)
Early		87 (29.2%)
Mccann		39 (13.1%)
Other		5 (1.7%)
Lawsuit settlement	**273**	
No		240 (87.9%)
Yes		27 (9.9%)
Attempted		6 (2.2%)

(continued)

TABLE A2.1. Descriptive Statistics for Measures for Person Shot, Officers Who Shot, Shooting-Related Factors for All Police Shooting Cases in Denver, Colorado, 1983–2020 (N=298) (*Continued*)

Sociodemographic characteristics of the person shot	N	Frequency (%) median (q1, q3)
Lawsuit settlement amount (USD)	18	332500 (70000, 1230000)
Shooting incident level of critique	298	
Problematic		62 (20.8%)
Questionable		144 (48.3%)
Less controversial		92 (30.9%)
Data sources		
Decision letter	298	278 (93.3%)
Review of DA file	298	183 (61.4%)
Review of video	298	38 (12.8%)
Copy of autopsy (among those who died)	150	109 (72.7%)
News coverage	298	255 (85.6%)
Number of news articles	298	3 (1, 5)

Note: A copy of the autopsy was requested for those who died as a result of the shooting or soon after due to suicide (N=150).

INDIVIDUAL-, INTERPERSONAL-, COMMUNITY-, AND INSTITUTIONAL-LEVEL FACTORS TO ASSESS IN OFFICER-INVOLVED SHOOTING RESEARCH BASED ON THE SOCIAL ECOLOGICAL MODEL

INDIVIDUAL-LEVEL FACTORS

Individual-level factors include sociodemographic characteristics, determinants of health, and known risk factors that lead to police contact.

Sources

- Interviews, autopsy data, medical records, death certificates, coroners, or mortuary reports[1]
- Current sources of data for police violence or police shootings, including mortality, are *Fatal Encounters*, *The Counted*, *Fatal Force*, and *Mapping Police Violence*

Sociodemographic Characteristics of the Person Shot

- Name
- Date of birth
- Age
- Sex
- Gender identity†[2]
- Race/ethnicity
- Foreign-born status
- Where person reportedly lived
- Relationship status: single, married, cohabitating
- Health insurance status†
- Education level†
- Source of income/employment†
- Income†
- Number of dependents†

Alcohol and Drug Use of the Person Shot on the Day of the Shooting

- Alcohol
- Marijuana/THC
- Crack†/cocaine
- Heroin/opiates
- Methamphetamine/amphetamine
- Fentanyl†
- Prescription medication†

Factors for the Person Shot at Time of Shooting

- Mental health outcomes
- Suicidality
- Carrying a weapon
- Gang membership

Factors for the Person Shot Before Shooting

- Criminal record
- Prison history
- Past gang membership†
- History of substance use treatment†
- History of physical, emotional, and/or sexual abuse†
- Adverse childhood events (ACEs)†

Sociodemographic Characteristics of the Officers Who Shot

- Name
- Date of birth†
- Age
- Sex
- Gender identity†
- Race/ethnicity
- Foreign-born status†
- Military veteran
- Attitudes and beliefs‡
- History of substance use treatment†
- History of physical, emotional, and sexual abuse†
- Adverse childhood events (ACEs)†

Officer Occupational Characteristics

- Academy year
- Number of years on the force
- Work assignment
- Commendations

- Rank§
- Number of prior shootings§
- Administrative complaints§

INTERPERSONAL-LEVEL FACTORS

Interpersonal-level factors include measures that describe interactions with police and other individuals at the time of the shooting.

Sources

- Police records, 911 data, decision letter, DA file, police camera video
- Media[3]

Shooting-Related Measures

- Time wave
- Day of the week
- Time of day of shooting
- Number of other people shot
- Police response time (minutes)
- 911, community-initiated engagement
- Person(s) who contacted the police
- Officer: reason for action
- Shooting indoor/outdoor location
- Shooting location details
- Witness reports

Officers Who Shot

- Number of officers at scene
- Number of officers who shot
- Number of shots fired
- Number of times hit suspect
- At least one officer was off duty
- Nonlethal alternative used by officer

- Type of nonlethal alternative by officer
- Officer injured during shooting
- Type of injury
- Officer partner or self previous exposure to violence last six months

Incident-Related Factors for the Person Shot

- Seriousness of offense
- Possible offense type
- Behavior when shot
- Fled from officer(s) in different neighborhood
- Gunshot wound location(s) on body
- Victimized other individual(s)
- Injured other individual(s)
- Suspect resisted arrest§

COMMUNITY-LEVEL FACTORS

Community-level factors include measures for the setting of the shooting as well as for the people who live in that area at the census tract level and officer agency information.

Sources

- American Community Survey (ACS) of the US Census[4]
- Population records, local government records, other institutional records, agency records[5]

Census Tract–Level Shooting Measures

- Census tract of shooting
- Proportion of race/ethnicity >50% in the neighborhood where shooting occurred
- Proportion of poverty in the neighborhood where shooting occurred
- Proportion of houselessness in the neighborhood where shooting occurred†

- Density of alcohol outlets†
- Population size‡
- Average income‡
- Average education level‡
- Unemployment rate‡

Geographic Identifiers

- State
- County
- City§

Law Enforcement Agency

- Police district for the area of the census tract of shooting
- Law enforcement agency
- Average number of complaints against police behavior
- Police chief

INSTITUTIONAL-LEVEL FACTORS

Institutional-level factors include shooting outcomes from the agency and judicial system and policies and programs that create, maintain, and sustain or support policies on shootings and dictate the consequences that police officers face.

Sources

- Decision letter, DA file
- Media, government, and legislative records[6]

Post-Shooting Outcomes

- Person shot
- Outcome
- Reported dispute

- Incident resulted in incarceration in jail or prison
- Death-penalty-eligible case
- Prison (currently or in the past)
- Survivors of death: children, partner, family
- Injury outcome: health costs, impact on life
- District attorney (DA)
- Officer discipline
- File charges
- Lawsuit settlement
- Shooting incident level of critique

Data Release Policies

- Decision letter
- DA file
- Autopsy
- Police camera video†

Media Coverage

- News coverage
- Number of news articles

Organizational Within Law Enforcement Institutions§

- Contribution to national database of police shootings
- Professionalizing the police
- Strengthening early intervention systems
- Diversifying the police force
- Empowering civilian review boards
- Expanding the use of body-worn cameras

Laws and Policies

- Independent monitor‡
- Laws‡
- Institutional policies‡

- Institutional practices‡
- Public policy§
- Evidence-based policies for reducing racial bias in officer-involved shootings§

The measures without a symbol were included in the current study.

† These measures were not included in the current study but are recommended by the authors.

‡ These measures are presented by Linda L. Dahlberg and Etienne G. Krug, "Violence: A Global Public Health Problem," *Ciência and Saúde Coletiva* 11 (2006).

§ These measures are presented by Roger G. Dunham and Nick Petersen, "Making Black Lives Matter," *Criminology and Public Policy* 16, no. 1 (2017): 341–48.

NOTES

INTRODUCTION

1. Selected cases were incorporated to develop the storytelling method of sharing information developed by critical race theory. See Richard Delgado, "Legal Storytelling: Storytelling for Oppositionists and Others: A Plea for Narrative," *Michigan Law Review* 87 (1989): 2411–41; Richard Delgado and Jean Stefancic, eds., *The Derrick Bell Reader* (New York University Press, 2005); Richard Delgado and Jean Stefancic, *Critical Race Theory: An Introduction* (New York University Press, 2012). However, rather than create fictionalized characters responding to real issues, we chose to focus on actual cases involving real participants. This type of storytelling matches the vision of W. E. B. Du Bois, *The Philadelphia Negro: A Social Study* (University of Pennsylvania Press, 1996), and the encouraged importance described in Alfredo Mirandé, *Rascuache Lawyer: Toward a Theory of Ordinary Litigation* (University of Arizona Press, 2011), and *Ordinary Injustice: Rascuache Lawyering and the Anatomy of a Criminal Case* (University of Arizona Press, 2023).

2. The terms Hispanic, Latino, Latina, Latinx, and Latina/o/x are used interchangeably in this book, although the authors acknowledge that this is not widely accepted. Terminology to describe race and ethnicity has been problematic and not always inclusive or representative of racial and ethnic diversity in the United States. See Luis Noe-Bustamante, Ana Gonzalez-Barrera, Khadijah Edwards, Lauren Mora, and Mark Hugo Lopez, "Measuring the Racial Identity of Latinos," Pew Research Center, 2021, https://www.pewresearch.org/hispanic/2021/11/04/measuring-the-racial-identity-of-latinos/ (in the bibliography under Reports; subsections of the bibliography will be noted in parentheses). The term *Latino* is gendered, implying the person is male or a man. Similarly, *Latina* implies the person is female or a woman. *Latinx* is the gender-neutral form of the term, but it erases male and female identities. It is reported that 3 percent of

Latinos use the term *Latinx* in comparison to other labeling terms such as "Hispanic." See Luis Noe-Bustamante, Lauren Mora, and Mark Hugo Lopez. "About One-in-Four U.S. Hispanics Have Heard of Latinx, but Just 3% Use It," Pew Research Center, 2020 (Reports).

3. Michael was pronounced dead at 5:39 PM, but this was not reported by the media until the next day.

4. Charles Lepley, Decision Letter: Michael Grimaldo, July 21, 2003. There was some lack of clarity on whether one of the shots occurred in the initial encounter with police or the second encounter.

5. Officer Christopher Mace had been a police officer for seven years, including service at the Westminster Police Department, Ft. Lupton Police Department, and Louisville Police Department. Before his law enforcement service, he had been in the US Marine Corps for eight years. On the Officer Down Memorial Page, he wrote a tribute to a fellow officer who had been killed transporting a prisoner just one month before this shooting, stating: "Jason serves as a constant reminder to me how dangerous our job is and how evil some people are out there. I pray for Jason and his family." Officer Down Memorial Page, https://www.odmp.org/officer/reflections/15771-deputy-sheriff -jason-schwartz/75.

6. Officer Karl Scherck had been with the Westminster Police Department for one year. Before this was an officer for the Northglenn Police Department, Parker Police Department, and Arapahoe County Sheriff's Office. It was unknown whether he participated in any officer-involved shootings with these other agencies.

7. Stephen J. Cina, "Autopsy Report: Grimaldo, Michael," Adams County Coroner's Office, April 26, 2003, Brighton, CO, describes the first two shots by Officer Scherck entering the abdomen and chest. In his statement to law enforcement officials, Officer Scherck did not mention the third shot, but officers arriving on the scene reported that the third shot came when Officer Scherck was closer to Mr. Grimaldo on the passenger side of the vehicle. The autopsy also seems to indicate that it was this third shot by Officer Scherck that resulted in Michael's death.

8. Lepley, Decision Letter: Michael Grimaldo, 23.

9. The doctors who performed the autopsy labeled Michael as white, thus, reflecting an example of the official underrepresentation of Latina/o/x victimization to police violence. Michael was born in Carrizo Springs, Texas, along the US-Mexico border, a geographic space and life that was nowhere near anything close to a white Anglo reality.

10. Phillip Dray, *At the Hands of Persons Unknown: The Lynching of Black America* (Random House, 2002); Shaun L. Gabbidon, "W. E. B. Du Bois: Pioneering American Criminologist," *Journal of Black Studies* 31, no. 5 (2001), 581–99; David Levering Lewis, *W. E. B. Du Bois: Biography of a Race: 1968–1919* (Owl Books, 1993), and *W. E. B. Du Bois: The Fight for Equality and the American Century, 1919–1963* (Henry Holt, 2001).

11. William D. Carrigan, *The Making of a Lynching Culture: Violence and Vigilantism in Central Texas 1836–1916* (University of Illinois Press, 2004); Monica Muñoz Martinez, *The Injustice Never Leaves You: Anti-Mexican Violence in Texas* (Harvard University Press, 2018).

12. Paul Takagi, "A Garrison State in Democratic Society," *Crime and Social Justice* (Spring/ Summer 1974): 27–32.

13. Philip J. Cook and Jens Ludwig, *Gun Violence: The Real Costs* (Oxford University Press, 2002); Phil Cook, Mark Moore, and Anthony Braga. "Gun Control," Working Paper, John F. Kennedy School of Government, Harvard University Faculty Research Working Paper Series (2000); David Hemenway, *Private Guns: Public Health* (University of Michigan Press, 2004).

14. Small Arms Survey, *Chapter 7: Reducing Armed Violence: The Public Health Approach* (Cambridge University Press, 2008).

15. Vivek Murthy, "Firearm Violence: A Public Health Crisis in America," The US Surgeon General's Advisory, 2024 (Reports).

16. Andrea M. Burch, Arrest-Related Deaths, 2003–2009, NCJ 235385, US Department of Justice, Bureau of Justice Statistics, Washington, DC, 2011 (Reports).

17. Arnold Binder and Peter Scharf, "Deadly Force in Law Enforcement," *Crime and Delinquency* 28 (1982), 1–23; David I. Caplan, "Even Deadly Force: Fully Justifiable Homicide vs. Barely Excusable Homicide," *Journal on Firearms and Public Policy* 7 (2000), 7–16; William M. Ravkind, "Justifiable Homicide in Texas," *Southwestern Law Journal* 13 (1959), 508–24; Lawrence Southwick, "Guns and Justifiable Homicide: Deterrence and Defense," *St. Louis University Public Law Review* 18 (1999), 217–46.

18. Stephen B. Bright, "Counsel for the Poor: The Death Sentence Not for the Worst Crime but for the Worst Lawyer," *Yale Law Journal* 103 (1994), 1835–83; Death Penalty Information Center, Executions in the United States, http://www.deathpenaltyinfo.org /executions-united-states; Federal Bureau of Investigation, Uniform Crime Reports, http://www.fbi.gov/about-us/cjis/ucr/ucr.

19. For individuals shot by the police under thirty years of age, the first name will be used to highlight that this injury or death is much less than the average life expectancy.

20. James J. Fyfe, "Police Use of Deadly Force: Research and Reform," *Justice Quarterly* 5 (1988), 165–205; and "Too Many Missing Cases: Holes in Our Knowledge About Police Use of Force," *Justice Research and Policy* 4 (2002): 87–102.

21. Fyfe, "Police Use of Deadly Force," 166.

22. Fyfe, "Too Many Missing Cases."

23. Michael D. White and David Klinger, "Contagious Fire? An Empirical Assessment of the Problem of Multi-Shooter, Multi-Shot Deadly Force Incidents in Police Work," *Crime and Delinquency* 58, no. 2: 196–221.

24. Lawrence W. Sherman and Robert H. Langworthy, "Measuring Homicide by Police Officers," *Journal of Criminal Law and Criminology* 70, no. 4 (1979): 546–60.

25. Alexander Alvarez, "Trends and Patterns of Justifiable Homicide: A Comparative Analysis," *Violence and Victims* 7, no. 4 (1992): 347–56; Sidney L. Harring, Tony Platt, Richard Speiglman, and Paul Takagi, "The Management of Police Killings," *Crime and Social Justice* 8, (Fall–Winter 1977): 34–43; David Jacobs and David Britt, "Inequality and Police Use of Deadly Force: An Empirical Assessment of a Conflict Hypothesis," *Social Problems* 26, no. 4 (1979): 403–12; David Jacobs and Robert M. O'Brien, "The Determinants of Deadly Force: A Structural Analysis of Police Violence," *American*

Journal of Sociology 103, no. 4 (1998): 837–62; John M. MacDonald, Robert J. Kaminski, Geoffrey P. Alpert, and Abraham N. Tennenbaum, "The Temporal Relationship Between Police Killings of Civilians and Criminal Homicide: A Refined Version of the Danger-Perception Theory," *Crime and Delinquency* 47, no. 2 (2001): 155–72; Sherman and Langworthy, "Measuring Homicide by Police Officers"; Jonathan R. Sorensen, James W. Marquart, and Deon E. Brock, "Factors Related to Killings of Felons by Police Officers: A Test of the Community Violence and Conflict Hypotheses," *Justice Quarterly* 10, no. 3 (1993): 417–40; Paul Takagi, "A Garrison State in Democratic Society," *Crime and Social Justice* (Spring/Summer 1974): 27–32.

26. Chicago: William A. Geller and Kevin J. Karales, "Shootings of and by Chicago Police: Uncommon Crises Part I: Shootings by Chicago Police," *Journal of Criminal Law and Criminology* 72, no. 4 (1981): 1813–66; and "Shootings of and by Chicago Police: Uncommon Crises Part II: Shootings of Police, Shooting Correlates and Control Strategies," *Journal of Criminal Law and Criminology* 73 (1982): 331–78. Los Angeles: Marshall W. Meyer, "Police Shootings at Minorities: The Case of Los Angeles," *Annals of the American Academy of Political and Social Science* 452 (1980): 98–110. Memphis: James J. Fyfe, "Blind Justice: Police Shootings in Memphis," *Journal of Criminal Law and Criminology* 73, no. 2 (1982): 707–22. New York City: James J. Fyfe, "Geographic Correlates of Police Shooting: A Microanalysis," *Journal of Research in Crime and Delinquency* 17 (1980): 101–13; "Always Prepared: Police Off-duty Guns," *Annals of the American Academy* 452 (1980): 72–81; and "Blind Justice." Philadelphia: Gerald D. Robin, "Justifiable Homicide by Police Officers." *Journal of Criminal Law and Criminology* 54 (1963): 225–31; William B. Waegel, "How Police Justify the Use of Deadly Force," *Social Problems* 32, no. 2 (1984): 146–55; Michael D. White, "Assessing the Impact of Administrative Policy on Use of Deadly Force by On- and Off-Duty Police," *Evaluation Review* 24, no. 3 (2000): 295–318; and "Controlling Police Decisions to Use Deadly Force: Reexamining the Importance of Administrative Policy," *Crime and Delinquency* 47 (2001): 131–51.

27. The Stolen Lives Project book, *Stolen Lives: Killed and Brutalized by Police* (Stolen Lives, 1997), was sold for five dollars plus shipping fees. Durán picked up a copy while attending a Movimiento Estudiantil Chicano de Aztlán (MEChA) national conference at the University of California, Los Angeles, in 1998. At the time he picked up a copy, he had no idea this research topic would become such a significant piece of his life work.

28. Stolen Lives Project, *Stolen Lives: Killed by Law Enforcement* (October 22nd Coalition to Stop Police Brutality, Repression and the Criminalization of a Generation, 1999), 3.

29. My mind can't remove the autopsy photos or the description regarding undigested French fries in his gastrointestinal tract. This was just a kid, someone with no idea he could be killed by the police.

30. Stolen Lives Project, *Stolen Lives: Killed by Law Enforcement.*

31. Jennifer E. Cobbina, *Hands Up: Don't Shoot: Why the Protests in Ferguson and Baltimore Matter, and How They Changed America* (New York University Press, 2019).

32. Comparison between average annual deaths per year of 373: Jodi M. Brown and Patrick A. Langan, *Policing and Homicide, 1976–98: Justifiable Homicide by Police, Police*

Officers Murdered by Felons, NCJ 180987, US Department of Justice, Bureau of Justice Statistics, Washington, DC, 2001 (Reports).

33. Catherine Barber, Deborah Azrael, Amy Cohen, Mathew Miller, Deonza Thymes, David Enxe Wang, and David Hemenway, "Homicides by Police: Comparing Counts from the National Violent Death Reporting System, Vital Statistics, and Supplementary Homicide Reports," *American Journal of Public Health* 106, no. 5 (2016): 922–27.

34. John S. Goldkamp, "Minorities as Victims of Police Shootings: Interpretations of Racial Disproportionality and Police Use of Deadly Force," *Justice System Journal* (1976): 169–83, reported a framework of two items, including a quasi-labeling view of which certain groups are monitored more closely or disproportionately higher rates of minority involvement in crime. Goldkamp found both arguments inadequate, but determining which one was more accurate was left unresolved in his analysis.

35. Other names for blaming the community include the "community violence" hypothesis, "environmental explanations," "ratio-threat hypothesis," or "reactive hypotheses."

36. David Jacobs and Robert M. O'Brien, "The Determinants of Deadly Force: A Structural Analysis of Police Violence," *American Journal of Sociology* 103, no. 4 (1998): 837–62.

37. John M. MacDonald, Robert J. Kaminski, Geoffrey P. Alpert, and Abraham N. Tennenbaum, "The Temporal Relationship Between Police Killings of Civilians and Criminal Homicide: A Refined Version of the Danger-Perception Theory," *Crime and Delinquency* 47, no. 2 (2001): 155–72, reviewed FBI supplementary homicide reports over a twenty-one-year period. See also Jonathan R. Sorensen, James W. Marquart, and Deon E. Brock, "Factors Related to Killings of Felons by Police Officers: A Test of the Community Violence and Conflict Hypotheses," *Justice Quarterly* 10, no. 3 (1993): 417–40.

38. Goldkamp, "Minorities as Victims of Police Shootings"; MacDonald et al., ""The Temporal Relationship Between Police Killings of Civilians and Criminal Homicide"; Sorensen, Marquart, and Brock, "Factors Related to Killings of Felons by Police Officers."

39. Marshall W. Meyer, "Police Shootings at Minorities: The Case of Los Angeles," *Annals of the American Academy of Political and Social Science* 452 (1980): 98–110; Gerald D. Robin, "Justifiable Homicide by Police Officers," *Journal of Criminal Law and Criminology* 54 (1963): 225–31.

40. Fyfe, "Geographic Correlates of Police Shooting"; Fyfe, "Police Use of Deadly Force: Research and Reform."

41. William B. Waegel, "How Police Justify the Use of Deadly Force," *Social Problems* 32, no. 2 (1984): 146–55.

42. James J. Fyfe, "Who Shoots? A Look at Officer Race and Police Shooting," *Journal of Police Science and Administration* 9, no. 4 (1981b): 367–82.

43. Sidney L. Harring, Tony Platt, Richard Speiglman, and Paul Takagi, "The Management of Police Killings," *Crime and Social Justice* 8 (Fall–Winter 1977): 34–43.

44. Paul Takagi, "A Garrison State in Democratic Society," *Crime and Social Justice* (Spring/Summer 1974): 27–32.

45. Paul Takagi, "LEAA's Research Solicitation: Police Use of Deadly Force," *Crime and Social Justice* (Spring/Summer 1979): 55.

46. Harring, Platt, Speiglman, and Takagi, "The Management of Police Killings."

47. Harring, Platt, Speiglman, and Takagi, "The Management of Police Killings," 14.

48. Fyfe, "Police Use of Deadly Force: Research and Reform," 190.

49. Robin Kelley, "Slangin' Rocks . . . Palestinian Style:' Dispatches from the Occupied Zones of North America," in *Police Brutality: An Anthology*, ed. J. Nelson (Norton, 2000), 21–59.

50. Paul Takagi, "Race, Crime, and Social Policy: A Minority Perspective," *Crime and Delinquency* 27, no. 1 (1981): 48–63.

51. Alvin W. Gouldner, "The Sociologist as Partisan: Sociology and the Welfare State," *American Sociologist* 3, no. 2 (1968): 103–16.

52. Gouldner, "The Sociologist as Partisan."

53. Aldon D. Morris, *The Scholar Denied: W. E. B. Du Bois and the Birth of Modern Sociology* (University of California Press, 2015).

54. Ida B. Wells, *Southern Horrors: Lynch Law in All Its Phases* (Satya Books, 2017); and *The Red Record: Tabulated Statistics and Alleged Causes of Lynching in the United States* (1895; Cavalier Classics, 2015).

55. Morris, *The Scholar Denied*, 135.

56. Josh Hardman, "UC Berkeley: The Closure of the School of Criminology, 1976," 2016, FoundSF, https://www.foundsf.org/index.php?title=UC_Berkeley:_The_Closure_of _the_School_of_Criminology,_1976 (Reports); Zhandarka Kurti, "Starting a Dialogue: From Radical Criminology to Critical Resistance," *Journal of World-Systems Research* 27, no. 1 (2021): 136–48; Osagie K. Obasogie and Peyton Provenzano. "Race, Racism, and Police Use of Force in 21st Century Criminology: An Empirical Examination," *UCLA Law Review* 69 (2023): 1206–69.

57. Richard Delgado and Jean Stefancic, *Critical Race Theory: An Introduction*, 3rd ed. (New York University Press, 2017).

58. Coretta Phillips and Benjamin Bowling, "Racism, Ethnicity and Criminology: Developing Minority Perspectives," *British Journal of Criminology* 43 (2003): 269–90.

59. Emile Durkheim, *Suicide* (Free Press, 1951), 276.

60. Emile Durkheim, *The Division of Labor in Society* (Free Press, 1984), 310.

61. Julian Go, *Postcolonial Thought and Social Theory* (Oxford University Press, 2016).

62. Robert J. Durán, "Fatalistic Social Control: The Reproduction of Oppression Through the Medium of Gangs," PhD diss., University of Colorado at Boulder, 2006; *Gang Life in Two Cities: An Insider's Journey* (Columbia University Press, 2013).

63. Sandra Bass, "Policing Space, Policing Race: Social Control Imperatives and Police Discretionary Decisions," *Social Justice* 28, no. 1 (2001): 156–76.

64. Michelle Alexander, *The New Jim Crow: Mass Incarceration in the Age of Colorblindness* (New Press, 2012).

65. Hillary Haley and Jim Sidanius, "Person-Organization Congruence and the Maintenance of Group-Based Social Hierarchy: A Social Dominance Perspective," *Group Processes and Intergroup Relations* 8, no. 2 (2005): 187–203.

66. American Public Health Association, https://www.apha.org/what-is-public-health.

67. David Hemenway, *Private Guns: Public Health* (University of Michigan Press, 2004).

68. Kelly Lytle Hernández, *Migra! A History of the U.S. Border Patrol* (University of California Press, 2010); Walter L. Hixson, *American Settler Colonialism: A History* (Palgrave Macmillan, 2013).

69. C. Wright Mills, *The Power Elite* (Oxford University Press, 2000), 171.

70. Lisa Marie Cacho, *Social Death: Racialized Rightlessness and the Criminalization of the Unprotected* (New York University Press, 2012).

71. Stanley Cohen, *States of Denial: Knowing About Atrocities and Suffering* (Polity, 2001).

72. Geoffrey P. Alpert and William C. Smith, "How Reasonable Is the Reasonable Man? Police and Excessive Force," *Journal of Criminal Law and Criminology* 85 (1994): 481–501; Fyfe, "Who Shoots?"; Geller and Karales, "Shootings of and by Chicago Police"; David N. Konstantin, "Homicides of American Law Enforcement Officers, 1978–1980," *Justice Quarterly* 1, no. 1 (1984): 29–45; Albert J. Reiss, "Controlling Police Use of Deadly Force," *Annals of the American Academy* 452 (1980): 122–34.

73. Ernesto B. Vigil, *The Crusade for Justice: Chicano Militancy and the Government's War on Dissent* (University of Wisconsin Press, 1999).

74. US Census Bureau, QuickFacts Denver City, Colorado; Denver, Colorado, 2022, https://www.census.gov/quickfacts/fact/table/denvercitycolorado,denvercountycolorado/PST045222.

75. CensusScope 2011, https://www.censusscope.org; Geolytics, National Change Database CD: 1970–2010 (Reports).

1. THE CONTEXT OF POLICE SHOOTINGS AND PROTEST: DENVER

1. Lynn Bartels, "Remembering Teen, Demanding Justice—Hundreds Grieve, Offer Support to Paul Child's Family," *Rocky Mountain News*, July 11, 2003.

2. William A. Ritter Jr., Decision Letter: Paul Nash Childs, October 16, 2003.

3. One of the participants interviewed at the vigil, a white person, wished more white people had attended the event and expressed the belief that whites needed to show more outrage at this incident. Lynn Bartels, "Remembering Teen, Demanding Justice—Hundreds Grieve, Offer Support to Paul Child's Family," *Rocky Mountain News*, July 11, 2003.

4. Sean Kelly and Kit Miniclier, "Hundreds Call for Justice—Peacefully Rally Honors Slain Teen After Community Leaders Decry Anti-cop Flier," *Denver Post*, July 11, 2003.

5. Wellington Webb and Cindy Brovsky, *Wellington Webb: The Man, the Mayor, and the Making of Modern Denver* (Fulcrum, 2007).

6. Sean Kelly, "Cop Cleared in Shooting—DA's Decision in Killing of 15-Year-Old Paul Childs Brings Outrage," *Denver Post*, October 17, 2003.

7. The reason for the arrests was interesting because the protestors simply sat next to the police department. It was as if crossing a magical line and sitting down resulted in an arrest. Watching the protestors sit there was very powerful. However, the consequence of getting arrested was a deterrent for most of the crowd, including me.

8. According to Ronald J. Stephens, La Wanna M. Larson, and the Black American West Museum, *Images of America: African Americans in Denver* (Arcadia, 2008). Wilma Webb, the wife of Wellington Webb, coined the term "marade" in 1986 by combining the words "march" and "parade."

9. The heckling and consistent community advocacy on behalf of Paul Childs may have influenced John Hickenlooper to form the task force and to provide his own independent evaluation.

10. Alvin LeCabe Jr., City and County of Denver, Department of Safety, "Public Statement of Manager of Safety Regarding Disciplinary Action Taken Against Officer James Turney Arising from Events That Occurred on July 4 and 5, 2003," 2004 (Reports).

11. John C. Ensslin, "Officer's Suspension Upheld," *Rocky Mountain News*, April 11, 2007; Michael Knievel, "Teaching Deadly Force: Collaborative Dynamics and the Rhetoric of Police Policy," *IEEE Transactions on Professional Communication* 51, no. 1 (2008): 95–109.

12. Javier Erik Olvera, "Shooting Haunts Child's Mom—Teen's Slaying by Cop in 2003 a 'Nightmare I Can't Escape,'" *Rocky Mountain News*, July 5, 2006. According to Timothy M. Rastello, "Landmark Civil Rights Case Results in $2.25 Million Verdict," *TortSource* 4, no. 1 (2001): 3–4, the largest lawsuit was $2.25 million for the killing of Randy Bartel, who died as a result of a Denver police officer running a red light at seventy miles per hour during a high-speed pursuit. Bartel was a twenty-two-year-old college student who was taking his date home. The officer, Michael Farr, had previously had his license revoked three times by the state of Colorado in addition to having numerous traffic violations. Despite being denied employment by four other law enforcement agencies, Farr was hired by the Denver Police Department against the recommendation of the executive director of the Civil Service Commission. When the accident occurred, there were even threats toward witnesses to not report what they had observed. Additional significant cases include lawsuits involving Emily Rice in 2008 ($3 million), Jamal Harris in 2011 ($3.25 million), Marvin Booker in 2014 ($6 million), and a settlement for Michael Marshall in 2017 ($4.65 million).

13. The scale for analyzing shootings will be described in chapter 2.

14. William A. Ritter A. Jr., Decision Letter: Sergio Alejandro Medrano, November 18, 2003, 11 (Reports).

15. Brian D. Crecente, "Man Cradled Can, Not Gun, in Hand—but Denver Police Officer Thought Otherwise, and Invalid, 64, Is Dead," *Rocky Mountain News*, July 13, 2004; Sean Kelly, Amy Herdy, and Kris Hudson, "Shooting Probe to Stay Secret—No Charges Against Cop," *Denver Post*, December 10, 2004. Officer Ranjan Ford passed away on March 22, 2020, at the age of forty-eight, from unlisted reasons.

16. US Department of Commerce, Bureau of the Census, 1980 (Reports); US Census Bureau, 2022 (Reports).

17. World Population Review, "The 200 Largest Cities in the United States by Population 2022," https://worldpopulationreview.com/us-cities.

18. US Census Bureau, 2022, QuickFacts: Denver County, Colorado (Reports).

19.   National Change Database CD, 1970–2000, Geolytics; Robert J. Durán, *Gang Life in Two Cities: An Insider's Journey* (Columbia University Press, 2013), analyzed census data by neighborhood through Geolytics and then conducted field observations.

20.   Mike Maciag, "Gentrification in America Report," 2015, https://www.governing.com /archive/gentrification-in-cities-governing-report.html (Reports); Brian Page and Eric Ross, "Legacies of a Contested Campus: Urban Renewal, Community Resistance, and the Origins of Gentrification in Denver," *Urban Geography* 38, no. 9 (2017): 1293–1328; Durán, *Gang Life in Two Cities*, noticed this issue during his ethnographic walks of neighborhoods during 2000 to 2006 and analysis of census tracts from 1970 to 2010.

21.   Maciag, "Gentrification in America Report."

22.   Laura M. Mauck, *Five Points Neighborhood of Denver* (Arcadia, 2001); Ernesto B. Vigil, *The Crusade for Justice: Chicano Militancy and the Government's War on Dissent* (University of Wisconsin Press, 1999). According to Stephens, Larson, and the Black American West Museum, *Images of America: African Americans in Denver*, Lauren Watson led the Black Panther Party of Denver.

23.   Louisa W. Arps, *Denver in Slices: A Historical Guide to the City* (Ohio University Press, 1998); Lyle Dorsett and Michael McCarthy, *The Queen City: A History of Denver* (Pruett, 1986); Thomas J. Noel, *The City and the Saloon: Denver 1858–1916* (University of Nebraska Press, 1982).

24.   Dorsett and McCarthy, *The Queen City*, 53.

25.   Treaty of Guadalupe-Hidalgo, National Archives Catalog, US National Archives, February 2, 1848; Laura E. Gómez, *Manifest Destinies: The Making of the Mexican American Race* (New York University Press, 2007).

26.   Colin G. Calloway, *First Peoples: A Documentary Survey of American Indian History* (St. Martin's, 1999).

27.   Mark D. Varien and Richard H. Wilshusen, *Seeking the Center Place: Archaeology and the Ancient Communities in the Mesa Verde Region* (University of Utah Press, 2002).

28.   Calloway, *First Peoples*; Richard White, *It's Your Misfortune and None of My Own: A New History of the American West* (University of Oklahoma Press, 1991).

29.   Gary L. Roberts, *Massacre at Sand Creek: How Methodists Were Involved in an American Tragedy* (Abingdon, 2016).

30.   Roberts, *Massacre at Sand Creek*, 231.

31.   Dorsett and McCarthy, *The Queen City*, 42.

32.   Roberts, *Massacre at Sand Creek*, 137.

33.   White, *It's Your Misfortune and None of My Own*.

34.   Walter L. Hixson, *American Settler Colonialism: A History* (Palgrave Macmillan, 2013). There are interesting records of soldiers who were part of another contingent of the battalion who were disgusted with the events that unfolded and testified against Chivington. Carol A. Turner, *Forgotten Heroes and Villains of Sand Creek* (History Press, 2010).

35.   In 1909, a statue was erected to memorialize Union soldiers, and it was placed in front of the Colorado State Capitol in Denver. However, it became synonymous with one of the soldiers whose name was included, John Chivington. During the national effort to

remove statues of the Confederacy that symbolized slavery, white supremacy, and genocide, the "Chivington" statue was toppled in 2020. Although some individuals claimed
the statue reflected all Union soldiers, the American Indian Movement, and other community members continued to see this object as a reflection of Colorado officials' not
taking full accountability for the wrongful actions that occurred at Sand Creek and
during other confrontations with Native Americans. Roberts, *Massacre at Sand Creek*,
reported how the Sand Creek massacre was seen as wrongful to people throughout the
country—with the exception of most residents of Colorado.

36. Noel, *The City and the Saloon.*
37. Lenny Ortiz, *Denver Behind Bars: The History of the Denver Sheriff Department and
     Denver's Jail System* (Aventine, 2004); Eugene Frank Rider, "The Denver Police Depart-
     ment: An Administrative, Organizational, and Operational History, 1858–1905," PhD
     diss., University of Denver, 1971. Denver's official legal charter was in 1861. Statehood
     was not achieved until 1876.
38. According to Rider, "The Denver Police Department," the sentence of death was given
     to James A. Gordon in 1860. The first legal execution (if that, as it was a self-created
     People's Court) was of John Stoefel/Stuffel in 1859. Stephen J. Leonard, *Lynching in Col-
     orado, 1859–1919* (University Press of Colorado, 2002); Mitch Morrissey and Norm
     Brisson, *Denver District Attorney's Office: A History of Crime in the Mile High City
     (1869–2021)* (n.p., 2022); Michael L. Radelet, *The History of the Death Penalty in Colo-
     rado* (University Press of Colorado, 2017).
39. Leonard, *Lynching in Colorado*; Rider, "The Denver Police Department." Radelet, *The
     History of the Death Penalty in Colorado*, did not report on the case of L. H. Musgrove.
     Rider, "The Denver Police Department," included newspaper articles describing how
     members of the mob should instead be considered as an assembly of the people because
     it was made up of good men who acted quietly and orderly to execute the law. Wil-
     liam W. King, *Going to Meet a Man: Denver's Last Legal Public Execution, 27 July 1886*
     (University Press of Colorado, 1990); Rider, "The Denver Police Department"; and
     Radelet, *The History of the Death Penalty in Colorado*, report on the killing of Myers/
     Miears, but Leonard, *Lynching in Colorado*, does not. Rider incorporated a news arti-
     cle that stated it is better for the law to carry out the execution compared to vigilantes.
40. Rider, "The Denver Police Department."
41. Rider, "The Denver Police Department"; Morrissey and Brisson, *Denver District Attor-
     ney's Office.*
42. Dorsett and McCarthy, *The Queen City: A History of Denver.* Arps, *Denver in Slices*,
     stated the neighborhood was referred to as "Chink Alley."
43. Noel, *The City and the Saloon.*
44. Leonard, *Lynching in Colorado*, stated the injustice even included city journalists and
     historians, who got Look Young's name wrong, referring to him as Sing Lee. Ortiz, *Den-
     ver Behind Bars*, reported that the individuals charged with killing Look Young were
     acquitted and set free.
45. Noel, *The City and the Saloon.* Rider, "The Denver Police Department." The history
     books reviewed provide little information on Officer Isaac Brown. Stephens, Larson,

and the Black American West Museum, *Images of America*, reported that a Civil War veteran named Francis T. Bruce, a Black man, was listed on the Denver Police roster in 1892. He also helped organize the Black Masonic Lodge and was known affectionately as "Daddy." Additional officers in the early 1900s include William Baker and his brother Ulysses Baker. They both remained in law enforcement into the 1920s.

46. Leonard, *Lynching in Colorado, 1859–1919*; Radelet, *The History of the Death Penalty in Colorado*. Strangely, John Chivington was also the sheriff who escorted Green to the gallows and conducted his autopsy.

47. King, *Going to Meet a Man*, provided an Afrocentric perspective. He focused on race, crime, and justice and how this hanging was a moral travesty despite being considered legal.

48. Rider, "The Denver Police Department," 280. The officer involved in the shooting was Police Captain Swain. The surname of the person shot was Fitzgerald. Rider reported differing accounts of what transpired in the shooting. Morrissey and Brisson, *Denver District Attorney's Office*, mistakenly listed this shooting as occurring on February 26, 1896, but it was 1886, as reflected in the three news citations used.

49. Morrissey and Brisson, *Denver District Attorney's Office*, describe numerous corruption scandals involving members of the Denver Police Department.

50. Morrissey and Brisson, *Denver District Attorney's Office*. The Denver police officer's name was Robert J. Boykin and the Arapahoe County deputy sheriff's name was Milton Smith. Additional information is available from the Colorado Supreme Court case: 22 Colo. 496; 45 P. 419; 1896 Colo. LEXIS 275. It was unclear why there was not more information about this incident, because it appears to be a landmark case in terms of a feud between law enforcement agencies, an interracial killing of a Black officer by a white officer, and a legal examination of self-defense and use of lethal force.

51. Rider, "The Denver Police Department," 466, with citation given to *Rocky Mountain News*, November 24, 1897, 10. Durán was curious about the language stating "escaping criminals charged with great crimes, such as murder, burglary, arson, etc." because of the lack of clarity around the use of the term "charged." It seems to be simply an accusation rather than a criminal conviction for committing a particular crime. In addition, the statement included crimes such as burglary, which could result in a potential death sentence if the officer decided to use his firearm. *Tennessee v. Garner*, which was decided in 1985, changed the legal guidelines, removing the discretion to shoot at a person fleeing a burglary unless there was a deadly threat to the officer or another party.

52. Rider, "The Denver Police Department, 499, reported that as of 1969, target practice was held once a month for Denver police officers and that they were required to shoot for the record.

53. Morrissey and Brisson, *Denver District Attorney's Office*. The man shot and killed by Officer Secrest was Henry Reed.

54. "Denver Murder: Engineer Shot by Policeman in Saloon," *Twin Lakes Miner*, February 17, 1906. News article coverage stated that the man killed was a steam engineer from Minnesota who had done nothing wrong. On Ancestry.com, Charles Sumner Secrest

was found and the information provided stated he was paroled in 1913 but later violated his parole and was sent back to prison before being re-released in 1917.

55.   Rider, "The Denver Police Department," 591.

56.   The Denver Sheriff's Office was created in 1902 to manage the court and jail. Denver became independent from Arapahoe County to become its own city and county in 1902. Ortiz, *Denver Behind Bars*, reports that the jail had been run by the police department until 1951 and was not independently run by the sheriff's office until 1968. Sheriff's officers have a limited law enforcement capacity in the city and county and cannot work as off-duty security inside the city limits.

57.   Moya Hansen, "Entitled to Full and Equal Enjoyment: Leisure and Entertainment in the Denver Black Community, 1900 to 1930," *Historical Studies Journal* 10, no. 1 (1993): 47–77.

58.   Hansen, "Entitled to Full and Equal Enjoyment"; Lionel Dean Lyles, "An Historical-Urban Geographical Analysis of Black Neighborhood Development in Denver, 1860–1970." PhD diss., University of Colorado at Boulder, 1977; Laura M. Mauck, *Five Points Neighborhood of Denver* (Arcadia, 2001). Stephens, Larson, and the Black American West Museum, *Images of America*, refer to Five Points as the heart of the Black community.

59.   Lynda Faye Dickson, "The Early Club Movement Among Black Women in Denver: 1890–1925," PhD diss., University of Colorado at Boulder, 1982, 115.

60.   Mauck, *Five Points Neighborhood of Denver*.

61.   Noel, *The City and the Saloon*.

62.   Noel, *The City and the Saloon*; Leonard, *Lynching in Colorado, 1859–1919*.

63.   Rider, "The Denver Police Department," 379. Rider and Leonard used different sources to provide a slightly dissimilar account of the lynching. Italians became organized in response to a shooting of a World War I veteran named Jerry Corbetta, who was shot in the back by Denver police detective George Klein during a bootlegging raid. Corbetta was shot for running away during the raid, and the DA charged the officer with first-degree murder. According to Morrissey and Brisson, *Denver District Attorney's Office*, two thousand Italians protested the detective being able to post bond. Detective Klein was cleared by a jury; the officer reported the shooting was accidental. Detective Klein was later shot to death by an unknown assailant.

64.   Morrissey and Brisson, *Denver District Attorney's Office*; Noel, *The City and the Saloon*.

65.   David Cunningham, *Klansville, U.S.A.: The Rise and Fall of the Civil Rights–Era Ku Klux Klan* (Oxford University Press, 2013); Rory McVeigh and Kevin Estep, *The Politics of Losing: Trump, the Klan, and the Mainstreaming of Resentment* (Columbia University Press, 2019).

66.   Phil Goodstein, *In the Shadow of the Klan: When the KKK Ruled Denver, 1920–1926* (New Social Publications, 2006). In 1921, Denver's manager of safety ordered members of the Denver police department to "shoot to kill" bandits fleeing from officers. Morrissey and Brisson, *Denver District Attorney's Office*. It was reported that criminals had relocated from other large cities to set up in Denver.

67.   Goodstein, *In the Shadow of the Klan*; Morrissey and Brisson, *Denver District Attorney's Office*; Vigil, *The Crusade for Justice*.

68. According to Morrissey and Brisson, *Denver District Attorney's Office*, Denver residents of the Stapleton neighborhood voted to change the name to Central Park in 2020 so it would no longer be named after the Klan-elected mayor.

69. James Harlan Davis, "The Rise and Fall of Dr. John Galen Locke," KOA Radio Station, 1962, https://www.worldcat.org/title/rise-and-fall-of-dr-john-galen-locke/oclc /53481553. Interview can be heard at the University of Denver's oral history archives: https://mediaspace.du.edu/media/The+rise+and+fall+of+Dr.+John+Galen+Locke +oral+history+interviews/1_7azyki3f;   https://mediaspace.du.edu/media/The%20 rise%20and%20fall%20of%20Dr.%20John%20Galen%20Locke%20oral%20his-tory%20interviews/1_w4agtx1h. Ku Klux Klan Membership Ledger Book 2020 (Reports); Morrissey and Brisson, *Denver District Attorney's Office*, reported that the DA at the time, Philip S. Van Cise (1921 to 1924), vigorously pursued the Klan, and he was replaced by Foster W. Cline (1925 to 1928), a more sympathetic DA.

70. This information was provided by Morrissey and Brisson, *Denver District Attorney's Office*. To confirm, Durán reviewed the KKK ledger and confirmed Judge Henry Bray's name and address.

71. McVeigh and Estep, *The Politics of Losing*, described the third national wave occurring in the 1960s and the fourth wave evolving after the 2016 election of Donald J. Trump.

72. Hansen, "Entitled to Full and Equal Enjoyment"; Dickson, "The Early Club Movement Among Black Women in Denver," reported that the Black population in Denver was 2.5 percent in 1930.

73. Sierra Standish, "Beet Borderland: Hispanic Workers, the Sugar Beet, and the Making of a Northern Colorado Landscape," master's thesis, Colorado State University, 2002.

74. US Government Printing Office, 1960, "Number of Inhabitants: Colorado," https:// www2.census.gov/prod2/decennial/documents/17598731v1p7ch2.pdf (Reports).

75. Adult Education Council of Denver, "The Youth Problem in Denver," a Report by the Youth Survey Committee of the Adult Education Council of Denver 14(2), in clippings file, Denver Public Library, 1938 (Reports).

76. Durán, *Gang Life in Two Cities*.

77. Durán *Gang Life in Two Cities*; James Patrick Walsh, "Young and Latino in a Cold War Barrio: Survival, the Search for Identity, and the Formation of Street Gangs in Denver, 1945–1955," master's thesis, University of Colorado at Denver, 1995.

78. Leonard, *Lynching in Colorado, 1859–1919*; Noel, *The City and the Saloon*. The Denver Police Department encountered scrutiny when seventeen officers received grand jury indictments in 1946 for charges ranging from burglary to brutality. The officers were exonerated in separate trials, and the DA's office dismissed the seventeenth case. George V. Kelly, *The Old Gray Mayors of Denver* (Pruett, 1974). Morrissey and Brisson, *Denver District Attorney's Office*, 188, stated that the district attorney, James T. Burke, who reported charges against the officers stated the mayor and police chief were "doing nothing to weed misfits out the police department." *Rocky Mountain News*, August 12, 1946.

79. 1947 Report by Mayor Newton's Interim Committee on Human Relations as reported by Richard Delgado and Jean Stefancic, "Home Grown Racism: Colorado's Historic

Embrace—and Denial—of Equal Opportunity in Higher Education," The Latino/a Research and Policy Center, University of Colorado at Denver, 1999 (Reports).

80. Morrissey and Brisson, *Denver District Attorney's Office.*

81. *Rocky Mountain News*, October 13, 1944; *Rocky Mountain News*, November 23, 1947; *Denver Post*, November 17, 1950; City and County of Denver, 1958 (Reports).

82. Delgado and Stefancic, "Home Grown Racism."

83. *Rocky Mountain News*, January 31 to February 6, 1954; *Rocky Mountain News*, October 10, 1957.

84. *Denver Post*, April 5, 1959.

85. Officer John W. Ford Jr. was found guilty of burglarizing the Pink Lady Tavern and was sentenced to prison in the mid-1950s. Kelly, *The Old Gray Mayors of Denver*. However, additional burglaries based on other officers continued. Morrissey and Brisson, *Denver District Attorney's Office*, reported that Officer Ford admitted to a dozen burglaries since he joined the Denver Police Department in 1952. He was arrested in 1954 and sentenced to prison for one to five years.

86. This statement was made in a supplemental editorial the same day.

87. Leonard, *Lynching in Colorado, 1859–1919*; Noel, *The City and the Saloon*. Kelly, *The Old Gray Mayors of Denver*, describes the burglary of a Denver meat market and the stealing of a safe. The safe fell out the back of a vehicle as the police officers were fleeing. Additional police officers arrived at the scene and let the fleeing officers go.

88. Kelly, *The Old Gray Mayors of Denver.*

89. Mort Stern, "What Makes a Policeman Go Wrong," *Journal of Criminal Law, Criminology, and Police Science* 53, no. 1 (1962): 97–101.

90. Kelly, *The Old Gray Mayors of Denver.*

91. Morrissey and Brisson, *Denver District Attorney's Office.*

92. Vigil, *The Crusade for Justice*. The other key organizations were focused on land grants, farm workers, and forming a political party.

93. David H. Bayley and Harold Mendelsohn, *Minorities and the Police: Confrontation in America* (Free Press, 1968).

94. Vigil, *The Crusade for Justice.*

95. The officer who shot and killed Edward Larry Romero was Officer Gordon L. Thomas. No gun was ever found. A news article later contradicted the officer's claim that he was shot in the chest, instead claiming he was shot in the back.

96. Warren Beard was the officer who killed Alfred Salazar. He was working off duty.

97. Piñedo was killed by patrolman John E. Cain. George Seaton became police chief after Harold Dill resigned. A 1967 *El Gallo* newspaper article described the court proceedings as a "farce." They reported that the judge dismissed the case because the DA failed to provide sufficient evidence and did not call witnesses.

98. Elizabeth Hinton, *From the War on Poverty to the War on Crime: The Making of Mass Incarceration in America* (Harvard University Press, 2016); and *America on Fire: The Untold History of Police Violence and Black Rebellion Since the 1960s* (Liveright, 2021).

99. Del W. Harding, "Police Policy Set on Line-of-Duty Killing," *Rocky Mountain News*, December 16, 1965.

100. "Controversy Over Civil Suits Against Policemen Deepens," *Rocky Mountain News*, November 10, 1966.

101. "Plan to Recruit and Train Minority Policemen Studied," *Denver Post*, August 24, 1967; "Negroes Feel Bias a Fact on Denver Force," *Denver Post*, October 24, 1967.

102. Don Lyle, "Police Promotion Changes Sought," *Rocky Mountain News*, April 30, 1968.

103. Vigil, *The Crusade for Justice*. In addition to the police shootings reported by Vigil, news articles also reported a significant number, including the shootings of Andrew Garcia (1967), Richard Medina (1967), Nathan Earl Jones (1968), Joseph Martin Archuleta (fifteen years of age in 1968), and Ronald Harrison (eighteen years of age in 1975). There was also a probe of several officers selling drugs in 1970.

104. Cindy Parmenter, "Jury Indicts 1, Clear 2 in Curtis Incident," *Denver Post*, December 9, 1977.

105. Vigil, *The Crusade for Justice*, 341–42.

106. Cecil Jones, "Council Considering Police Review Board," *Rocky Mountain News*, June 30, 1974.

107. Suzanne Weiss, "Mayor Forms Committee to Monitor Police Conduct," *Rocky Mountain News*, October 10, 1976.

108. Tim McGovern and Bill McBean, "Review Panel Critical of Police," *Denver Post* September 16, 1977. The committee was chaired by Hiawatha Davis Jr.; the vice chair was Carol Tempest; and other committee members included Irving Hook, Wally Beckler, and Paul Sandoval.

109. Suzanne Weiss, "Council Seeks Police Conduct Reports," *Rocky Mountain News*, April 21, 1978.

110. City and County of Denver, "Denver Police Officers Receive 'Citizens Appreciate Police' Award for Acts of Kindness," 2020, https://www.denvergov.org/content/denvergov/en /police-department/news/2020/officers-receive-award.html.

111. Colorado Revised Statutes, Title 18, Criminal Code, 18-1-707 (2013).

112. Morrissey and Brisson, *Denver District Attorney's Office*.

113. Erickson Commission, "Report of the Erickson Commission," 1997 (Reports).

114. James B. Meadow, "Police Shoot, Kill Man Outside Club—Off-Duty Cops Working Security Open Fire After Car Backs Into Officer," *Rocky Mountain News*, March 21, 1996. More coverage will be provided in chapter 4.

115. Erickson Commission, "Report of the Erickson Commission," 55.

116. Michael Knievel, "Teaching Deadly Force: Collaborative Dynamics and the Rhetoric of Police Policy," *IEEE Transactions on Professional Communication* 51, no. 1 (2008): 95–109. Michael Knievel reconstructed the task force's 104-day existence and analyzed the group's struggle to work together. Differing opinions between the community activists and law enforcement officers was the biggest difficulty. The final report captures disagreements in language and law enforcement officers' fears regarding increased oversight and how it may conflict with the officers' ability to manage various situations.

117. Denvergov.org, https://www.denvergov.org/Government/Agencies-Departments-Offi ces/Agencies-Departments-Offices-Directory/Office-of-the-Independent-Monitor.

118. Merrick Bobb, Bernard K. Melekian, Oren Root, Mathew Barge, and Camelia Naguib, "The Denver Report on Use of Deadly Force," Police Assessment Resource Center, Los Angeles, 2008.

119. Bobb et al., "The Denver Report on Use of Deadly Force," 15.

120. *Graham v. Connor*, 490 U.S. 386. (1989); Bobb et al., "The Denver Report on Use of Deadly Force," 19.

121. This was definitely transparent in the video recording of officers and the suspects involved in the Frankie Brabo (January 3, 2006) shooting. Police thought he possessed a gun, but it was actually his cell phone.

122. Bobb et al., "The Denver Report on Use of Deadly Force," 138. It appears that after the PARC report, the Denver Police Department moved toward developing a policy that refrained from shooting at people in vehicles; however, incidents have continued. It has become more administratively frowned upon but not removed as a potential legal recourse.

123. King, *Going to Meet a Man*.

124. Leonard, *Lynching in Colorado, 1859–1919*.

2. DIVERGENT LIFE CHANCES FOR GETTIN' SHOT BY THE POLICE

1. Beth McCann, "Officer Involved Shooting Protocol," State of Colorado, Office of the District Attorney, Denver, 2017, 3 (Reports).

2. Mitchell R. Morrissey, Officer-Involved Shooting Protocol, State of Colorado, Office of the District Attorney, Denver, 2011 (Reports). After I asked to move the process forward by receiving the confidentiality agreement, the communications director stated the lawyers would need to prepare the document. The document was never sent to Durán.

3. Bridget DuPey, Margaret B. Kwoka, and Christopher McMichael, "Access Denied: Colorado Law Enforcement Refuses Public Access to Records of Police Misconduct," University of Denver Legal Studies Research Paper 18-05, 2018.

4. For an overview of the difficulty of obtaining internal affairs files in Colorado, see DuPey, Kwoka, and McMichael, "Access Denied." In this study, the researchers from the University of Denver Sturm College of Law submitted requests to forty-three of the 180 law enforcement agencies in Colorado asking for information regarding internal affairs investigations conducted between 2015 and 2016. More than half of the agencies did not respond or reject the requests. An effort to follow up with agencies that were minimally, moderately, or substantially supportive resulted in cost-prohibitive estimates. For example, the Denver Sheriff's Department and the Denver Police Department stated a cost of $1,500 to obtain eight files, based on an estimate of time of thirty-five to fifty hours at a rate of $35 per hour. In our study, Durán used research funds of $825 to obtain additional information on twenty-five of the officers included in chapter 5 at the cost of $33 per hour for twenty-five hours of labor.

5. The largest gap in coverage was during the 1980s when the local news agencies were not electronically searchable and when many officer-involved shootings were not reported in the news. Despite this challenge, Durán used microfiche archives at the Denver Public Library to look at newspapers for the two to three days following a reported shooting. Many of the shootings did not receive media attention.

6. Autopsy data was not requested by the Denver medical examiner for the year 2020, as data collection for analysis had already been completed. Quantitative data is not as flexible as qualitative data when adding new information.

7. From the 1980 census for 1983 to 1984, 1990 census for 1985 to 1994, 2000 census for 1995 to 2004, 2010 census for 2005 to 2014, and the 2020 census for 2015 to 2020. The Geolytics National Change Database CD was used for these analyses.

8. Jon M. Shane, Brian Lawton, and Zoe Swenson, "The Prevalence of Fatal Police Shootings by U.S. Police, 2015–2016: Patterns and Answers from a New Data Set," *Journal of Criminal Justice* 52 (2017): 101–11.

9. Nancy Whittier, Tina Wildhagen, and Howard J. Gold, *Statistics for Social Understanding: With Stata and SPSS* (Rowman & Littlefield, 2020), 650.

10. Addresses for the individuals shot were not provided in DA reports or autopsies. They were compiled by incorporating all available forms of data.

11. Historical US Census data for 1980 to 2010 were gathered from Geolytics, National Change Database CD, 1970–2010.

12. These numbers may be higher because autopsies were the best source for postmortem toxicology tests, whereas other cases where the individual survived were not as consistently reported or available in the DA letters or case files.

13. A small number of cases reported that this was assessed by the law enforcement agency before interviewing.

14. Denver Police Department Operations Manual 2020 (Reports).

15. National Institute on Alcohol Abuse and Alcoholism (NIAAA), "Alcohol's Effects on the Body," 2022, https://www.niaaa.nih.gov/alcohols-effects-health/alcohols-effects-body (Reports).

16. Beth McCann, "Decision Letter: Mac McPherson," January 19, 2021 (Reports). According to the Denver Police Department Operations Manual 2020, a blood alcohol level of 0.08 or higher can result in a DUI.

17. Jacky M. Jennings, Adam J. Milam, Amelia Greiner, et al., "Neighborhood Alcohol Outlets and the Association with Violent Crime in One Mid-Atlantic City: The Implications for Zoning Policy," *Journal of Urban Health* 91, no. 1 (2014): 62–71.

18. Abron F. Franklin II, Thomas A. Laveist, Daniel W. Webster, and William K. Pan, "Alcohol Outlets and Violent Crime in Washington D.C," *Western Journal of Emergency Medicine* 11, no. 3 (2010): 283–90.

19. Li Zhu, Dennis M. Gorma, and Stéphane Horel, "Alcohol Outlet Density and Violence: A Geospatial Analysis," *Alcohol and Alcoholism* 39, no. 4 (2004): 369–75.

20. Xingyou Zhang, Bonnie Hatcher, Lydia Clarkson, et al., "Changes in Density of on-Premises Alcohol Outlets and Impact on Violent Crime, Atlanta, Georgia, 1997–2007," *Preventing Chronic Disease* 12, no. 140317 (2015).

21. Pamela J. Trangenstein, Frank C. Curriero, Daniel Webster, et al., "Outlet Type, Access to Alcohol, and Violent Crime," *Alcohol: Clinical and Experimental Research* 42, no. 11 (2018): 2234–45.

22. In 2012, Colorado legalized recreational use of marijuana for adults over the age of twenty-one.

23. National Institute on Drug Abuse (NIDA), "Drugfacts," 2019, https://nida.nih.gov/drug topics/publications/drug-facts (Reports).

24. Centers for Disease Control and Prevention (CDC), "Polysubstance Use Facts," 2022, https://www.cdc.gov/stopoverdose/polysubstance-use/index.html (Reports).

25. Erich Goode, *Drugs in American Society* (McGraw-Hill, 2008).

26. National Institute on Alcohol Abuse and Alcoholism 2022, "Alcohol's Effects on the Body" (Reports).

27. Substance Abuse and Mental Health Services Administration, "Highlights for 2020 National Survey on Drug Use and Health," 2022, https://www.samhsa.gov/data/release /2020-national-survey-drug-use-and-health-nsduh-releases (Reports).

28. Eugene A. Paoline III, William Terrill, and Logan J. Somers, "Police Officer Use of Force Mindset and Street-Level Behavior," *Police Quarterly* 24, no. 4 (2021): 547–77; William Terrill and Stephen D. Mastrofski, "Situational and Officer-Based Determinants of Police Coercion," *Justice Quarterly* 19, no. 2 (2002): 215–48.

29. We were unable to obtain official files before 1983. We do have unofficial numbers that indicate that at least eleven individuals were shot by the police in 1982. Organized alphabetically by surname, these cases include the following: Amos, Darrow, Gallimore, Garcia, Goodwin, King, Martinez, Pyne, Rivera, West, and Williams. In 1981, at least eight individuals were shot by the police: Collier, Gonzalez, Shanholtz, and five with an unknown surname. In 1980, at least ten individuals were shot by the police: Barchfer, Bazil, Caranza, Evans, Giron, Gonzales, Guerrero, Joyner, and Mathew. In addition, Durán has information for fifty-eight additional persons shot by law enforcement between 1905 and 1979 if additional research information becomes available to analyze these cases more comprehensively.

30. Michael Sierra-Arévalo, "American Policing and the Danger Imperative," *Law and Society Review* 55, no. 1 (2021): 70–103; John M. Violanti, Desta Fekedulegn, Michael E. Andrew, et al., "Shift Work and the Incidence of Injury Among Police Officers," *American Journal of Industrial Medicine* 55 (2012): 217–27.

31. Mitchell Morrisey, "Decision Letter: Phuong Van Dang," January 17, 2008 (Reports).

32. The authors chose to use the first name of the individual shot by the police to provide a more humanistic account for those under thirty years of age and Mr. or Ms. for those aged thirty years or older as a sign of respect. The individuals shot by the police were not punished legally via a court of law but rather at the discretion of individual police officers. The purpose is not to condone the actions of the individuals shot or vilify the law enforcement officer but to emphasize the public health risk that exists for the greatest chance of loss of life at the hands of the criminal justice system.

33. William A. Ritter Jr., "Decision Letter: Kathleen Stege," 1994 (Reports).

34. We defined "high poverty" as equal or greater than 20 percent to lower than 40 percent. "Medium poverty" was defined as equal or greater than 10 percent to lower than
20 percent. See William Julius Wilson, *When Work Disappears: The World of the New
Urban Poor* (Vintage, 1996), to learn more about the impact of poverty and joblessness.

35. Durán has a physical map where he has labeled the location of each shooting. As the
location for each shooting is in the dataset, it is the hope of Durán to later use GIS mapping to greater analyze these patterns.

36. This analysis was based upon previous college courses taught by Durán in criminal law,
constitutional law, and prison law. The texts that supplement these courses include the
following publications: Clair A. Cripe, *Legal Aspects of Corrections Management* (Aspen,
1997); Daniel E. Hall, *Criminal Law and Procedure*, 2nd ed. (Delmar, 1996); Jerold H.
Israel and Wayne R. LaFave, *Criminal Procedure: Constitutional Limitations* (West
Group, 2001); Yale Kamisar, Wayne R. LaFave, Jerold H. Israel, and Nancy J. King,
Basic Criminal Procedure: Cases, Comments, and Questions, 10th ed. (West Group,
2002).

37. Denver Police Department Operations Manual 2020, 176 (Reports).

38. Denver Police Department Operations Manual 2020 (Reports).

39. Pew Research Center, "Key Facts About Americans and Guns," 2021, https://www
.pewresearch.org/fact-tank/2021/09/13/key-facts-about-americans-and-guns/ (Reports).

40. Norman S. Early Jr., "Decision Letter: Richard Z. Davis," 1991, 4–5 (Reports). A study
by William L. Sandel, M. Hunter Martaindale, and J. Pete Blair, "A Scientific Examination of the 21-Foot Rule," *Police Practice and Research: An International Journal* 22,
no. 3 (2020): 1314–29, found the twenty-one-foot rule did not provide law enforcement
officers a safe distance to stop a charging suspect. They found thirty-two feet safer but
also did not want to suggest that such a policy change would mitigate all the other factors that go into someone's approaching an officer in a way that may justify the use of
deadly force.

41. Merrick Bobb, Bernard K. Melekian, Oren Root, Mathew Barge, and Camelia Naguib,
"The Denver Report on Use of Deadly Force," Police Assessment Resource Center, Los
Angeles, 2008 (Reports).

42. David Hemenway, *Private Guns: Public Health* (University of Michigan Press,
2004), 47.

43. Michael A. Vella, Alexander Warshauer, Gabriella Tortorello, et al., "Long-Term Functional, Psychological, Emotional, and Social Outcomes in Survivors of Firearm Injuries," *JAMA Surgery* 155, no. 1 (2019): 51–59.

44. Gracie R. Baum, Jaxon T. Baum, Dan Hayward, and Brendan J. MacKay, "Gunshot
Wounds: Ballistics, Pathology, and Treatment Recommendations, with a Focus on
Retained Bullets," *Orthopedic Research and Reviews* 14 (2022): 293–317; Antonio
Pinto, Anna Russo, Alfonso Reginelli, et al., "Gunshot Wounds: Ballistics and Imag-
ing Findings," *Seminars in Ultrasound, CT and MRI* 40, no. 1 (2019): 25–35; Peter M.
Rhee, Ernest E. Moore, Bellal Joseph, et al., "Gunshot Wounds: A Review of Ballis-
tics, Bullets, Weapons, and Myths," *Journal of Trauma Acute Care Surgery* 80, no. 6

(2016): 853–67. A forthcoming book by Craig Uchida on the Los Angeles Police Department had data on not only shooting deaths and injuries but also cases where officers fired their weapon. Such data could be important for analyzing cases where a police officer fired their weapon but may have missed the suspect. Later chapters will also present how the state of California made the reporting of such data a legal requirement.

45. Justin Nix and John A. Shjarback, "Factors Associated with Police Shooting Mortality: A Focus on Race and a Plea for More Comprehensive Data," *PLOS One* (2021): https://doi.org/10.1371/journal.pone.0259024.

46   Durán believes that the drop from 2011 to 2020 was partially attributable to not having access to the complete files at the DA's office.

47. Future research could benefit from interviewing people shot, witnesses, and officers.

48. This evaluation was based upon the reading of several scholarly works: James R. Acker, Robert M. Bohm, and Charles S. Lanier, eds., *America's Experiment with Capital Punishment: Reflections on the Past, Present, and Future of the Ultimate Penal Sanction* (Carolina Academic Press, 1998); Jay Lifton and Greg Mitchell, *Who Owns Death? Capital Punishment, the American Conscience, and the End of Executions* (HarperPerennial, 2002); R. J. Maratea, *Killing with Prejudice: Institutionalized Racism in American Capital Punishment* (New York University Press, 2019); Michael L. Radelet, *The History of the Death Penalty in Colorado* (University Press of Colorado, 2017).

49. Radelet, *The History of the Death Penalty in Colorado.*

50. The three officers terminated were Denver police officers Gary Brooke and Robert Fitzgibbons and Federal Bureau of Investigation officer Chase Bishop.

51. The decision to change the name of this category to "less controversial" compared to "legitimate" was based on a statement by Sister Helen Prejean in the foreword to Radelet's 2017 book *The History of the Death Penalty in Colorado.* Sister Prejean was countering an argument for the death penalty based upon "he deserves it." She stated, "As I see it, human beings do not have the wisdom or skills to determine what other people 'deserve' with the accuracy necessary to separate who shall live and who shall die. There are too many unknowns and unknowables." In essence we are "making these godlike decisions without godlike skills" (xiii).

52. Scores between −11 and −3 were considered problematic, −2 to +2 questionable, and +3 to +7 less controversial.

53. Nancy Whittier, Tina Wildhagen, and Howard J. Gold, *Statistics for Social Understanding: With Stata and SPSS* (Rowman & Littlefield, 2020), 649.

54. John H. Laub and Robert J. Sampson, *Shared Beginnings, Divergent Lives: Delinquent Boys to Age 70* (Harvard University Press, 2003).

55. In terms of the data sources used to gather the data for this analysis, there were age group differences in whether there was a copy of the autopsy for those who died as a result of the shooting or soon after from suicide, news coverage, and the number of news articles. A copy of an autopsy was less frequent for individuals below 18 years old (57.1 percent) compared to older age groups who received a copy of the autopsy over 64 percent of the time (18 to 27: 73.5 percent; 28 to 37: 77.1 percent; 38 to 47: 72.4 percent; 48+: 64.7 percent). Although there were high rates of news coverage across all age

groups, individuals 48 years and older received the least coverage (68.0 percent) and a median of 2 (0, 3) newspaper articles, while the other age groups had 80.0 percent or higher and a median of three to four newspaper articles.

56. Paul Colomy and Laura Ross Greiner, "Making Youth Violence Visible: The News Media and the Summer of Violence," *Denver University Law Review* 77 (2000): 661–88; Robert J. Durán, *Gang Life in Two Cities: An Insider's Journey* (Columbia University Press, 2013).

57. Federico Coccolini, Camilla Cremonini, Francesco Arces, et al., "Trauma in Elderly," in *Emergency General Surgery in Geriatrics*, ed. Rifat Latifi, Fausto Catena, and Federico Coccolini (Springer, 2021), 231–41; Kimberly K. Nagy, Robert F. Smith, Roxanne R. Roberts, et al., "Prognosis of Penetrating Trauma in Elderly Patients: A Comparison with Younger Patients," *Journal of Trauma and Acute Care Surgery* 49, no. 2 (2000): 190–94; Peter M. Rhee, Ernest E. Moore, Bellal Joseph, et al., "Gunshot Wounds: A Review of Ballistics, Bullets, Weapons, and Myths," *Journal of Trauma Acute Care Surgery* 80, no. 6 (2016): 853–67.

58. Elizabeth Arias, Betzaida Tejada-Vera, Kenneth D. Kochanek, and Farida B. Ahmad, "Provisional Life Expectancy Estimates for 2021," National Vital Statistics System Rapid Release, Report 23, US Department of Health and Human Services, Centers for Disease Control and Prevention, 2022 (Reports).

59. Joanne Belknap, *The Invisible Woman: Gender, Crime, and Justice* (Sage, 2015); James W. Messerschmidt, *Masculinities and Crime: Critique and Reconceptualization of Theory* (Rowman and Littlefield, 1993).

60. Christine L. Williams and Arlene Stein, eds., *Sexuality and Gender* (Blackwell, 2002).

61. Pew Research Center, "About 5% of Young Adults in the U.S. Say Their Gender Is Different from Their Sex Assigned at Birth," 2022, https://www.pewresearch.org/fact-tank/2022/06/07/about-5-of-young-adults-in-the-u-s-say-their-gender-is-different-from-their-sex-assigned-at-birth/ (Reports).

62. Virginia Prince, "Sex vs. Gender," *International Journal of Transgenderism* 8, no. 4 (2005): 29–32; Kristen W. Springer, Jeanne Mager Stellman, and Rebecca M. Jordan-Young, "Beyond a Catalogue of Differences: A Theoretical Frame and Good Practice Guidelines for Researching Sex/Gender in Human Health," *Social Science and Medicine* 74, no. 11 (2012): 1817–24.

63. Brian Burghart, *Fatal Encounters*, University of Southern California, 2023, https://fatalencounters.org/ (Reports). "The Counted: People Killed by Police in the US," 2015, https://www.theguardian.com/us-news/ng-interactive/2015/jun/01/the-counted-police-killings-us-database. *Fatal Force*, 2015, https://www.washingtonpost.com/graphics/investigations/police-shootings-database/; Campaign Zero, "Mapping Police Violence," 2013, https://mappingpoliceviolence.org/.

64. Merriam-Webster.com, s.v. "cisgender" (2023), https://www.merriam-webster.com/dictionary/cisgender. News coverage of this case can be found on "Denver Police Killing of LGBT Teen Jessica Hernandez Sparks Outcry as Officers' Claims Disputed," *Democracy Now*, February 13, 2015, https://www.democracynow.org/2015/2/13/denver_police_killing_of_lgbt_teen.

65. There were no significant sex differences in sociodemographic characteristics of the person shot, alcohol and drug use of the person shot, incident-related factors, and sociodemographic characteristics of the officers who shot.

66. Norman S. Early, "Decision Letter: Anne D. Barnett," 1992 (Reports).

67. Kevin Simpson, "Changing Story of Mom's Death Shakes Son's Faith in Cops," *Denver Post*, May 19, 1992.

68. The closest exception was the shooting of Ms. Barnett. The female officer attempted to shoot Ms. Barnett, but the bullet ricocheted off a metal railing and instead hit her male partner.

69. Walter L. Hixson, *American Settler Colonialism: A History* (Palgrave Macmillan, 2013).

70. Kevin R. Johnson, *Opening the Floodgates: Why America Needs to Rethink Its Borders and Immigration Laws* (New York University Press, 2007).

71. Migration Policy Institute, "Colorado: Demographics and Social," 2019, https://www.migrationpolicy.org/data/state-profiles/state/demographics/CO (Reports).

72. Denver Police Department Operations Manual 2020 (Reports). This manual also recognizes various reasons, including language differences, for noncompliance with verbal directives.

73. There were no significant differences in measures for sociodemographic characteristics of the officers who shot by foreign-born status.

74. William Armando Vega, Ethel Alderete, Bohdan Kolody, and Sergio Augilar-Gaxiola, "Illicit Drug Use Among Mexicans and Mexican Americans in California: The Effects of Gender and Acculturation," *Addiction* 93, no. 12 (1998): 1847.

75. Maritza Pérez, "A History of Anti-Latino State-Sanctioned Violence," in *Gringo Injustice: Insider Perspectives on Police, Gangs, and Law*, ed. Alfredo Mirandé (Routledge, 2020), 25–43.

76. Kirk Mitchell and Annette Espinoza, "March for Immigrants," *Denver Post*, March 25, 2006, https://www.denverpost.com/2006/03/25/march-for-immigrants/. For an overview of right-wing attacks on immigrants, Latinos, and the US-Mexico border, see Cristal N. Hernandez and Miltonette Olivia Craig, "Deadly Force by U.S. Customs and Border Protection: An Analysis of Fatal Encounters with Latinos," *Sociology of Race and Ethnicity* (2024); Gilberto Rosas, *Unsettling: The El Paso Massacre, Resurgent White Nationalism, and the US-Mexico Border* (John Hopkins University Press, 2023).

77. Shytierra Gaston, April D. Fernandes, and Rashaan A. DeShay, "A Macrolevel Study of Police Killings at the Intersection of Race, Ethnicity, and Gender," *Crime and Delinquency* 67, no. 8 (2021): 1075–102.

78. Asha Layne, "It's Not Just Black and White: How Black Immigrants Continue to Influence the Fight Against Police Violence," *Journal of Liberal Arts and Humanities* 2, no. 6 (2021): 1–7.

79. Kimberle Crenshaw, "Demarginalizing the Intersection of Race and Sex: A Black Feminist Critique of Antidiscrimination Doctrine, Feminist Theory, and Antiracist Politics," *University of Chicago Legal Forum* 1, no. 8 (1989): 139–67.

80. Patricia Hill Collins, *Intersectionality as Critical Social Theory* (Duke University Press, 2019).

3. TWO TRIGGER FINGERS: AN EXAMINATION OF RACIAL AND ETHNIC DIFFERENCES

1. Robert J. Durán, "Pinta Fearz: A Chicano Sociologist's Life on the Edge of the Law," *Bad Subjects: Political Education for Everyday Life* 71 (2004); and *Gang Life in Two Cities: An Insider's Journey* (Columbia University Press, 2013).

2. For a great overview of Latinos always perceived as banditos or criminals, see the work of Pat Rubio Goldsmith, Mary Romero, Raquel Rubio Goldsmith, et al., "Ethno-Racial Profiling and State Violence in a Southwest Barrio," *Aztlán* 34, no. 1 (2009): 93–123; and Alfredo Mirandé, *The Chicano Experience: An Alternative Perspective*, 2nd ed. (University of Notre Dame Press, 2022). In the white, Latter-Day Saints space of Utah, such perceptions of inclusion and exclusion were tied into the history of the state. Durán, *Gang Life in Two Cities*; Leslie G. Kelen and Eileen Hallet Stone, *Missing Stories: An Oral History of Ethnic and Minority Groups in Utah* (University of Utah Press, 1996).

3. See Robert J. Durán, "An Attempt to Change Disproportionate Minority Contact by Working in Youth Corrections," in *Experiencing Corrections: Lessons from the Field*, ed. M. Johnson (Sage, 2011), 149–64, for an overview of my efforts and frustrations working for the juvenile justice system.

4. This relationship between Copwatch and police departments did not necessarily begin or end this way, as described by Robert J. Durán and Charlene M. Shroulote-Durán, "Institutionalizing Community Oversight of the Police: Copwatch," in *Justice and Legitimacy in Policing: Transforming the Institution*, ed. M. O. Craig and K. L. Blount-Hill (Routledge, 2023), 76–90. For example, in one of the first Denver Copwatch events, occurring on 16th Street Mall, an officer tried to confiscate a camera. The news media was there to observe and record the interaction. The public backlash that ensued led the police department to alter its approach. Nevertheless, the Denver Police Department maintained an undercover officer within the group, which later resulted in the "Denver Spy Files" lawsuit led by the American Civil Liberties Union. ACLU of Colorado, "ACLU and Denver Officials Agree to Resolve Lawsuit Over Notorious Police 'Spy Files,'" April 17, 2003.

5. Durán, *Gang Life in Two Cities*; Durán and Shroulote-Durán, "Institutionalizing Community Oversight of the Police: Copwatch." Jocelyn Simonson, "Beyond Body Cameras: Defending a Robust Right to Record the Police," *Georgetown Law Journal* 104, no. 6 (2016): 1559–80, outlines the First Amendment right to observe and the importance of copwatching.

6. James D. Cockcroft, *Outlaws in the Promised Land: Mexican Immigrant Workers and America's Future* (Grove, 1986). Cockcroft focused on the legally unprotected status of Mexican immigrants. He used the term "outlaw" to refer to how this population was "outside the law" of protection. Another critical analysis of marginalized groups being omitted from protection includes the literature on social death. Lisa Marie Cacho, *Social Death: Racialized Rightlessness and the Criminalization of the Unprotected* (New York University Press, 2012); Orlando Patterson, *Slavery and Social Death: A Comparative Study* (Harvard University Press, 2018).

7.   Jerold H. Israel and Wayne R. LaFave, *Criminal Procedure: Constitutional Limitations* (West Group, 2001); Yale Kamisar, Wayne R. LaFave, Jerold H. Israel, and Nancy J. King, *Basic Criminal Procedure: Cases, Comments, and Questions*, 10th ed. (West Group, 2002).

8.   Paul A. Jargowsky, "The Persistence of Segregation in the 21st Century," *Minnesota Journal of Law and Inequality* 36, no. 2 (2018): 207–30; Douglas S. Massey, "Still the Linchpin: Segregation and Stratification in the USA," *Race and Social Problems* 12, no. 1 (2020): 1–12; Ruth D. Peterson and Lauren J. Krivo, *Divergent Social Worlds: Neighborhood Crime and the Racial-Spatial Divide* (Russell Sage Foundation, 2012).

9.   Denver Police Department Annual Report 1982, 2007. In 1982, DPD was 6.7 percent female and in 2007 11.4 percent.

10. Eduardo Bonilla-Silva, *Racism Without Racists: Color-Blind Racism and the Persistence of Racial Inequality in America*, 6th ed. (Rowman and Littlefield, 2022).

11. Eduardo Bonilla-Silva, "From Bi-Racial to Tri-Racial: Towards a New System of Racial Stratification in the USA," *Ethnic and Racial Studies* 27, no. 6 (2004): 931–50; Joe R. Feagin, *The White Racial Frame: Centuries of Racial Framing and Counter-Framing*, 2nd ed. (Routledge, 2013); Reanne Frank, Illana Redstone Akresh, and Bo Lu, "Latino Immigrants and the U.S. Racial Order: How and Where Do They Fit In?," *American Sociological Review* 75, no. 3 (2010): 378–401; Tanya Maria Golash-Boza, *Race and Racisms: A Critical Approach*, 3rd ed. (Oxford University Press, 2022); Laure E. Gómez, *Manifest Destinies: The Making of the Mexican American Race* (New York University Press, 2007); Ian F. Haney-López, *Racism on Trial: The Chicano Fight for Justice* (Belknap, 2003); Douglas S. Massey, "The Racialization of Mexicans in the United States? Racial Stratification in Theory and Practice," *Migración y Desarrollo* 10 (2008): 59–95; Juan F. Perea, "Ethnicity and the Constitution: Beyond the Black and White Binary Constitution," *William and Mary Law Review* 571, no. 2 (1995): 571–611; and "The Black/White Binary Paradigm of Race: The Normal Science of American Racial Thought," *California Law Review* 85, no. 5 (1997): 127–72.

12. Statement adopted from Robert Blauner, *Racial Oppression in America* (Harper and Row, 1972).

13. Matthew R. Durose, Erica L. Smith, and Patrick A. Langan, "Contacts Between Police and the Public, 2005," Bureau of Justice Statistics, 2007 (Reports). Andrew Gelman, Jeffrey Fagan, and Alex Kiss, "An Analysis of the New York City Police Department's 'Stop-and-Frisk' Policy in the Context of Claims of Racial Bias," *Journal of the American Statistical Association* 102, no. 479 (2007): 813–23; Andrew Golub, Bruce D. Johnson, and Eloise Dunlap, "The Race/Ethnicity Disparity in Misdemeanor Marijuana Arrests in New York City," *Criminology and Public Policy* 6, no. 1 (2007): 131–64; Human Rights Watch, *Shielded from Justice: Police Brutality and Accountability in the United States* (Human Rights Watch, 1998); Brad W. Smith and Malcolm D. Holmes, "Police Use of Excessive Force in Minority Communities: A Test of the Minority Threat, Place, and Community Accountability Hypotheses," *Social Problems* 61, no. 1 (2014): 83–104.

14. Rob Voigt, Nicholas P. Camp, Vinodkumar Prabhakaran, et al., "Language from Police Body Camera Footage Shows Racial Disparities in Officer Respect," *Proceedings of the National Academy of Sciences* 114, no. 25 (2017): 6521–26.

15. Raúl Peréz and Geoff Ward, "From Insult to Estrangement and Injury: The Violence of Racist Police Jokes," *American Behavioral Scientist* 63, no. 13 (2019): 1810–29. For particular marginalized groups in society, there has even been reported the use by law enforcement of the term "NHI," or "No Human Involved." Celeste Fremon, *Father Greg and the Homeboys: The Extraordinary Journey of Father Greg Boyle and His Work with the Latino Gangs of East L.A* (Hyperion, 1995); Cheryl L. Neely, *No Human Involved: The Serial Murder of Black Women and Girls and the Deadly Cost of Police Indifference* (Beacon, 2025).

16. As academia is primarily a white space that has included primarily white researchers researching white officers, it is difficult to imagine how they could objectively realize how their own backgrounds may be playing a role in how they perceived society. There have only been a small number of scholars of color, whether Black, Latino, Native American, or Asian, who have studied law enforcement, but this has begun to change.

17. Gerald D. Robin, "Justifiable Homicide by Police Officers," *Journal of Criminal Law and Criminology* 54 (1963): 231.

18. Andres Inn, Alan C. Wheeler, and Cynthia L. Sparling, "The Effects of Suspect Race and Situation Hazard on Police Officer Shooting Behavior," *Journal of Applied Social Psychology* 7, no. 1 (1977): 27–37.

19. Bonilla-Silva, *Racism Without Racists*, 152. Research has found whites are the most segregated racial and ethnic group in the United States. John R. Logan and Brian Stults, "The Persistence of Segregation in the Metropolis: New Findings from the 2010 Census," Census Brief Prepared for Project US2010, 2011; and "Metropolitan Segregation: No Breakthrough in Sight," Working Paper 22-14, Center for Economic Studies, US Census Bureau, 2022 (Reports).

20. John S. Goldkamp, "Minorities as Victims of Police Shootings: Interpretations of Racial Disproportionality and Police Use of Deadly Force," *Justice System Journal* (1976): 169–83; John M. MacDonald, Robert J. Kaminski, Geoffrey P. Alpert, and Abraham N. Tennenbaum, "The Temporal Relationship Between Police Killings of Civilians and Criminal Homicide: A Refined Version of the Danger-Perception Theory," *Crime and Delinquency* 47, no. 2 (2001): 155–72; Robin, "Justifiable Homicide by Police Officers"; William B. Waegel, "How Police Justify the Use of Deadly Force," *Social Problems* 32, no. 2 (1984): 146–55.

21. Katheryn Russell-Brown, *Underground Codes: Race, Crime, and Related Fires* (New York University Press, 2004).

22. Such was the impetus for the creation of *Stolen Lives: Killed by Law Enforcement*, October 22nd Coalition to Stop Police Brutality, Repression and the Criminalization of a Generation, New York, 1999.

23. Alexander Alvarez, "Trends and Patterns of Justifiable Homicide: A Comparative Analysis," *Violence and Victims* 7, no. 4 (1992): 347–56; James J. Fyfe, "Observations on Police Deadly Force," *Crime and Delinquency* 27 (1981): 376–89, "Blind Justice: Police Shootings in Memphis," *Journal of Criminal Law and Criminology* 73, no. 2 (1982): 707–22, "Police Use of Deadly Force: Research and Reform," *Justice Quarterly* 5 (1988): 165–205; Sidney L. Harring, Tony Platt, Richard Speiglman, and Paul Takagi, "The

Management of Police Killings," *Crime and Social Justice* 8 (Fall–Winter 1977): 34–43; David Jacobs and Robert M. O'Brien, "The Determinants of Deadly Force: A Structural Analysis of Police Violence," *American Journal of Sociology* 103, no. 4 (1998): 837–62; Arthur L. Kobler, "Figures (and Perhaps Some Facts) on Police Killing of Civilians in the United States, 1965–1969," *Journal of Social Issues* 31, no. 1 (1975): 185–91; Paul Takagi, "A Garrison State in Democratic Society," *Crime and Social Justice* (Spring/Summer 1974): 27–32.

24. Jodi M. Brown and Patrick A. Langan, *Policing and Homicide, 1976–98: Justifiable Homicide by Police, Police Officers Murdered by Felons,* NCJ 180987, US Department of Justice, Bureau of Justice Statistics, 2001 (Reports).

25. *Fatal Force,* 2015, https://www.washingtonpost.com/graphics/investigations/police -shootings-database/.

26. David Hemenway, John Berrigan, Deborah Azrael, et al., "Fatal Police Shootings of Civilians, by Rurality," *Preventive Medicine* 134 (2020): 106046.

27. Elle Lett, Emmanuella Ngozi Asabor, Theodore Corbin, and Dowin Boatright, "Racial Inequity in Fatal US Police Shootings, 2015–2020," *Journal of Epidemiology and Community Health* 75 (2020): 394–97.

28. Brian Burghart, *Fatal Encounters,* University of Southern California, 2023, https:// fatalencounters.org/.

29. Frank Edwards, Michael H. Esposito, and Hedwig Lee, "Risk of Police-Involved Death by Race/Ethnicity and Place, United States, 2012–2018," *American Journal of Public Health* 108, no. 9 (2018): 1241–48. Although women, children, and transgender people were also documented by the database, they were excluded from the final sample because of the lower numbers for statistical analysis.

30. Frank Edwards, Hedwig Lee, and Michael Esposito, "Risk of Being Killed by Police Use of Force in the United States by Age, Race-Ethnicity, and Sex," *Proceedings of the National Academy of Sciences* 116, no. 34 (2019): 16793–98.

31. Alex E. Crosby and Bridget Lyons, "Assessing Homicides by and of U.S. Law Enforcement Officers," *New England Journal of Medicine* 375, no. 16 (2016): 1509–11.

32. Catherine Barber, Deborah Azrael, Amy Cohen, et al., "Homicides by Police: Comparing Counts from the National Violent Death Reporting System, Vital Statistics, and Supplementary Homicide Reports," *American Journal of Public Health* 106, no. 5 (2016): 922–27.

33. Disproportionate Minority Contact Technical Assistance Manual, US Department of Justice, 2009, https://www.ncjrs.gov/html/ojjdp/dmc_ta_manual/index.html (Reports).

34. James W. Buehler, "Racial/Ethnic Disparities in the Use of Lethal Force by US Police, 2010–2014," *American Journal of Public Health* 107, no. 2 (2017): 295–97.

35. Campaign Zero 2013, *Mapping Police Violence,* 2023, https://mappingpoliceviolence .org/.

36. Aldina Mesic, Lydia Franklin, Alev Cansever, et al., "The Relationship Between Structural Racism and Black-White Disparities in Fatal Police Shootings at the State Level," *Journal of the National Medical Association* 110, no. 2 (2018): 106–16.

37. Takagi, "A Garrison State in Democratic Society," 30.

38. Harold D. Lasswell, "Sino-Japanese Crisis: The Garrison State Versus the Civilian State," *China Quarterly* 11 (1937): 643–49; and "The Garrison State," *American Journal of Sociology* 46, no. 4 (1941): 455–68.

39. Lasswell, "Sino-Japanese Crisis."

40. Radley Balko, *Rise of the Warrior Cop: The Militarization of America's Police Forces* (PublicAffairs, 2013); Daryl Meeks, "Police Militarization in Urban Areas: The Obscure War Against the Underclass," *The Black Scholar* 35, no. 4 (2006): 33–41.

41. When determining differences, it involves comparing rates of an outcome, such as police shootings, across groups, such as racial and ethnic groups in a specific geographical area. For example, you can report the rate at which police shootings occurred among whites (20 percent), Blacks (40 percent), Latinos (30 percent), or other racial and ethnic groups (10 percent) in a city. A statistical test can be used to determine if these rates differ. A disparity refers to an imbalance. When determining disparities, it involves comparing the rate of the outcome, such as police shootings, in a group in a specific geographical area to the proportions that group represents in the general population in that particular geographical area. For example, if the rate of police shootings for Blacks in a city was 40 percent but Blacks represent 20 percent of the population in that city, we can say that Blacks were overrepresented in police shootings.

42. The population of males between the ages of fourteen and sixty was used to develop a comparative risk, drawn from the 1980 census for the years of 1983 to 1984, 1990 census for 1985 to 1994, 2000 census for 1995 to 2004, 2010 census for 2005 to 2014, and the 2020 census for 2015 to 2020. For the censuses of 1980, 1990, 2000, and 2010, the National Change Database by Geoyltics was used for the age group of fourteen to sixty. The 2020 Census data was obtained online for Denver County, but the ages acquired were less able to be isolated; thus the years fifteen to sixty-four were used.

43. Edwards, Lee, and Esposito, "Risk of Being Killed by Police Use of Force in the United States by Age, Race-Ethnicity, and Sex"; Lett et al., "Racial Inequity in Fatal US Police Shootings, 2015–2020."

44. William A. Ritter Jr., "Decision Letter: James Fleck," June 16, 1997 (Reports).

45. Neighborhood census tract data was based on the closest decennial census to the year of the incident.

46. Norman S. Early Jr., "Decision Letter: Antonio Castillo," February 9, 1988 (Reports).

47. The finding of .25-caliber firearms has been sketchy when involved with police shootings. Officers planting guns on suspects after a shooting is not an unheard-of practice. Russell Covey, "Police Misconduct as a Cause of Wrongful Convictions," *Washington University Law Review* 90, no. 4 (2013): 1133–90; Arthur L. Kobler, "Police Homicide in a Democracy," *Journal of Social Issues* 31, no. 1 (1975): 163–84.

48. Michelle Alexander, *The New Jim Crow: Mass Incarceration in the Age of Colorblindness* (The New Press, 2012).

49. Avelardo Valdez, Zenong Yin, and Charles D. Kaplan, "A Comparison of Alcohol, Drugs, and Aggressive Crime Among Mexican-American, Black, and White Male Arrestees in Texas," *American Journal of Drug Alcohol Abuse* 23, no. 2 (1997): 249–65.

50. Alfredo Mirandé, *The Chicano Experience: An Alternative Perspective*, 2nd ed. (University of Notre Dame Press, 2022); Rogelio Sáenz and Maria Cristina Morales, *Latinos in the United States: Diversity and Change* (Polity, 2015); Edward E. Telles and Vilma Ortiz, *Generations of Exclusion: Mexican Americans, Assimilation, and Race* (Russell Sage Foundation, 2008).

51. William A. Ritter Jr., "Decision Letter: Ralph Baca-Salcido," May 10, 2000 (Reports).

52. Rahwa Haile, Tawandra Rowell-Cunsolo, Marie-Fatima Hyacinthe, and Sirry Alang, "'We (Still) Charge Genocide': A Systematic Review and Synthesis of the Direct and Indirect Health Consequences of Police Violence in the United States," *Social Science and Medicine* 322 (2023): 115784. Marlene Mercado, "Chicana/x Carework: Invisible Feminized Labor, Chicana/x Carceral Community, and the Variegated Nature of Feminist Agency in Carceral Contexts," PhD diss., University of California at Davis, 2022; Satomi Nakajima, Masaya Ito, Akemi Shirai, and Takako Konishi, "Complicated Grief in Those Bereaved by Violent Death: The Effects of Post-Traumatic Stress Disorder on Complicated Grief," *Dialogues in Clinical Neuroscience* 14, no. 2 (2012): 210–14; Rafael L. Outland, Thomas Noel Jr., Kris Rounsville, et al., "Living with Trauma: Impact of Police Killings on the Lives of the Family and Community of Child and Teen Victims," *Current Psychology* 41 (2020): 7059–73.

53. William A. Ritter Jr., "Decision Letter: Joseph P. Ashley," January 25, 2000 (Reports).

54. Tommy J. Curry, *The Man-Not: Race, Class, Genre, and the Dilemmas of Black Manhood* (Temple University Press, 2017).

55. Norman S. Early Jr., "Decision Letter: Miguel Angel Ochoa," February 11, 1993 (Reports).

56. Early, "Decision Letter: Miguel Angel Ochoa" (Reports).

57. Marilyn Robinson, "Off-Duty Cop Shoots Suspect in Bank Heist," *Denver Post*, October 29, 1992.

58. Alexander, *The New Jim Crow*; Sandra Bass, "Policing Space, Policing Race: Social Control Imperatives and Police Discretionary Decisions," *Social Justice* 28, no. 1 (2001): 156–76; Marc Mauer, *Race to Incarcerate* (New Press, 1999).

59. Norman S. Early Jr., "Decision Letter: Alfonso Mitchell," October 20, 1986 (Reports).

60. William A. Ritter Jr., "Decision Letter: Luis Almedia-Ponce," April 29, 2003 (Reports).

61. Denver Police Department Operations Manual, 2020; Denver Police Department 2009 Annual Report (Reports).

62. James Alan Fox, Jack Levin, and Kenna Quinet, *The Will to Kill: Making Sense of Senseless Murder* (Pearson, 2008); Mark S. Hamm and Ramón Spaaij, *The Age of Lone Wolf Terrorism* (Columbia University Press, 2017); Katherine S. Newman, Cybelle Fox, David Harding, et al., *Rampage: The Social Roots of School Shootings* (Basic Books, 2004).

63. Hamm and Spaaij, *The Age of Lone Wolf Terrorism*.

64. Jonas R. Kunst, Lisa S. Myhren, and Ivuoma N. Onyeador, "Simply Insane? Attributing Terrorism to Mental Illness (Versus Ideology) Affects Mental Representation of Race," *Criminal Justice and Behavior* 45, no. 12 (2018): 1888–902.

65. Durán, *Gang Life in Two Cities*; *The Gang Paradox*.

66. Nonwhite Other was not applicable.

67. The eight officers involved in the shooting included Joe Rodarte, James Smith, Randy Steinke, Kristy Garcia, Jeff Motz, Robert Pine, Raymond Sheridan, and Robert Waidler.

68. William A. Ritter Jr., "Decision Letter: Shaun Gilman," December 16, 2003 (Reports).

69. John Ingold, "There Has to Be Something Other Than a Bullet," *Denver Post*, July 29, 2003.

70. Kirk Mitchell, "Cops: Man Killed as He Turned with Gun," *Denver Post*, May 26, 2005.

71. Hector Gutierrez, "Victim's Kin Vow to Hire Investigator: Cousin Speaks Out Against Police at Candlelight Vigil," *Rocky Mountain News*, May 28, 2005.

72. Video link: https://www.facebook.com/denverpolice/videos/396196541716796/. This information was also featured in Andrew Kenney, "Lt. Michael Wyatt Is Denver's Police Ambassador to LGBTQ People," *Denverite*, December 1, 2016, https://denverite.com/2016/12/01/michael-wyatt-denvers-police-ambassador-lgbtq-people/.

73. Norman S. Early Jr., "Decision Letter: William B. Harper," November 2, 1983 (Reports).

74. Early, "Decision Letter: William B. Harper" (Reports).

75. Norman S. Early Jr., "Decision Letter: Louis Melendez," April 21, 1993 (Reports).

76. Early, "Decision Letter: Louis Melendez" (Reports).

77. Takagi, "A Garrison State in Democratic Society," 27–32.

78. Lett et al., "Racial Inequity in Fatal US Police Shootings, 2015–2020."

79. For an overview of locations in the United States with higher levels of Asian populations, see Robert Gebeloff, Denise Lu, and Miriam Jordan, "Inside the Diverse and Growing Asian Population in the U.S.," *New York Times*, August 21, 2021.

80. Grace S. Liu, Brenda L. Nguyen, Bridget H. Lyons, et al., "Surveillance for Violent Deaths—National Violent Death Reporting System, 48 States, the District of Columbia, and Puerto Rico, 2020," Surveillance Summaries, Centers for Disease Control, *Morbidity and Mortality Weekly Report* (*MMWR*), 2023 (Reports).

4. TYPES OF SHOOTINGS: PROBLEMATIC, QUESTIONABLE, AND LESS CONTROVERSIAL

1. In my review of the case, there is no decision letter provided for Steven Gant because the DA pursued criminal charges. There are many news articles, but to develop a more comprehensive viewpoint, a Colorado Open Records request was sent to the Denver Police Department to obtain additional records on Michael Blake. The information for this section combines these various sources of official records, public news reports, and the autopsy provided by the medical examiner's office.

2. Actually, Steven is biracial, with a white mother and Black father, but visibly perceived as Black. His mother believed he was killed in part because of his race and asserted that such an outcome would not have occurred with a white suspect and a Black officer. Ann Carnahan, "Jury Acquits Patrolman in Man's Death," *Rocky Mountain News*, December 18, 1993.

3. Steve Lipsher, "Man Pleaded, 'Don't Shoot,' Witnesses Say," *Denver Post*, September 2, 1992.

4. Marilyn Robinson and Steve Lipsher, "Earlier Threat by Cop? Allegation Probed in Fatal Shooting," *Denver Post*, September 4, 1992.

5. Katie Kerwin, "Single Shot Ends a Life, Jeopardizes a Career," *Rocky Mountain News*, March 20, 1993.

6. Alan Gottlieb, "Officer in Killing Called Liar," *Denver Post*, December 2, 1993.

7. Katie Kerwin, "Grand Jury Indicts Cop in Fatal Shooting," *Rocky Mountain News*, March 20, 1993.

8. Steve Lipsher, "Shooting Details Under Wraps—Police, DA Tell No More About Unarmed Suspect's Death," *Denver Post*, September 3, 1992.

9. Lipsher, "Man Pleaded, 'Don't Shoot,' Witnesses Say."

10. Ann Carnahan, "Witnesses Differ on Slaying by Cop—Prosecutors Say Officer Had Grudge Against Victim, but Defendant Says He Was Threatened in Stairwell," *Rocky Mountain News*, December 3, 1993.

11. Denver Coroner, Amy Martin, "Steven Gant," September 2, 1992 (Reports).

12. Kevin Simpson, "Unconscionable Delays Taint DA's Probe of Cop Shooting," *Denver Post*, December 17, 1992.

13. Marilyn Robinson and Tracy Seipel, "Cop Could Be Indicted in Shooting," *Denver Post*, February 12, 1993; Kevin Simpson, "Grand Jury Does Early's Work, Dares to Indict a Cop," *Denver Post*, March 23, 1993.

14. Kerwin, "Single Shot Ends a Life, Jeopardizes a Career."

15. Ann Carnahan, "Acquittal Embitters Mother of Capitol Hill Shooting Victim," *Rocky Mountain News*, December 18, 1993.

16. Ann Carnahan, "DA Drops Last Charge Against Cop," *Rocky Mountain News*, January 7, 1994.

17. George Lane, "Officer Won't Face New Trial in Death," *Denver Post*, January 7, 1994.

18. George Lane, "Lawsuit in Fatal Shooting Settled," *Denver Post*, June 9, 1998. One report had listed that $55,000 was awarded in damages.

19. Information obtained from Ancestry.com.

20. See the appendix for the process of evaluating police shootings.

21. There were eighteen problematic shootings from 1983 to 1990, nineteen between 1991 to 2000, twelve between 2001 and 2010, and thirteen between 2011 and 2020. It is important to note that additional data reporting could alter these forms of evaluation, shifting them to be more problematic or less controversial, but based upon the information gathered from various data sources as of 2023, this is the conclusion reached as of this writing.

22. Katheryn Russell-Brown, *Underground Codes: Race, Crime, and Related Fires* (New York University Press, 2004); Stolen Lives Project, *Stop Police Brutality, Repression and the Criminalization of a Generation* (New York, 1999) (Reports).

23. Jennifer Hunt and Peter K. Manning, "The Social Context of Police Lying," *Symbolic Interaction* 14, no. 1 (1991): 51–70; Jeff Rojek, Geoffrey P. Alpert, and Hayden P. Smith, "Examining Officer and Citizen Accounts of Police Use-of-Force Incidents," *Crime and Delinquency* 58, no. 2 (2010): 301–27.

24. David Weisburd, Rosann Greenspan, Edwin E. Hamilton, et al., *Police Attitudes Toward Abuse of Authority: Findings from a National Study* (National Institute of Justice, 2000) (Reports).

25. Robert J. Durán and Charlene Shroulote-Durán, "Institutionalizing Community Oversight of the Police: Copwatch," in *Justice and Legitimacy in Policing: Transforming the Institution*, ed. M. O. Craig and K. L. Blount-Hill (Routledge, 2023), 76–90; Mary D. Fan, *Camera Power: Proof, Policing, Privacy, and Audiovisual Big Data* (Cambridge University Press, 2019); Katheryn Russell-Brown, "Body Cameras, Police Violence, and Racial Credibility," *Florida Law Review Forum* 67 (2015): 207–13; Howard M. Wasserman, "Police Misconduct, Video Recording, and Procedural Barriers to Rights Enforcement," *North Carolina Law Review* 96, no. 5 (2017): 1313–62.

26. Not all of these firearms were real (i.e., BB guns), contained bullets, or were capable of firing.

27. Keith B. Payne, "Prejudice and Perception: The Role of Automatic and Controlled Processes in Misperceiving a Weapon," *Journal of Personality and Social Psychology* 81, no. 2 (2001): 181–92; and "Weapon Bias: Split-Second Decisions and Unintended Stereotyping," *Current Directions in Psychological Science* 15, no. 6 (2006): 287–91.

28. Philip J. Cook and Kristin A. Goss, *The Gun Debate: What Everyone Needs to Know* (Oxford University Press, 2014).

29. Reggie Rivers, "An Innocent Victim," *Denver Post*, July 16, 2004.

30. Alvin J. LaCabe Jr., "Public Statement of Manager of Safety Regarding Discipline of Officer Ranjan Ford Arising from the Shooting Death of Frank Lobato on July 11, 2004," City and County of Denver Department of Safety, August 5, 2005 (Reports).

31. Denver Coroner, Amy Martin, "Lobato, Frank," July 12, 2004 (Reports).

32. LaCabe, "Public Statement of Manager of Safety," 2005 (Reports).

33. Felix Doligosa Jr., "Pact Shortens Cop's Penalty," *Rocky Mountain News*, January 10, 2006.

34. David Olinger, "Shooting Victim Had Long Police Record—He Had Been Sentenced to Rehab Center and Was Violating a Judge's Order by Being at the Residence," *Denver Post*, July 13, 2004.

35. Christopher N. Osher, " 'Trigger Happy,' Woman Who Dated Him Says," *Denver Post*, April 24, 2007.

36. Christopher N. Osher, "Council Oks Settlement in Lobato Death—$900,000 Goes to the Family Lawyer and the Man's Four Children. The Unarmed Victim Was Shot by Police," *Denver Post*, December 18, 2007.

37. "Police Identify Cops on Leave for DUIs," *Denver Post*, June 17, 2014; *Daily Camera*, April 5, 2020.

38. Information for the Ismael Mena killing was developed from newspaper articles, interviews with community activists, the autopsy report, newspaper articles on each officer, and a public talk given by Leroy Lemos at a police accountability meeting. Leroy Lemos was a leader involved in the Justice for Mena Committee. The documentary titled *The Holes in the Door* by Alan Dominguez (2007) provided a great overview of this case. There is also a scholarly chapter written by Ernesto B. Vigil (2020) on this case in the book *Gringo Injustice*.

39. Alan Dominguez, *The Holes in the Door*, Documentary (Loco Lane Filmworks, 2007).

40. John C. Ensslin and Hector Gutierrez, "Man's Slaying in No-Knock Raid Puts Him in Public Eye. Father of Nine Children Had Gun but No Drugs," *Rocky Mountain News*, December 2, 1999; Denver Coroner, Amy Martin, "Mena, Ismael," September 30, 1999 (Reports).

41. Hector Gutierrez, "FBI Probes Cop Shooting of Immigrant No-Knock Drug Raid in September Led to Slaying of Mexican Worker," *Rocky Mountain News*, December 16, 1999.

42. Amy Herdy, "Findings Complicate Mena Case Sworn Testimony Raises Questions Over 1999 Denver Police Shooting," *Denver Post*, January 23, 2003.

43. John C. Ensslin, "Suit Alleges Conspiracy in Mena's Death," *Rocky Mountain News*, January 24, 2003; Howard Pankratz, "Bini Pleads Guilty to Lesser Charge in Fatal Raid," *Denver Post*, October 26, 2000.

44. Kevin Vaughan, "Cops Allegation Brings Swift Action," *Rocky Mountain News*, January 29, 2000.

45. Kevin Flynn, "Denver Pays $712,000 in Claims Against the Police," *Rocky Mountain News*, April 12, 2000.

46. Howard Pankratz, "Affidavit: Ex-Cop Locked Girls In—Joseph Bini Is Being Investigated for Child Enticement in the Case," *Denver Post*, June 5, 2008.

47. Information for the Lelani Lucero shooting was obtained from newspaper articles, the DA decision letter, and a review of the case file.

48. Norman S. Early Jr., "Decision Letter: Leilani Lucero," February 22, 1983 (Reports).

49. Information for the Antonio Reyes-Rojas shooting was obtained by reviewing the case file, the Denver DA decision letter, and newspaper articles.

50. Mitchell R. Morrissey, "Decision Letter: Diamond Demmer," 2010 (Reports).

51. Wayne Harrison, "Firing of Denver Officer Who Brought AR-15, Ammo from Home Is Upheld," *7News*, January 31, 2013.

52. Tom McGhee, "Lawyer: Fired Cop Mistakenly Loaded Incorrect Ammo," *Denver Post*, February 22, 2012; Jeremy P. Meyer, "City May Settle Cop-Shooting Suit," *Denver Post*, May 19, 2012.

53. James J. Fyfe, "Always Prepared: Police Off-Duty Guns," *Annals of the American Academy* 452 (1980): 72–81.

54. Michael D. White, "Assessing the Impact of Administrative Policy on Use of Deadly Force by On- and Off-Duty Police," *Evaluation Review* 24, no. 3 (2000): 295–318.

55. David Hemenway, Chloe Shawah, and Elizabeth Lites, "Defensive Gun Use: What Can We Learn from News Reports?," *Injury Epidemiology* 9, no. 19 (2022); Karol Mazur, "The 'Good Guy with a Gun' Concept in the American Gun Culture and Gun Control Policy," *Scientific Journal of Bielsko-Biala School of Finance and Law* 25, no. 2 (2021): 5–10. Andrew Stover, "An Examination of Mass Shooting Site Selection: Suggestions for Environmental Crime Prevention," Presentation at the American Society of Criminology, 2022 (Reports).

56. Denver Coroner, Amy Martin, "Ochoa, Miguel," November 9, 1992 (Reports).

57. Norman S. Early Jr., "Decision Letter: Miguel Angel Ochoa," February 11, 1993 (Reports).

58.   William A. Ritter Jr., "Decision Letter: Manuel Moreno-Delgado," April 7, 1997 (Reports).

59.   Brian D. Crecente, "Expert: Officer Likely Lied About Fatal Shooting—Commission Will Seek Reprimand After It Hears That the Evidence Doesn't Support Lawman's Story," *Rocky Mountain News*, December 21, 2001.

60.   Peggy Lowe, "Glass, Gun, and Blood Focus of 'Forensic Battle,'" *Rocky Mountain News*, November 24, 2001.

61.   Denver Coroner, Amy Martin, "Delgado, Manuel M.," December 22, 1996 (Reports).

62.   Patricia Callahan, "DA Panel to Study Shooting Decision Prompted by Truax Incident," *Denver Post*, June 26, 1996.

63.   James B. Meadow, "Police Shoot, Kill Man Outside Club—Off-Duty Cops Working Security Open Fire After Car Backs Into Officer," *Rocky Mountain News*, March 21, 1996.

64.   Tillie Fong, "Friends of Slain Bar Patron Hold Vigil—Police Shooting Angers Those Who Knew Victim," *Rocky Mountain News*, March 23, 1996.

65.   Alan Snel and Marilyn Robinson, "Driver Killed by Cops—Off-Duty Officers Fire Near Club," *Denver Post*, March 21, 1996.

66.   Robert Garrison, "Victim in FBI Shooting at Mile High Spirits in Denver Speaks Out," *ABC News*, June 6, 2018.

67.   Sam Tabachnik, "No Jail for Dancing FBI Agent—He Plead Guilty to Third-Degree Assault in Club Shooting," *Denver Post*, December 22, 2018.

68.   The omission of some shootings from this page became a concern when one shooting described in chapter 7 was discovered. It should have been listed, raising questions as to how often these incidents may have occurred from 1983 to 2020.

69.   Data sources did not differ significantly by type of shooting.

70.   Russell-Brown made this point in her book *Underground Codes*.

71.   Oscar Zeta Acosta, *The Revolt of the Cockroach People* (Bantam Books, 1973). https://www.facebook.com/ChicanoSecretService/videos/la-cucarachathe-revolt-of-the-cockroach-people-reading-part-1/1399682390047345/.

72.   Acosta, *The Revolt of the Cockroach People*, 106–7.

5. LAW ENFORCEMENT OFFICERS AND THE PRISTINE FOURTEEN

1.   It was reported that a 1975 federal consent decree, known as the Hogue Decree, required the Denver Police Department to hire from the "available workforce." Christopher N. Osher, "Black, Latino Hiring Rates Rise: Police, Fire Departments Cite Procedural Changes," *Denver Post*, September 26, 2007; Sarah Langbein, "Hispanic Cops File Federal Complaint: Denver Police Latino Group Claims Job Bias, Threatens Lawsuit," *Rocky Mountain News*, March 7, 2006. At the time, 10.1 percent of hires were mandated to be Black and 14.25 percent Latino. Officer Rufino Trujillo argued that the Latino population had grown since this decision was made and therefore the percentage should be more reflective of current population numbers.

2.   This interview was conducted for Durán's dissertation and later book titled *Gang Life in Two Cities*. In *Gang Life in Two Cities* Durán interviewed seven law enforcement officers, and he interviewed nineteen officers in *The Gang Paradox* (n=26). Between both sites, observations occurred of nearly 350 police-resident interactions for infractions or potential delinquent/criminal activity. These books were primarily focused on marginalized community experiences (n=137) with the police or practitioner efforts (n=57) to help youth, but law enforcement was always a major part of the story. A future aspect of research should include interviews of individuals shot by the police along with family members, friends, witnesses, and law enforcement officers. The criminologist David Klinger interviewed eighty officers from nineteen different police departments in four states for his book *Into the Kill Zone*. Identifying with a law enforcement perspective, Klinger describes his experience as a law enforcement officer killing an armed suspect. He did not report interviewing anyone shot by the police who had survived or any of their family members, friends, or witnesses.

3.   Robert J. Durán, "An Attempt to Change Disproportionate Minority Contact by Working in Youth Corrections," in *Experiencing Corrections: Lessons from the Field*, ed. M. Johnson (Sage, 2011), 149–64. For insider perspectives of working in law enforcement as a Latino, see Eric Gamino, "Racialized Policing on the South Texas-Mexico Border: Mexican American Police Officers' Racialization of Latin-Origin Unauthorized Immigrants," PhD diss., Texas A&M University, 2015. For perspectives on racial and ethnic identity and how it shapes the interviewing of law enforcement officers, see Claudio G. Vera Sanchez and Edwardo L. Portillos, "Insiders and Outsiders: Latino Researchers Navigating the Studying of the Police," *Race and Justice* 11, no. 4 (2021): 384–406.

4.   Jim Sidanius, James H. Liu, John S. Shaw, and Felicia Pratto, "Social Dominance Orientation, Hierarchy Attenuators and Hierarchy Enhancers: Social Dominance Theory and the Criminal Justice System," *Journal of Applied Social Psychology* 24, no. 4 (1994): 338–66.

5.   Jim Sidanius and Felicia Pratto, *Social Dominance: An Intergroup Theory of Social Hierarchy and Oppression* (Cambridge University Press, 1999), 223.

6.   Vicky M. Wilkins and Brian N. Williams, "Black or Blue: Racial Profiling and Representative Bureaucracy," *Public Administration Review* 68, no. 4 (2008): 654–64; "Representing Blue: Representative Bureaucracy and Racial Profiling in the Latino Community," *Administration and Society* 40, no. 8 (2009): 775–98.

7.   Elizabeth Hinton, *America on Fire: The Untold History of Police Violence and Black Rebellion Since the 1960s* (Liveright, 2021).

8.   The criminologists Samuel Walker and Charles Katz, *The Police in America: An Introduction*, 6th ed. (McGraw-Hill, 2008), 4, reported: "The crime-fighter image, however, is not an accurate description of what the police do. Only about one-third of a patrol officer's activities are devoted to criminal law enforcement. The typical officer rarely makes a felony arrest and almost never fires a weapon in his or her entire career. Most police work is best described as peacekeeping, order maintenance, or problem solving." Police in racialized minority communities experience a more aggressive type of policing than may have been presented by these authors. Although

firing a bullet may not always occur, there should be additional insight into how many times officers pull their firearm to demand submission from suspects to assert authority. In Rory Kramer and Brianna Remster, "Stop, Frisk, and Assault? Racial Disparities in Police Use of Force During Investigatory Stops," *Law and Society Review* 52, no. 4 (2018), 960–93, the analysis of New York City police encounter data from 2007 to 2014 found that Black residents were more likely to experience fundamentally different interactions with police, especially with the potential use of lethal force. John L. Worrall, Stephen A. Bishopp, and William Terrill, "The Effect of Suspect Race on Police Officers' Decision to Draw Their Weapons," *Justice Quarterly* 38, no. 7 (2021): 1428–47, analyzed Dallas Police Department data and found that Black suspects were two-thirds as likely as non-Blacks to have a weapon drawn against them. These authors, however, dismissed this overrepresentation because they argued that Blacks have higher arrest rates, which results in a higher number of interactions with Black suspects. Such an argument justifies systemic racism as common sense. Ian F. Haney-López, *Racism on Trial: The Chicano Fight for Justice* (Belknap, 2003). Haney-López reported: "When we uncritically rely on racial ideas, we often, in turn, practice racism. We treat people according to their place in the racial hierarchies created by society, and, by doing so, perpetuate those hierarchies. . . . Today, after several decades of declining overt prejudice, it is likely that most racism is unconsidered and reflexive, the product of thoughtless reliance on background ideas of race. Racism is now most often common sense" (7). Therefore, the structural racial inequality that has resulted in racially segregated neighborhoods and the concentration of wealth and poverty differentially should not then be utilized as establishing the benchmark for whether Blacks or Latinos are more likely to be shot by the police. The benchmark should be the county demographics and not arrest rates, as the overlap of crime and neighborhoods is reflective of these divergent social worlds. See Ruth D. Peterson and Lauren J. Krivo, *Divergent Social Worlds: Neighborhood Crime and the Racial-Spatial Divide* (Russell Sage Foundation, 2012).

9.   Most scholarly studies lack the data to include officer shots fired and suspect subsequent injury or death. The outcome of death is most commonly reported, and its limitations have been addressed by other researchers. Justin Nix and John A. Shjarback, "Factors Associated with Police Shooting Mortality: A Focus on Race and a Plea for More Comprehensive Data," *PLOS One* (2021), https://doi.org/10.1371/journal.pone.0259024. A forthcoming book by Craig D. Uchida, *Policing the Streets of Los Angeles: Controversy, Change, and Continuity* (Southern Illinois University Press), included all three (shots fired, injury, and death) in a study involving shootings by the Los Angeles Police Department. Uchida reported that from 2006 to 2021 there were 641 officer-involved shootings by the LAPD, of which 28 percent involved an officer firing a shot and missing the suspect. In 2015, California passed legislation requiring all law enforcement agencies to collect data on use-of-force incidents. Data collection has been ongoing from 2016 and required submission of this data since 2017. Several new research studies have begun analyzing these data.

10. *Graham v. Connor*, 490 U.S. 386. (1989).

11. Kaitlin Durbin, "Law Agencies Inconsistent in Naming Officers in Shootings," *The Gazette*, July 1, 2016.

12. James Alan Fox, Jack Levin, and Kenna Quinet, *The Will to Kill: Making Sense of Senseless Murder* (Pearson, 2008).

13. Erving Goffman, *The Presentation of Self in Everyday Life* (Doubleday Anchor, 1959).

14. Jeffrey Reiman, *The Rich Get Richer and the Poor Get Prison* (Pearson, 2007).

15. Everett C. Hughes, "Dilemmas and Contradictions of Status," *American Journal of Sociology* 50, no. 5 (1945): 353–59.

16. Goffman, *The Presentation of Self in Everyday Life*.

17. The cost to obtain these records was $825.

18. Walker and Katz, *The Police in America*.

19. Herman Goldstein, *Policing a Free Society* (Ballinger, 1977). A major flaw in Goldstein's analysis was his presumption that we live in a free society. He definitely must not have analyzed Black, Latino, or Native American history in the United States.

20. Frank Eugene Rider, "The Denver Police Department: An Administrative, Organizational, and Operational History, 1858–1905," PhD diss., University of Denver, 1971.

21. Captain Charles Hawley was attacked by two men in 1891. Officer Richie Rose was ambushed and murdered. Mitch Morrissey and Norm Brisson, *Denver District Attorney's Office: A History of Crime in the Mile High City (1869–2021)* (n.p., 2022).

22. Denver Police Officer John C. Phillips, the first line of duty death, was fatally wounded by a burglar during questioning on July 16, 1889. Morrissey and Brisson, *Denver District Attorney's Office*. Charles Wanless was killed responding to a disturbance. Detective Alpheus Moore was shot and killed on March 19, 1895, by, it was assumed, James McDonald during an arrest for burglary. McDonald was later arrested and found not guilty. In 1896, Denver Police Officer Wendell Smith was shot and killed when attempting to arrest a burglar. Officer William Beck was killed interrupting a burglary in 1908, as was Officer William Stephens in a separate incident. Officer Roy Downing was shot and killed attempting to intervene in a burglary in 1920.

23. On September 18, 1890, Officer Charles F. Wanless was shot and killed by Joseph N. Barnes during a domestic dispute with his wife and mother. Barnes received a nonfatal wound. Barnes was sentenced to ten years in prison. Morrissey and Brisson, *Denver District Attorney's Office*.

24. Denver Special Policeman Gustave Gisin was killed on January 24, 1892. The officer attempted to mediate a dispute between an employee who had been fired the day before. Morrissey and Brisson, *Denver District Attorney's Office*.

25. Officer Emerson McKinnon died on duty while assisting in fighting a fire. Officers Clarence Zietz and Forrest Ross died in car crashes in 1921. Officer Arthur Pinkerton was electrocuted moving an electric light for pedestrians in 1921. Morrissey and Brisson, *Denver District Attorney's Office*.

26. Shooting deaths of Thomas C. Clifford and William Griffiths on August 13, 1899, in an attempt to arrest an unruly soldier. In 1894, Denver Police Officer Robert Boykin shot and killed Arapahoe County Deputy Sheriff Milton Smith. An officer killed

William Griffith. A Black deputy sheriff was shot and killed on November 7, 1900. Plus, two Black officers were shot and wounded in 1905: Police Surgeon Frank Dulin and Captain William Bohanna were shot and killed when responding to a barricaded suspect. In 1900, a shootout between the Denver Police Department and Arapahoe County Sheriff's Department resulted in the death of four law enforcement officers. The law enforcement agencies were battling jurisdictional disputes on Election Day. John Spellman was shot and killed in 1906 attempting to arrest three drunken men. Morrissey and Brisson, *Denver District Attorney's Office*.

27. Paul Wilson was shot and killed in 1968 by an officer who was showing a gun to a third officer when it accidently discharged.

28. Norman S. Early Jr., "Decision Letter: Norman Anthony 'Tony' Silva," February 4, 1993 (Reports).

29. Early, "Decision Letter: Norman Anthony 'Tony' Silva" (Reports).

30. Early, "Decision Letter: Norman Anthony 'Tony' Silva" (Reports).

31. Tustin Amole, "Family, Friends Say Farewell to Fallen Deputy," *Rocky Mountain News*, February 9, 1993.

32. Marilyn Robinson, "Tragic Gun Accident Kills Deputy," *Rocky Mountain News*, February 4, 1993.

33. http://memorialwebsites.legacy.com/DeputyTonySilva1993/Subpage.aspx?mod=1.

34. https://www.odmp.org/agency/984-denver-police-department-colorado.

35. https://www.odmp.org/agency/984-denver-police-department-colorado. A brief overview of the names and circumstances are provided in these endnotes. On December 12, 1986, Officer Patrick Pollock was killed as a result of gunfire. Pollock's partner, Daniel Saracino, shot and killed the suspect. On June 3, 1987, Patrolman James Edward Wier was hit by a shotgun blast. Robert W. Wallis was killed by Phillip Hutchinson, who ran him down while attempting to flee the scene of a crime. Shawn Leinen was killed by Raymond Gone in 1995 and was sentenced to life in prison. Officer Bruce VanderJagt was murdered by Mattheus Jahning in 1997; he ambushed the officer, who was attempting to make an arrest for a burglary. Vehicle accidents resulting in death included Officer Michael Licata in September 2000 and Officer Ron DeHerrera in April 1997. Detective Michael Dowd died in December 1997 as a result of injuries sustained from gunfire twenty-eight years earlier. Detective Donald "Donnie" Young was killed on May 8, 2005, working off-duty at a private event. Patrolman David Roberts died on March 29, 1985, as a result of injuries from being shot by an arrest suspect. The incident left him paralyzed on the left side of his body, and his condition continued to deteriorate until his death. Celena Charise Hollis was killed attempting to break up a fight on June 24, 2012. Patrolman Robert Eugene Sandoval was killed on October 29, 2020, by gunfire from a homeowner who thought he was being robbed. Other law enforcement deaths in the area included Denver Deputy Sheriff Daniel Stillwell, who was killed at Denver General Hospital by an escaped suspect using the officer's own gun.

36. US Bureau of Labor Statistics, "Injuries, Illnesses, and Fatalities. Fact Sheet, Police Officers 2018," April 2020, https://www.bls.gov/iif/oshwc/cfoi/police-2018.htm (Reports).

37. Jodi M. Brown and Patrick A. Langan, *Policing and Homicide, 1976–98: Justifiable Homicide by Police, Police Officers Murdered by Felons*, NCJ 180987, US Department of Justice, Bureau of Justice Statistics, 2001 (Reports).

38. US Department of Justice, 2012 (Reports).

39. FBI National Press Office, "FBI Releases 2019 Statistics on Law Enforcement Officers Killed in the Line of Duty," May 4, https://www.fbi.gov/news/pressrel/press-releases /fbi-releases-2019-statistics-on-law-enforcement-officers-killed-in-the-line-of duty (Reports).

40. "FBI Releases Officers Killed and Assaulted in the Line of Duty, 2023 Special Report and Law Enforcement Employee Counts," FBI National Press Office, May 14, 2024.

41. Guy Toscano, "Dangerous Jobs. Compensation and Working Conditions," https://www .bls.gov/iif/oshwc/cfar0020.pdf; US Bureau of Labor Statistics. "Injuries, Illnesses, and Fatalities. Fact Sheet, Police Officers 2018," https://www.bls.gov/iif/oshwc/cfoi/police -2018.htm (Reports).

42. Michael Sierra-Arévalo, "The Commemoration of Death, Organizational Memory, and Police Culture," *Criminology* 57, no. 4 (2019): 632–58; and "American Policing and the Danger Imperative," *Law and Society Review* 55, no. 1 (2021): 70–103. Walker and Katz, *The Police in America*.

43. Caitlin G. Lynch, "Don't Let Them Kill You on Some Dirty Roadway: Survival, Entitled Violence, and the Culture of Modern American Policing," *Contemporary Justice Review: Issues in Criminal, Social, and Restorative Justice* 21, no. 1 (2018): 33–43.

44. Sierra-Arévalo, "American Policing and the Danger Imperative."

45. William B. Waegal, "How Police Justify the Use of Deadly Force," *Social Problems* 32, no. 2 (1984): 146–55.

46. Mitchell R. Morrissey, "Decision Letter: Daniel Abeyta," October 11, 2013 (Reports).

47. "Man Sentenced for Neighborhood Rampage: 'Incredible Danger,'" *Denver CBS4*, July 28, 2015.

48. DignityMemorial.com, 2013.

49. David Mitchell and Julie Hayden, "Housing Officials Say Federal Rules Forced Eviction of Murder Victim's Family," *FOX 31*, August 20, 2013; *Daily Mail.com*, August 20, 2013.

50. David Mitchell and Tak Landrock, "Couple at Center of SW Denver Shooting Have Troubled, Criminal Past," *FOX31*, August 16, 2013.

51. Dave Young, "Bomb-Toting Suspect Who Shot, Killed Denver Woman Appears in Court," *FOX31*, August 23, 2013.

52. Kieran Nicholson, "Daniel Abeyta Testifies at Trial," *Denver Post*, May 29, 2015.

53. Jim Kirksey and Felisa Cardona, "Man Dies After Denver Police Shoot Him with Taser," *Denver Post*, August 20, 2004.

54. "Police Have Killed More Than 1,000 People with Tasers Since 2000," *PBS NewsHour*, September 23, 2017. The data source used by PBS was *Reuters Investigates*, which released a six-part series on this topic. The first one can be viewed here: https://www.reuters .com/investigates/special-report/usa-taser-911/ . *Fatal Encounters* has tallied 927 killings from Tasers in their database.

55. Denver Police Department Operations Manual (Reports).

56. Kevin Flynn, "Police Line Up to Oppose Idea of Off-Duty Liability Insurance," *Rocky Mountain News*, November 26, 1998.

57. Kevin Flynn, "Official: Taxpayers Shouldn't Pay for Off-Duty Cops' Actions," *Rocky Mountain News*, November 14, 1998.

58. Kevin Vaughan, "Cop Moonlighting Called 'Mixed Bag': Some Suggest It's Time for a New Look at a Longtime Practice," *Rocky Mountain News*, March 10, 2003.

59. See note 35.

60. Mitchell R. Morrissy, "Decision Letter: Jason Wood," February 23, 2016 (Reports).

61. The stop sounds questionable.

62. Jesse Paul, "Man Who Shot, Critically Wounded Denver Police Officer Gets 52 Years in Prison," *Denver Post*, June 17, 2016.

63. Jaclyn Allen, "Denver Police Officer Tony Lopez Jr., Shot 2 Years Ago, Says Love Saved His Life," *ABC, Denver 7*, December 7, 2017.

64. The perceived sex of each officer was found for 100 percent of the officers. The race and ethnicity was determined for 92 percent of officers.

65. Since data collection was focused on a geographic area (Denver) and a timeframe (1983 to 2020), it is possible some officers may have had a shooting outside of Denver and outside of this timeframe. When possible, these data were included if discovered.

66. Beth McCann, "Decision Letter: Jamie Fernandez," July 20, 2020 (Reports).

67. There were questions regarding whether this vehicle was really wanted for eluding the police or simply used as a pretext to interact with the suspects.

68. Officer Lopez fired nineteen rounds with his gun magazine holding fifteen rounds and one in the chamber. He carried three spare magazines and reloaded once. Corporal Reyes fired eleven rounds from a magazine that held seventeen rounds. Since Ms. Fernandez was killed, it was not clear whether she shot to hit officers or simply to distract officers so she could escape.

69. David J. Johnson, Trevor Tress, Nicole Burkel, Carley Taylor, and Joseph Cesario, "Officer Characteristics and Racial Disparities in Fatal Officer-Involved Shootings," *Proceedings of the National Academy of Sciences* 116, no. 32 (2019): 15877–82.

70. Johnson et al., "Officer Characteristics and Racial Disparities in Fatal Officer-Involved Shootings," 15877.

71. Dean Knox, "Revealing Racial Bias," *Science* 374 (2021): 6568; Dean Knox and Jonathan Mummolo, "Making Inference About Racial Disparities in Police Violence," *PNAS* 117, no. 3 (2020): 1261–62; Dean Knox and Jonathan Mummolo, "It Took Us Months to Contest a Flawed Study on Police Bias. Here's Why That's Dangerous," *Washington Post*, January 28, 2020; Dean Knox and Jonathan Mummolo, "A Widely Touted Study Found No Evidence of Racism in Police Shootings. It's Full of Errors," *Washington Post*, July 15, 2020.

72. Eduardo Bonilla-Silva, *Racism Without Racists: Color-Blind Racism and the Persistence of Racial Inequality in America*, 6th ed. (Rowman and Littlefield, 2022).

73. The term "datasets of convenience" was adopted from Knox, "Revealing Racial Bias."

74. Bocar A. Ba, Dean Knox, Jonathan Mummolo, and Roman Rivera, "The Role of Officer Race and Gender in Police-Civilian Interactions in Chicago," *Science* 371, no. 6530 (2021): 696–702.

75. The only Black officer found to have two or more shootings was Jimmy Sheppard. He passed away on November 29, 2021, at the age of forty-seven.

76. John H. Laub and Robert J. Sampson, *Shared Beginnings, Divergent Lives: Delinquent Boys to Age 70* (Harvard University Press, 2003).

77. Belen Ward, "National Guard the Route for Veteran's 36-Year-Long Career," *Fort Lupton Press*, December 7, 2021.

78. *Rocky Mountain News*, May 28, 1991.

79. Kevin Simpson, "Verdict's in, but Cop Still on the Loose," *Denver Post*, August 17, 1995.

80. Howard Pankratz, "Basketball Fracas Ends Up in Court—Officer Says Teammate Punched Him," *Denver Post*, August 16, 1995. *Rocky Mountain News*, August 17, 1995.

81. Ward, "National Guard the Route for Veteran's 36-Year-Long Career."

82. CORA data for Officer Chavez lists fifty-three commendations, two citizen complaints, and three internal complaints.

83. Ward, "National Guard the Route for Veteran's 36-Year-Long Career."

84. Finn McNally, "Police Chief Moves on From Interim Role," *Herald Democrat*, October 23, 2023.

85. Data was not available regarding the race or ethnicity of the other three individuals.

86. Sarah Huntley, "Violence Yet to Scar Cop's Career," *Rocky Mountain News*, February 15, 2002.

87. Huntley, "Violence Yet to Scar Cop's Career."

88. Doug Mcinnis, Gary Massaro, and Tillie Fong, "Robbery Suspect Slain in Police Shootout Cop Wounded, Another Man Shot 3 Times," *Rocky Mountain News*, February 1, 1991.

89. Staff, "Denver Man Sues City Over Beating by Cop," *Rocky Mountain News*, August 16, 1997.

90. Ann Imse, "City May Pay Up in Shooting—Police Review Panel Says Killing Was Unjustified," *Rocky Mountain News*, March 28, 1998.

91. John Ingold and David Migoya, "Denver 'Dangerous' Officers Fly Under Radar of Denver Police," *Denver Post*, December 3, 2001.

92. According to the Colorado Open Records Act (CORA) request, there were four listed citizen complaints and scheduled disciplinary acts, but they don't seem to overlap with the *Denver Post*'s report, so somewhere, there is a discrepancy problem. We chose to run the publicly reported information because it did not list any information that was publicly retracted.

93. Nicole Vap and Jeremy Jojola, "Denver Firefighter Disciplined, Police Officer Fired Over City's COVID Mandate," *9NEWS*, January 10, 2022.

94. *Officer Down*, memorial page, https://www.odmp.org/search/year?year=2021.

95. "Decision Letter: Michael Ferguson," January 9, 2017.

96. Felisa Cardona, "Latino Officers to File Bias Suit vs. Department: Hiring, Promotion Among Issues," *Denver Post*, February 9, 2007.

97.   "Latinos' Police-Bias Claims Growing: Thirty-One Officers Have Filed Complaints Since March Against the Denver Police Department Over Alleged Discrimination," *Denver Post*, July 19, 2006; Christopher N. Osher, "Latino Officers Seek Probe by FBI: A White Policeman Is Accused of Using Excessive Force in Arresting a Latino Teenager Last Month," *Denver Post*, May 8, 2008.

98.   Tom McGhee, "Cops Try to Sort Out Lie—Teen Assault—Denver's Monitor Says at Least One Officer May Have Perjured Himself," *Denver Post*, March 22, 2009.

99.   Michael Roberts, "Charles Porter, Cop Involved in Juan Vasquez Stomping, Fired by Outgoing Manager of Safety," *Westword*, June 30, 2010.

100. Tom McGhee, "Denver Police Officer's Firing Upheld in the Stomping of a Teenage Boy in 2008," *Denver Post*, March 13, 2012.

101. Afterall.com/obituaries/RufinoTrujillo.

102. *Denver Post*, September 21, 2003.

103. *Denver Post*, September 21, 2003.

104. *Denver Post*, September 21, 2003.

105. Meret S. Hofer, Allison R. Gilbert, and Marvin S. Swartz, "Police Mental Health: A Neglected Element of Police Reform," *Psychiatric Services* 72, no. 9 (2021): 985.

106. Katelyn K. Jetelina, Rebecca J. Molsberry, Jennifer Reingle Gonzalez, et al., "Prevalence of Mental Illness and Mental Health Care Use Among Police Officers," *JAMA Network Open* 3, no. 10 (2020): e2019658.

107. Multidisciplinary Association for Psychedelic Studies (MAPS), "MDMA: Read Our Research," 2022, https://maps.org/mdma/ (Reports).

108. Michael C. Mithoefer, Ann T. Mithoefer, Allison A. Feduccia, et al., "3,4-Methylenedioxymethamphetamine (MDMA)-Assisted Psychotherapy for Post-Traumatic Stress Disorder in Military Veterans, Firefighters, and Police Officers: A Randomised, Double-Blind, Dose-Response, Phase 2 Clinical Trial," *Lancet Psychiatry* 5, no. 6 (2018): 486–97.

109. Marcia Wagner and Richard J. Brzeczek, "Alcoholism and Suicide: A Fatal Connection," *FBI Law Enforcement Bulletin* 52, no. 8 (1983): 8–15.

110. Sabrina Rubin Erdely, "Police Violence: Cops on Steroids," *Men's Health*, November 8, 2013.

111. John M. Violanti, "The Mystery Within: Understanding Police Suicide," *FBI Law Enforcement Bulletin* 64, no. 2 (1995): 19–26; Wagner and Brzeczek, "Alcoholism and Suicide."

112. Labeling of law enforcement as a gang: William T. Armaline, Claudio G. Vera Sanchez, and Mark Correia, " 'The Biggest Gang in Oakland': Re-thinking Police Legitimacy," *Contemporary Justice Review* 17, no. 3 (2014): 375–99; Robert J. Durán, "Fatalistic Social Control: The Reproduction of Oppression Through the Medium of Gangs," PhD diss., University of Colorado at Boulder, 2006; *Gang Life in Two Cities: An Insider's Journey* (Columbia University Press, 2013).

113. Durán, "Fatalistic Social Control," 189.

114. Durán, *Gang Life in Two Cities*; *The Gang Paradox*.

115. There has been some interesting research that has been examining policing culture: Linda Zhao and Andrew V. Papachristos, "Network Position and Police Who Shoot," *Annals of the American Academy of Political and Social Science* 687, no. 1 (2020): 89–112.

116. This quotation is attributed to Zora Neale Hurston.

6. A PUBLIC HEALTH PROBLEM FOR THE UNITED STATES: PLACES, PRACTICES, AND POLICIES

1. Although we do not wish to boost the shooter's fame or recognition, for research purposes, we believe that Salvador Rolando Ramos's (born May 16, 2004) story needs to be studied. We chose not to print his name on the main pages of the book but instead place it here as an endnote. However, to name the shooter at all, we felt it important also to recognize the victims who had their lives stolen: Makenna Lee Elrod, 10; Layla Salazar, 11; Maranda Mathis, 11; Nevaeh Bravo, 10; Jose Manuel Flores Jr., 10; Xavier Lopez, 10; Tess Marie Mata, 10; Rojelio Torres, 10; Eliahna "Ellie" Amyah Garcia, 9; Eliahna A. Torres, 10; Annabell Guadalupe Rodriguez, 10; Jackie Cazares, 9; Uziya Garcia, age unlisted; Jayce Carmelo Luevanos, 10; Maite Yuleana Rodriguez, 10; Jailah Nicole Silguero, 10; Irma Garcia, 48; Eva Mireles, 44; Amerie Jo Garza, 10; Alexandria "Lexi" Aniyah Rubio, 10; and Alithia Ramirez, 10. Sneha Dey, Erin Douglas, Andrew Zhang, and Brooke Park, "21 Lives Lost: Uvalde Victims Were a Cross-Section of a Small, Mostly Latino Town in South Texas," *Texas Tribune*, May 27, 2022. It was reported that seventeen other individuals were injured from the shooting, and a husband whose wife was killed in the shooting died from a broken heart. " 'Day by Day:' Uvalde Survivors Recover from Wounds, Trauma," Associated Press, June 2, 2022. The individuals and families have had their lives completely altered by this incident.
2. News media often reports seventy-seven minutes. The Investigative Committee on the Robb Elementary Shooting listed seventy-three minutes. Dustin Burrows, Joe Moody, and Eva Guzman, "Interim Report 2022," Investigative Committee on the Robb Elementary Shooting, Texas House of Representatives, 2022. In contrast, others have reported that since the first 911 call to the conclusion of the event took eighty minutes.
3. Burrows, Moody, and Guzman, "Interim Report 2022" (Reports).
4. The investigative report cited the campaign dontnamethem.org, which encourages not using the names of shooters to prevent future events and instead to tell the stories of the victims, the heroes, and the communities that come together to heal. The dontnamethem campaign cited the "No Notoriety" campaign, which shares a similar message, which was organized after the shooting at the Aurora Colorado movie theater.
5. Jack Morphet and David Propper, "Texas Shooter Salvador Ramos' Grandma 'May Never Be Able to Talk Again': Kin," *New York Post*, May 29, 2022. It was reported that if the bullet had been an inch in another direction, it would have decapitated the shooter's grandmother.
6. Lee Brown, "Funeral Homes Refused to Take Uvalde School Shooter Salvador Ramos' Body," *New York Post*, August 24, 2022.
7. "Autopsies Sealed in Ongoing Investigation," *Uvalde Leader-News*, November 24, 2022. Reviewing autopsies, although morbid, was beneficial for analyzing shootings in Denver, Colorado.
8. Burrows, Moody, and Guzman, "Interim Report 2022" (Reports).
9. Mark S. Hamm and Ramón Spaaij, *The Age of Lone Wolf Terrorism* (Columbia University Press, 2017), outline that the greatest point for intervention in the

radicalization model was "broadcasting intent," wherein the shooter shares information with others about his intentions. It was reported that the shooter in Uvalde regularly expressed in online gaming and social media posts a desire to shoot up a school
and that he was preparing to do so. At this point, there were no expressed writings or
statements to link the Uvalde school shooter with an ideological purpose for carrying
out this attack; there was no explicit reason to label this as an act of lone-wolf
terrorism.

10. Patricia A. Adler, *Wheeling and Dealing: An Ethnography of an Upper-Level Drug
Dealing and Smuggling Community* (Columbia University Press, 1993); Paul Atkin-
son, Amanda Coffey, Sara Delamont, et al., *Handbook of Ethnography* (SAGE, 2001);
Jeff Ferrell and Mark S. Hamm, *Ethnography at the Edge: Crime, Deviance, and Field
Research* (Northeastern University Press, 1998); John Lofland, David Snow, Leon
Anderson, and Lyn H. Lofland, *Analyzing Social Settings: A Guide to Qualitative
Observation and Analysis* (Waveland, 2006).

11. As a son to parents who were devoted Catholics and having attended private Catholic
school from kindergarten through sixth grade, a rosary was symbolically a source of
prayer and a belief that, with faith, both personal and public problems can be resolved.

12. A very common statement that was given by community members to Katherine
Newman and her team of researchers studying school shootings was "how could it
happen here?" Katherine S. Newman, Cybelle Fox, David Harding, et al., *Rampage:
The Social Roots of School Shootings* (Basic Books, 2004), report in their book that
despite the rarity of school shootings, malevolence can exist anywhere, especially
when individuals are not paying attention to the warning signs. A study proposed by
an unknown author in the journal *Symbolic Interactionism* has emphasized how most
school shootings did not result in anyone being killed. The author referred to those
that did as outliers.

13. Robert Klemko, Silvia Foster-Frau, and Shawn Boburg, "Gunman Bought Two Rifles,
Hundreds of Rounds in Days Before Massacre," *Washington Post*, May 25, 2022.

14. Burrows, Moody, and Guzman, "Interim Report 2022" (Reports).

15. Kiah Collier and Jeremy Schwartz, "Why 18-Year-Olds Can Buy AR-15s in Texas but
Not Handguns," *Texas Tribune*, May 26, 2022. Although probably not the shooter's preferred weapon, he could not purchase a handgun until the age of twenty-one because
of federal law.

16. Straw purchases, as they are called, were a federal crime.

17. According to the US Census Bureau, QuickFacts, Uvalde County, Texas, had 24,940
residents in July 2022, of which 72.4 percent were Latino and 24.8 percent white.

18. For an analysis of harm and how it goes beyond the study of crime, see Lo Presser, *Why
We Harm* (Rutgers University Press, 2013).

19. Alvin J. LaCabe Jr., "Public Statement of the Manager of Safety Regarding an Officer-
Involved Shooting by Technician Ryan Grothe and Technician James Sewald on
June 25, 2006, at 4600 Stapleton Drive South Which Resulted in the Death of Michael
Ford," City and County of Denver, 2007 (Reports); Mitchell R. Morrissey, "Decision
Letter: Michael Julius Ford," June 29, 2006 (Reports).

20. Michael Ford killed Mauricio DeHaro; DeHaro's family reported he had no conflicts with anyone. Mr. DeHaro was tragically taken from his wife and two young children. "Warehouse Gunman Wasn't on Drugs," *Denver Post*, October 12, 2006.

21. Mark Follman, Gavin Aronsen, and Deanna Pan, "US Mass Shootings, 1982–2023: Data from *Mother Jones'* Investigation," *Mother Jones*, July 5, 2023. An interesting story in *Politifact* includes an interview with the criminologist Grant Duwe, who wrote a book on mass shootings titled *Mass Murder in the United States: A History* (McFarland, 2007). Duwe expressed some concerns with *Mother Jones's* data collection efforts but believed, based on his data, that white males were actually more likely to account for 63 percent of mass shooters, which was more comparable to the white male population in the United States. *Politifact*, October 6, 2017, https://www.politifact.com/factchecks/2017/oct/06/newsweek/are-white-males-responsible-more-mass-shootings-an/.

22. Hamm and Spaaij, *The Age of Lone Wolf Terrorism*.

23. We are interested in how often whites may be involved in mass shootings and escape being shot by law enforcement. A full systematic study of these cases deserves greater attention. An analysis of the *Mother Jones* data could help in these efforts. Some notable recent shootings that come to mind where the white shooter was arrested without being killed include the shootings by Patrick Crusius in El Paso, Texas; Payton S. Gendron in Buffalo, New York; James Eagan Holmes in Aurora, Colorado; and Kyle Rittenhouse in Kenosha, Wisconsin.

24. These data, as mentioned earlier in the book, were compiled based on the benefit of DA decision letters that reported the times of the incident, notification of law enforcement, arrival, and reports of shots fired.

25. Unfortunately, it was not until the writing of this book that Durán reviewed the downloadable data from these websites to see how they compared to the data he had acquired in each geographic site. Durán was very pleased to see the development of these data, and they were very beneficial for cross-checking the data already collected by Durán and his students. Another unfortunate reality was that Durán's data collection phase before publishing this book took a long period of time, from 2003 to 2025. Collaboration with Loza began in 2014, but converting the data from Excel to SPSS, cleaning, and categorizing for analysis took additional time. This book's original deadline was October 2021, but too many events surrounding COVID-19 were occurring at that point. It should be noted that Durán and Loza did have other publications on police shootings that were published during this time.

26. *Disproportionate Minority Contact Technical Assistance Manual* (US Department of Justice, 2009), https://www.ncjrs.gov/html/ojjdp/dmc_ta_manual/index.html (Reports).

27. Nancy Krieger, Jarvis T. Chen, Pamela D. Waterman, et al., "Police Killings and Police Deaths Are Public Health Data and Can Be Counted," *PLOS Medicine* 12, no. 12 (2015): e1001915.

28. Krieger et al., "Police Killings and Police Deaths Are Public Health Data and Can Be Counted."

29. Brian Burghart, *Fatal Encounters*, University of Southern California, 2023, https://fatalencounters.org/; "The Counted: People Killed by Police in the US," *Guardian*,

June 1, 2015, https://www.theguardian.com/us-news/ng-interactive/2015/jun/01/the -counted-police-killings-us-database; *Fatal Force, Washington Post*, 2015, https://www .washingtonpost.com/graphics/investigations/police-shootings-database/; Campaign Zero, *Mapping Police Violence*, https://mappingpoliceviolence.org/. An additional data source, the *Gun Violence Archive*, https://www.gunviolencearchive.org, was also found to include some officer-involved shootings, but that dataset was less developed in comparison to these other sources.

30.   *Fatal Encounters.*

31.   As reported in chapter 2, the data sources of *Fatal Encounters, Fatal Force, The Counted*, and *Mapping Police Violence* may have chosen to use the term "Gender" as the column title, but instead the databases used the term "Sex," as gender identity was most often not available for the data sources utilized for compiling these data. Thus, Durán and Loza have changed every instance of "gender" to "sex" for consistency.

32.   "The Counted."

33.   *Fatal Force.*

34.   *Mapping Police Violence.*

35.   National Violent Death Reporting System (NVDRS), https://www.cdc.gov/violence prevention/datasources/nvdrs/index.html.

36.   Andrew Conner, Deborah Azrael, Vivian H. Lyons, et al., "Validating the National Violent Death Reporting System as a Source of Data on Fatal Shootings of Civilians by Law Enforcement Officers," *American Journal of Public Health* 109, no. 4 (2019): 578–84.

37.   See https://www.cdc.gov/violenceprevention/datasources/nvdrs/stateprofiles.html.

38.   Benjamin P. Comer and Jason R. Ingram, "Comparing Fatal Encounters, Mapping Police Violence, and *Washington Post* Fatal Police Shooting Data from 2015–2019: A Research Note," *Criminal Justice Review* 48, no. 2 (2022). Despite the inclusion of the intertwining of these data sources, the key information presented for the counties was collected and analyzed by Durán and his graduate students. Future research will be required to determine the full benefits of NVDRS and whether it can be publicly accessible.

39.   Death Penalty Information Center, "Executions in the United States," http://www .deathpenaltyinfo.org/executions-united-states. This website also has a downloadable Excel file regarding all death penalty executions.

40.   Robert J. Durán, *Gang Life in Two Cities: An Insider's Journey* (Columbia University Press, 2013); *The Gang Paradox: Inequalities and Miracles on the U.S.-Mexico Border* (Columbia University Press, 2018).

41.   Joel Garreau, *The Nine Nations of North America* (Houghton Mifflin, 1981); Colin Woodard, *American Nations: A History of the Eleven Rival Regional Cultures of North America* (Penguin, 2011).

42.   As all data was triangulated, *Fatal Encounters* began in 2000, and thus, there was no other way to compare the data I had collected with any other source that occurred before this database became available, so they were omitted for comparison purposes.

43.   Garreau, *The Nine Nations of North America.*

44.   Woodard, *American Nations.*

45.   US Census Bureau, QuickFacts: Colorado, "Population Estimates, July 1, 2022."

46.   After comparing Durán and Loza's dataset with *Fatal Encounters*, it was determined that their dataset included suicides that occurred during a police interaction. We did not include these data in our dataset unless we could determine that the person had been shot by the officer based upon district attorney findings or autopsy results. Another discrepancy with *Fatal Encounters* was that the city or county where the death reportedly occurred was not always in the city and county of Denver. In total, *Fatal Encounters* included ten more individuals than we did, and we were missing three killings. Based on the review, there was one shooting not included in our dataset that should have been, the off-duty killing of an unarmed teenager Alexis Mendez-Perez by a correctional officer. Elise Schmelzer, "No Charges for Department of Corrections Employee in Fatal Shooting of Suspected Burglar," *Denver Post*, June 10, 2020. In Colorado, correctional officers were considered peace officers with law enforcement powers, and thus this omission from DA Beth McCann's police shooting list was noteworthy. Not only did the DA not pursue charges despite the teenager being shot in the back, but the shooting was also omitted from the officer-involved-shooting webpage. The family was urging the DA to reconsider charging the officer. It was reported that the officer was fired by the state of Colorado due to conduct unbecoming and hired as a police officer, but his firing was under administrative review. Julia Cardi, "Analysis Reinstating a Corrections Employee for Off-Duty Fatal Shooting Made Mistakes: Appeals Court," *Denver Gazette*, December 19, 2022.

47.   Death Penalty Information Center, https://deathpenaltyinfo.org/state-and-federal-info/state-by-state/colorado.

48.   SB15-217. These data were helpful in the creation of a report outlining shootings in the state of Colorado between January 1, 2010 and June 30, 2019. Colorado Division of Criminal Justice, 2020.

49.   Colorado Division of Criminal Justice, https://ors.colorado.gov/ors-coll-ois.

50.   SB20-217. However, it is unclear to the authors regarding where this data is held and how to access the information.

51.   Denver DA, "Officer Involved Shooting Investigations and Decision Letters," https://www.denverda.org/officer-involved-shooting-investigations-decision-letters-2/.

52.   Durán, *Gang Life in Two Cities.*

53.   US Census Bureau, QuickFacts, Weber County, Utah, https://www.census.gov/quickfacts/fact/table/UT/PST045222.

54.   Erin Alberty, "Killings by Utah Police Outpacing Gang, Drug, Child-Abuse Homicides," *Salt Lake Tribune*, November 24, 2014.

55.   Durán, *Gang Life in Two Cities.*

56.   US Census Bureau, QuickFacts, Weber County, Utah.

57.   In addition, it appears some journalists have reported success utilizing a Government Records Access and Management Act (GRAMA) request to obtain officer-involved-shooting data in Utah.

58.   Andy Howell, "Matthew David Stewart Case to Leave Lasting Impression," *Standard-Examiner*, June 1, 2013.

59. Loretta Park, "Stewart Says He Feared for His Life," *Standard-Examiner*, February 4, 2012.

60. Jamie Lampros, "Officials: Accused Cop-Killer Stewart Refused Jail's Mental Health Services, Committed Suicide," *Standard Examiner*, May 25, 2013.

61. Jessica Miller and Bob Mims, "Alleged Cop Killer Matthew Stewart Hangs Self in Jail Cell," *Salt Lake Tribune*, May 24, 2013.

62. Andreas Rivera, "Salt Lake City 'Peace Officer' Screening to Include Director Q&A," *Standard Examiner*, October 2, 2015; Brad Barber and Scott Christopherson, "Peace Officer," Soro Films, 2015.

63. Mark Shenefelt, "Friends, Family Note Francom's Legacy 5 Years After Deadly Ogden Shootout," *Standard Examiner*, January 16, 2017.

64. Mark Shenefelt, "5 Years After Shootout, Ogden Police Better Equipped, 'More Cautious,'" *Standard Examiner*, January 16, 2017b; Jessica Miller, "Ogden Public Safety Building Renamed for Fallen Officer: The Ceremony Marks First Anniversary of Jared Francom's Death," *Salt Lake Tribune*, January 5, 2013. Naming the public safety center in Officer Francom's name is reflective of the commemoration of death, organizational memory, and police culture as outlined by Michael Sierra-Arévalo, "The Commemoration of Death, Organizational Memory, and Police Culture," *Criminology* 57, no. 4 (2019): 632–58.

65. Cathy Mckitrick, "5 Years After Matthew Stewart's Death, Mother Still Hopes to Clear Son's Name," *Standard Examiner*, January 16, 2017.

66. Derrick A. Bell, "*Brown v. Board of Education* and the Interest-Convergence Dilemma," *Harvard Law Review* 93, no. 3 (1980): 518–53.

67. For example, the bodycam video footage of the shooting of Todd Blair in 2010. The police enter the dwelling shouting "police search warrant." Mr. Blair grabs a golf club and is immediately shot to death. Despite many states having a "castle doctrine" law, which permits homeowners to protect themselves, such a law does not include protection from law enforcement.

68. Weber County Attorney, Critical Incident Community Briefing, https://www.webercountyutah.gov/Attorney/video/index.php.

69. Garreau, *The Nine Nations of North America*.

70. Garreau, *The Nine Nations of North America*, 229.

71. Ian F. Haney-Lopez, *Racism on Trial: The Chicano Fight for Justice* (Belknap, 2003); Monica Muñoz Martinez, *The Injustice Never Leaves You: Anti-Mexican Violence in Texas* (Harvard University Press, 2018); Alfredo Mirandé, *Gringo Justice* (University of Notre Dame Press, 1987); Alfredo Mirandé, ed., *Gringo Injustice: Insider Perspectives on Police, Gangs, and Law* (Routledge, 2020); Armando Navarro, *Mexicano Political Experience in Occupied Aztlán: Struggles and Change* (AltaMira, 2005).

72. Durán, *The Gang Paradox*.

73. The Southern Border Communities Coalition, http://southernborder.org.

74. A forthcoming journal article in the *Sociology of Race and Ethnicity* focuses on deaths at the hands of police by US Customs and Border Protection. Durán is also working on an article that focuses on officer-involved shootings on the Texas side of the

US-Mexico border, which includes data on shootings in fourteen counties from 2015 to 2023. This study involves all law enforcement agencies.

75. Durán, *The Gang Paradox*.

76. Additional research on New Mexico can be found in Durán, *The Gang Paradox*; Laura E. Gómez, *Manifest Destinies: The Making of the Mexican American Race* (New York University Press, 2007); and other works.

77. John Acosta, "New Mexico Has the Second-Highest Fatal Police Shooting Rate in the US—Is It Ready to Change?," *Guardian*, May 6, 2021. This article listed Alaska as having the highest rate.

78. Durán had acquired data in Albuquerque that was not ready to be analyzed by the time this book went to press, but a future article or book chapter will cover these trends. Durán's paternal side of his family has lived in New Mexico and southern Colorado for more than three centuries.

79. US Department of Justice Civil Rights Division, Office of the Assistant Attorney General, "Re: Albuquerque Police Department," April 10, 2014.

80. Walt Rubel, "Walt Rubel: Panel Thursday Will Look at Transparency After Police Shootings," *Las Cruces Sun-News*, March 28, 2015. Mary Carmack-Altwies, Officer Involved Shooting Review and Evaluation, First Judicial District Attorney, state of New Mexico, n.d.

81. "Hispanic" instead of "Latino" was the preferred identity term in southern New Mexico.

82. US Census Bureau, QuickFacts, Doña Ana County, New Mexico, https://www.census .gov/quickfacts/fact/table/donaanacountynewmexico/PST045222.

83. Unfortunately, there was also a Las Cruces Police Department officer, Jonah Hernandez, who was killed by an individual with a knife on February 11, 2024. The attacker had a reported history of mental illness, and he was killed by a bystander who observed the officer getting victimized. As Durán has not been back to Las Cruces since this event, it is unclear how this officer's killing has affected police training, morale, and subsequent use of force on residents. The officer's bodycam footage was very difficult and sad to watch.

84. One of the most egregious killings was by the Las Cruces Police Department officer Christopher Smelser, who placed Antonio Valenzuela, forty, in a chokehold on February 29, 2020. A judge dismissed the case charging the officer, but the city agreed to pay the family $6.5 million and ban the use of chokeholds by officers. Associated Press, "Judge Dismisses Charge Against New Mexico Officer Accused of Killing Man with Chokehold," *NBC News*, July 14, 2022. Watching the video of Mr. Valenzuela's murder was disturbing and followed a pattern reflected in the killings of George Floyd and Eric Garner. Tragically, the murder of Mr. Valenzuela did not result in the criminal prosecution of the officer. Additional coverage of this case can be found in Marlené Mercado, "Chicana/x Carework: Invisible Feminized Labor, Chicana/x Carceral Community, and the Variegated Nature of Feminist Agency in Carceral Contexts," PhD diss., University of California at Davis, 2022.

85. Andy Stiny, "Police: Deputy Fleeing When Killed by Fellow Deputy—the Two Were Staying in Hotel After Transporting Prisoner," *Albuquerque Journal*, October 29, 2014.

86. Andy Stiny, "Autopsy: Deputy Was Shot in Back—Report Says Santa Fe Deputy Died from Four or Five Gunshots," *Albuquerque Journal*, January 9, 2015.

87. Phaedra Haywood, "Chan May Claim Self-Defense in Colleague's Death," *Santa Fe New Mexican*, March 9, 2015.

88. Carlos Andes Lopez, "Chan Takes Stand to Defend Actions—'He Was Going to Kill Me,' He Says of Martin," *Las Cruces Sun-News*, June 4, 2016.

89. Lauren Villagran, "Mistrial Declared in Murder Case Against Former SF Deputy," *Albuquerque Journal*, June 8, 2016.

90. Andy Stiny, "Judge Throws Out Charges in Long-Running Chan Case," *Albuquerque Journal*, July 29, 2020.

91. William D. Carrigan, *The Making of a Lynching Culture: Violence and Vigilantism in Central Texas, 1836–1916* (University of Illinois Press, 2004); Kelly Lytle Hernández, *Migra! A History of the U.S. Border Patrol* (University of California Press, 2010); Monica Muñoz Martinez, *The Injustice Never Leaves You: Anti-Mexican Violence in Texas* (Harvard University Press, 2018); Julian Samora, Joe Bernal, and Albert Peña, *Gunpowder Justice: A Reassessment of the Texas Rangers* (University of Notre Dame Press, 1979).

92. Carrigan, *The Making of a Lynching Culture* (University of Illinois Press, 2004), 175.

93. Hernández, *Migra!*; Muñoz Martinez, *The Injustice Never Leaves You*; David Dorado Romo, *Ringside Seat to a Revolution: An Underground Cultural History of El Paso and Juárez: 1893–1923* (Cinco Puntos, 2005). A high level of violence has also been enacted against Native Americans in Texas. Gary Clayton Anderson, *The Conquest of Texas: Ethnic Cleansing in the Promised Land, 1820–1875* (University of Oklahoma Press, 2005).

94. Death Penalty Information Center, https://deathpenaltyinfo.org/state-and-federal-info/state-by-state/texas.

95. Based on the numbers per 100,000, it appears that Texas had the second highest rate per 100,000 residents for the use of the death penalty after Oklahoma.

96. Wetchler Texas Justice Initiative, Fact Sheet, "Officer-Involved Shootings and Custodial Deaths in Texas, 2018" (Reports).

97. The Other category was 3 percent of all shootings.

98. Hongsup Shin and Eva Ruth Moravec, Texas Justice Initiative, "Officer-Involved Shootings in Texas: 2016–2019."

99. Durán, *The Gang Paradox*.

100. Jo Tuckman, "Mexican, 15, Shot Dead by US Border Patrol Officer," *Guardian*, June 10, 2010.

101. Kimberly Dvorak, "Mexico Claims Racism in the U.S. Is on the Rise," *San Diego Examiner*, July 16, 2010.

102. "Family of Mexican Boy Killed by Border Agent Sues," Associated Press State Wire: Texas, January 17, 2011.

103. Jerry Seper, "Border Agent Will Not Be Charged in Teen's Killing—Justice Department Cites Insufficient Evidence," *Washington Times*, May 1, 2012.

104. Julián Aguilar, "Border Patrol Union: Ruling Could Harm Agents," *Texas Tribune*, July 1, 2014.

105. Charles Davis, "U.S. Customs and Border Protection Has Killed Nearly 50 People in 10 Years. Most Were Unarmed. And Not One Officer Has Been Disciplined," *New Republic*, January 4, 2015.

106. *Hernandez et al. v. Mesa* (2020).

107. *Hernandez et al. v. Mesa*, 8.

108. Aaron Martinez, "Officer Indicted in Fatal '15 Shooting—Burglary Suspect Was Allegedly Shot Three Times in the Back," *El Paso Times*, April 18, 2017.

109. Daniel Borunda, "El Paso Police Officer Acquitted of Manslaughter in Fatal Shooting Back on Duty," *El Paso Times*, November 1, 2019.

110. Elida S. Perez, "City Council, in Unprecedented Move, Settles Police Shooting Lawsuit on Eve of Trial," *El Paso Matters*, March 30, 2022.

111. Such implications may also implicate the state of Texas in undercounting the number of police shootings occurring in this state. Other places in the Borderlands, such as Arizona and California, also have a variety of data-collection efforts. For example, in Arizona, the newspaper *Arizona Republic* has been collecting and analyzing data from 2011 to 2018 and reporting on various police shootings up to the present day: https:// www.azcentral.com/storytelling/arizona-police-shootings/. In California, 89.3 KPCC, a National Public Radio station, shares data in CSV format and has a dashboard that displays aggregated data on officer-involved shootings in Los Angeles County with filters for the outcome (fatal, nonfatal), weapon (unarmed, firearm, other weapon), and sex for all cases and race and ethnicity (Latino, Black, white, Asian, or other) for fatal shootings. It also shows data by incident filters, including officer self-defense, officer defense of other officers, officer defense of civilians, and car stops.

112. John Hope Franklin and Alfred A. Moss, *From Slavery to Freedom: A History of African Americans* (Knopf, 2004).

113. Manning Marable, *Race, Reform, and Rebellion: The Second Reconstruction and Beyond in Black America, 1945–2006* (University Press of Mississippi, 2007).

114. Garreau, *The Nine Nations of North America*.

115. Garreau, *The Nine Nations of North America*, 130.

116. James H. Cone, *Martin and Malcolm and America: A Dream or a Nightmare* (Orbis, 1998).

117. Cone, *Martin and Malcolm and America*, 96.

118. Tennessee Bureau of Investigation, "Officer-Involved Shootings," https://www.tn.gov /tbi/crime-issues/crime-issues/officer-involved-shootings.html.

119. Durán originally created a data collection circle for collecting official and ethnographic data that went counterclockwise from Knoxville, Nashville, and Memphis, Tennessee, to Jackson, Mississippi; Birmingham, Alabama; Atlanta, Georgia; Columbia, South Carolina; and Charlotte, North Carolina. Thus, with the help of students, Durán has officer-involved shooting data in these cities and the counties they are in. After moving to Texas, he has collected data on Houston (Harris County) and the 1,300 miles of border counties between Texas and Mexico. More research and data collection will be required to write up these comparisons.

120. Rounding up percentages resulted in a sum slightly over 100 percent.

121. Don Jacobs, "Police Tape on Shooting Released—Audio Indicates Officers Warned Teen for 10 Seconds Before Shooting," *Knoxville News Sentinel*, May 21, 2003.

122. Don Jacobs, "Shooting Site Has History of Problems—Police, Weigel's Tried Variety of Methods to Control Late Crowds," *Knoxville News Sentinel*, May 24, 2003.

123. Lola Alapo, "Vigil Stirs Anger, Hope," *Knoxville News Sentinel*, May 28, 2003.

124. Lola Alapo, "Officer Cleared in Shooting—Family Lawyer: 'Disappointed' Relatives May Pursue Civil-Rights Lawsuit," *Knoxville News Sentinel*, September 10, 2003; Don Jacobs, "Officer Cleared in Shooting—District Attorney: Death Shows 'Drugs, Alcohol, Guns a Deadly Combination,'" *Knoxville News Sentinel*, September 10, 2003.

125. Jamie Satterfield, "Mother of 19-Year-Old Man Shot to Death KPD Officer Sues City," *Knoxville News Sentinel*, May 19, 2004.

126. "Witnesses: Teen Was Unarmed." *Daily Times*, May 20, 2003.

127. *Gillispie v. City of Knoxville*, Court of Appeals of Tennessee, at Knoxville, 2006.

128. Théoden Janes, "NASCAR—Wallace's Mother, Father Talk Trump Tweet, Noose Flag," *The Herald*, July 13, 2020.

129. "NASCAR Bans Confederate Flags from All Racetracks," *ESPN News Services*, June 10, 2020.

130. This was the shooting of Anthony Thompson Jr. See Neil Vigdor, "Tennessee Student Killed by Police Did Not Fire Bullet That Hit Officer, Officials Say," *New York Times*, April 14, 2021.

131. Living in Knoxville and working as a gang expert for gang enhancement cases, Durán began collecting data on the overrepresentation of Blacks charged with gang enhancement charges in comparison to whites. The plan is to finish either a book chapter or article on the topic.

7. ACCOUNTABILITY THROUGH LEGISLATIVE ACTION, INSTITUTIONAL POLICIES, AND RESEARCH

1. For an example of how widespread issues of rebellion were in regard to police violence, see the appendix in Elizabeth Hinton, *America on Fire: The Untold History of Police Violence and Black Rebellion Since the 1960s* (Liveright, 2021). Jennifer E. Cobbina, *Hands Up: Don't Shoot: Why the Protests in Ferguson and Baltimore Matter, and How They Changed America* (New York University Press, 2019), also provides a great overview of protest of police violence since the killing of Mike Brown in Ferguson, Missouri.

2. Hinton, *America on Fire.*

3. Ernesto B. Vigil, *The Crusade for Justice: Chicano Militancy and the Government's War on Dissent* (University of Wisconsin Press, 1999).

4. To learn more about Brother Jeff, see Museum of Contemporary Art Denver, https://mcadenver.org/blog/community-spotlight-interview-brother-jeff.

5. Kim Muhammad, "Police Brutality Concerns Addressed on MLK Holiday," *Denver Weekly News*, January 29–February 5, 2004.

6.   Robert J. Durán and Charlene Shroulote-Durán, "Institutionalizing Community Oversight of the Police: Copwatch," in *Justice and Legitimacy in Policing: Transforming the Institution*, ed. M. O. Craig and K. L. Blount-Hill (Routledge, 2023), 76–90.

7.   See chapter 1; see also Michael Knievel, "Teaching Deadly Force: Collaborative Dynamics and the Rhetoric of Police Policy," *IEEE Transactions on Professional Communication* 51, no. 1 (2008): 95–109.

8.   *Tennessee v. Garner*, 1985.

9.   *Graham v. Connor*, 1988.

10. *Graham v. Connor*, 1988, 386.

11. See Jerome H. Skolnick and James J. Fyfe, *Above the Law: Police and the Excessive Use of Force* (Free Press, 1993).

12. Jerry R. Sparger and David J. Giacopassi, "Memphis Revisited: A Reexamination of Police Shootings After the Garner Decision," *Justice Quarterly* 9, no. 2 (1992): 211–25.

13. Samuel Walker, Cassia Spohn, and Miriam DeLone, *The Color of Justice: Race, Ethnicity, and Crime in America*, 6th ed. (Cengage Learning, 2018).

14. Derrick A. Bell, "*Brown v. Board of Education* and the Interest-Convergence Dilemma," *Harvard Law Review* 93, no. 3 (1980): 518–53; Mari J. Matsuda, "Public Response to Racist Speech: Considering the Victim's Story," *Michigan Law Review* 87, no. 8 (1989): 2320–81; Alfredo Mirandé, *Gringo Justice* (University of Notre Dame Press, 1987); *Rascuache Lawyer: Toward a Theory of Ordinary Litigation* (University of Arizona Press, 2011); *Ordinary Injustice: Rascuache Lawyering and the Anatomy of a Criminal Case* (University of Arizona Press, 2023); Richard Quinney, *Class, State, and Crime: On the Theory and Practice of Criminal Justice* (D. McKay, 1977).

15. Wendy Leo Moore, "The *Stare Decisis* of Racial Inequality: Supreme Court Race Jurisprudence and the Legacy of Legal Apartheid in the United States," *Critical Sociology* 40, no. 1 (2014): 67–88. See Anna Swanson, "Revisiting *Garner* with *Garner*: A Look at Deadly Force and the Use of Chokeholds and Neck Restraints by Law Enforcement," *South Texas Law Review* 57, no. 3 (2016): 401–48, for the problems with the *Tennessee v. Garner* decision.

16. Jordan E. DeVylder, Deidre M. Anglin, Lisa Bowleg, et al., "Police Violence and Public Health," *Annual Review of Clinical Psychology* 18 (2022): 527–52.

17. Walter L. Hixson, *American Settler Colonialism: A History* (Palgrave Macmillan, 2013).

18. Hannah L. F. Cooper and Mindy Fullilove, "Editorial: Excessive Police Violence as a Public Health Issue," *Journal of Urban Health: Bulletin of the New York Academy of Medicine* 93, suppl. 1 (2016): 1–7; Jordan E. DeVylder, Hans Oh, Boyoung Nam, et al., "Prevalence, Demographic Variation and Psychological Correlates of Exposure to Police Victimisation in Four US Cities," *Epidemiology and Psychiatric Sciences* 26, no. 5 (2017): 466–77; Global Burden of Diseases, Injuries, and Risk Factors Study (GBD), Police Violence US Subnational Collaborators, "Fatal Police Violence by Race and State in the USA, 1980–2019: A Network Meta-Regression," *Lancet* 398, no. 10307 (2021): 1239–55; Editorial Board, "Winter HPHR Editorial: Racism Is a Public Health Problem," *Harvard Public Health Review* 3 (2015), https://hphr.org/3-article-hphr/.

19. Rahwa Haile, Tawandra Rowell-Cunsolo, Marie-Fatima Hyacinthe, and Sirry Alang, "'We (Still) Charge Genocide': A Systematic Review and Synthesis of the Direct and Indirect Health Consequences of Police Violence in the United States," *Social Science and Medicine* 322 (2023): 115784.

20. National Academy of Medicine, "Racism and Associated Heath Impacts," 2022, https://nam.edu/racism-and-associated-health-impacts/.

21. National Academy of Medicine, "Racism and Associated Heath Impacts," 1.

22. Osagie K. Obasogie and Zachary Newman, "Police Violence, Use of Force Policies, and Public Health," *American Journal of Law and Medicine* 43, no. 2–3 (2017): 279–95.

23. Aaron J. Kivisto, Bradley Ray, and Peter L. Phalen, "Firearm Legislation and Fatal Police Shootings in the United States," *American Journal of Public Health* 107, no. 7 (2017): 1068–75.

24. This research merges with the studies by David Hemenway attempting to reduce firearm violence.

25. John A. Shjarback, "State-Mandated Transparency: A Discussion and Examination of Deadly Force Data Among Law Enforcement Agencies in Texas," *Journal of Crime and Justice* 42, no. 1 (2019): 3–17; John A. Shjarback and Justin Nix, "Considering Violence Against Police by Citizen Race/Ethnicity to Contextualize Representation in Officer Involved Shootings," *Journal of Criminal Justice* 66 (2020): 101653.

26. Joanna C. Schwartz, "How Qualified Immunity Fails." *Yale Law Journal* 127 (2017): 2–76.

27. Leigh Paterson, "Company Pitches Liability Insurance for Colorado Cops, Following Passage of Police Reform Law," KUNC, NPR for Northern Colorado, September 10, 2021.

28. Stephen Wulff, "Flipping the 'New Penology' Script: Police Misconduct Insurance, Grassroots Activism, and Risk Management-Based Reform," *Law and Social Inquiry* 47, no. 1 (2022): 162–204.

29. Morgan J. Steele and Ziwei Qui, "The Impact of State Laws on Officer-Involved Deaths (OIDs)," *Criminology, Criminal Justice, Law, and Society* 25, no. 3 (2024): 1–20.

30. Lisabeth Pérez Castle, "2023 Semiannual Report," Denver Office of the Independent Monitor, 2023 (Reports).

31. See Mir Usman Ali and Maureen Pirog, "Social Accountability and Institutional Change: The Case of Citizen Oversight of Police," *Public Administration Review* 79, no. 3 (2019): 411–26; Joseph G. Sandoval, "Preliminary Observations on Civilian Oversight in Denver," presented at the SWACJ Conference, 2002; Samuel Walker, *Role Accountability: The Role of Citizen Oversight* (Wadsworth, 2000).

32. Yves Cabannes, "Participatory Budgeting: A Significant Contribution to Participatory Democracy," *Environment and Urbanization* 16, no. 1 (2004): 27–46; Nelson Dias and Simone Júlio, "The Next Thirty Years of Participatory Budgeting in the World Start Today," in *Hope for Democracy: 30 Year of Participatory Budgeting Worldwide* (Epopeia Records, 2018) (Reports).

33. Lodewijk Gelauff and Ashish Goel, "Opinion Change or Differential Turnout: Changing Opinions on the Austin Police Department in a Budget Feedback Process," *Digital Government: Research and Practice* 5, no. 3 (2024): 1–32. The *Texas Tribune* reported

the Austin City Council cut the police department budget by one-third, which was estimated to be $21.5 million dollars, and redistributed the money toward other services. Meena Venkataramanan, "Austin City Council Cuts Police Department Budget by One-Third, Mainly Through Reorganizing Some Duties Out from Law Enforcement Oversight," *Texas Tribune*, August 13, 2020.

34.   Megan Munce, "Gov. Greg Abbott Signs Slate of Legislation to Increase Criminal Penalties for Protestors, Punish Cities That Reduce Police Budgets," *Texas Tribune*, June 1, 2021.

35.   See Miltonette Olivia Craig and Kwan-Lamar Blount-Hill, *Justice and Legitimacy in Policing: Transforming the Institution* (Routledge, 2023).

36.   Gelauff and Goel, "Opinion Change or Differential Turnout"; Li Sian Goh, "Going Local: Do Consent Decrees and Other Forms of Federal Intervention in Municipal Police Departments Reduce Police Killings?," *Justice Quarterly* 37, no. 5 (2020): 900–29; Sam McCann, "Everything You Need to Know About Consent Decrees: Understanding Federal Oversight of the Criminal Legal System," *Vera*, August 30, 2023.

37.   Victor Ray, "A Theory of Racialized Organizations," *American Sociological Review* 84, no. 1 (2019): 26–53.

38.   Office of Community Oriented Policing Services, "The President's Task Force on 21st Century Policing: Implementation Guide Moving from Recommendations to Action," 2015.

39.   Obasogie and Newman, "Police Violence, Use of Force Policies, and Public Health."

40.   Obasogie and Newman, "Police Violence, Use of Force Policies, and Public Health," 286.

41.   Obasogie and Newman, "Police Violence, Use of Force Policies, and Public Health."

42.   Jay T. Jennings and Meghan E. Rubado, "Preventing the Use of Deadly Force: The Relationship Between Police Agency Policies and Rates of Officer-Involved Gun Deaths," *Public Administration Review* 77, no. 2 (2017): 217–26.

43.   A study by John A. Shjarback, Michael D. White, and Stephen A. Bishopp, "Can Police Shootings Be Reduced by Requiring Officers to Document When They Point Firearms at Citizens," *Injury Prevention* 27 (2021): 508–13, found similar results for one large police department.

44.   Paul Takagi, "A Garrison State in Democratic Society," *Crime and Social Justice* (Spring/ Summer 1974): 27–32.

45.   Amelia Cheatham and Lindsay Maizland, "How Police Compare in Different Democracies," Council on Foreign Relations, 2022 (Reports); Melissa Godin, "What the U.S. Can Learn from Countries Where Cops Don't Carry Guns," *Time*, June 19, 2020; Paul J. Hirschfield, "Exceptionally Lethal: American Police Killings in a Comparative Perspective," *Annual Review of Criminology* 6 (2023): 471–98.

46.   Trevor Bechtel, Mara C. Ostfeld, and H. Luke Shaefer, "Evidence on Measures to Reduce Excessive Use of Force by the Police," Center for Racial Justice, University of Michigan, 2023 (Reports).

47.   Emily D. Buehler, "State and Local Law Enforcement Training Academics, 2018— Statistical Tables," US Department of Justice, Office of Justice Programs, Bureau of Justice Statistics, NCJ 255915, 2021 (Reports).

48.   Robin S. Engel, Nicholas Corsaro, Gabrielle T. Isaza, and Hannah D. McManus, "Assessing the Impact of De-escalation Training on Police Behavior: Reducing Police Use of Force in the Louisville, KY Metro Police Department," *Criminology and Public Policy* 21 (2022): 199–233; Robin S. Engel, Hannah D. McManus, and Tamara D. Herold, "Does De-escalation Training Work? A Systematic Review and Call for Evidence in Police Use of Force," *Criminology and Public Policy* 19 (2020): 721–59.

49.   Engel et al., "Assessing the Impact of De-escalation Training on Police Behavior."

50.   Engel, McManus, and Herold, "Does De-escalation Training Work?"

51.   Samantha J. Simon, "Training for War: Academy Socialization and Warrior Policing," *Social Problems* 70 (2023): 1021–43.

52.   Sierra Arévalo, "American Policing and the Danger Imperative."

53.   Danyao Li, Sean Nicholson-Crotty, and Jill Nicholson-Crotty, "Creating Guardians or Warriors? Examining the Effects of Non-Stress Training on Policing Outcomes," *American Review of Public Administration* 51, no. 1 (2021): 3–16.

54.   Jennifer Carlson, "Police Warriors and Police Guardians: Race, Masculinity, and the Construction of Gun Violence," *Social Problems* 67 (2020): 399–417; Justin E. Holz, Roman G. Rivera, and Bocar A. Ba, "Peer Effects in Police Use of Force," *Amerian Economic Journal: Economic Policy* 15, no. 2 (2023): 256–91; Linda Zhao and Andrew V. Papachristos, "Network Position and Police Who Shoot," *Annals of the American Academy of Political and Social Science* 687, no. 1 (2020): 89–112.

55.   Craig Bennell, Geoffrey Alpert, Judith P. Andersen, et al., "Advancing Police Use of Force Research and Practice: Urgent Issues and Prospects," *Legal and Criminological Psychology* 26, no. 2 (2021): 121–44.

56.   Bennell et al., "Advancing Police Use of Force Research and Practice," 125–28.

57.   Lois James, "The Stability of Implicit Racial Bias in Police Officers," *Police Quarterly* 21, no. 1 (2018): 30–52.

58.   Alison N. Cooke and Amy G. Halberstadt, "Adultification, Anger Bias, and Adult's Different Perceptions of Black and White Children," *Cognition and Emotion* 35, no. 7 (2021): 1416–22.

59.   Amy C. Watson, Leah G. Pope and Michael T. Compton, "Police Reform from the Perspective of Mental Health Services and Professionals: Our Role in Social Change," *Psychiatric Services* 72, no. 9 (2021): 1085–87.

60.   Jams D. Livingston, "Contact Between Police and People with Mental Disorders: A Review of Rates," *Psychiatric Services* 67, no. 8 (2016): 850–57.

61.   Doris A. Fuller, H. Richard Lamb, Michael Biasotti, and John Snook, "Overlooked in the Undercounted: The Role of Mental Illness in Fatal Law Enforcement Encounters," Treatment Advocacy Center, a Report from the Office of Research and Public Affairs, 2015, https://www.treatmentadvocacycenter.org/storage/documents/overlooked-in-the-undercounted.pdf (Reports).

62.   Wesley Lowery, Kimberly Kindy, Keith L. Alexander, and Steven Rich. "Distraught People, Deadly Results," *Washington Post*, May 30, 2015, https://www.washingtonpost.com/sf/investigative/2015/06/30/distraught-people-deadly-results/.

63. Michael Compton and Amy Watson, "Research to Improve Law Enforcement Responses to Persons with Mental Illnesses and Intellectual/Developmental Disabilities," Bureau of Justice Assistance, US Department of Justice, slide 14, https://bjatta.bja.ojp.gov /system/files/documents/training_resources/Research%20to%20Improve%20Law%2 0Enforcement%20Responses%20to%20Persons%20with%20Mental%20Illnesses%20 and%20Developmental%20Disabilities.pdf (Reports).

64. Amy C. Watson, Melissa Schaefer Morabito, Jeffrey Draine, and Victor Ottati, "Improving Police Response to Persons with Mental Illness: A Multi-Level Conceptualization of CIT," *International Journal of Law and Psychiatry* 31, no. 4 (2008): 359–68.

65. Michael S. Rogers, Dale E. McNiel, and Renée L. Binder, "Effectiveness of Police Crisis Intervention Training Programs," *Journal of the American Academy of Psychiatry and the Law Online* (2019): 003863-19; Eric Westervelt, "Mental Health and Police Violence: How Crisis Intervention Teams Are Failing," NPR, September 18, 2020, https://www .npr.org/2020/09/18/913229469/mental-health-and-police-violence-how-crisis-inter vention-teams-are-failing.

66. Meret S. Hofer, Allison R. Gilbert, and Marvin S. Swartz, "Police Mental Health: A Neglected Element of Police Reform," *Psychiatric Services* 72, no. 9 (2021): 985; Mark D. Stephenson, Ben Schram, Elisa F. D. Canetti, and Robin Orr, "Effects of Acute Stress on Psychophysiology in Armed Tactical Occupations: A Narrative Review," *International Journal of Environmental Research and Public Health* 19, no. 3 (2022): 1802.

67. Stephanie Schweitzer Dixon, "Law Enforcement Suicide: The Depth of the Problem and Best Practices for Suicide Prevention Strategies," *Aggression and Violent Behavior* 61 (2021): 101649; Leigh S. Goodmark, "Hands Up at Home: Militarized Masculinity and Police Officers Who Commit Intimate Partner Abuse," *Brigham Young University Law Review* 1183 (2015); Annelise M. Mennicke and Katie Ropes, "Estimating the Rate of Domestic Violence Perpetrated by Law Enforcement Officers: A Review of Methods and Estimates," *Aggression and Violent Behavior* 31 (2016): 157–64; John M. Violanti, Desta Fekedulegn, Michael E. Andrew, et al., "Shift Work and the Incidence of Injury Among Police Officers," *American Journal of Industrial Medicine* 55 (2012): 217–27.

68. Katelyn K. Jetelina, Rebecca J. Molsberry, Jennifer Reingle Gonzalez, et al., "Prevalence of Mental Illness and Mental Health Care Use Among Police Officers," *JAMA Network Open* 3, no. 10 (2020): e2019658; Ruth E. Marshall, Josie Milligan-Saville, Katherine Petrie, et al., "Mental Health Screening Among Police Officers: Factors Associated with Under-Reporting of Symptoms," *BMC Psychiatry* 21 (2021): 135.

69. James P. McElvain and Augustine J. Kposowa, "Police Officer Characteristics and Internal Affairs Investigations for Use of Force Allegations," *Journal of Criminal Justice* 32 (2004): 265–79.

70. Barbara E. Armacost, "Organizational Culture and Police Misconduct," *George Washington Law Review* 72, no. 3 (2004): 453–546.

71. Ben Grunwald and John Rappaport, "The Wandering Officer," *Yale Law Journal* 129, no. 6 (2020): 1600–195; Jerome H. Skolnick and James J. Fyfe, *Above the Law: Police and the Excessive Use of Force* (Free Press, 1993).

72. The concept of vision and nerve originates from the scholarship of Dr. Harry Reed, for whom Durán served as a teaching assistant at the University of Colorado for the Ethnic Studies course titled "Contemporary Black Protest Movements (The Long Historical Record)."

73. Curtis J. Austin, *Up Against the wall: Violence in the Making and Unmaking of the Black Panther Party* (University of Arkansas Press, 2006); Jocelyn Simonson, "Filming the Police as an Act of Resistance: Remarks Given at the Smartphoned Symposium," *University of St. Thomas Journal of Law and Public Policy* 10, no. 2 (2016): 83–88; Ernesto B. Vigil, *The Crusade for Justice: Chicano Militancy and the Government's War on Dissent* (University of Wisconsin Press, 1999).

74. Durán and Shroulote-Durán, "Institutionalizing Community Oversight of the Police."

75. John D. Márquez, *Black-Brown Solidarity: Racial Politics in the New Gulf South* (University of Texas Press, 2013); Jeffrey Reiman, *The Rich Get Richer and the Poor Get Prison* (Pearson, 2007).

76. Betty Shabazz, *Malcolm X, February 1965: The Final Speeches* (Pathfinder, 1992), 37.

77. Hinton, *America on Fire.*

78. National Library of Medicine, keyword "Police Violence," 2024.

79. National Library of Medicine, keyword "Police Shootings," 2024.

80. National Institutes of Health, keyword "Police Violence," 2024.

81. National Institutes of Health, keyword "Police Shootings," 2024.

82. Justin Nix, "On the Challenges Associated with the Study of Police Use of Deadly Force in the United States: A Response to Schwartz and Jahn," *PLOS One* 15, no. 7 (2020).

83. National Library of Medicine, keyword "Police Violence," 2024.

84. National Library of Medicine, keyword "Police Shootings," 2024.

85. Gun Violence Archive, https://www.gunviolencearchive.org.

86. Naomi G. Goldberg, Christy Mallory, Amira Hasenbush, et al., "Police and the Criminalization of LGBT People," in *The Cambridge Handbook of Policing in the United States*, ed. E. J. Miller and T. R. Lave (Cambridge University Press, 2019), 374–91.

87. Sharon Lipperman-Kreda, Ida Wilson, Geoffrey P. Hunt, et al., "Substance Use Among Sexual and Gender Minorities: Association with Police Discrimination and Police Mistrust," *Sexuality, Gender and Policy* 3, no. 2 (2020): 92–104.

88. David L. Carter, "Hispanic Perception of Police Performance: An Empirical Assessment," *Journal of Criminal Justice* 13, no. 6 (1985): 487–500; Malcolm D. Holmes, "Minority Threat and Police Brutality: Determinants of Civil Rights Criminal Complaints in U.S. Municipalities," *Criminology* 38 (2000): 343–67; Ramiro Martínez, "Incorporating Latinos and Immigrants Into Policing Research," *Criminology and Public Policy* 6, no. 1 (2007): 57–64; Cecilia Menjívar and Cynthia Bejarano, "Latino Immigrants' Perception of Crime and Police Authorities in the United States: A Case Study from the Phoenix Metropolitan Area," *Ethnic and Racial Studies* 2, no. 1 (2004): 120–48; Alfredo Mirandé, *Gringo Justice* (University of Notre Dame Press, 1987); Ronald Weitzer, "The Puzzling Neglect of Hispanic Americans in Research on Police-Citizen Relations," *Ethnic and Racial Studies* 37, no. 11 (2014): 1995–2013.

89. Frances Negrón-Muntaner, Chelsea Abbas, Luis Figueroa, and Samuel Robson, "The Latino Media Gap: A Report on the State of Latinos in U.S. Media," Center for the Study of Ethnicity and Race, Columbia University, 2014, https://www.columbia.edu/cu/cser /downloads/Latino_Media_Gap_Report.pdf.

90. Rogelio Sáenz and Maria Cristina Morales, *Latinos in the United States: Diversity and Change* (Polity, 2015); Alfredo Mirandé, *The Chicano Experience: An Alternative Perspective*, 2nd ed. (University of Notre Dame Press, 2022).

91. Grace S. Liu, Brenda L. Nguyen, Bridget H. Lyons, et al., "Surveillance for Violent Deaths—National Violent Death Reporting System, 48 States, the District of Columbia, and Puerto Rico, 2020," Surveillance Summaries, Centers for Disease Control, *Morbidity and Mortality Weekly Report* (*MMWR*), 2023 (Reports).

92. Gary Clayton Anderson, *The Conquest of Texas: Ethnic Cleansing in the Promised Land, 1820–1875* (University of Oklahoma Press, 2005); David E. Stannard, *American Holocaust: Columbus and the Conquest of the New World* (Oxford University Press, 1992).

93. Abby Budiman, "Income Inequality Is Greater Among Chinese Americans Than Any Other Asian Origin Group in the U.S," Pew Research Center, May 31, 2024 (Reports).

94. Jennifer Lee and Min Zhou, *The Asian American Achievement Paradox* (Russell Sage Foundation, 2015).

95. James J. Fyfe, "Police Use of Deadly Force: Research and Reform," *Justice Quarterly* 5 (1988): 165–205.

96. Timothy A. Akers and Mark M. Lanier, "'Epidemiological Criminology': Coming Full Circle," *American Journal of Public Health* 99, no. 3 (2009): 397–402.

97. Etienne G. Krug, James A. Mercy, Linda L. Dahlberg and Anthony B. Zwi, "The World Report on Violence and Health," *Lancet* 360, no. 9339 (2002): 1083–88.

98. Nancy Krieger, "Theories for Social Epidemiology in the 21st Century: An Ecosocial Perspective," *International Journal of Epidemiology* 30, no. 4 (2001): 668–77.

99. Kenneth R. McLeroy, Daniel Bibeau, Allan Steckler, and Karen Glanz, "An Ecological Perspective on Health Promotion Programs," *Health Education Quarterly* 15, no. 4 (1988): 351–77.

100. Centers for Disease Control and Prevention (CDC) Agency for Toxic Substances and Disease Registry, 2015; Centers for Disease Control and Prevention (CDC), "The Social-Ecological Model: A Framework for Prevention," 2022, https://www.cdc.gov /violenceprevention/about/social-ecologicalmodel.html.

101. CDC, "The Social-Ecological Model."

102. Christian M. Connell, Tamika D. Gilreath, Will M. Aklin, and Robert A. Brex, "Social-Ecological Influences on Patterns of Substance Use Among Non-Metropolitan High School Students," *American Journal of Community Psychology* 45, no. 1–2 (2010): 36–48; Danielle Horyniak, Karla D. Wagner, Richard F. Armenta, et al., "Cross-Border Injection Drug Use and HIV and Hepatitis C Virus Seropositivity Among People Who Inject Drugs in San Diego, California," *International Journal of Drug Policy* 47 (September 2017): 9–17.

103. Devin E. Banks, Devon J. Hensel, and Tamika C. B. Zapolski, "Integrating Individual and Contextual Factors to Explain Disparities in HIV/STI Among Heterosexual

African American Youth: A Contemporary Literature Review and Social Ecological Model," *Archives of Sexual Behavior* 49, no. 6 (2020): 1939–64. Sandra E. Larios, Remedios Lozada, Steffanie A. Strathdee, et al., "An Exploration of Contextual Factors That Influence HIV Risk in Female Sex Workers in Mexico: The Social Ecological Model Applied to HIV Risk Behaviors," *AIDS Care* 21, no. 10 (2009): 1335–42.

104. Etienne G. Krug, James A. Mercy, Linda L. Dahlberg, and Anthony B. Zwi, "The World Report on Violence and Health," *Lancet* 360, no. 9339 (2002): 1083–88.

105. Allison Durkin, Christopher Schenck, Yamini Narayan, et al., "Prevention of Firearm Injury Through Policy and Law: The Social Ecological Model," *Journal of Law, Medicine and Ethics* 48, no. 4, suppl. (2020): 191–97.

106. Adelyn Allchin, Vicka Chaplin, and Joshua Horwitz, "Limiting Access to Lethal Means: Applying the Social Ecological Model for Firearm Suicide Prevention," *Injury Prevention* 25, suppl. 1 (2019): i44–i48.

107. Robert J. Kane, "The Social Ecology of Police Misconduct," *Criminology* 40, no. 4 (2002): 867–96.

108. Roger G. Dunham and Nick Petersen, "Making Black Lives Matter," *Criminology and Public Policy* 16, no. 1 (2017): 341–48.

109. Dunham and Petersen, "Making Black Lives Matter," 343.

110. Jordan E. DeVylder, Deidre M. Anglin, Lisa Bowleg, et al., "Police Violence and Public Health," *Annual Review of Clinical Psychology* 18 (2022): 527–52.

111. DeVylder et al., "Police Violence and Public Health," 528.

112. Durán and Shroulote-Durán, "Institutionalizing Community Oversight of the Police."

CONCLUSION

1. Writing a book can take a long time. Writing that has influenced each component of this book has covered a time period of twenty-two years, from 2003 to 2025. The killing of George Floyd was a key motivator in completing this book, and despite the killing occurring before the Uvalde shooting presented in chapter 6, it could not be omitted from inclusion despite not occurring in a linear timeframe.

2. Sadly, this statement was in direct contrast to my conclusions for creating change eleven years prior: Robert J. Durán, *Gang Life in Two Cities: An Insider's Journey* (Columbia University Press, 2013). It is a sad commentary to think about the disillusionment that can occur with age and thus the happiness and pride felt when seeing youth challenge structural powers and demand change.

3. Kenny Wiley, "Bryan Demonstration Against Racism, Police Violence Draws Hundreds," *The Eagle*, June 1, 2020.

4. Emile Durkheim, *Suicide* (Free Press, 1951); *The Division of Labor in Society* (Free Press, 1984).

5. The white male in the truck was later arrested and charged with reckless driving.

6. See differences between the Chicago School (Jean-Michel Chapoulie, *Chicago Sociology* [Columbia University Press, 2020]) and Atlanta School (Aldon D. Morris, *The Scholar*

Denied: W. E. B. Du Bois and the Birth of Modern Sociology [University of California Press, 2015]), in addition to the discussion on social justice (Patricia Hill Collins, *Intersectionality: A Critical Social Theory* [Duke University Press, 2019]; and Mary Romero, "Sociology Engaged in Social Justice," *American Sociological Review* 85, no. 1 (2020): 1–30).

7. Howard S. Becker, "Whose Side Are We On?," *Social Problems* 14, no. 3 (1967): 239–47. Joe R. Feagin and Hernan Vera, *Liberation Sociology* (Westview, 2001); Paulo Freire, *Pedagogy of the Oppressed* (Continuum, 2000); Alvin W. Gouldner, "The Sociologist as Partisan: Sociology and the Welfare State," *American Sociologist* 3, no. 2 (1968): 103–16; Romero, "Sociology Engaged in Social Justice"; Willie F. Tolliver, Bernadette R. Hadden, Fabienne Snowden, and Robyn Brown-Manning, "Police Killings of Unarmed Black People: Centering Race and Racism in Human Behavior and the Social Environment," *Journal of Human Behavior in the Social Environment* 26, no. 3–4 (2016): 279–86.

8. Alex Samuels, "Anger, Anguish and Calls for Change Mark George Floyd's Memorial in Houston," *Texas Tribune*, June 8, 2020.

9. National Association of Buffalo Soldiers and Troopers Motorcycle Club, https://www.nabstmc.com/.

10. Probably too many years devoted to my Catholic upbringing.

11. Robert J. Durán and Charlene Shroulote-Durán, "Institutionalizing Community Oversight of the Police: Copwatch," in *Justice and Legitimacy in Policing: Transforming the Institution*, ed. M. O. Craig and K. L. Blount-Hill (Routledge, 2023), 76–90. Mary D. Fan, *Camera Power: Proof, Policing, Privacy, and Audiovisual Big Data* (Cambridge University Press, 2019).

12. Edward J. Escobar, *Race, Police, and the Making of a Political Identity: Mexican Americans and the Los Angeles Police Department, 1900–1945* (University of California Press, 1999); Roberto Rodriguez, *Justice: A Question of Race* (Bilingual Press, 1997).

13. *Fatal Force*, https://www.washingtonpost.com/graphics/investigations/police-shootings-database/.

14. James J. Fyfe, "Police Use of Deadly Force: Research and Reform," *Justice Quarterly* 5 (1988): 165–205; and "Too Many Missing Cases: Holes in Our Knowledge About Police Use of Force," *Justice Research and Policy* 4, no. 1–2 (2002): 87–102. Paul Takagi, "A Garrison State in Democratic Society," *Crime and Social Justice* (Spring/Summer 1974): 27–32.

15. Phillip Dray, *At the Hands of Persons Unknown: The Lynching of Black America* (Random House, 2002); David Levering Lewis, *W. E. B. Du Bois: Biography of a Race: 1968–1919* (Owl, 1993). Other studies of public lynchings concur with the public spectacle: William W. King, *Going to Meet a Man: Denver's Last Legal Public Execution, 27 July 1886* (University Press of Colorado, 1990); Stephen J. Leonard, *Lynching in Colorado, 1859–1919* (University Press of Colorado, 2002); Monica Muñoz Martinez, *The Injustice Never Leaves You: Anti-Mexican Violence in Texas* (Harvard University Press, 2018).

16. Phillip Dray, *At the Hands of Persons Unknown: The Lynching of Black America* (Random House, 2002); Lewis, *W. E. B. Du Bois*.

17. Katheryn Russell-Brown, *Underground Codes: Race, Crime, and Related Fires* (New York University Press, 2004); *Stolen Lives: Killed by Law Enforcement*, October 22nd Coalition to Stop Police Brutality, Repression and the Criminalization of a

Generation, New York, 1999; Paul Takagi, "LEAA's Research Solicitation: Police Use of Deadly Force," *Crime and Social Justice* (Spring/Summer 1979): 51–59.

18. Ben Grunwald and John Rappaport, "The Wandering Officer," *Yale Law Journal* 129, no. 6 (2020): 1600–195.

19. See Tommy J. Curry, *The Man-Not: Race, Class, Genre, and the Dilemmas of Black Manhood* (Temple University Press, 2017), for a very disturbing analysis of the killing of Black men. In addition, we could probably also add individuals of Mexican descent, Puerto Ricans, and Native Americans with tribal affiliation.

20. Tami Gold and Kelly Anderson, *Every Mother's Son*, New Day Films, 2004; John D. Márquez, *Black-Brown Solidarity: Racial Politics in the New Gulf South* (University of Texas Press, 2013).

21. Robin Kelley, " 'Slangin' Rocks . . . Palestinian Style' Dispatches from the Occupied Zones of North America," in *Police Brutality: An Anthology*, ed. J. Nelson (Norton, 2000), 21–59.

22. David Klinger, *Into the Kill Zone: A Cop's Eye View of Deadly Force* (Jossey-Bass, 2004).

23. Jennifer Carlson, "Police Warriors and Police Guardians: Race, Masculinity, and the Construction of Gun Violence," *Social Problems* 67 (2020): 399–417; Justin E. Holz, Roman G. Rivera, and Bocar A. Ba, "Peer Effects in Police Use of Force," *Amerian Economic Journal: Economic Policy* 15, no. 2 (2023): 256–91; Linda Zhao and Andrew V. Papachristos, "Network Position and Police Who Shoot," *Annals of the American Academy of Political and Social Science* 687, no. 1 (2020): 89–112.

24. Raúl Pérez and Geoff Ward, "From Insult to Estrangement and Injury: The Violence of Racist Police Jokes," *American Behavioral Scientist* 63, no. 13 (2019): 1810–29.

25. The star example is Serpico; see Peter Maas, *Serpico* (Bantam, 1973).

26. Hill Collins, *Intersectionality*.

27. John Gramlich, "What the Data Says About Gun Deaths in the U.S.," Pew Research Center, https://www.pewresearch.org/short-reads/2023/04/26/what-the-data-says-about-gun-deaths-in-the-u-s/ (Reports).

28. Alex Piquero, "Racial Inequality in Firearm Homicide Victimization—but Not Other Types of US Violence," *Cambridge Journal of Evidence-Based Policing* 8, no. 1 (2023).

29. Márquez, *Black-Brown Solidarity*, 44.

30. Walter L. Hixon, *American Settler Colonialism: A History* (Palgrave Macmillan, 2013); Márquez, *Black-Brown Solidarity*.

31. Gary Clayton Anderson, *The Conquest of Texas: Ethnic Cleansing in the Promised Land, 1820–1875* (University of Oklahoma Press, 2005); Richard Slotkin, *Regeneration Through Violence: The Mythology of the American Frontier, 1600–1860* (Wesleyan University Press, 1973); Patrick Wolfe, "Settler Colonialism and the Elimination of the Native," *Journal of Genocide Research* 8, no. 4 (2006): 387–409.

32. Alexander Alvarez, "Trends and Patterns of Justifiable Homicide: A Comparative Analysis," *Violence and Victims* 7, no. 4 (1992): 347–56; James J. Fyfe, "Observations on Police Deadly Force," *Crime and Delinquency* 27 (1981): 376–89; "Blind Justice: Police Shootings in Memphis," *Journal of Criminal Law and Criminology* 73, no. 2 (1982): 707–22; William A. Geller and Kevin J. Karales, "Shootings of and by Chicago Police:

Uncommon Crises—Part I: Shootings by Chicago Police," *Journal of Criminal Law and Criminology* 72, no. 4 (1981): 1813–66; Sidney L. Harring, Tony Platt, Richard Speiglman, and Paul Takagi, "The Management of Police Killings," *Crime and Social Justice* 8 (Fall–Winter 1977): 34–43; Andres Inn, Alan C. Wheeler, and Cynthia L. Sparling, "The Effects of Suspect Race and Situation Hazard on Police Officer Shooting Behavior," *Journal of Applied Social Psychology* 7, no. 1 (1977): 27–37; Arthur L. Kobler, "Figures (and Perhaps Some Facts) on Police Killing of Civilians in the United States, 1965–1969," *Journal of Social Issues* 31, no. 1 (1975): 185–91; Marshall W. Meyer, "Police Shootings at Minorities: The Case of Los Angeles," *Annals of the American Academy of Political and Social Science* 452 (1980): 98–110.

33.   Eduardo Bonilla-Silva, *Racism Without Racists: Color-Blind Racism and the Persistence of Racial Inequality in America*, 6th ed. (Rowman and Littlefield, 2022); Joe R. Feagin, *The White Racial Frame: Centuries of Racial Framing and Counter-Framing*, 2nd ed. (Routledge, 2013).

34.   Takagi, "A Garrison State in Democratic Society."

35.   Other researchers who share the opinion of Latinos experiencing a nonwhite experience include Laura E. Gómez, *Manifest Destinies: The Making of the Mexican American Race* (New York University Press, 2007); Ian F. Haney-López, *Racism on Trial: The Chicano Fight for Justice* (Belknap, 2003); Alfredo Mirandé, *Gringo Justice* (University of Notre Dame Press, 1987); *The Chicano Experience: An Alternative Perspective*, 2nd ed. (University of Notre Dame Press, 2022).

36.   Gary Clayton Anderson, *The Conquest of Texas: Ethnic Cleansing in the Promised Land, 1820–1875* (University of Oklahoma Press, 2005); Robert J. Durán, *The Gang Paradox: Inequalities and Miracles on the U.S.-Mexico Border* (Columbia University Press, 2018).

37.   A strange paradox whenever witnessing white supremacists preaching the great replacement theory.

38.   Richard Delgado and Jean Stefancic, *The Derrick Bell Reader* (New York University Press, 2005); *Critical Race Theory: An Introduction* (New York: New York University Press, 2012); Jim Sidanius and Felicia Pratto, *Social Dominance: An Intergroup Theory of Social Hierarchy and Oppression* (Cambridge University Press, 1999).

39.   Mari J. Matsuda, "Public Response to Racist Speech: Considering the Victim's Story," *Michigan Law Review* 87, no. 8 (1989): 2325.

40.   Elizabeth Hinton, *America on Fire: The Untold History of Police Violence and Black Rebellion Since the 1960s* (Liveright, 2021).

41.   Richard Slotkin, *Regeneration Through Violence: The Mythology of the American Frontier, 1600–1860* (Wesleyan University Press, 1973).

42.   Sandra Bass, "Policing Space, Policing Race: Social Control Imperatives and Police Discretionary Decisions," *Social Justice* 28, no. 1 (2001): 156–76; David Hemenway, *Private Guns: Public Health* (University of Michigan Press, 2004); Katheryn Russell-Brown, *Underground Codes: Race, Crime, and Related Fires* (New York University Press, 2004); Takagi, "A Garrison State in Democratic Society."

43.   USCensus,https://www.census.gov/data/tables/time-series/demo/popest/2020s-counties-total.html.

44. Durán does have such a physical map pinpointing each shooting, but we believe additional analyses could be performed using GIS.
45. King, *Going to Meet a Man*, 156.
46. Gary L. Roberts, *Massacre at Sand Creek: How Methodists Were Involved in An American Tragedy* (Abingdon, 2016).
47. It is reported that Mahatma Gandhi provided this paraphrased quote. However, it has also been attributed to Dr. Martin Luther King Jr.

ACKNOWLEDGMENTS

1. Drake, "Started from the Bottom (explicit)," YouTube video, DrakeVEVO, 2013, https://www.youtube.com/watch?v=RubBzkZzpUA. Plus, shout out to my homie Xavier Perez, who wrote an article with that title: Xavier Perez, "Started from the Bottom, Now We're Here: Reflections of a Latinx Scholar-Activist," *Journal of Criminal Justice Education* 34, no. 3 (2023): 451–59.
2. "Enhanced Interdisciplinary Research Training Institute on Hispanic Substance Abuse (IRTI), 2013 Fellows," http://www.irtiusc.org/fellows/2013-fellows/.

APPENDIX 1: DATA SOURCES AND ANALYSIS

1. Mitchell R. Morrissey, "Officer-Involved Shooting Protocol," State of Colorado, Office of the District Attorney, Denver, 2011, 1.
2. It was my desire to go back fifty years, but the District Attorney's office only began writing and collecting decision letters in 1983, and newspaper articles were often incomplete in providing comprehensive coverage.
3. Morrissey, "Officer-Involved Shooting Protocol," 2.
4. Paul J. Hirschfield and Daniella Simon, "Legitimating Police Violence: Newspaper Narratives of Deadly Force," *Theoretical Criminology* 14 (2010): 155–82.
5. The *Rocky Mountain News* published its final paper on February 27, 2009.
6. Robert J. Durán, *Gang Life in Two Cities: An Insider's Journey* (Columbia University Press, 2013).
7. Robert J. Durán, *The Gang Paradox: Inequalities and Miracles on the U.S.-Mexico Border* (Columbia University Press, 2018).
8. Durán, Robert J., and Oralia Loza, "Exploring the Two Trigger Fingers Thesis: Racial and Ethnic Differences in Officer Involved Shootings," *Contemporary Justice Review: Issues in Criminal, Social, and Restorative Justice* 20, no. 1 (2017): 71–94.
9. International Business Machines (IBM), "IBM SPSS Statistics for Mac, Version 25.0, Released 2012," Armonk, New York.
10. Qualitative Research Software (QSR) International, "NVivo, Version 10, Released 2014," Burlington, Massachusetts.

APPENDIX 2: DATA TABLES

1. Linda L. Dahlberg and Etienne G. Krug, "Violence: A Global Public Health Problem," *Ciência and Saúde Coletiva* 11 (2006).
2. The measures without a symbol were included in the current study.

    † These measures were not included in the current study but are recommended by the authors.

    ‡ These measures are presented by Dahlberg and Krug, "Violence."

    § These measures are presented by Roger G. Dunham and Nick Petersen, "Making Black Lives Matter," *Criminology and Public Policy* 16, no. 1 (2017): 341–48.
3. Dahlberg and Krug, "Violence."
4. US Census, American Community Survey (ACS): https://www.census.gov/programs -surveys/acs.
5. Dahlberg and Krug, "Violence."
6. Dahlberg and Krug, "Violence."

BIBLIOGRAPHY

Acker, James R., Robert M. Bohm, and Charles S. Lanier, eds. *America's Experiment with Capital Punishment: Reflections on the Past, Present, and Future of the Ultimate Penal Sanction.* Carolina Academic Press, 1998.

Acosta, Oscar Zeta. *The Revolt of the Cockroach People.* Bantam Books, 1973.

Adler, Patricia A. *Wheeling and Dealing: An Ethnography of an Upper-Level Drug Dealing and Smuggling Community.* Columbia University Press, 1993.

Akers, Timothy A., and Mark M. Lanier. "'Epidemiological Criminology': Coming Full Circle." *American Journal of Public Health* 99, no. 3 (2009): 397–402.

Alang, Sirry, Taylor B. Rogers, Lillie D. Williamson, Cherrell Green, and April J. Bell. "Police Brutality and Unmet Need for Mental Health Care." *Health Services Research* 56, no. 6 (2021): 1104–13.

Alexander, Michelle. *The New Jim Crow: Mass Incarceration in the Age of Colorblindness.* The New Press, 2012.

Ali, Mir Usman, and Maureen Pirog. "Social Accountability and Institutional Change: The Case of Citizen Oversight of Police." *Public Administration Review* 79, no. 3 (2019): 411–26.

Allchin, Adelyn, Vicka Chaplin, and Joshua Horwitz. "Limiting Access to Lethal Means: Applying the Social Ecological Model for Firearm Suicide Prevention." *Injury Prevention* 25, suppl. 1 (2019): i44–i48.

Alpert, Geoffrey P., and William C. Smith. "How Reasonable Is the Reasonable Man? Police and Excessive Force." *Journal of Criminal Law and Criminology* 85 (1994): 481–501.

Alvarez, Alexander. "Trends and Patterns of Justifiable Homicide: A Comparative Analysis." *Violence and Victims* 7, no. 4 (1992): 347–56.

American Public Health Association. https://www.apha.org/what-is-public-health.

Anderson, Gary Clayton. *The Conquest of Texas: Ethnic Cleansing in the Promised Land, 1820–1875.* University of Oklahoma Press, 2005.

Armacost, Barbara E. "Organizational Culture and Police Misconduct." *George Washington Law Review* 72, no. 3 (2004): 453–546.

Armaline, William T., Claudio G. Vera Sanchez, and Mark Correia. "'The Biggest Gang in Oakland': Re-thinking Police Legitimacy." *Contemporary Justice Review* 17, no. 3 (2014): 375–99.

Arps, Louisa, W. *Denver in Slices: A Historical Guide to the City.* Ohio University Press, 1998.

Atkinson, Paul, Amanda Coffey, Sara Delamont, John Lofland, and Lyn Lofland. *Handbook of Ethnography.* SAGE, 2001.

Austin, Curtis J. *Up Against the Wall: Violence in the Making and Unmaking of the Black Panther Party.* University of Arkansas Press, 2006.

Ba, Bocar A., Dean Knox, Jonathan Mummolo, and Roman Rivera. "The Role of Officer Race and Gender in Police-Civilian Interactions in Chicago." *Science* 371, no. 6530 (2021): 696–702.

Balko, Radley. *Rise of the Warrior Cop: The Militarization of America's Police Forces.* PublicAffairs, 2013.

Banks, Devin E., Devon J. Hensel, and Tamika C. B. Zapolski. "Integrating Individual and Contextual Factors to Explain Disparities in HIV/STI Among Heterosexual African American Youth: A Contemporary Literature Review and Social Ecological Model." *Archives of Sexual Behavior* 49, no. 6 (2020): 1939–64.

Barber, Catherine, Deborah Azrael, Amy Cohen, Mathew Miller, Deonza Thymes, David Enxe Wang, and David Hemenway. "Homicides by Police: Comparing Counts from the National Violent Death Reporting System, Vital Statistics, and Supplementary Homicide Reports." *American Journal of Public Health* 106, no. 5 (2016): 922–27.

Bass, Sandra. "Policing Space, Policing Race: Social Control Imperatives and Police Discretionary Decisions." *Social Justice* 28, no. 1 (2001): 156–76.

Baum, Gracie R., Jaxon T. Baum, Dan Hayward, and Brendan J. MacKay. "Gunshot Wounds: Ballistics, Pathology, and Treatment Recommendations, with a Focus on Retained Bullets." *Orthopedic Research and Reviews* 14 (2022): 293–317.

Bayley, David H., and Harold Mendelsohn. *Minorities and the Police: Confrontation in America.* Free Press, 1968.

Becker, Howard S. "Whose Side Are We On?" *Social Problems* 14, no. 3 (1967): 239–47.

Belknap, Joanne. *The Invisible Woman: Gender, Crime and Justice.* Sage, 2015.

Bell, Derrick A. "*Brown v. Board of Education* and the Interest-Convergence Dilemma." *Harvard Law Review* 93, no. 3 (1980): 518–53.

Bennell, Craig, Geoffrey Alpert, Judith P. Andersen, Joseph Arpaia, Juha-Matti Huhta, Kimberly B. Kahn, et al. "Advancing Police Use of Force Research and Practice: Urgent Issues and Prospects." *Legal and Criminological Psychology* 26, no. 2 (2021): 121–44.

Binder, Arnold, and Peter Scharf. "Deadly Force in Law Enforcement." *Crime and Delinquency* 28 (1982): 1–23.

Blauner, Robert. *Racial Oppression in America.* Harper and Row, 1972.

Bonilla-Silva, Eduardo. "From Bi-Racial to Tri-Racial: Towards a New System of Racial Stratification in the USA." *Ethnic and Racial Studies* 27, no. 6 (2004): 931–50.

——. *Racism Without Racists: Color-Blind Racism and the Persistence of Racial Inequality in America.* 6th ed. Rowman and Littlefield, 2022.

Bright, Stephen B. "Counsel for the Poor: The Death Sentence Not for the Worst Crime but for the Worst Lawyer." *Yale Law Journal* 103 (1994): 1835–83.

Buehler, James W. "Racial/Ethnic Disparities in the Use of Lethal Force by US Police, 2010–2014." *American Journal of Public Health* 107, no. 2 (2017): 295–97.

Cabannes, Yves. "Participatory Budgeting: A Significant Contribution to Participatory Democracy." *Environment and Urbanization* 16, no. 1 (2004): 27–46.

Cacho, Lisa Marie. *Social Death: Racialized Rightlessness and the Criminalization of the Unprotected.* New York University Press, 2012.

Calloway, Colin G. *First Peoples: A Documentary Survey of American Indian History.* St. Martin's, 1999.

Caplan, David I. "Even Deadly Force: Fully Justifiable Homicide vs. Barely Excusable Homicide." *Journal on Firearms and Public Policy* 7 (2000): 7–16.

Carlson, Jennifer. "Police Warriors and Police Guardians: Race, Masculinity, and the Construction of Gun Violence." *Social Problems* 67 (2020): 399–417.

Carrigan, William D. *The Making of a Lynching Culture: Violence and Vigilantism in Central Texas, 1836–1916.* University of Illinois Press, 2004.

Carter, David L. "Hispanic Perception of Police Performance: An Empirical Assessment." *Journal of Criminal Justice* 13, no. 6 (1985): 487–500.

Chapoulie, Jean-Michel. *Chicago Sociology.* Columbia University Press, 2020.

City and County of Denver. "Denver Police Officers Receive 'Citizens Appreciate Police' Award for Acts of Kindness." 2020. https://www.denvergov.org/content/denvergov/en/police-department/news/2020/officers-receive-award.html.

Cobbina, Jennifer E. *Hands Up, Don't Shoot: Why the Protests in Ferguson and Baltimore Matter, and How They Changed America.* New York University Press, 2019.

Coccolini, Federico, Camilla Cremonini, Francesco Arces, Dario Tartaglia, and Massimo Chiarugi. "Trauma in Elderly." In *Emergency General Surgery in Geriatrics,* ed. Rifat Latifi, Fausto Catena, and Federico Coccolini, 231–41. Springer, 2021.

Cockcroft, James D. *Outlaws in the Promised Land: Mexican Immigrant Workers and America's Future.* Grove, 1986.

Cohen, Stanley. *States of Denial: Knowing About Atrocities and Suffering.* Polity, 2001.

Collins, Patricia Hill. *Intersectionality as Critical Social Theory.* Duke University Press, 2019.

Colomy, Paul, and Laura Ross Greiner. "Making Youth Violence Visible: The News Media and the Summer of Violence." *Denver University Law Review* 77 (2000): 661–88.

Comer, Benjamin P., and Jason R. Ingram. "Comparing Fatal Encounters, Mapping Police Violence, and Washington Post Fatal Police Shooting Data from 2015–2019: A Research Note." *Criminal Justice Review* 48, no. 2 (2022).

Cone, James H. *Martin and Malcolm and America: A Dream or a Nightmare.* Orbis, 1998.

Connell, Christian M., Tamika D. Gilreath, Will M. Aklin, and Robert A. Brex. 2010. "Social-Ecological Influences on Patterns of Substance Use Among Non-Metropolitan High School Students." *American Journal of Community Psychology* 45, no. 1–2 (2010): 36–48.

Conner, Andrew, Deborah Azrael, Vivian H. Lyons, Catherine Barber, and Matthew Miller. "Validating the National Violent Death Reporting System as a Source of Data on Fatal

Shootings of Civilians by Law Enforcement Officers." *American Journal of Public Health* 109, no. 4 (2019): 578–84.

Cook, Philip J., and Kristin A. Goss. *The Gun Debate: What Everyone Needs to Know.* Oxford University Press, 2014.

Cook, Philip J., and Jens Ludwig. *Gun Violence: The Real Costs.* Oxford University Press, 2002.

Cook, Phil, Mark Moore, and Anthony Braga. "Gun Control." Faculty Research Working Paper Series, John F. Kennedy School of Government, Harvard University. 2000.

Cooke, Alison N., and Amy G. Halberstadt. "Adultification, Anger Bias, and Adult's Different Perceptions of Black and White Children." *Cognition and Emotion* 35, no. 7 (2021): 1416–22.

Cooper, Hannah L. F., and Mindy Fullilove. "Editorial: Excessive Police Violence as a Public Health Issue." *Journal of Urban Health: Bulletin of the New York Academy of Medicine* 93, suppl. 1 (2016): 1–7.

Covey, Russell. "Police Misconduct as a Cause of Wrongful Convictions." *Washington University Law Review* 90, no. 4 (2013): 1133–90.

Craig, Miltonette Olivia, and Kwan-Lamar Blount-Hill. *Justice and Legitimacy in Policing: Transforming the Institution.* Routledge, 2023.

Crenshaw, Kimberle. "Demarginalizing the Intersection of Race and Sex: A Black Feminist Critique of Antidiscrimination Doctrine, Feminist Theory, and Antiracist Politics." *University of Chicago Legal Forum* 1, no. 8 (1989): 139–67.

Cripe, Clair A. *Legal Aspects of Corrections Management.* Aspen, 1997.

Crosby, Alex E., and Bridget Lyons. "Assessing Homicides by and of U.S. Law Enforcement Officers." *New England Journal of Medicine* 375, no. 16 (2016): 1509–11.

Cunningham, David. *Klansville, U.S.A.: The Rise and Fall of the Civil Rights–Era Ku Klux Klan.* Oxford University Press, 2013.

Curry, Tommy J. *The Man-Not: Race, Class, Genre, and the Dilemmas of Black Manhood.* Temple University Press, 2017.

Dahlberg, Linda L., and Etienne G. Krug. "Violence: A Global Public Health Problem." *Ciência and Saúde Coletiva* 11 (2006).

Death Penalty Information Center. "Executions in the United States." http://www .deathpenaltyinfo.org/executions-united-states.

Delgado, Richard. "Legal Storytelling: Storytelling for Oppositionists and Others: A Plea for Narrative." *Michigan Law Review* 87 (1989): 2411–41.

Delgado, Richard, and Jean Stefancic, eds. *Critical Race Theory: An Introduction.* New York University Press, 2012.

——. *Critical Race Theory: An Introduction.* 3rd ed. New York University Press, 2017.

——. *The Derrick Bell Reader.* New York University Press, 2005.

DeVylder, Jordan E., Deidre M. Anglin, Lisa Bowleg, Lisa Fedina, and Bruce G. Link. "Police Violence and Public Health." *Annual Review of Clinical Psychology* 18 (2022): 527–52.

DeVylder, Jordan E., Hans Oh, Boyoung Nam, Tanya L. Sharpe, Meshan Lehmann, and Bruce G. Link. "Prevalence, Demographic Variation, and Psychological Correlates of Exposure to Police Victimisation in Four US Cities." *Epidemiology and Psychiatric Sciences* 26, no. 5 (2017): 466–77.

Dickson, Lynda Faye. "The Early Club Movement Among Black Women in Denver: 1890–1925." PhD diss., University of Colorado at Boulder, 1982.

Dixon, Stephanie Schweitzer. "Law Enforcement Suicide: The Depth of the Problem and Best Practices for Suicide Prevention Strategies." *Aggression and Violent Behavior* 61 (2021): 101649.

Dorsett, Lyle, and Michael McCarthy. *The Queen City: A History of Denver.* Pruett, 1986.

Dray, Phillip. *At the Hands of Persons Unknown: The Lynching of Black America.* Random House, 2002.

Du Bois, W. E. B. *The Philadelphia Negro: A Social Study.* University of Pennsylvania Press, 1996.

Dunham, Roger G., and Nick Petersen. "Making Black Lives Matter." *Criminology and Public Policy* 16, no. 1 (2017): 341–48.

Durán, Robert J. "An Attempt to Change Disproportionate Minority Contact by Working in Youth Corrections." In *Experiencing Corrections: Lessons from the Field*, ed. M. Johnson, 149–64. Sage, 2011.

——. "Fatalistic Social Control: The Reproduction of Oppression Through the Medium of Gangs." PhD diss., University of Colorado at Boulder, 2006.

——. *Gang Life in Two Cities: An Insider's Journey.* Columbia University Press, 2013.

——. *The Gang Paradox: Inequalities and Miracles on the U.S.-Mexico Border.* Columbia University Press, 2018.

——. "Pinta Fearz: A Chicano Sociologist's Life on the Edge of the Law." *Bad Subjects: Political Education for Everyday Life* 71 (2004).

Durán, Robert J., and Charlene M. Shroulote-Durán. "Institutionalizing Community Oversight of the Police: Copwatch." In *Justice and Legitimacy in Policing: Transforming the Institution*, ed. M. O. Craig and K. L. Blount-Hill, 76–90. Routledge, 2023.

Durán, Robert J., and Oralia Loza. "Exploring the Two Trigger Fingers Thesis: Racial and Ethnic Differences in Officer Involved Shootings." *Contemporary Justice Review: Issues in Criminal, Social, and Restorative Justice* 20, no. 1 (2017): 71–94.

Durkheim, Emile. *The Division of Labor in Society.* Free Press, 1984.

——. *Suicide.* Free Press, 1951.

Durkin, Allison, Christopher Schenck, Yamini Narayan, Kate Nyhan, Kaveh Khoshnood, and Sten H. Vermund. "Prevention of Firearm Injury Through Policy and Law: The Social Ecological Model." *Journal of Law, Medicine, and Ethics* 48, no. 4, suppl. (2020): 191–97.

Duwe, Grant. *Mass Murder in the United States: A History.* McFarland and Co., 2007.

Edwards, Frank, Hedwig Lee, and Michael Esposito. "Risk of Being Killed by Police Use of Force in the United States by Age, Race-Ethnicity, and Sex." *Proceedings of the National Academy of Sciences* 116, no. 34 (2019): 16793–98.

Edwards, Frank, Michael H. Esposito, and Hedwig Lee. "Risk of Police-Involved Death by Race/Ethnicity and Place, United States, 2012–2018." *American Journal of Public Health* 108, no. 9 (2018): 1241–48.

Engel, Robin S., and Eric Silver. "Policing Mentally Disordered Suspects: A Reexamination of the Criminalization Hypothesis." *Criminology* 39, no. 2 (2001): 225–52.

Engel, Robin S., Hannah D. McManus, and Tamara D. Herold. "Does De-escalation Training Work? A Systematic Review and Call for Evidence in Police Use of Force." *Criminology and Public Policy* 19 (2020): 721–59.

Engel, Robin S., Nicholas Corsaro, Gabrielle T. Isaza, and Hannah D. McManus. "Assessing the Impact of De-escalation Training on Police Behavior: Reducing Police Use of Force in the Louisville, KY Metro Police Department." *Criminology and Public Policy* 21 (2022): 199–233.

Escobar, Edward J. *Race, Police, and the Making of a Political Identity: Mexican Americans and the Los Angeles Police Department, 1900–1945.* University of California Press, 1999.

Fan, Mary D. *Camera Power: Proof, Policing, Privacy, and Audiovisual Big Data.* Cambridge University Press, 2019.

Feagin, Joe R. *The White Racial Frame: Centuries of Racial Framing and Counter-Framing.* 2nd ed. Routledge, 2013.

Feagin, Joe R., and Hernan Vera. *Liberation Sociology.* Westview, 2001.

Federal Bureau of Investigation. Uniform Crime Reports. http://www.fbi.gov/about-us/cjis/ucr/ucr.

Ferrell, Jeff, and Mark S. Hamm. *Ethnography at the Edge: Crime, Deviance, and Field Research.* Northeastern University Press, 1998.

Fox, James Alan, Jack Levin, and Kenna Quinet. *The Will to Kill: Making Sense of Senseless Murder.* Pearson, 2008.

Frank, Reanne, Illana Redstone Akresh, and Bo Lu. "Latino Immigrants and the U.S. Racial Order: How and Where Do They Fit In?" *American Sociological Review* 75, no. 3 (2010): 378–401.

Franklin, F. Abron II, Thomas A. Laveist, Daniel W. Webster, and William K. Pan. "Alcohol Outlets and Violent Crime in Washington D.C." *Western Journal of Emergency Medicine* 11, no. 3 (2010): 283–90.

Franklin, John Hope, and Alfred A. Moss Jr. *From Slavery to Freedom: A History of African Americans.* Knopf, 2004.

Freire, Paulo. *Pedagogy of the Oppressed.* 1970; Continuum, 2000.

Fremon, Celeste. *Father Greg and the Homeboys: The Extraordinary Journey of Father Greg Boyle and His Work with the Latino Gangs of East L.A.* Hyperion, 1995.

Fyfe, James J. "Always Prepared: Police Off-duty Guns." *Annals of the American Academy* 452 (1980b): 72–81.

——. "Blind Justice: Police Shootings in Memphis." *Journal of Criminal Law and Criminology* 73, no. 2 (1982): 707–22.

——. "Geographic Correlates of Police Shooting: A Microanalysis." *Journal of Research in Crime and Delinquency* 17 (1980): 101–13.

——. "Observations on Police Deadly Force." *Crime and Delinquency* 27 (1981): 376–89.

——. "Police Use of Deadly Force: Research and Reform." *Justice Quarterly* 5 (1988): 165–205.

——. "Too Many Missing Cases: Holes in Our Knowledge About Police Use of Force." *Justice Research and Policy* 4 (2002): 87–102.

——. "Who Shoots? A Look at Officer Race and Police Shooting." *Journal of Police Science and Administration* 9, no. 4 (1981): 367–82.

Gabbidon, Shaun L. "W. E. B. Du Bois: Pioneering American Criminologist." *Journal of Black Studies* 31, no. 5 (2001): 581–99.

Gamino, Eric. "Racialized Policing on the South Texas-Mexico Border: Mexican American Police Officers' Racialization of Latin-Origin Unauthorized Immigrants." PhD diss., Texas A&M University, 2015.

Garreau, Joel. *The Nine Nations of North America.* Houghton Mifflin, 1981.

Gascón, Luis Daniel, and Aaron Roussell. *The Limits of Community Policing: Civilian Power and Police Accountability in Black and Brown Los Angeles.* New York University Press, 2019.

Gaston, Shytierra, April D. Fernandes, and Rashaan A. DeShay. "A Macrolevel Study of Police Killings at the Intersection of Race, Ethnicity, and Gender." *Crime and Delinquency* 67, no. 8 (2021): 1075–102.

Gelauff, Lodewijk, and Ashish Goel. "Opinion Change or Differential Turnout: Changing Opinions on the Austin Police Department in a Budget Feedback Process." *Digital Government: Research and Practice* 5, no. 3 (2024): 1–32.

Geller, William A., and Kevin J. Karales. "Shootings of and by Chicago Police: Uncommon Crises. Part I: Shootings by Chicago Police." *Journal of Criminal Law and Criminology* 72, no. 4 (1981): 1813–66.

——. "Shootings of and by Chicago Police: Uncommon Crises. Part II: Shootings of Police, Shooting Correlates, and Control Strategies." *Journal of Criminal Law and Criminology* 73 (1982): 331–78.

Gelman, Andrew, Jeffrey Fagan, and Alex Kiss. "An Analysis of the New York City Police Department's 'Stop-and-Frisk' Policy in the Context of Claims of Racial Bias." *Journal of the American Statistical Association* 102, no. 479 (2007): 813–23.

Global Burden of Diseases, Injuries, and Risk Factors Study (GBD), Police Violence US Subnational Collaborators. "Fatal Police Violence by Race and State in the USA, 1980–2019: A Network Meta-Regression." *Lancet* 398, no. 10307 (2021): 1239–55.

Go, Julian. *Postcolonial Thought and Social Theory.* Oxford University Press, 2016.

Goffman, Erving. *The Presentation of Self in Everyday Life.* Doubleday Anchor, 1959.

Goh, Li Sian. "Going Local: Do Consent Decrees and Other Forms of Federal Intervention in Municipal Police Departments Reduce Police Killings?" *Justice Quarterly* 37, no. 5 (2020): 900–29.

Golash-Boza, Tanya Maria. *Race and Racisms: A Critical Approach.* 3rd ed. Oxford University Press, 2022.

Goldberg, Naomi G., Christy Mallory, Amira Hasenbush, Lara Stemple, and Ilan H. Meyer. "Police and the Criminalization of LGBT People." In *The Cambridge Handbook of Policing in the United States,* ed. E. J. Miller and T. R. Lave, 374–91. Cambridge University Press, 2019.

Goldkamp, John S. "Minorities as Victims of Police Shootings: Interpretations of Racial Disproportionality and Police Use of Deadly Force." *Justice System Journal* (1976): 169–83.

Goldsmith, Pat Rubio, Mary Romero, Raquel Rubio Goldsmith, Manual Escobedo, and Laura Khoury. "Ethno-Racial Profiling and State Violence in a Southwest Barrio." *Aztlán* 34, no. 1 (2009): 93–123.

Goldstein, Herman. *Policing a Free Society.* Ballinger, 1977.

Golub, Andrew, Bruce D. Johnson, and Eloise Dunlap. "The Race/Ethnicity Disparity in Misdemeanor Marijuana Arrests in New York City." *Criminology and Public Policy* 6, no. 1 (2007): 131–64.

Gómez, Laura E. *Manifest Destinies: The Making of the Mexican American Race.* New York University Press, 2007.

Goode, Erich. *Drugs in American Society.* McGraw-Hill, 2008.

Goodmark, Leigh S. "Hands Up at Home: Militarized Masculinity and Police Officers Who Commit Intimate Partner Abuse." *Brigham Young University Law Review* 1183 (2015).

Goodstein, Phil. *In the Shadow of the Klan: When the KKK Ruled Denver, 1920–1926.* New Social Publications, 2006.

Gouldner, Alvin W. "The Sociologist as Partisan: Sociology and the Welfare State." *American Sociologist* 3, no. 2 (1968): 103–16.

Grunwald, Ben, and John Rappaport. "The Wandering Officer." *Yale Law Journal* 129, no. 6 (2020): 1600–195.

Gun Violence Archive. https://www.gunviolencearchive.org.

Haile, Rahwa, Tawandra Rowell-Cunsolo, Marie-Fatima Hyacinthe, and Sirry Alang. "We (Still) Charge Genocide": A Systematic Review and Synthesis of the Direct and Indirect Health Consequences of Police Violence in the United States." *Social Science and Medicine* 322 (2023): 115784.

Haley, Hillary, and Jim Sidanius. "Person-Organization Congruence and the Maintenance of Group-Based Social Hierarchy: A Social Dominance Perspective." *Group Processes and Intergroup Relations* 8, no. 2 (2005): 187–203.

Hall, Daniel E. *Criminal Law and Procedure.* 2nd ed. Delmar, 1996.

Hamm, Mark S., and Ramón Spaaij. *The Age of Lone Wolf Terrorism.* Columbia University Press, 2017.

Haney-López, Ian F. *Racism on Trial: The Chicano Fight for Justice.* Belknap, 2003.

Hansen, Moya. "Entitled to Full and Equal Enjoyment: Leisure and Entertainment in the Denver Black Community, 1900 to 1930." *Historical Studies Journal* 10, no. 1 (1993): 47–77.

Harring, Sidney L., Tony Platt, Richard Speiglman, and Paul Takagi. "The Management of Police Killings." *Crime and Social Justice* 8 (Fall–Winter 1977): 34–43.

Harvard Public Health Review Editorial Board. "HPHR Editorial: Racism Is a Public Health Problem." *Harvard Public Health Review* 3 (2015). https://hphr.org/3-article-hphr/.

Hemenway, David. *Private Guns: Public Health.* University of Michigan Press, 2004.

Hemenway, David, Chloe Shawah, and Elizabeth Lites. "Defensive Gun Use: What Can We Learn from News Reports?" *Injury Epidemiology* 9, no. 19 (2022).

Hemenway, David, John Berrigan, Deborah Azrael, Catherine Barber, and Matthew Miller. "Fatal Police Shootings of Civilians, by Rurality." *Preventive Medicine* 134 (2020): 106046.

Hernandez, Cristal N., and Miltonette Olivia Craig. "Deadly Force by U.S. Customs and Border Protection: An Analysis of Fatal Encounters with Latinos." *Sociology of Race and Ethnicity* (2024).

Hernández, Kelly Lytle. *Migra! A History of the U.S. Border Patrol.* University of California Press, 2010.

Hinton, Elizabeth. *America on Fire: The Untold History of Police Violence and Black Rebellion Since the 1960s.* Liveright, 2021.

——. *From the War on Poverty to the War on Crime: The Making of Mass Incarceration in America.* Harvard University Press, 2016.

Hirschfield, Paul J. "Exceptionally Lethal: American Police Killings in a Comparative Perspective." *Annual Review of Criminology* 6 (2023): 471–98.

Hirschfield, Paul J., and Daniella Simon. "Legitimating Police Violence: Newspaper Narratives of Deadly Force." *Theoretical Criminology* 14 (2010): 155–82.

Hixson, Walter L. *American Settler Colonialism: A History.* Palgrave Macmillan, 2013.

Hofer, Meret S., Allison R. Gilbert, and Marvin S. Swartz. "Police Mental Health: A Neglected Element of Police Reform." *Psychiatric Services* 72, no. 9 (2021): 985.

Holmes, Malcolm D. "Minority Threat and Police Brutality: Determinants of Civil Rights Criminal Complaints in U.S. Municipalities." *Criminology* 38 (2000): 343–67.

Holz, Justin E., Roman G. Rivera, and Bocar A. Ba. "Peer Effects in Police Use of Force." *American Economic Journal: Economic Policy* 15, no. 2 (2023): 256–91.

Hong, Jun Song, Hyunkag Cho, and Alvin Shiulain Lee. "Revisiting the Virginia Tech Shootings: An Ecological Systems Analysis." *Journal of Loss and Trauma* 15, no. 6 (2010): 561–75.

Hong, Jun Song, Hyunkag Cho, Paula Allen-Meares, and Dorothy L. Espelage. "The Social Ecology of the Columbine High School Shootings." *Children and Youth Services Review* 33, no. 6 (2011): 861–68.

Horyniak, Danielle, Karla D. Wagner, Richard F. Armenta, Jazmine Cuevas-Mota, Erik Hendrickson, and Richard S. Garfein. "Cross-Border Injection Drug Use and HIV and Hepatitis C Virus Seropositivity Among People Who Inject Drugs in San Diego, California." *International Journal of Drug Policy* 47 (2017): 9–17.

Hughes, Everett C. "Dilemmas and Contradictions of Status." *American Journal of Sociology* 50, no. 5 (1945): 353–59.

Human Rights Watch. *Shielded from Justice: Police Brutality and Accountability in the United States.* Human Rights Watch, 1998.

Hunt, Jennifer, and Peter K. Manning. "The Social Context of Police Lying." *Symbolic Interaction* 14, no. 1 (1991): 51–70.

Inn, Andres, Alan C. Wheeler, and Cynthia L. Sparling. "The Effects of Suspect Race and Situation Hazard on Police Officer Shooting Behavior." *Journal of Applied Social Psychology* 7, no. 1 (1977): 27–37.

Israel, Jerold H., and Wayne R. LaFave. *Criminal Procedure: Constitutional Limitations.* West Group, 2001.

Jacobs, David, and David Britt. "Inequality and Police Use of Deadly Force: An Empirical Assessment of a Conflict Hypothesis." *Social Problems* 26, no. 4 (1979): 403–12.

Jacobs, David, and Robert M. O'Brien. "The Determinants of Deadly Force: A Structural Analysis of Police Violence." *American Journal of Sociology* 103, no. 4 (1998): 837–62.

James, Lois. "The Stability of Implicit Racial Bias in Police Officers." *Police Quarterly* 21, no. 1 (2018): 30–52.

Jargowsky, Paul A. "The Persistence of Segregation in the 21st Century." *Minnesota Journal of Law and Inequality* 36, no. 2 (2018): 207–30.

Jennings, Jacky M., Adam J. Milam, Amelia Greiner, C. Debra Furr-Holden, Frank C. Curriero, and Rachel J. Thornton. "Neighborhood Alcohol Outlets and the Association with Violent Crime in One Mid-Atlantic City: The Implications for Zoning Policy." *Journal of Urban Health* 91, no. 1 (2014): 62–71.

Jennings, Jay T., and Meghan E. Rubado. "Preventing the Use of Deadly Force: The Relationship Between Police Agency Policies and Rates of Officer-Involved Gun Deaths." *Public Administration Review* 77, no. 2 (2017): 217–26.

Jetelina, Katelyn K., Rebecca J. Molsberry, Jennifer Reingle Gonzalez, Alaina M. Beauchamp, and Trina Hall. "Prevalence of Mental Illness and Mental Health Care Use Among Police Officers." *JAMA Network Open* 3, no. 10 (2020): e2019658.

Johnson, David J., Trevor Tress, Nicole Burkel, Carley Taylor, and Joseph Cesario. "Officer Characteristics and Racial Disparities in Fatal Officer-Involved Shootings." *Proceedings of the National Academy of Sciences* 116, no. 32 (2019): 15877–82.

Johnson, Kevin R. *Opening the Floodgates: Why America Needs to Rethink Its Borders and Immigration Laws.* New York University Press, 2007.

Kamisar, Yale, Wayne R. LaFave, Jerold H. Israel, and Nancy J. King. *Basic Criminal Procedure: Cases, Comments, and Questions.* 10th ed. West Group, 2002.

Kane, Robert J. "The Social Ecology of Police Misconduct." *Criminology* 40, no. 4 (2002): 867–96.

Kelen, Leslie G., and Eileen Hallet Stone. *Missing Stories: An Oral History of Ethnic and Minority Groups in Utah.* University of Utah Press, 1996.

Kelley, Robin. "Slangin' Rocks . . . Palestinian Style': Dispatches from the Occupied Zones of North America." In *Police Brutality: An Anthology*, ed. J. Nelson, 21–59. Norton, 2000.

Kelly, George V. *The Old Gray Mayors of Denver.* Pruett, 1974.

King, William W. *Going to Meet a Man: Denver's Last Legal Public Execution, 27 July 1886.* University Press of Colorado, 1990.

Kivisto, Aaron J., Bradley Ray, and Peter L. Phalen. "Firearm Legislation and Fatal Police Shootings in the United States." *American Journal of Public Health* 107, no. 7 (2017): 1068–75.

Klinger, David. *Into the Kill Zone: A Cop's Eye View of Deadly Force.* Jossey-Bass, 2004.

Knievel, Michael. "Teaching Deadly Force: Collaborative Dynamics and the Rhetoric of Police Policy." *IEEE Transactions on Professional Communication* 51, no. 1 (2008): 95–109.

Knox, Dean. "Revealing Racial Bias." *Science* 374 (2021): 6568.

Knox, Dean, and Jonathan Mummolo. "Making Inference About Racial Disparities in Police Violence." *PNAS* 117, no. 3 (2020): 1261–62.

Kobler, Arthur L. "Figures (and Perhaps Some Facts) on Police Killing of Civilians in the United States, 1965–1969." *Journal of Social Issues* 31, no. 1 (1975): 185–91.

——. "Police Homicide in a Democracy." *Journal of Social Issues* 31, no. 1 (1975): 163–84.

Konstantin, David N. "Homicides of American Law Enforcement Officers, 1978–1980." *Justice Quarterly* 1, no. 1 (1984): 29–45.

Kozlov, Xenia J. "School Shootings as a Multi-Faceted Phenomenon: Social-Ecological Model-Based Review." *Psychology in Education* 2, no. 4 (2020): 349–57.

Kramer, Rory, and Brianna Remster. "Stop, Frisk, and Assault? Racial Disparities in Police Use of Force During Investigatory Stops." *Law and Society Review* 52, no. 4 (2018): 960–93.

Krieger, Nancy. "Theories for Social Epidemiology in the 21st Century: An Ecosocial Perspective." *International Journal of Epidemiology* 30, no. 4 (2001): 668–77.

Krieger, Nancy, Jarvis T. Chen, Pamela D. Waterman, Mathew V. Kiang, and Justin Feldman.
"Police Killings and Police Deaths Are Public Health Data and Can Be Counted." *PLOS
Medicine* 12, no. 12 (2015): e1001915.

Krug, Etienne G., James A. Mercy, Linda L. Dahlberg, and Anthony B. Zwi. "The World Report
on Violence and Health." *Lancet* 360, no. 9339 (2002): 1083–88.

Kunst, Jonas R., Lisa S. Myhren, and Ivuoma N. Onyeador. "Simply Insane? Attributing Terrorism to Mental Illness (Versus Ideology) Affects Mental Representation of Race." *Criminal Justice and Behavior* 45, no. 12 (2018): 1888–902.

Kurti, Zhandarka. "Starting a Dialogue: From Radical Criminology to Critical Resistance."
Journal of World-Systems Research 27, no. 1 (2021): 136–48.

Larios, Sandra E., Remedios Lozada, Steffanie A. Strathdee, Shirley J. Semple, Scott Roesch,
Hugo Staines, et al. "An Exploration of Contextual Factors That Influence HIV Risk in
Female Sex Workers in Mexico: The Social Ecological Model Applied to HIV Risk Behav-
iors." *AIDS Care* 21, no. 10 (2009): 1335–42.

Lasswell, Harold D. "The Garrison State." *American Journal of Sociology* 46, no. 4 (1941):
455–68.

——. "Sino-Japanese Crisis: The Garrison State Versus the Civilian State." *China Quarterly* 11
(1937): 643–49.

Laub, John H., and Robert J. Sampson. *Shared Beginnings, Divergent Lives: Delinquent Boys to
Age 70.* Harvard University Press, 2003.

Layne, Asha. "It's Not Just Black and White: How Black Immigrants Continue to Influence
the Fight Against Police Violence." *Journal of Liberal Arts and Humanities* 2, no. 6 (2021):
1–7.

Lee, Jennifer, and Min Zhou. *The Asian American Achievement Paradox.* Russell Sage Foundation, 2015.

Lett, Elle, Emmanuella Ngozi Asabor, Theodore Corbin, and Dowin Boatright. "Racial Inequity in Fatal US Police Shootings, 2015–2020." *Journal of Epidemiology and Community
Health* 75 (2020): 394–97.

Lewis, David Levering. *W. E. B. Du Bois: Biography of a Race: 1968–1919.* Owl Books, 1993.

——. *W. E. B. Du Bois: The Fight for Equality and the American Century, 1919–1963.* Henry Holt,
2001.

Lifton, Jay, and Greg Mitchell. *Who Owns Death? Capital Punishment, the American Conscience, and the End of Executions.* HarperPerennial, 2002.

Leonard, Stephen J. *Lynching in Colorado, 1859–1919.* University Press of Colorado, 2002.

Leonard, Stephen J., and Thomas J. Noel. *Denver: Mining Camp to Metropolis.* University Press
of Colorado, 1990.

Li, Danyao, Sean Nicholson-Crotty, and Jill Nicholson-Crotty. "Creating Guardians or Warriors? Examining the Effects of Non-Stress Training on Policing Outcomes." *American
Review of Public Administration* 51, no. 1 (2021): 3–16.

Lipperman-Kreda, Sharon, Ida Wilson, Geoffrey P. Hunt, Rachelle Annechino, and
Tamar M. J. Antin. "Substance Use Among Sexual and Gender Minorities: Association

with Police Discrimination and Police Mistrust." *Sexuality, Gender, and Policy* 3, no. 2 (2020): 92–104.

Livingston, James D. "Contact Between Police and People with Mental Disorders: A Review of Rates." *Psychiatric Services* 67, no. 8 (2016): 850–57.

Lofland, John, David Snow, Leon Anderson, and Lyn H. Lofland. *Analyzing Social Settings: A Guide to Qualitative Observation and Analysis.* Waveland, 2006.

Lyles, Lionel Dean. "An Historical-Urban Geographical Analysis of Black Neighborhood Development in Denver, 1860–1970." PhD diss., University of Colorado at Boulder, 1977.

Lynch, Caitlin G. "Don't Let Them Kill You on Some Dirty Roadway: Survival, Entitled Violence, and the Culture of Modern American Policing." *Contemporary Justice Review: Issues in Criminal, Social, and Restorative Justice* 21, no. 1 (2018): 33–43.

Maas, Peter. *Serpico.* Bantam Books, 1973.

MacDonald, John M., Robert J. Kaminski, Geoffrey P. Alpert, and Abraham N. Tennenbaum. "The Temporal Relationship Between Police Killings of Civilians and Criminal Homicide: A Refined Version of the Danger-Perception Theory." *Crime and Delinquency* 47, no. 2 (2001): 155–72.

Marable, Manning. *Race, Reform, and Rebellion: The Second Reconstruction and Beyond in Black America, 1945–2006.* University Press of Mississippi, 2007.

Maratea, R. J. *Killing with Prejudice: Institutionalized Racism in American Capital Punishment.* New York University Press, 2019.

Márquez, John D. *Black-Brown Solidarity: Racial Politics in the New Gulf South.* University of Texas Press, 2013.

Marshall, Ruth E., Josie Milligan-Saville, Katherine Petrie, Richard A. Bryant, Philip B. Mitchell, and Samuel B. Harvey. "Mental Health Screening Among Police Officers: Factors Associated with Under-Reporting of Symptoms." *BMC Psychiatry* 21 (2021): 135.

Martinez, Monica Muñoz. *The Injustice Never Leaves You: Anti-Mexican Violence in Texas.* Harvard University Press, 2018.

Martínez, Ramiro. "Incorporating Latinos and Immigrants Into Policing Research." *Criminology and Public Policy* 6, no. 1 (2007): 57–64.

Massey, Douglas S. "The Racialization of Mexicans in the United States? Racial Stratification in Theory and Practice." *Migración y Desarrollo* 10 (2008): 59–95.

——. "Still the Linchpin: Segregation and Stratification in the USA." *Race and Social Problems* 12, no. 1 (2020): 1–12.

Matsuda, Mari J. "Public Response to Racist Speech: Considering the Victim's Story." *Michigan Law Review* 87, no. 8 (1989): 2320–81.

Mauck, Laura M. *Five Points Neighborhood of Denver.* Arcadia, 2001.

Mauer, Marc. *Race to Incarcerate.* New Press, 1999.

Mazur, Karol. "The 'Good Guy with a Gun' Concept in the American Gun Culture and Gun Control Policy." *Scientific Journal of Bielsko-Biala School of Finance and Law* 25, no. 2 (2021): 5–10.

McElvain, James P., and Augustine J. Kposowa. "Police Officer Characteristics and Internal Affairs Investigations for Use of Force Allegations." *Journal of Criminal Justice* 32 (2004): 265–79.

McLeroy, Kenneth R., Daniel Bibeau, Allan Steckler, and Karen Glanz. "An Ecological Perspective on Health Promotion Programs." *Health Education Quarterly* 15, no. 4 (1988): 351–77.

McVeigh, Rory, and Kevin Estep. *The Politics of Losing: Trump, the Klan, and the Mainstreaming of Resentment.* Columbia University Press, 2019.

Meeks, Daryl. "Police Militarization in Urban Areas: The Obscure War Against the Underclass." *The Black Scholar* 35, no. 4 (2006): 33–41.

Menjívar, Cecilia, and Cynthia Bejarano. "Latino Immigrants' Perception of Crime and Police Authorities in the United States: A Case Study from the Phoenix Metropolitan Area." *Ethnic and Racial Studies* 2, no. 1 (2004): 120–48.

Mennicke, Annelise M., and Katie Ropes. "Estimating the Rate of Domestic Violence Perpetrated by Law Enforcement Officers: A Review of Methods and Estimates." *Aggression and Violent Behavior* 31 (2016): 157–64.

Mercado, Marlené. "Chicana/x Carework: Invisible Feminized Labor, Chicana/x Carceral Community, and the Variegated Nature of Feminist Agency in Carceral Contexts." PhD diss., University of California at Davis, 2022.

Mesic, Aldina, Lydia Franklin, Alev Cansever, Fiona Potter, Anika Sharma, Anita Knopov, and Michael Siegel. "The Relationship Between Structural Racism and Black-White Disparities in Fatal Police Shootings at the State Level." *Journal of the National Medical Association* 110, no. 2 (2018): 106–16.

Messerschmidt, James W. *Masculinities and Crime: Critique and Reconceptualization of Theory.* Rowman and Littlefield, 1993.

Meyer, Marshall W. "Police Shootings at Minorities: The Case of Los Angeles." *Annals of the American Academy of Political and Social Science* 452 (1980): 98–110.

Mills, C. Wright. *The Power Elite.* Oxford University Press, 2000.

Mirandé, Alfredo. *The Chicano Experience: An Alternative Perspective.* 2nd ed. University of Notre Dame Press, 2022.

——, ed. *Gringo Injustice: Insider Perspectives on Police, Gangs, and Law.* Routledge, 2020.

——. *Gringo Justice.* University of Notre Dame Press, 1987.

——. *Ordinary Injustice: Rascuache Lawyering and the Anatomy of a Criminal Case.* University of Arizona Press, 2023.

——. *Rascuache Lawyer: Toward a Theory of Ordinary Litigation.* University of Arizona Press, 2011.

Mithoefer, Michael C., Ann T. Mithoefer, Allison A. Feduccia, Lisa Jerome, Mark Wagner, Joy Wymer, et al. "3,4-Methylenedioxymethamphetamine (MDMA)-Assisted Psychotherapy for Post-Traumatic Stress Disorder in Military Veterans, Firefighters, and Police Officers: A Randomised, Double-Blind, Dose-Response, Phase 2 Clinical Trial." *Lancet Psychiatry* 5, no. 6 (2018): 486–97.

Moore, Wendy Leo. "The *Stare Decisis* of Racial Inequality: Supreme Court Race Jurisprudence and the Legacy of Legal Apartheid in the United States." *Critical Sociology* 40, no. 1 (2014): 67–88.

Morris, Aldon D. *The Scholar Denied: W. E. B. Du Bois and the Birth of Modern Sociology.* University of California Press, 2015.

Morrissey, Mitch, and Norm Brisson. *Denver District Attorney's Office: A History of Crime in the Mile High City (1869–2021).* N.p., 2022.

Nagy, Kimberly K., Robert F. Smith, Roxanne R. Roberts, Kimberly T. Joseph, Faran Bokhari, and John Barrett. "Prognosis of Penetrating Trauma in Elderly Patients: A Comparison with Younger Patients." *Journal of Trauma and Acute Care Surgery* 49, no. 2 (2000): 190–94.

Nakajima, Satomi, Masaya Ito, Akemi Shirai, and Takako Konishi. "Complicated Grief in Those Bereaved by Violent Death: The Effects of Post-Traumatic Stress Disorder on Complicated Grief." *Dialogues in Clinical Neuroscience* 14, no. 2 (2012): 210–14.

Navarro, Armando. *Mexicano Political Experience in Occupied Aztlán: Struggles and Change.* AltaMira, 2005.

Neely, Cheryl L. *No Human Involved: The Serial Murder of Black Women and Girls and the Deadly Cost of Police Indifference.* Beacon, 2025.

Newman, Katherine S., Cybelle Fox, David Harding, Jal Mehta, and Wendy Roth. *Rampage: The Social Roots of School Shootings.* Basic Books, 2004.

Nix, Justin. "On the Challenges Associated with the Study of Police Use of Deadly Force in the United States: A Response to Schwartz and Jahn." *PLOS One* 15, no. 7 (2020).

Nix, Justin, and John A. Shjarback. "Factors Associated with Police Shooting Mortality: A Focus on Race and a Plea for More Comprehensive Data." *PLOS One* (2021): https://doi.org/10.1371/journal.pone.0259024.

Noel, Thomas J. *The City and the Saloon: Denver, 1858–1916.* University of Nebraska Press, 1982.

Obasogie, Osagie K., and Peyton Provenzano. "Race, Racism, and Police Use of Force in 21st Century Criminology: An Empirical Examination." *UCLA Law Review* 69 (2023): 1206–69.

Obasogie, Osagie K., and Zachary Newman. "Police Violence, Use of Force Policies, and Public Health." *American Journal of Law and Medicine* 43, no. 2–3 (2017): 279–95.

Ortiz, Lenny. *Denver Behind Bars: The History of the Denver Sheriff Department and Denver's Jail System.* Aventine, 2004.

Outland, Rafael L., Thomas Noel Jr., Kris Rounsville, Tomas Boatwright, Craig Waleed, and Asia Abraham. "Living with Trauma: Impact of Police Killings on the Lives of the Family and Community of Child and Teen Victims." *Current Psychology* 41 (2020): 7059–73.

Page, Brian, and Eric Ross. "Legacies of a Contested Campus: Urban Renewal, Community Resistance, and the Origins of Gentrification in Denver." *Urban Geography* 38, no. 9 (2017): 1293–328.

Paoline III, Eugene A., William Terrill, and Logan J. Somers. "Police Officer Use of Force Mindset and Street-Level Behavior." *Police Quarterly* 24, no. 4 (2021): 547–77.

Patterson, Orlando. *Slavery and Social Death: A Comparative Study.* Harvard University Press, 2018.

Payne, B. Keith. "Prejudice and Perception. The Role of Automatic and Controlled Processes in Misperceiving a Weapon." *Journal of Personality and Social Psychology* 81, no. 2 (2001): 181–92.

——. "Weapon Bias: Split-Second Decisions and Unintended Stereotyping." *Current Directions in Psychological Science* 15, no. 6 (2006): 287–91.

Perea, Juan F. "The Black/White Binary Paradigm of Race: The Normal Science of American Racial Thought." *California Law Review* 85, no. 5 (1997): 127–72.

——. "Ethnicity and the Constitution: Beyond the Black and White Binary Constitution." *William and Mary Law Review* 571, no. 2 (1995): 571–611.

Pérez, Maritza. "A History of Anti-Latino State-Sanctioned Violence." In *Gringo Injustice: Insider Perspectives on Police, Gangs, and Law*, ed. Alfredo Mirandé, 25–43. Routledge, 2020.

Peréz, Raúl, and Geoff Ward. "From Insult to Estrangement and Injury: The Violence of Racist Police Jokes." *American Behavioral Scientist* 63, no. 13 (2019): 1810–29.

Perez, Xavier. "Started from the Bottom, Now We're Here: Reflections of a Latinx Scholar-Activist." *Journal of Criminal Justice Education* 34, no. 3 (2023): 451–59.

Peterson, Ruth D., and Lauren J. Krivo. *Divergent Social Worlds: Neighborhood Crime and the Racial-Spatial Divide*. Russell Sage Foundation, 2012.

Phillips, Coretta, and Benjamin Bowling. "Racism, Ethnicity, and Criminology: Developing Minority Perspectives." *British Journal of Criminology* 43 (2003): 269–90.

Piquero, Alex. "Racial Inequality in Firearm Homicide Victimization—but Not Other Types of US Violence." *Cambridge Journal of Evidence-Based Policing* 8, no. 1 (2023).

Pinto, Antonio, Anna Russo, Alfonso Reginelli, Francesca Iacobellis, Marco Di Serafino, Sabrina Giovine, and Luigia Romano. "Gunshot Wounds: Ballistics and Imaging Findings." *Seminars in Ultrasound, CT and MRI* 40, no. 1 (2019): 25–35.

Presser, Lo. *Why We Harm*. Rutgers University Press, 2013.

Prince, Virginia. "Sex vs. Gender." *International Journal of Transgenderism* 8, no. 4 (2005): 29–32.

Quinney, Richard. *Class, State, and Crime: On the Theory and Practice of Criminal Justice*. D. McKay, 1977.

Radelet, Michael L. *The History of the Death Penalty in Colorado*. University Press of Colorado, 2017.

Rastello, Timothy M. "Landmark Civil Rights Case Results in $2.25 Million Verdict." *TortSource* 4, no. 1 (2001): 3–4.

Ravkind, William M. "Justifiable Homicide in Texas." *Southwestern Law Journal* 13 (1959): 508–24.

Ray, Victor. "A Theory of Racialized Organizations." *American Sociological Review* 84, no. 1 (2019): 26–53.

Reiman, Jeffrey. *The Rich Get Richer and the Poor Get Prison*. Pearson, 2007.

Reiss, Albert J. "Controlling Police Use of Deadly Force." *The Annals of the American Academy* 452 (1980): 122–34.

Rhee, Peter M., Ernest E. Moore, Bellal Joseph, Andrew Tang, Viraj Pandit, and Gary Vercruysse. "Gunshot Wounds: A Review of Ballistics, Bullets, Weapons, and Myths." *Journal of Trauma Acute Care Surgery* 80, no. 6 (2016): 853–67.

Rider, Eugene Frank. "The Denver Police Department: An Administrative, Organizational, and Operational History, 1858–1905." PhD diss., University of Denver, 1971.

Roberts, Gary L. *Massacre at Sand Creek: How Methodists Were Involved in an American Tragedy*. Abingdon, 2016.

Robin, Gerald D. "Justifiable Homicide by Police Officers." *Journal of Criminal Law and Criminology* 54 (1963): 225–31.

Rodriguez, Roberto. *Justice: A Question of Race.* Bilingual, 1997.

Rogers, Michael S., Dale E. McNiel, and Renée L. Binder. "Effectiveness of Police Crisis Intervention Training Programs." *Journal of the American Academy of Psychiatry and the Law Online* (2019): 003863-19.

Rojek, Jeff, Geoffrey P. Alpert, and Hayden P. Smith. "Examining Officer and Citizen Accounts of Police Use-of-Force Incidents." *Crime and Delinquency* 58, no. 2 (2010): 301–27.

Romero, Mary. "Sociology Engaged in Social Justice." *American Sociological Review* 85, no. 1 (2020): 1–30.

Romo, David Dorado. *Ringside Seat to a Revolution: An Underground Cultural History of El Paso and Juárez: 1893–1923.* Cinco Puntos, 2005.

Rosas, Gilberto. *Unsettling: The El Paso Massacre, Resurgent White Nationalism, and the US-Mexico Border.* John Hopkins University Press, 2023.

Rubens, Muni, and Nancy Shehadeh. "Gun Violence in United States: In Search for a Solution." *Frontiers in Public Health* 2, no. 17 (2014): 1–4.

Russell-Brown, Katheryn. "Body Cameras, Police Violence, and Racial Credibility." *Florida Law Review Forum* 67 (2015): 207–13.

——. *The Color of Crime: Racial Hoaxes, White Fear, Black Protectionism, Police Harassment, and Other Macroaggressions.* New York University Press, 1998.

——. *Underground Codes: Race, Crime, and Related Fires.* New York University Press, 2004.

Sáenz, Rogelio, and Maria Cristina Morales. *Latinos in the United States: Diversity and Change.* Polity, 2015.

Samora, Julian, Joe Bernal, and Albert Peña. *Gunpowder Justice: A Reassessment of the Texas Rangers.* University of Notre Dame Press, 1979.

Sandel, William L., M. Hunter Martaindale, and J. Pete Blair. "A Scientific Examination of the 21-Foot Rule." *Police Practice and Research: An International Journal* 22, no. 3 (2020): 1314–29.

Schwartz, Joanna C. "How Qualified Immunity Fails." *Yale Law Journal* 127 (2017): 2–76.

Shabazz, Betty. *Malcolm X, February 1965: The Final Speeches.* Pathfinder, 1992.

Shane, Jon M., Brian Lawton, and Zoe Swenson. "The Prevalence of Fatal Police Shootings by U.S. Police, 2015–2016: Patterns and Answers from a New Data Set." *Journal of Criminal Justice* 52 (2017): 101–11.

Shapiro, Gilla K., Andree Cusi, Maritt Kirst, Patricia O'Campo, Arash Nakhost, and Vicky Stergiopoulos. "Co-Responding Police-Mental Health Programs: A Review." *Administration and Policy in Mental Health and Mental Health Services Research* 42, no. 5 (2015): 606–20.

Sherman, Lawrence W., and Robert H. Langworthy. "Measuring Homicide by Police Officers." *Journal of Criminal Law and Criminology* 70, no. 4 (1979): 546–60.

Shjarback, John A. "State-Mandated Transparency: A Discussion and Examination of Deadly Force Data Among Law Enforcement Agencies in Texas." *Journal of Crime and Justice* 42, no. 1 (2019): 3–17.

Shjarback, John A., and Justin Nix. "Considering Violence Against Police by Citizen Race/Eth-
nicity to Contextualize Representation in Officer Involved Shootings." *Journal of Criminal Justice* 66 (2020): 101653.

Shjarback, John A., Michael D. White, and Stephen A. Bishopp. "Can Police Shootings be
Reduced by Requiring Officers to Document when they Point Firearms at Citizens." *Injury
Prevention* 27 (2021): 508–13.

Sidanius, Jim, and Felicia Pratto. *Social Dominance: An Intergroup Theory of Social Hierarchy
and Oppression.* Cambridge University Press, 1999.

Sidanius, Jim, James H. Liu, John S. Shaw, and Felicia Pratto. "Social Dominance Orientation,
Hierarchy Attenuators and Hierarchy Enhancers: Social Dominance Theory and the Criminal Justice System." *Journal of Applied Social Psychology* 24, no. 4 (1994): 338–66.

Sierra-Arévalo, Michael. "American Policing and the Danger Imperative." *Law and Society
Review* 55, no. 1 (2021): 70–103.

——. "The Commemoration of Death, Organizational Memory, and Police Culture." *Criminology* 57, no. 4 (2019): 632–58.

Simon, Samantha J. "Training for War: Academy Socialization and Warrior Policing." *Social
Problems* 70 (2023): 1021–43.

Simonson, Jocelyn. "Beyond Body Cameras: Defending a Robust Right to Record the Police."
Georgetown Law Journal 104, no. 6 (2016): 1559–80.

——. "Filming the Police as an Act of Resistance: Remarks Given at the Smartphoned Symposium." *University of St. Thomas Journal of Law and Public Policy* 10, no. 2 (2016): 83–88.

Skolnick, Jerome H., and James J. Fyfe. *Above the Law: Police and the Excessive Use of Force.*
Free Press, 1993.

Slotkin, Richard. *Regeneration Through Violence: The Mythology of the American Frontier,
1600–1860.* Wesleyan University Press, 1973.

Small Arms Survey. *Chapter 7: Reducing Armed Violence: The Public Health Approach.* Cambridge University Press, 2008.

Smith, Brad W., and Malcolm D. Holmes. "Police Use of Excessive Force in Minority Communities: A Test of the Minority Threat, Place, and Community Accountability Hypotheses." *Social Problems* 61, no. 1 (2014): 83–104.

Sorensen, Jonathan R., James W. Marquart, and Deon E. Brock. "Factors Related to Killings
of Felons by Police Officers: A Test of the Community Violence and Conflict Hypotheses." *Justice Quarterly* 10, no. 3 (1993): 417–40.

Southwick, Lawrence. "Guns and Justifiable Homicide: Deterrence and Defense." *St. Louis University Public Law Review* 18 (1999): 217–46.

Sparger, Jerry R., and David J. Giacopassi. "Memphis Revisited: A Reexamination of Police
Shootings After the Garner Decision." *Justice Quarterly* 9, no. 2 (1992): 211–25.

Springer, Kristen W., Jeanne Mager Stellman, and Rebecca M. Jordan-Young. "Beyond a Catalogue of Differences: A Theoretical Frame and Good Practice Guidelines for Researching Sex/Gender in Human Health." *Social Science and Medicine* 74, no. 11 (2012): 1817–24.

Standish, Sierra. "Beet Borderland: Hispanic Workers, the Sugar Beet, and the Making of a
Northern Colorado Landscape." Master's thesis, Colorado State University, 2002.

Stannard, David E. *American Holocaust: Columbus and the Conquest of the New World.* Oxford University Press, 1992.

Steele, Morgan J. and Ziwei Qui. "The Impact of State Laws on Officer-Involved Deaths (OIDs)." *Criminology, Criminal Justice, Law, and Society* 25, no. 3 (2024): 1–20.

Stephens, Ronald J., La Wanna M. Larson, and the Black American West Museum. *Images of America: African Americans in Denver.* Arcadia, 2008.

Stephenson, Mark D., Ben Schram, Elisa F. D. Canetti, and Robin Orr. "Effects of Acute Stress on Psychophysiology in Armed Tactical Occupations: A Narrative Review." *International Journal of Environmental Research and Public Health* 19, no. 3 (2022): 1802.

Stern, Mort. "What Makes a Policeman Go Wrong." *Journal of Criminal Law, Criminology and Police Science* 53, no. 1 (1962): 97–101.

Swanson, Anna. "Revisiting Garner with Garner: A Look at Deadly Force and the Use of Chokeholds and Neck Restraints by Law Enforcement." *South Texas Law Review* 57, no. 3 (2016): 401–48.

Takagi, Paul. "A Garrison State in Democratic Society." *Crime and Social Justice* (Spring/Summer 1974): 27–32.

——. "LEAA's Research Solicitation: Police Use of Deadly Force." *Crime and Social Justice* (Spring/Summer 1979): 51–59.

——. "Race, Crime, and Social Policy: A Minority Perspective." *Crime and Delinquency* 27, no. 1 (1981): 48–63.

Telles, Edward E., and Vilma Ortiz. *Generations of Exclusion: Mexican Americans, Assimilation, and Race.* Russell Sage Foundation, 2008.

Terrill, William, and Stephen D. Mastrofski. "Situational and Officer-Based Determinants of Police Coercion." *Justice Quarterly* 19, no. 2 (2002): 215–48.

Tolliver, Willie F., Bernadette R. Hadden, Fabienne Snowden, and Robyn Brown-Manning. "Police Killings of Unarmed Black People: Centering Race and Racism in Human Behavior and the Social Environment." *Journal of Human Behavior in the Social Environment* 26, no. 3–4 (2016): 279–86.

Trangenstein, Pamela J., Frank C. Curriero, Daniel Webster, Jacky M. Jennings, Carl Latkin, Raimee Eck, and David H. Jernigan. "Outlet Type, Access to Alcohol, and Violent Crime." *Alcohol: Clinical and Experimental Research* 42, no. 11 (2018): 2234–45.

Turner, Carol A. *Forgotten Heroes and Villains of Sand Creek.* History Press, 2010.

Uchida, Craig D. *Policing the Streets of Los Angeles: Controversy, Change, and Continuity.* Under review at Southern Illinois University Press.

Valdez, Avelardo, Zenong Yin, and Charles D. Kaplan. "A Comparison of Alcohol, Drugs, and Aggressive Crime Among Mexican-American, Black, and White Male Arrestees in Texas." *American Journal of Drug Alcohol Abuse* 23, no. 2 (1997): 249–65.

Varien, Mark D., and Richard H. Wilshusen. *Seeking the Center Place: Archaeology and the Ancient Communities in the Mesa Verde Region.* University of Utah Press, 2002.

Vega, William Armando, Ethel Alderete, Bohdan Kolody, and Sergio Augilar-Gaxiola. "Illicit Drug Use Among Mexicans and Mexican Americans in California: The Effects of Gender and Acculturation." *Addiction* 93, no. 12 (1998): 1839–150.

Vella, Michael A., Alexander Warshauer, Gabriella Tortorello, Joseph Fernandez-Moure, Joseph Giacolone, Bofeng Chen, et al. "Long-term Functional, Psychological, Emotional, and Social Outcomes in Survivors of Firearm Injuries." *JAMA Surgery* 155, no. 1 (2019): 51–59.

Vera Sanchez, Claudio G., and Edwardo L. Portillos. "Insiders and Outsiders: Latino Researchers Navigating the Studying of the Police." *Race and Justice* 11, no. 4 (2021): 384–406.

Vigil, Ernesto B. *The Crusade for Justice: Chicano Militancy and the Government's War on Dissent.* University of Wisconsin Press, 1999.

——. "Killing Ismael Mena: "The SWAT Teams Feared for Their Lives . . ."" In *Gringo Injustice: Insider Perspectives on Police, Gangs, and Law,* ed. Alfredo Mirandé, 80–102. Routledge, 2020.

Violanti, John M. "The Mystery Within: Understanding Police Suicide." *FBI Law Enforcement Bulletin* 64, no. 2 (1995): 19–26.

Violanti, John M., Desta Fekedulegn, Michael E. Andrew, Luenda E. Charles, Tara A. Hartley, Bryan Vila, and Cecil M. Burchfiel. "Shift Work and the Incidence of Injury Among Police Officers." *American Journal of Industrial Medicine* 55 (2012): 217–27.

Violanti, John M., Sherry L. Owens, Erin McCanlies, Desta Fekedulegn, and Michael E. Andrew. "Law Enforcement Suicide: A Review." *Policing: An International Journal* 42, no. 2 (2017): 141–64.

Voigt, Rob, Nicholas P. Camp, Vinodkumar Prabhakaran, William L. Hamilton, Rebecca C. Hetey, Camilla M. Griffiths, et al. "Language from Police Body Camera Footage Shows Racial Disparities in Officer Respect." *Proceedings of the National Academy of Sciences* 114, no. 25 (2017): 6521–26.

Waegel, William B. "How Police Justify the Use of Deadly Force." *Social Problems* 32, no. 2 (1984): 146–55.

Wagner, Marcia, and Richard J. Brzeczek. "Alcoholism and Suicide: A Fatal Connection." *FBI Law Enforcement Bulletin* 52, no. 8 (1983): 8–15.

Walker, Samuel. *Role Accountability: The Role of Citizen Oversight.* Wadsworth, 2000.

Walker, Samuel, Cassia Spohn, and Miriam DeLone. *The Color of Justice: Race, Ethnicity, and Crime in America.* 6th ed. Cengage Learning, 2018.

Walker, Samuel, and Charles M. Katz. *The Police in America: An Introduction.* 6th ed. McGraw-Hill, 2008.

Walsh, James Patrick. "Young and Latino in a Cold War Barrio: Survival, the Search for Identity, and the Formation of Street Gangs in Denver, 1945–1955." Master's thesis, University of Colorado at Denver, 1995.

Wasserman, Howard M. "Police Misconduct, Video Recording, and Procedural Barriers to Rights Enforcement." *North Carolina Law Review* 96, no. 5 (2017): 1313–62.

Watson, Amy C., Leah G. Pope, and Michael T. Compton. "Police Reform from the Perspective of Mental Health Services and Professionals: Our Role in Social Change." *Psychiatric Services* 72, no. 9 (2021): 1085–87.

Watson, Amy C., Melissa Schaefer Morabito, Jeffrey Draine, and Victor Ottati. "Improving Police Response to Persons with Mental Illness: A Multi-Level Conceptualization of CIT." *International Journal of Law and Psychiatry* 31, no. 4 (2008): 359–68.

Webb, Willington, and Cindy Brovsky. *Wellington Webb: The Man, the Mayor, and the Making of Modern Denver.* Fulcrum, 2007.

Weitzer, Ronald. "The Puzzling Neglect of Hispanic Americans in Research on Police-Citizen Relations." *Ethnic and Racial Studies* 37, no. 11 (2014): 1995–2013.

Wells, Ida B. *Southern Horrors: Lynch Law in All Its Phases.* Satya, 2017.

Wells-Barnett, Ida B. *The Red Record: Tabulated Statistics and Alleged Causes of Lynching in the United States.* 1895; Cavalier Classics, 2015.

White, Michael D. "Assessing the Impact of Administrative Policy on Use of Deadly Force by On- and Off-Duty Police." *Evaluation Review* 24, no. 3 (2000): 295–318.

——. "Controlling Police Decisions to Use Deadly Force: Reexamining the Importance of Administrative Policy." *Crime and Delinquency* 47 (2001): 131–51.

White, Michael D., and David Klinger. "Contagious Fire? An Empirical Assessment of the Problem of Multi-Shooter, Multi-Shot Deadly Force Incidents in Police Work." *Crime and Delinquency* 58, no. 2: 196–221.

White, Richard. *It's Your Misfortune and None of My Own: A New History of the American West.* University of Oklahoma Press, 1991.

Whittier, Nancy, Tina Wildhagen, and Howard J. Gold. *Statistics for Social Understanding: With Stata and SPSS.* Rowman & Littlefield, 2020.

Wilkins, Vicky M., and Brian N. Williams. "Black or Blue: Racial Profiling and Representative Bureaucracy." *Public Administration Review* 68, no. 4 (2008): 654–64.

——. "Representing Blue: Representative Bureaucracy and Racial Profiling in the Latino Community." *Administration and Society* 40, no. 8 (2009): 775–98.

Williams, Christine L., and Arlene Stein, eds. *Sexuality and Gender.* Blackwell, 2002.

Wilson, William Julius. *When Work Disappears: The World of the New Urban Poor.* Vintage, 1996.

Wolfe, Patrick. "Settler Colonialism and the Elimination of the Native." *Journal of Genocide Research* 8, no. 4 (2006): 387–409.

Woodard, Colin. *American Nations: A History of the Eleven Rival Regional Cultures of North America.* Penguin, 2011.

Worrall, John L., Stephen A. Bishopp, and William Terrill. "The Effect of Suspect Race on Police Officers' Decision to Draw Their Weapons." *Justice Quarterly* 38, no. 7 (2021): 1428–47.

Wulff, Stephen. "Flipping the 'New Penology' Script: Police Misconduct Insurance, Grassroots Activism, and Risk Management-Based Reform." *Law and Social Inquiry* 47, no. 1 (2022): 162–204.

Zhang, Xingyou, Bonnie Hatcher, Lydia Clarkson, James Holt, Suparna Bagchi, Dafna Kanny and Robert D. Brewer. "Changes in Density of On-Premises Alcohol Outlets and Impact on Violent Crime, Atlanta, Georgia, 1997–2007." *Preventing Chronic Disease* 12, no. 140317 (2015).

Zhao, Linda, and Andrew V. Papachristos. "Network Position and Police Who Shoot." *Annals of the American Academy of Political and Social Science* 687, no. 1 (2020): 89–112.

Zhu, Li, Dennis M. Gorma, and Stéphane Horel. "Alcohol Outlet Density and Violence: A Geospatial Analysis." *Alcohol and Alcoholism* 39, no. 4 (2004): 369–75.

REPORTS AND DATA SOURCES

Adult Education Council of Denver. "The Youth Problem in Denver." Report by the Youth Survey Committee of the Adult Education Council of Denver 14(2). In clippings file, Denver Public Library, 1938.

Arias, Elizabeth, Betzaida Tejada-Vera, Kenneth D. Kochanek and Farida B. Ahmad. "Provisional Life Expectancy Estimates for 2021." National Vital Statistics System Rapid Release. Report 23. US Department of Health and Human Services, Centers for Disease Control and Prevention, 2022.

Bechtel, Trevor, Mara C. Ostfeld, and H. Luke Shaefer. "Evidence on Measures to Reduce Excessive Use of Force by the Police." Center for Racial Justice, University of Michigan, 2023.

Bobb, Merrick, Bernard K. Melekian, Oren Root, Mathew Barge, and Camelia Naguib. "The Denver Report on Use of Deadly Force." Police Assessment Resource Center, Los Angeles, 2008.

Brown, Jodi M., and Patrick A. Langan. "Policing and Homicide, 1976–98: Justifiable Homicide by Police, Police Officers Murdered by Felons." NCJ 180987. US Department of Justice, Bureau of Justice Statistics, 2001.

Budiman, Abby. "Income Inequality Is Greater Among Chinese Americans Than Any Other Asian Origin Group in the U.S." Pew Research Center, May 31, 2024.

Buehler, Emily D. "State and Local Law Enforcement Training Academics, 2018—Statistical Tables." NCJ 255915. US Department of Justice, Office of Justice Programs, Bureau of Justice Statistics, 2021.

Burch, Andrea M. "Arrest-Related Deaths, 2003–2009." NCJ 235385. US Department of Justice, Bureau of Justice Statistics, 2011.

Burghart, Brian. "Fatal Encounters." University of Southern California, 2023. https://fatalen counters.org/.

Burrows, Dustin, Joe Moody, and Eva Guzman. "Interim Report 2022." Investigative Committee on the Robb Elementary Shooting, Texas House of Representatives, 2022.

Campaign Zero. *Mapping Police Violence.* 2013. https://mappingpoliceviolence.org/.

Carmack-Altwies, Mary. Officer Involved Shooting Review and Evaluation. First Judicial District Attorney, State of New Mexico, n.d.

Castle, Lisabeth Pérez. 2023 Semiannual Report. Denver Office of the Independent Monitor, 2023.

Centers for Disease Control and Prevention (CDC). "Polysubstance Use Facts." 2022. https:// www.cdc.gov/stopoverdose/polysubstance-use/index.html.

——. "The Social-Ecological Model: A Framework for Prevention." 2022. https://www.cdc.gov /violenceprevention/about/social-ecologicalmodel.html.

Centers for Disease Control and Prevention, Agency for Toxic Substances and Disease Registry (CDC—ATSDR). "Principles of Community Engagement—Second Edition. Chapter 1—Community Engagement: Definitions and Organizing Concepts from the Literature." 2015. https://www.atsdr.cdc.gov/communityengagement/pdf/PCE_Report _508_FINAL.pdf.

Cheatham, Amelia, and Lindsay Maizland. "How Police Compare in Different Democracies." Council on Foreign Relations, 2022.

Cina, Stephen J. "Autopsy Report: Grimaldo, Michael." Adams County Coroner's Office, Brighton, CO, April 26, 2003.

City and County of Denver. "Problems in Relation to Work with Spanish Speaking People in Denver." 1958.

Colorado Division of Criminal Justice. "A Report of Officer Involved Shootings in Colorado: January 1, 2010–June 30, 2019." Colorado Department of Public Safety, 2020.

Compton, Michael, and Amy Watson. "Research to Improve Law Enforcement Responses to Persons with Mental Illnesses and Intellectual/Developmental Disabilities." Bureau of Justice Assistance, US Department of Justice. https://bja.ojp.gov/sites/g/files/xyckuh186/files/media/document/Research_to_Improve_Law_Enforcement_Responses_to_Persons_with_Mental_Illnesses_and_Developmental_Disabilities.pdf.

Delgado, Richard, and Jean Stefancic. "Home Grown Racism: Colorado's Historic Embrace—and Denial—of Equal Opportunity in Higher Education." Latino/a Research and Policy Center, University of Colorado at Denver, 1999.

Dias, Nelson, and Simone Júlio. "The Next Thirty Years of Participatory Budgeting in the World Start Today." Hope for Democracy: 30 Year of Participatory Budgeting Worldwide. Epopeia Records, Faro, Portugal, 2018.

Disproportionate Minority Contact Technical Assistance Manual. US Department of Justice, 2009. https://www.ncjrs.gov/html/ojjdp/dmc_ta_manual/index.html.

DuPey, Bridget, Margaret B. Kwoka, and Christopher McMichael. "Access Denied: Colorado Law Enforcement Refuses Public Access to Records of Police Misconduct." University of Denver Legal Studies Research Paper No. 18-05, 2018.

Durose, Matthew R., Erica L. Smith, and Patrick A. Langan. "Contacts Between Police and the Public, 2005." Bureau of Justice Statistics, 2007.

89.3 KPCC. "Explore the Data." https://projects.scpr.org/officer-involved/explore/.

Erickson Commission. "Report of the Erickson Commission." Denver, Colorado, 1997.

Fallis, David, Sarah Childress, Reuben Fischer-Baum, Meghan Hoyer, Courtney Kan, and Angela Mecca. "Fatal Force: Police Shootings Database." Washington Post. https://www.washingtonpost.com/graphics/investigations/police-shootings-database/.

Fuller, Doris A., H. Richard Lamb, Michael Biasotti, and John Snook. "Overlooked in the Undercounted: The Role of Mental Illness in Fatal Law Enforcement Encounters." A Report from the Office of Research and Public Affairs, Treatment Advocacy Center, 2015. https://www.treatmentadvocacycenter.org/storage/documents/overlooked-in-the-undercounted.pdf.

Geolytics. National Change Database CD: 1970–2010.

Gramlich, John. "What the Data Says About Gun Deaths in the U.S." Pew Research Center. https://www.pewresearch.org/short-reads/2023/04/26/what-the-data-says-about-gun-deaths-in-the-u-s/.

Hardman, Josh. 2016. "UC Berkeley: The Closure of the School of Criminology, 1976." FoundSF. https://www.foundsf.org/index.php?title=UC_Berkeley:_The_Closure_of_the_School_of_Criminology,_1976.

International Business Machines (IBM). "IBM SPSS Statistics for Mac, Version 25.0, Released 2012." Armonk, NY, 2012.

Ku Klux Klan Membership Ledger Book 2020. https://www.historycolorado.org/kkkledgers.

Krug, Etienne G., Linda L. Dahlberg, James A. Mercy, Anthony B. Zwi, and Rafael Lozano. "World Report on Violence and Health. Chapter 1. Violence—a Global Public Health Problem." World Health Organization, Geneva, Switzerland, 2002. https://apps.who.int/iris/bitstream/handle/10665/42495/9241545615_eng.pdf.

LeCabe, Alvin J., Jr. "Public Statement of Manager of Safety Regarding Disciplinary Action Taken Against Officer James Turney Arising from Events that Occurred on July 4 and 5, 2003." City and County of Denver, Department of Safety, 2004.

——. Public Statement of Manager of Safety Regarding Discipline of Officer Ranjan Ford Arising from the Shooting Death of Frank Lobato on July 11, 2004. City and County of Denver, Department of Safety, August 5, 2005.

——. "Public Statement of the Manager of Safety Regarding an Officer-Involved Shooting by Technician Ryan Grothe and Technician James Sewald on June 25, 2006 at 4600 Stapleton Drive South Which Resulted in the Death of Michael Ford." City and County of Denver, 2007.

Liu, Grace S., Brenda L. Nguyen, Bridget H. Lyons, Kameron J. Sheats, Rebecca F. Wilson, Carter J. Betz, and Katherine A. Fowler. "Surveillance for Violent Deaths—National Violent Death Reporting System, 48 States, the District of Columbia, and Puerto Rico, 2020." Surveillance Summaries. Centers for Disease Control, *Morbidity and Mortality Weekly Report (MMWR)*, 2023.

Logan, John R., and Brian Stults. "Metropolitan Segregation: No Breakthrough in Sight." Working Paper 22-14. Center for Economic Studies, US Census Bureau, 2022.

——. "The Persistence of Segregation in the Metropolis: New Findings from the 2010 Census." Census Brief Prepared for Project US2010, 2011.

Maciag, Mike. "Gentrification in America Report." 2015. https://www.governing.com/archive/gentrification-in-cities-governing-report.html.

McCann, Beth. "Officer Involved Shooting Protocol." State of Colorado, Office of the District Attorney, Denver, 2017.

Migration Policy Institute. "Colorado: Demographics and Social." 2019. https://www.migrationpolicy.org/data/state-profiles/state/demographics/CO.

Multidisciplinary Association for Psychedelic Studies (MAPS). "MDMA: Read Our Research." 2022. https://maps.org/mdma/.

Murthy, Vivek. "Firearm Violence: A Public Health Crisis in America." US Surgeon General's Advisory, 2024.

National Academy of Medicine. "Racism and Associated Heath Impacts." 2022. https://nam.edu/racism-and-associated-health-impacts/.

National Institute on Alcohol Abuse and Alcoholism (NIAAA). "Alcohol's Effects on the Body." 2022. https://www.niaaa.nih.gov/alcohols-effects-health/alcohols-effects-body.

——. "Alcohol Facts and Statistics." 2022. https://www.niaaa.nih.gov/publications/brochures-and-fact-sheets/alcohol-facts-and-statistics.

National Institute on Drug Abuse (NIDA). "Drugfacts." 2019. https://nida.nih.gov/drug-topics /publications/drug-facts.

National Library of Medicine. "Pubmed.Gov (Keyword "Police Shootings")." May 29, 2024. https://pubmed.ncbi.nlm.nih.gov/?term=%22police+shootings%22.

——. "Pubmed.Gov (Keyword: "Police Violence")." May 29, 2024. https://pubmed.ncbi.nlm.nih .gov/?term=%22police%20violence%22.

——. "Reporter (Keyword: "Police Shootings")." May 29, 2024. https://reporter.nih.gov/search /UOI9lepNBUCheO7j4592rw/projects/charts.

——. "Reporter (Keyword: "Police Violence")." May 29, 2024. https://reporter.nih.gov/search /uXUll_TuuUqZTWICQDh4qg/projects.

Negrón-Muntaner, Frances, Chelsea Abbas, Luis Figueroa, and Samuel Robson. "The Latino Media Gap: A Report on the State of Latinos in U.S. Media." Center for the Study of Ethnicity and Race, Columbia University, 2014. https://www.columbia.edu/cu/cser/downloads /Latino_Media_Gap_Report.pdf.

Noe-Bustamante, Luis, Ana Gonzalez-Barrera, Khadijah Edwards, Lauren Mora, and Mark Hugo Lopez. "Measuring the Racial Identity of Latinos." Pew Research Center, 2021. https://www.pewresearch.org/hispanic/2021/11/04/measuring-the-racial-identity-of -latinos/.

Noe-Bustamante, Luis, Lauren Mora, and Mark Hugo Lopez. "About One-in-Four U.S. Hispanics Have Heard of Latinx, but Just 3% Use It." Pew Research Center, 2020.

Office of Community Oriented Policing Services. "The President's Task Force on 21st Century Policing: Implementation Guide Moving from Recommendations to Action." Washington, DC, 2015.

Pew Research Center. "About 5% of Young Adults in the U.S. Say Their Gender Is Different from Their Sex Assigned at Birth." 2022. https://www.pewresearch.org/fact-tank/2022 /06/07/about-5-of-young-adults-in-the-u-s-say-their-gender-is-different-from-their-sex -assigned-at-birth/.

——. "Key Facts About Americans and Guns." 2021. https://www.pewresearch.org/fact-tank /2021/09/13/key-facts-about-americans-and-guns/.

——. "Majority of Latinos Say Skin Color Impacts Opportunity in America and Shapes Daily Life: Measuring the Racial Identity of Latinos." 2021. https://www.pewresearch.org /hispanic/2021/11/04/measuring-the-racial-identity-of-latinos/.

Police Assessment Resource Center. "The Denver Report on Use of Deadly Force." Los Angeles, 2008.

Sandoval, Joseph G. "Preliminary Observations on Civilian Oversight in Denver." Presented at the SWACJ Conference, 2002.

Shin, Hongsup, and Eva Ruth Moravec. "Officer-Involved Shootings in Texas: 2016–2019." Texas Justice Initiative.

Sinyangwe, Samuel, DeRay McKesson, and Johnetta Elzie. *Mapping Police Violence*. 2023. https://mappingpoliceviolence.org/.

Stolen Lives Project. *Stolen Lives: Killed and Brutalized by Police.* Stolen Lives Project, 1997.

——. *Stolen Lives: Killed by Law Enforcement.* October 22nd Coalition to Stop Police Brutality, Repression and the Criminalization of a Generation, 1999.

Stover, Andrew. "An Examination of Mass Shooting Site Selection: Suggestions for Environmental Crime Prevention." Presentation at the American Society of Criminology, 2022.

Substance Abuse and Mental Health Services Administration. "Highlights for 2020 National Survey on Drug Use and Health." Rockville, MD, 2022. https://www.samhsa.gov/data/release/2020-national-survey-drug-use-and-health-nsduh-releases.

Swaine, Jon, Oliver Laughland, Jamiles Lartey, and Ciara McCarthy. "The Counted: People Killed by Police in the US." 2015.

——. "The Counted: People Killed by Police in the US." 2016.

Toscano, Guy. "Dangerous Jobs. Compensation and Working Conditions." 1997. https://www.bls.gov/iif/oshwc/cfar0020.pdf.

US Bureau of Labor Statistics. "Injuries, Illnesses, and Fatalities. Fact Sheet, Police Officers 2018." April 2020. https://www.bls.gov/iif/oshwc/cfoi/police-2018.htm.

US Census. American Community Survey (ACS). https://www.census.gov/programs-surveys/acs.

——. "QuickFacts Denver City, Colorado." 2022. https://www.census.gov/quickfacts/fact/table/denvercitycolorado,denvercountycolorado/PST045222.

——. "QuickFacts: Denver County, Colorado." 2020. https://www.census.gov/quickfacts/fact/table/denvercountycolorado,US/RHI125221.

——. "QuickFacts: Denver County, Colorado." 2022. https://www.census.gov/quickfacts/denvercountycolorado.

US Department of Commerce. Bureau of the Census. "1980 Census of Population." https://www2.census.gov/prod2/decennial/documents/1980a_coABC-01.pdf.

US Government Printing Office. "Number of Inhabitants: Colorado." 1960. https://www2.census.gov/prod2/decennial/documents/17598731v1p7ch2.pdf.

US Department of Health and Human Services. "Provisional Life Expectancy Estimates for 2021." National Vital Statistics System Rapid Release. Report 23. Centers for Disease Control and Prevention, 2022.

Weber County Attorney. Critical Incident Community Briefing. https://www.webercountyutah.gov/Attorney/video/index.php.

Weisburd, David, Rosann Greenspan, Edwin E. Hamilton, Hubert Williams, and Kellie A. Bryant. *Police Attitudes Toward Abuse of Authority: Findings from a National Study.* Washington, DC: National Institute of Justice, 2000.

Wetchler Texas Justice Initiative. Officer-Involved Shootings and Custodial Deaths in Texas, 2018. Fact Sheet.

COURT CASES

Boykin v. The People. 22 Colo. 496; 45 P. 419; 1896 Colo. LEXIS 275.

Colorado Revised Statutes. Title 18, Criminal Code. 18-1-707 (2013).

Gillispie v. City of Knoxville. Court of Appeals of Tennessee, at Knoxville.

Graham v. Connor, 490 U.S. 386 (1989).

Hernandez et al. v. Mesa (2020).
Tennessee v. Garner, 471 U.S. 1 (1985).

MEDIA

Barber, Brad and Scott Christopherson. "Peace Officer." 2015. Soro Films.
Dominguez, Alan. "The Holes in the Door." 2007. Documentary. Loco Lane Filmworks.
Drake. "Drake—Started from the Bottom." VEVO. February 13, 2013. https://www.youtube
     .com/watch?v=RubBzkZzpUA.
Gold, Tami, and Kelly Anderson. *Every Mother's Son.* 2004. New Day Films.

INDEX

GPSR Authorized Representative: Easy Access System Europe, Mustamäe tee
50, 10621 Tallinn, Estonia, gpsr.requests@easproject.com

www.ingramcontent.com/pod-product-compliance
Lightning Source LLC
Chambersburg PA
CBHW021847020426
42334CB00013B/218